THE MAKING *of* THE ENGLISH GARDENER

THE MAKING *of* THE
English Gardener

MARGARET WILLES

YALE UNIVERSITY PRESS
NEW HAVEN AND LONDON

Publication was made possible by a grant from the Scouloudi Foundation in association with the Institute of Historical Research.

For information about this and other Yale University Press publication please contact:
U.S. Office: sales.press@yale.edu   www.yalebooks.com
Europe Office: sales@yaleup.co.uk   www.yalebooks.co.uk

Set in Arno Pro by IDSUK (DataConnection) Ltd
Printed in Great Britain by TJ International Ltd, Padstow, Cornwall

Library of Congress Cataloging-in-Publication Data

Willes, Margaret.
   The making of the English gardener / Margaret Willes.
      p. cm.
Includes bibliographical references and index.
ISBN 978-0-300-16382-7 (alk. paper)
1. Gardens--England--History--16th century. 2. Gardeners--England-History--16th century.
3. Gardens--England--History--17th century. 4. Gardeners--England--History--17th century.
I. Title.
SB451.36.G7W55 2011
712.0942--dc23
                                                                    2011014431
A catalogue record for this book is available from the British Library

10 9 8 7 6 5 4 3 2 1

Contents

List of Illustrations

Figures

Introduction
The Pattern in the Quilt

ONE OF MY FAVOURITE BOOKS AS A CHILD was *A Traveller in Time* by Alison Uttley, in which a twentieth-century girl experienced a simultaneous sixteenth-century life in a manor house in Derbyshire.[1] The plot hatched by Anthony Babington to rescue the captive Mary Queen of Scots takes centre stage, but it was the background of the daily life of a Tudor household that enthralled me. When Uttley described the herb garden, I could see the parterres 'like a patterned quilt' and smell the fragrance of the lavender and the roses. When she entered the kitchen, I could savour the herbs gathered for the possets and for strewing on pillows and floors. So began my fascination with Elizabethan history, and my subsequent exploration of the early Stuarts.

This is a book about people, their gardens, their plants and the books they used to find out about botany, horticulture and design. It is not, however, a chronological account of the development of design, and although the gardens and their creators are mostly English, the story is by no means confined to England. Rather, it examines the networks of communication and circles of cultivation that enabled ideas about gardens and horticulture to travel around Europe, and indeed all parts of the known world.

At the very mention of historical gardens in England, Capability Brown and his contemporaries usually spring to mind. However, I wanted to look at the period before the creation of the great landscape gardens. As I explored the subject, so I realised that in 1560, just after the accession of Elizabeth I, England was not in the gardening vanguard of Europe: the Italians and the

French were the leaders in garden design; the Dutch and the Flemish were the experts in horticulture; and the Portuguese and the Spanish were introducing the latest in exotic plants and flowers from their overseas empires. William Harrison in his *Description of England* published in 1577 recognised how his nation was lagging behind the rest of the world. He blamed it on the political upheavals of the fourteenth and fifteenth centuries, though it was more complex than this. And he would have been astonished, had he still been alive in 1660 when Charles II was restored to the throne, how England had developed into a major horticultural nation, poised to lead the world in the design of gardens. How the revolution took place is another major theme of the book.

We can get a sense of the span of this revolution by looking at the title pages from two of the many books about various aspects of the horticultural scene that began to be published at this period. One is a botanical work published in London in 1570, the second a gardening book published in 1664, again in London. *Stirpium Adversaria* was the work of Matthias L'Obel from Lille and Peter Pena from Aix en Provence, from the northern and southern parts of Europe.[2] The book's title indicates that it is a new register of plants, yet the reader would be hard put to it to realise this if they had no Latin, for the reference to plants is limited to a small urn filled with flowers to be found in the centre of the page. At the top is a reproduction of the cosmographical system of Ptolemy, with the Tudor rose, portcullis and crown, showing that the book was published in London and dedicated to Elizabeth I. Flanking the planets and elements are shields enclosing devices of the two authors, using punning emblems, so popular at this period. At the bottom of the page is a map, a close copy of one drawn by Giralmo Porro of Padua in 1567, and one of the earliest to show in detail the Scandinavian peninsula and the Baltic Sea, areas of particular interest to sixteenth-century London merchants. Above the map are two kneeling figures of philosophers with scientific instruments, one in European dress representing mathematics and astronomy, the second in Turkish cap and robes as the representation of alchemy.

In the 1570s London was not a centre for international publishing, nor in the forefront of printing techniques, but L'Obel and Pena had taken refuge here to escape religious persecution in Europe. The design of the title page, only the third in England to use engraving in copper, has been attributed to the Dutchman Remigius Hogenberg. Perhaps this pictorial

1 The title page of L'Obel and Pena's register of plants, *Stirpium Adversaria*, published in London in 1570.

statement of a complete world philosophy was too advanced for the London market, for the edition of *Stirpium Adversaria* was not a commercial success, with L'Obel complaining of unsold copies for many years thereafter. However, it succinctly shows in pictorial form the new and fascinating world that was opening up.

Pena and L'Obel were distinguished botanists and physicians who had studied together under the great teacher Guillaume Rondelet at Montpellier University. Medicine was the driving force in the development of the study of botany, where the accurate identification of plants was vital. Botanical gardens had been established as part of the medical faculties of universities in Italy in the 1540s, and into these were introduced native plants, but also exotics from all parts of the world. This was an era of rapid expansion in discovery of new worlds driven by a thirst for knowledge, but also a desire for profit. Spain and Portugal had established colonies in the Americas, while the Dutch were creating mercantile outposts in the Far East.

Moving forward less than a hundred years, and looking at the second title page, for John Evelyn's *Sylva*, the picture is very different. Although the title is in Latin, the subtitle, 'A Discourse of Forest-Trees', is in English, as is the text of the book. Like *Stirpium Adversaria*, the book is dedicated to the monarch, this time the newly restored Charles II, but this royal connection is firmly underlined, unlike its predecessor, with reference to 'His Majesties Dominions', and the fact that the text was delivered to the Royal Society as a result of concerns about the viability of naval timber supplies. In fact, *Sylva* was the first book to be published by the Society for Improving of Natural Knowledge, which had received its royal charter from Charles II two years earlier. He also approved the coat of arms that illustrates the title page, with the three lions from the royal arms, one of a series of sketches made by Evelyn for the King. The motto 'Nullius in Verba' ('Take nobody's word for it') came from the Epistles of Horace, but was particularly appropriate for a society whose primary motive was knowledge through practical experimentation.

The author, John Evelyn, is described as 'J.E. Esq'. He was a member of the gentry who travelled widely in Europe in the 1640s, taking the opportunity to observe the gardens of the learned and the wealthy in France, the Low Countries and Italy. Appended to the discourse of forest trees is a treatise on the growing of fruit trees to make cider, and a gardener's almanac, providing a thorough grounding in the horticultural year. There had been practical gardening manuals in Tudor England, but these were not by

SYLVA,

Or A DISCOURSE Of

FOREST-TREES,

AND THE

Propagation of Timber

In His MAJESTIES Dominions.

By *J. E.* Esq;

As it was Deliver'd in the *ROYAL SOCIETY* the xv[th] of *October*, CIƆIƆCLXII. upon Occasion of certain *Quæries* Propounded to that *Illustrious Assembly*, by the *Honorable* the Principal *Officers*, and *Commissioners* of the *Navy*.

To which is annexed

POMONA Or, An *Appendix* concerning *Fruit-Trees* in relation to *CIDER*; The *Making* and several ways of *Ordering* it.

Published by express Order *of the* ROYAL SOCIETY.

ALSO

KALENDARIUM HORTENSE; Or, *Gard'ners Almanac*; Directing *what* he is to do *Monethly* throughout the *Year*.

———Tibi res antiquæ laudis & artis
Ingredior, tantos aufus recludere fonteis.   Virg.

LONDON, Printed by *Jo. Martyn*, and *Ja. Allestry*, Printers to the *Royal Society*, and are to be sold at their Shop at the *Bell* in S. *Paul's* Church-yard, MDCLXIV.

2 The title page of John Evelyn's *Sylva*, published in London in 1664.

wealthy, well-travelled individuals, and their target audience was very different. Unlike the London edition of *Stirpium Adversaria*, Evelyn's *Sylva* proved a great success: when a second edition was issued in 1669, the proud author informed the King in the dedication that 'more than a thousand copies had been bought up ... of the first impression, in much lesse time than two years' which according to booksellers was 'a very extraordinary thing in volumes of this bulk'. Moreover, the book was known throughout Europe, thanks to being advertised in the autumn catalogue of books exhibited at the Frankfurt Book Fair, the very heart of the international trade.

John Evelyn was later to compare Britain with a bouquet,

> cull'd and compos'd, not from any one single Beauty of the flowry-Parterre, but from the Rose and the Lily, the Jasmine, Tuberose and the rest ... so the Inclinations of the English seem to result from the great Variety of the people, which as so many glorious Flowers from time to time, have been transplanted into our British Elysium: Few Nations that I know of under Heaven (in so short a time) consisting of so many Ingredients, by Revolutions, and Successions.[3]

In this remarkable tribute to multiculturalism, he considered the ingredients of the recipe to be the Britons, Romans, Saxons, Danes, Normans and Belgians. With the exception of the inhabitants of the Iberian peninsula, here were the people who could contribute to the development of a major horticultural nation. And by 1660 this nation had also become a major naval power, with settlements in North America and the Caribbean, sending back to the mother country all kinds of exciting exotic plants that could be cultivated in gardens thanks to Britain's temperate climate, aided by technical advances such as greenhouses with stoves.

The pages of my book are thronged with people – courtiers, gardeners, nurserymen, florists, medical men, designers, engineers, poets and plantsmen, and even occasionally women. Most of the records of gardens and gardeners are from the wealthier echelons of society, although I have tried, wherever possible, to look at what 'ordinary' gardeners might have been doing.

Of course many of the gardens of these men and women have vanished, overtaken by changes in fashion. When Sir Roy Strong wrote his groundbreaking *Renaissance Garden in England* in 1979, he dedicated it 'in memory of all those gardens destroyed by Capability Brown and his successors'. However, recreations of sixteenth- and seventeenth-century gardens have been undertaken in the last two hundred years, in keeping with the Romantic Revival. At Chastleton in Oxfordshire, for instance, the early seventeenth-century gardens that had been laid out as a series of courts around the house were transformed at the beginning of the nineteenth century into an 'old-fashioned garden' with topiary, rose arbours and espaliered fruit trees. A few years later the Phelips family recreated the flavour of the original Tudor garden at Montacute in Somerset, planting parterres with intricate arrangements of beds. At this time, too, books began to consider the history of gardens. The first devoted entirely to the subject was George William Johnson's *History of Gardening*, published in 1829. Two architects and garden designers published influential books at the turn of the twentieth century: Reginald Blomfield's *Formal Garden in England* and Inigo Triggs's *Formal Gardens in England and Scotland*. Both sought with their learned texts and good illustrations to advise country-house owners on how to create appropriate historic gardens.

Not everybody was as well-informed or rigorous as Blomfield and Triggs, and great was the temptation to produce 'olde worlde' pastiches. E.F. Benson in *Queen Lucia*, published in 1920, deliciously satirises gardens inspired by the flowers that Shakespeare introduced so often into his plays. Lucia lived in a Sussex village, where she planted an Ophelia border, 'for it consisted solely of those flowers which that distraught maiden distributed to her friends when she should have been in a lunatic asylum'.[4]

Although gardens of the sixteenth and seventeenth centuries have disappeared, their 'bones' often remain to be uncovered by the developing science of garden archaeology. In recent years, organisations such as English Heritage, the National Trust, and the National Trust for Scotland have adopted a firmly authoritative approach, though always beset with dilemmas. In 1951 Pitmedden in Aberdeenshire passed to the National Trust for Scotland, with the bones of its late seventeenth-century formal garden, inspired by the designs of the great French gardener, André le Nôtre. The Trust recreated the forms of the parterre with box hedging, but within this, instead of using coloured sand, planted brilliantly coloured annuals – Victorian and late Stuart combined. The National Trust south of the border made the opposite decision when creating a seventeenth-century garden at Moseley Old Hall in Staffordshire. This was based on the designs made by a Yorkshire rector, the Revd Walter Stonehouse, and surviving in the archives of Magdalen College, Oxford. To save on labour – and it has to be remembered that the complex schemes of the Tudor and Stuart great gardens were highly labour intensive – the Trust took the decision to set the box trees of the knot garden into box-edged beds of gravel and cobble.

Recently English Heritage has recreated the privy garden laid out by Robert Dudley for the visit of Elizabeth I to Kenilworth in Warwickshire in 1575. Meticulous research and archaeology have been brought into play to provide as accurate a recreation as possible. The National Trust is in the middle of an equally ambitious plan to restore parts of the remarkable garden at Lyveden New Bield in Northamptonshire, originally created by Thomas Tresham at the end of the sixteenth century. These gardens do give a feeling of what must have met the eyes of our Tudor and Stuart ancestors. Yet, as John Sales, the former chief gardens adviser for the National Trust, shrewdly pointed out: 'All restored gardens are products of the values and understanding of those who restore them, as well as being a reflection of the past'.[5]

Another way of recapturing the appearance and spirit of sixteenth- and seventeenth-century gardens is to turn to drawings, plans, and occasional glimpses in the background of portraits. These are indeed occasional glimpses, and give us only an idea of the appearance of the gardens of the wealthiest and grandest. In order to try to recreate a much wider spectrum, we must turn to books, and these have been given an important role in my text for, while they are not usually garden-specific, they provide a revealing source of how people gained knowledge and information and communicated it to others. I have tried also to find out what books were owned by whom, looking at libraries, catalogues, and references in contemporary records.

Today we are provided with a wealth of information about the various aspects of gardening, from books and journals to television, radio and the internet. Yet 400 years ago, the available sources of knowledge were very limited, especially for those who were not wealthy or did not have the benefit of a classical education, or indeed any education at all. As the years progressed, so the number of books grew. Women, who scarcely feature in the sixteenth century, begin to step out of the shadows in the seventeenth both as book owners and gardeners. The practical gardeners, whom I call 'the men on the ground', also gradually take on identity. Thus John Chapman, gardener to Cardinal Wolsey and Henry VIII and therefore responsible for extremely ambitious schemes at Hampton Court and Whitehall, appears in the house-hold accounts but nothing more is known about him than that he hailed from Kingston upon Thames. A century later, sufficient is known of the life of John

Tradescant the Elder to produce recent biographies and novels, even though we still don't know when exactly he was born, or details of his forefathers.[6]

I described above the groundbreaking work of Roy Strong in publishing books on sixteenth- and seventeenth-century English gardens. His first book, *The Renaissance Garden in England,* published in 1979, inspired others to investigate further, and to open up a whole series of debates. This can be clearly seen in the many papers that have been contributed to the journal of the Garden History Society, moving from an overwhelming interest in the eighteenth-century landscape gardens to look at a much wider world of historical horticultural endeavour. Without wishing to be invidious, I should also like to acknowledge the enormous debt we owe to John Harvey for his work on early gardeners and nurserymen, to Blanche Henrey for her monumental *British Botanical and Horticultural Literature before 1800,* and more recently Anna Pavord's *The Naming of Names,* and Paula Henderson's *The Tudor House and Garden.* The last is full of illustrations of gardens and designs to which I have referred, but which, given the even wider remit of my book, I could not include.

***

Paula Henderson's book was made possible by the generosity of the Paul Mellon Centre for Studies in British Art, and I too have received their support, for which I am deeply grateful. They have enabled me to include illustrations, a vital ingredient for a book on gardens. Thanks are also due to the Scouloudi Foundation for ensuring that some of the pictures can be reproduced in colour. The Wellcome Institute and the British Museum have also been particularly generous in their supply of images.

The staff of many libraries and archives have helped me with my research: Frances Harris and Giles Mandelbrote at the British Library; Dr Barker Banfield at the Bodleian; Andrew Peppitt at Chatsworth; Robin Harcourt Williams at Hatfield House; Sarah Cobbold at Jesus College, Oxford; Christine Ferdinand and Hilary Pattison at Magdalen College, Oxford; Sara Griffin at the Royal College of Physicians; Gerard Thijsse at the National Herbarium in Leiden; Charles Hinde at the RIBA; and Crispin Powell at the Northampton Record Office. I am also grateful to Mark Bradshaw at Lyveden New Bield and Fiona Sanders at Kenilworth Castle for their time and information.

I started my writing career proper rather late in the day, and I never cease to be amazed by how supportive and encouraging are the experts in the field. So I would also like to thank Sir Keith Thomas, Dr Stephen Harris, Professor David McKitterick, Dr John Hinks, Professor Batho, Professor Maurice Howard, Dr David Marsh, Adam Nicolson and Rory Stuart for their help. Christina Mackwell yet again interpreted fiendish secretary hand, and Michael Braeckman rescued me on some Latin titles. Thanks also to Kyle Cathie, Ros Alexander, Ans van Hille and Liz Morrison. Working with Yale University Press is such a pleasure, and special thanks to Robert Baldock, who came up with this wonderful subject, Rachael Lonsdale who has been such a responsive and helpful editor, and Kate Pocock with her wise advice. My beloved partner, Victor Morrison, died while I was working on the book, and his family have been very supportive, so my final thanks go to them.

CHAPTER 1

Fit for a Queen

D URING THE SUMMER MONTHS, to escape the heat and unhealthy
conditions of London, it was the custom of Queen Elizabeth I to go
on progress around her realm. Thus in late May 1583, she paid one
of her many visits to Theobalds, the great house built near St Albans in
Hertfordshire by William Cecil, Lord Burghley. One of those present noted:
'She was never in any place better pleased, and sure the house, garden and
walks may compare with any delicate place in Italy.'[1]

This was a great compliment, for although Elizabeth Tudor never visited
Italy – indeed, never left England – she appreciated that the most fashionable
ideas in design were being brought back and applied to architecture and to the
layout of gardens. She loved flowers, as can be seen in the iconography that
was adopted in her portraits, where the Queen is often depicted with her
favourites, such as the eglantine rose and the heartsease or pansy. And of
course the Tudor rose, the heraldic hybrid, is never far away. Elizabeth also
recognised how the symbolism of gardens could be used in the cult of
Gloriana that she so carefully nurtured.

However, unlike her father, Elizabeth was neither a great builder nor a
creator of gardens. At his death in 1547, it is estimated that Henry VIII owned
nearly sixty houses of varying sizes, all with accompanying gardens. Some
were sold or given away in the following decades, but Elizabeth was responsible for the upkeep of several elaborate examples, such as those at Hampton
Court, Richmond and Greenwich, with finances that were always perilous.
Instead she left her courtiers to create the exciting new gardens of the late

3 'Rosa Electa' by William Rogers, depicting Elizabeth I surrounded by eglantine and Tudor roses. Rogers made a series of engravings of the Queen in the last decade of the sixteenth century for sale as individual prints.

sixteenth century, bestowing upon them her patronage and favour. These courtiers responded by developing and elaborating upon the style of gardens that had been introduced by the Queen's grandfather, Henry VII, and by her father, Henry VIII.

In the 1560s there developed an inner circle of courtiers who were creating fine gardens around their 'prodigy' houses: William Cecil, Robert Dudley, Christopher Hatton and Bess of Hardwick. The early Elizabethan court might be divided into three groups. 'The old guard' of great families of the Middle Ages had had their wings severely clipped by the internecine conflicts of the Wars of the Roses, and by Henry VIII's pathological suspicion of overweening subjects. As a result, the Percies, the Nevilles, the Cliffords and above all the Howards were still recovering financially from these perilous years, and were not in the costly business of building great new houses or creating magnificent gardens.[2] This handed opportunity to the 'new men', like William Cecil, from relatively modest backgrounds but benefiting from a humanist education, who built their careers on service to the Crown. Lastly came the dashing courtiers who contributed to the heady and complex mythology of the Virgin Queen, such as Robert Dudley and Christopher Hatton. As a woman, Bess of Hardwick does not fit into this rough and ready categorisation, but her way of overcoming her modest background was to acquire four husbands, three of whom do represent the different groups: William Cavendish was a 'new man', William St Loe was a dashing courtier, and her last husband, George Talbot, Earl of Shrewsbury, came from one of the oldest noble families.

The chronicler William Harrison had some interesting observations to make about the development of gardens in England. In his *Description of England* dating from 1577, he argued that gardening flourished during the late thirteenth century, but with the civil wars that broke out in the fifteenth century, the cultivation of vegetables, herbs and flowers was neglected, and only late in the reign of Henry VII was gardening able to flourish again. Comparing old gardens to dunghills, Harrison noted with fervent pride how the introduction of flowers, 'medicinable herbs' and 'new seeds out of strange countries' had increased in the last forty years. Harrison was probably the son of a London merchant adventurer, and therefore had a particular message, emphasising the pride of the nation, and its trading links with the rest of the world. Yet the uneasy times imposed by the Wars of the Roses certainly diverted the Crown and the leading noblemen of England from keeping pace with the latest European developments in the design of gardens and in the range of plants to be cultivated. Moreover, Harrison was speaking from practical experience, for he had his own garden, more than 300 feet in length, where he cultivated over 300 different plants, 'no one of them being common or usually to be had.'[3]

Our knowledge of the early Tudor grand gardens is very patchy, reliant on occasional contemporary descriptions, and on portraits where a garden might be glimpsed in the distance. Despite his notoriety as a skinflint, Henry VII had a fine garden laid out at his palace of Richmond. He had spent many years of exile in Brittany, and latterly in France, but it was the lavish style of the Burgundian court that most influenced him. When his elder son Arthur, Prince of Wales, married Catherine of Aragon in 1501, it was recorded that under the windows of the royal apartments were 'most fair and pleasant gardens, with royal knots alleyed and herbed; many marvellous beasts, as lions, dragons and such other of divers kind, properly fashioned and carved in the ground ... with many vines, seeds and strange fruit, right goodly beset, kept and nourished with much labour and diligence'.[4]

The knots 'alleyed and herbed' are probably the compartments that were shown in a sketch of Richmond Palace by the Flemish artist Anthony van Wyngaerde, made in the 1550s. In the late fifteenth century grand gardens in Europe began to be organised into compartments containing beds for plants. These beds were usually about two metres in width, allowing gardeners ease of access from the surrounding paths, and the number of compartments and their shape varied according to the space available.[5] Intricate patterns, or knots, could be planted using herbs such as rosemary, hyssop or thyme, and Wyngaerde's drawing suggests that one of the compartments at Richmond was laid out in the form of a labyrinth or maze. The taste for carved beasts was a mediaeval one, but the Tudors particularly harnessed them as part of their iconography, as can be seen in Cambridge, on the gatehouse of St John's College, which displays the badges of Lady Margaret Beaufort and of her son Henry VII.

The chronicler of the marriage of Arthur and Catherine goes on to record 'pleasant galleries' in the lower part of the garden at Richmond. These galleries can also be seen in Wyngaerde's sketch – open below, and with large bay windows above, very much a feature of Burgundian garden palaces. Richmond Palace has long gone, but at Thornbury Castle in Gloucestershire, the canted galleries that would have looked down upon the garden have survived. Thornbury was built by Edward Stafford, third Duke of Buckingham, and remained unfinished when he was executed for treason by Henry VIII in 1521.

After Buckingham's fall, Thornbury was seized by the Crown, but left as a ruin – perhaps a reminder of the fate of over-ambitious nobles. But Henry VIII behaved quite differently with his other great acquisition, the palace and gardens at Hampton Court, ceded to him in 1528 by the very man who had engineered Buckingham's fall, Cardinal Wolsey. Over the next decade Henry ordered a major recreation of the gardens on the site between the palace and the river. A series of irregular walled compartments was developed, reminiscent of enclosed gardens within mediaeval castles, but with windows inserted in some of the walls to provide visual links. Beyond the privy garden was a triangular mount garden, a bowling alley and yet more compartments running down to the gate on the Thames. A veritable flurry of garden buildings was erected, some as viewing platforms, others as banqueting houses, the grandest of which was the 'Great Round Arbour'. Set on top of a mount that had been planted with thousands of trained shrubs, this remarkable building consisted of storeys of glittering glass, crowned by a bulbous dome according to another sketch made by Wyngaerde. Also scattered throughout the gardens were heraldic beasts, nearly one hundred in all, echoing those that rose above the roofs of the palace itself. The whole effect must have been highly theatrical, while there was no doubt that the leading actor was the King himself, a Renaissance prince in all his power and glory.

A detailed glimpse of the effect achieved at Hampton Court can be seen in the background of a painting of the family of Henry VIII, painted by an unknown artist towards the end of his reign, and now in the Royal Collection. In the outermost sections of the picture are two archways, with household servants peeping through. Behind them are rectangular beds of flowers surrounded by rails painted in the Tudor colours of green and white. Sitting atop decorated pillars are heraldic beasts holding banners. These details are thought to be from the privy gardens of the palace of Whitehall, another property seized from Cardinal Wolsey by the King. In the left-hand section the lodgings of Princess Mary are shown, painted externally with grotesques, giving an overall effect of an enormous amount of detailed decoration and colour.

Detail in the back of another painting provides another clue in this very patchy mosaic, and one to the style of more modest gardens. A miniature of the family of Sir Thomas More, painted in the late sixteenth century by Rowland Lockey as a copy of a lost painting by Holbein, shows in the distance a garden (Plate V). This is thought to be More's garden in Chelsea, on the bank of the Thames. Through an open arch, the garden is glimpsed surrounded by high brick walls, within which are low hedges enclosing individual beds. On one of the walls, overlooking the Thames, is a tall building that may have housed More's library and chapel, where 'he passed much of his time in

4 Detail from *The Family of Henry VIII*, painted by an unknown artist, *c.* 1545. Behind the maid peeping through an archway can be glimpsed gardens, possibly of Whitehall Palace. Raised beds of flowers are shown with striped rails, while heraldic beasts on columns hold tiny pennants.

retirement and devotion'.[6] According to Cicero, a man with a garden and a library has all he needs: unfortunately More also had a monarch with matrimonial problems.

The layout in the painting resembles the gardens depicted in the so-called 'Agas' map of Tudor London, where a whole series of details are shown, such as vineyards, orchards, and hedged plots. Strung out along the Strand are the houses belonging to various members of the Tudor court, including that built in the late 1540s for Edward Seymour, Duke of Somerset and Lord Protector to his nephew, Edward VI. One of the members of his household was the botanist William Turner, author of the first English herbal, who is credited with creating a physic garden for Somerset at Syon House, upstream on the

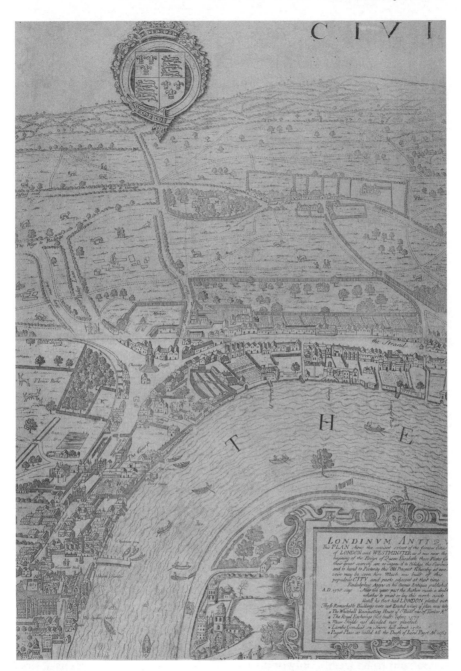

5 Detail from the 'Agas' map, a seventeenth-century copy of a lost map of London compiled in the mid-1550s. At the bottom left is Westminster Abbey and Hall and the palace of Whitehall with its garden laid out in compartments and a fountain in the centre. On the north bank of the Thames are the great mansions along the Strand, including Somerset House. William Cecil acquired his house on the north side of the Strand after this map was drawn, but the situation can be seen, looking out over countryside to the hills of Hampstead and Highgate.

Thames. He may well also have supervised the design and layout of the garden at Somerset House, which appears to be laid out in a series of compartments. Another member of the household at this period was William Cecil, and these gardens no doubt provided the inspiration for his lifelong love of gardens and plants.

William Cecil was born in 1520 in Bourne, a small town in Lincolnshire, the son of a middle-ranking officer in the royal household. After attending schools in Grantham and Stamford, he went up to Cambridge, to St John's College, joining a circle of leading classical scholars, including Roger Ascham and John Cheke, who were both to become tutors to the royal family. In 1540, soon after leaving Cambridge, he married Cheke's sister Mary. Cecil began to study law at Gray's Inn, but in 1543 Mary died, leaving the young lawyer with one son, Thomas. Two years later he married Mildred, the daughter of Sir Anthony Cooke, lawyer, soldier, member of Henry VIII's bodyguard, and a self-taught scholar. Mildred was one of a quartet of formidably clever daughters, and Cecil had now entered a cultivated circle enjoying excellent connections with the royal court.[7]

The 1540s and 1550s were perilous times in England, especially for anybody close to the court. Cecil managed to ride out the storms remarkably well. Although he was one of the secretaries to Lord Protector Somerset, he survived his fall, and instead became secretary to the King, Edward VI, through the favour of John Dudley, Duke of Northumberland. With the accession of the Catholic Mary Tudor in 1553, he retired from public life, building up his library and turning amateur architect, making modern improvements to the old house at Burghley in Northamptonshire that his father had purchased a quarter of a century earlier. He also made at least two visits to the Low Countries, keeping contact with Protestants who had fled there with the restoration of Catholicism in England. These journeys had, perforce, to be discreet, but it is thought that on one visit he stayed with the merchant and financier Sir Thomas Gresham in Antwerp and probably saw the garden of the castle of Wacquem with its elaborate use of water. Many castles and manor houses in this period were surrounded by moats, but Wacquem also had two gardens surrounded by water, one of which could be reached only by boat. These visits turned out to be Cecil's only opportunities to see Continental gardens at first hand. Thereafter he would have to rely on the descriptions of others, by word of mouth or through books and engravings.

Life changed radically for William Cecil with the accession of Elizabeth I in 1558. He became her secretary, and in 1561 was given the lucrative position

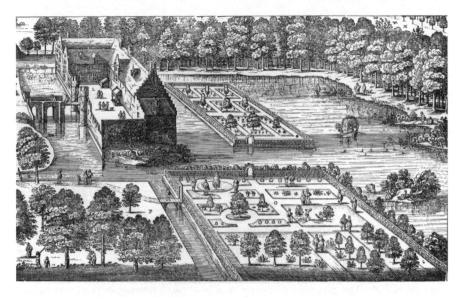

6 The château of Wacquem in Flanders. William Cecil probably saw the castle with its famous water gardens during one of his brief visits to the Low Countries during the reign of Mary Tudor, and used some of the features when creating his own gardens at Theobalds in Hertfordshire.

of Master of the Court of Wards. Now he had the money to be able to acquire properties, and to create fine gardens. He bought a house on the Strand in London, which became both his home and base of operations as Principal Secretary. Pulling down the old house, he created a model of architectural symmetry involving two courts, with extensive gardens running northwards to the open fields of Covent Garden. A recently discovered survey, now at Burghley House, has colour washes that give some indication of the appearance of the gardens. On the western side was a kitchen garden, on the east an L-shaped area which was probably Cecil's private garden. In the centre was his 'great garden' with a central path aligned to the main entrance of the house, an early example in England of the axiality held important by Renaissance architects. The 'great garden' was divided into three parts. To the west was a square enclosed by brick walls, with a mount in the centre, and four trees planted at the corners. To the east was an orchard laid out in a pattern of quincunxes. The central part had compartments divided by broad paths, and probably each compartment had an enclosing fence or trellis.

Three years after the acquisition of the London house, Cecil bought Theobalds, an old-fashioned moated manor house near St Albans on the main road northwards, now the A1. Elizabeth I paid her first visit to Theobalds in the July of 1564, but did not stay overnight because Cecil was planning improvements. And what improvements! Over the next thirty years he spent huge sums developing the house so that ultimately it boasted five courtyards. When the house was fit for the accommodation of the Queen, her apartments overlooked the gardens, which were as grand in scale as the house, and covered twice the area of Henry VIII's ambitious gardens at Hampton Court Palace. In one year alone, Cecil spent £955 on running costs for Theobalds, of which £148 were allotted to the gardens.[8]

Contemporary descriptions of gardens from English sources tended to focus on the overall impression of magnificence but remain rather vague about details. However, two German travellers who visited Theobalds right at the end of the sixteenth century have left a record of some of the features. In 1598 Paul Hentzner described entering the garden through an ornate loggia that Cecil had decorated with a genealogy of his family. From there he noted 'one goes into the garden, encompassed with a ditch full of water, large enough for one to have the pleasure of going in a boat, and rowing between shrubs.'[9] This is reminiscent of the garden that Cecil may have seen half a century earlier at the château of Wacquem.

The second German traveller, Baron Waldstein, made his visit in 1600, and recorded that there were 'columns and pyramids of wood and other materials up and down the garden', an echo of the ornaments in the gardens of Henry VIII. He also noted 'quite a large obelisk of alabaster surmounted by a figure of Christ'. Such religious iconography would have been so unusual in Protestant England that it has been suggested that Waldstein was mistaken, and this was in fact the statue of a gardener.[10] Much more characteristic of the age were hidden water pipes fed from a conduit that sprayed unwary visitors – the Tudors' idea of a good joke. Water again featured in a summer-house, 'in the lower part of which, built semi-circularly, are the twelve Roman emperors in white marble, and a table of touchstone; the upper part of it is set round with cisterns of lead, into which the water is conveyed through pipes, so that fish may be kept in them, and in summertime they are very convenient for bathing.'

Also mentioned was an extraordinary feature:

In the first room there is an overhanging rock or crag . . . made of different kinds of semi-transparent stone, and roofed over with pieces of coral, crystal, and all kinds of metallic ore. It is thatched with green grass, and inside can be seen a man and a woman dressed like wild men of the woods, and a number of animals creeping through the bushes. A bronze centaur stands at the base of it. A number of columns by the windows support the mighty structure of the room: these columns are covered with the bark of trees, so that they do in fact look exactly like oaks and pines.[11]

Grottoes, artificial rocky caves with water cascading into pools, had been created by the Romans and were taken up with enthusiasm in Italian Renaissance gardens. Cecil's grotto is the first recorded in England, and very like the famous one at Castello near Florence, created in the 1570s. Cecil was clearly a pioneering gardener, for he is also credited with erecting one of the first orangeries in England and was praised for 'a flourishing shew of sommer beauties in the middest of winters force'.[12]

When Cecil bought Theobalds in 1564, it was intended as the inheritance of Robert, his son by his marriage to Mildred Cooke. His estate at Burghley, which he had inherited from his father, and from which he took his title of Lord Burghley when he was ennobled by the Queen in 1571, was intended for his first son, Thomas. Gradually William changed Burghley from a courtyard house to one that looked outwards, with a great west wing opening onto extensive gardens. A visit by Elizabeth was planned for the summer of 1566 that had to be cancelled when Cecil's daughter Anne was suspected of contracting smallpox. But the gardens were laid out in preparation for the royal visit, with shaded walks and mounts, orchards and formal areas. The Queen would have arrived in late afternoon, so the windows of the west front were designed to catch the sun, glittering their welcome like an immense lantern.

Although we know quite a lot about the layout of Cecil's gardens, and about some of the features, there is hardly any indication of the plants cultivated therein. Yet William Cecil loved plants, as Thomas Hill makes clear in his dedication to him in his book, *The Gardeners Labyrinth*, published in 1577, in which he talked of the alleys and walks where he could 'diligently view the prosperity of his herbs and flowers' and get some relief from the heavy burdens of office. Cecil's biographer noted that his delight was 'riding in his garden walks, upon his little mule', and he is thus depicted in a charming portrait by an anonymous artist.[13] Instead of the formal pose of the Queen's Chief Secretary, he wears an embroidered crimson robe, trimmed with fur, and in his hand he holds a nosegay of pinks and honeysuckle. The landscape behind is filled with wild flowers (Plate I).

Cecil probably was the designer of his own gardens. He was kept informed of the planting and estate work at Burghley by his agent, Peter Kemp, and from the mid-1570s John Gerard acted as the supervisor of the collection of his plants, indigenous and exotic, in London and at Theobalds. Gerard was born in Cheshire in 1545 and attended school at Willaston near Nantwich, where he learnt Latin and possibly a smattering of Greek before being apprenticed to a London barber surgeon, Alexander Mason. Although he practised as a surgeon, it is clear from his herbal that Gerard's overriding interest was botany and horticulture. He travelled with the Company of Merchant Adventurers to Scandinavia, Poland and Estonia, though it is not known whether he did so professionally or as a passenger. Nor is it known how he came to be appointed by William Cecil as the supervisor of his gardens. Gerard was energetic, a man of talent and drive, not backwards in coming forward, overcoming his relatively modest background and sometimes courting controversy. His herbal of 1597 and the catalogue of contents of his own garden in Holborn published the previous year give us an idea of what plants he may have had in his care in Cecil's gardens. A consignment of bulbed flowers sent from Constantinople included the double white daffodil, 'whose rootes when they were planted in our London gardens, did bring foorth beautifull flowers'. William Harborne, who combined the roles of merchant and ambassador at the court of the Ottoman Sultan, dispatched to Cecil the 'red Lilly of Constantinople'. This martagon lily, according to Gerard, 'groweth wilde in the fields and mountains, many daies journeys beyond Constantinople, wither it is brought by the poore pesants to be solde, for the deckup of gardens'.[14]

When William Cecil died in August 1598, the Queen called him 'pater pacis patriae'. She had quarrelled many times over the years with this father figure, but their relationship had always remained close and she knew how important he had been in the government of her kingdom. Her relationship with Robert Dudley, Earl of Leicester, was equally close but on a different footing. William Camden described it as 'a sympathy of spirits between them, occasioned perhaps by some secret constellation'.[15] They were almost exactly the same age – Elizabeth was born in September 1533, Robert in the June of that year, or the previous year. Both knew privilege and peril at an early age. Elizabeth was only three when her mother Anne Boleyn was executed by her father Henry VIII. Robert's grandfather Edmund was executed in 1510 by Henry in a ruthless bid for popularity early in his reign, for Dudley, with Sir Richard Empson, had been the public faces of Henry VII's extortionate financial policy. Robert's father, John Dudley, Duke of Northumberland, having spectacularly revived the family's fortunes, equally spectacularly fell from power when he attempted to put Lady Jane Grey on the throne after the death of Edward VI. During the crisis both Robert and Elizabeth were imprisoned in the Tower of London by Mary Tudor, with a very real threat of death hanging over them both. Add to this a strong sexual attraction, and it is little wonder that they remained close throughout their turbulent lives.

Both Robert Dudley's parents were well educated. His father John was brought up in the cultured household of Sir Edward Guildford and married his daughter Jane, who had received her education in the royal school instituted by Catherine of Aragon and directed by Juan Luys Vives. The marriage between Jane Guildford and John Dudley proved a close and fruitful one, with eight sons and two daughters. Robert's childhood home was Ely Place in Holborn, the mediaeval residence of the Bishops of Ely, with twelve acres of garden. He was a man of action rather than bookish, fascinated by mathematics and the new sciences, especially cosmography. One poignant memorial may point to a family interest in botany. When Robert and four of his brothers were imprisoned in the Beauchamp Tower after their father's failed coup to put Lady Jane Grey on the throne, a carving was made on the wall of their cell, probably organised by his eldest brother, John. Around the Dudley badge of the bear and ragged staff are a rose for Ambrose, gillyflowers for Guildford, Lady Jane Grey's husband, honeysuckle for Henry, and oak leaves (*robur*) for Robert. Although Guildford was executed along with his tragic Queen of nine days, Robert escaped with his life, and within a year was sent to Europe with Mary Tudor's consort, Philip II of Spain. He received an unusually pan-European experience as part of a retinue of Spaniards, Flemings, Neapolitans, Dutch, Savoyards, and Germans travelling through the Low Countries, conveying reports from Philip to the various English ambassadors.

After years of peril, Elizabeth I came to the throne in 1558, and one of her first appointments was to make Robert Dudley Master of the Horse. This involved him in the organisation of court entertainments such as masques and plays, banquets and tournaments and brought him into almost daily contact with his sovereign. In 1563 his brother Ambrose was made Earl of Warwick, one of the titles that their father had held, and was given the castle at Warwick. In the same year Robert was given the castle of Kenilworth, and in 1564 he was made Earl of Leicester. The castle at Kenilworth, situated just five miles from Warwick, also represented an echo of the family's past, for it had belonged briefly to John Dudley.

Kenilworth was one of England's great castles, dating back to the twelfth century, with a massive keep and curtain walls standing high above a huge artificial lake, the 'Great Pool'. Although in the late fourteenth century John of

Gaunt had added a great hall and domestic apartments to make it into a residence fit for a prince, when Robert Dudley acquired the castle, much work needed to be done. In the late 1560s he spent some £60,000 on enlarging and improving the accommodation. This is an impressive sum – the equivalent today would be around a million pounds – but modest compared to William Cecil's annual expenditure of around a quarter of a million pounds over many years in developing Theobalds. A wooden bridge, 600 feet in length, was built to connect the castle to the deer park to the west, while a causeway to the south was developed into a tiltyard with viewing galleries. To the north he built a three-storey gatehouse, and opposite a rectangular tower, Leicester's Building, to provide apartments for visitors. His master mason, William Spicer, was very concerned that the castle lacked symmetry, beseeching 'yr lordship repent not hereafter what is left undone'.[16]

Dudley did not repent, for he was looking for rather a different effect to that achieved by Cecil at his houses. He would have been rather surprised by the categorisation of courtiers made at the beginning of this chapter, for the Dudleys were related to several 'old families' of mediaeval England. Thus Kenilworth represented for him a reminder of his noble ancestry and, like his brother Ambrose at Warwick Castle, he chose to retain the mediaeval character. By connecting the castle with the deer park and creating an area for the tilt, Robert Dudley was playing the role of Master of the Horse and emphasising his knightly qualities. He was also preparing the castle for the reception of his Queen, and for her he laid out magnificent formal gardens within the curtain wall.

Elizabeth's first sight of Kenilworth occurred in the summer of 1572, but even after this Robert Dudley continued to develop the gardens so that the horticultural climax came in July 1575 when the Queen stayed for nineteen days. A major recreation of the formal garden has recently been undertaken by English Heritage, based on archaeological investigation and a letter purportedly written by one of Dudley's servants, Robert Laneham, the keeper of the council chamber at Kenilworth, who contrived to get into the garden while Elizabeth was out hunting.[17]

An archway led from the castle above, and the Queen would have seen the pattern of the garden laid out below her as she descended to the high terrace walk. Along the walls of the walk were stone white bears, the emblems of the Dudley family, interspersed with obelisks, the latter making their first appearance in England. Obelisks, or pyramids as they were sometimes described, were symbols of the Egyptian sun god, and pairs would be set to guard the entrance to temples during the Middle Kingdom. The Romans had brought examples back to Italy, and they were a favourite feature of Renaissance gardens there. At each end of the terrace were arbours 'redolent by sweet trees and flowers', probably honeysuckle and rose. The garden itself was divided into four by walks of grass or sand, with low fences of wooden lattice enclosing the quarters. In the centre of each quarter stood an obelisk topped with an orb of porphyry. In the very centre of the garden was a great fountain with an octagonal basin of white marble surmounted by two figures of Atlas holding a globe. The eight sides of the basin were decorated with scenes taken from the watery stories in Ovid's *Metamorphoses*, such as Caenis, a beauty from Thessaly who was raped by Neptune, and Tethis riding naked on a dolphin. Laneham reported that if visitors became overheated by desire in seeing these scenes, spouts of water could be turned on to spray them – another example of the popular sixteenth-century joke. There was also an aviary, two-storied, twenty feet high, thirty feet long and fourteen feet broad, which Laneham described as being 'beautified with diamonds, emeralds, rubies, and sapphires ... and garnished with gold'. This extravagant structure was based on a design by the Roman architect Varro, from the first century BCE.

Laneham also talked of the 'fragrancy of sweet odours' and the 'taste of delicious strawberries, cherries and other fruits', and these can be savoured by modern visitors courtesy of the recreation of the privy garden. Around the perimeter fruit trees – apples, pears and cherries – have been planted, using varieties familiar to Thomas Tusser and other contemporary gardening writers. The layout of the four formal beds in the centre of the garden is based on contemporary illustrations such as the engravings of J. Vredeman de Vries in his *Hortorum viridariorum*, published in 1583. Filling the beds are flowers that were known to the Elizabethans, although a few probably did not appear in England until after 1575, and are first recorded by John Gerard in his herbal of 1597. In springtime many of the plants are natives, sweet violets, lily of the valley and primroses. In summer the native columbine is accompanied by the sweet william and the pot marigold that had been growing in English gardens for centuries. An exotic element is introduced with *Lychnis chalcedonica* that arrived from north Russia just at the time that Dudley was laying out his garden. Two flowers from the New World have been included: *Amaranthus paniculatis*, from South America, known familiarly as love-lies-bleeding and a nice allusion to Dudley's devotion to the Queen; and *Tagetes erecta*, the African marigold which is in fact a native of Central America, providing a splash of brilliant orange among the predominance of blues, whites and pinks.

The presence of the Queen at Kenilworth is symbolised by her favourite heartsease and eglantine rose, and the Tudor rose in the form of *Rosa damascena versicolor*. Carnations and the various kinds of roses provide the intense scent that must have greeted Elizabeth as she stepped down from the terrace during her visit in high summer (Plate II).

The visit that Elizabeth paid to Robert Dudley at Kenilworth in 1575 was without precedent in many ways. Most of her summer progresses were made in the south of England, and she never went further north than Warwickshire. The presence of her cousin, Mary Queen of Scots, in Derbyshire may have discouraged her from going further afield, or she may have felt that long journeys were inconvenient and expensive. Certainly it was rather a doubtful privilege to entertain the Queen, for she was a demanding guest. When she first stayed with William Cecil at Theobalds, she observed that her chamber was too small. A similar complaint was made on her visit to Cecil's brother-in-law, Nicholas Bacon, at his Hertfordshire house, Gorhambury. In a witty allusion to his own expanding girth, he replied, 'Madame, my house is well, but it is you that have made me too great for my house'.[18] By the time she came to stay again, he had built a new gallery, 120 feet long, especially for her. Tradition has it that the Queen on her first visit to Kenilworth expressed her disappointment that she could not see the gardens from her apartments. Overnight Robert Dudley ordered his gardeners to create a new garden below her bedchamber.

There were some courtiers who built great houses and created wonderful gardens in the hope that the Queen would afford them the privilege of her presence, only to have that hope dashed. One such was Sir Christopher Hatton. The son of a lesser gentry family from Northamptonshire, he first came to the Queen's notice when he appeared in a masque at the Inner Temple during the celebrations for the New Year of 1562. The play, *Gorboduc*, is regarded as one of the earliest tragedies in the English language, partly written by Thomas Sackville. 'Sometimes noble, and always dull' is the judgement of Sackville's descendant, Vita Sackville-West, which may explain why the Queen focused her attention on one of the participants rather than the drama itself.[19] According to William Camden, Hatton was 'a tall handsome young man, and of comely countenance', and some have unkindly suggested that it was his skills as a dancer that made him quickly gain the favour of the Queen.[20]

But Hatton was much more than a dancing partner. If Chaucer were to have cast the roles for the Elizabethan court, he might have made William Cecil the clerk, Robert Dudley the soldier, and Hatton the squire. Between the Queen and her squire developed an extraordinary relationship. As her constant suitor he worshipped her with a devotion that was unwavering. While Dudley was her 'Eyes', her pet names for Hatton were 'Lids' and 'Sheep'. When a new favourite appeared on the scene, Walter Raleigh, Hatton sent her a token, a silver bucket, symbol of 'wa[l]ter', indicating that water was an unstable element. The Queen responded by pointing out that Hatton was so dear that she had bounded the banks so that water would not overthrow him, and sent him a symbol, a dove, the biblical herald of receding flood. Hatton held many court offices, so was constantly at the Queen's side; unlike Dudley, whose romantic life was complex and perilous, he never married and, unlike Cecil, had no family ambitions.

In 1578 Hatton began rebuilding his hereditary home, Holdenby, around two great courts. Perhaps most spectacular was the south front, 350 feet in length, which, like Burghley, was dominated by great windows that glittered in the sun. The range overlooked an equally dramatic garden that was laid out on a huge flat platform that had been artificially raised from the sloping hillside. John Norden in 1595 noted:

> with what industrye and toyle of man, the garden have been raised, levelled, and formed out of a most craggye and unfitable lande now framed a most pleasante, sweete and princely place, with divers walks, many ascendings and descendings, replenished also with manie delightful Trees of Fruite, artificially composed Arbours and a Destilling House on the west end of the same garden, over which is a Ponde of Water, broughte by conduit pypes, out of the feylde adjoining on the west, quarter of a myle from the same house.[21]

This is the only written description of the gardens at Holdenby, but there is a visual record and one that shows the development in their layout. Ralph Treswell made an estate map in 1580, and a second one seven years later, both now in the record office at Northampton. In 1580 an area to the south of the house was described as 'ye Rosiary', possibly for rose trees, flanking a formal garden divided into quarters. A single large flower had been placed in each of the quarters, suggesting that these were filled with flower beds. To the west of the house was another large garden, divided into nine compartments, with a cistern or conduit house fed by a stream, and a mount in the north-west corner. By 1587 the 'Rosiary' remains, but the central garden is shown with more detailed planting designs. The nine compartments to the west have been replaced by a plantation of trees.

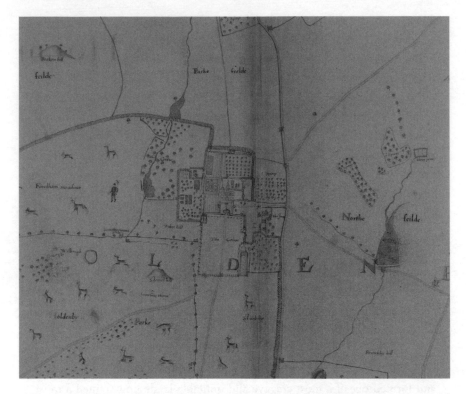

7 Detail of Ralph Treswell's map of Holdenby House, made in 1587. Around the house are the formal gardens, including one with an elaborate knot. The tall building standing in the top left corner of 'the Greene' is probably a banqueting house. Beyond the gardens is Sir Christopher Hatton's hunting park with rabbits, deer, and huntsmen with their falcons.

A designer has been attributed to the gardens at Holdenby – an unusual thing in itself, and made even more unusual by the identity of the person, Hugh Hall, a Catholic priest.[22] Throughout his career there were recurrent suggestions that Hatton held Catholic sympathies, never borne out by contemporary evidence. William Camden astutely suggested that he was opposed to fire and sword in matters of religion, and also described him as possessing a modest sweetness of character, so that it may have been out of kindness that he employed Hall as the designer of his garden. But it also seems possible that Hall helped to create the water gardens at Burghley, for a letter from William Cecil's steward, Peter Kemp, referred to a priest who would not dig holes in the orchard, as they would then stand full of water.[23] It would seem that in matters of gardening, religious prejudices could be overcome.

All the splendour at Holdenby remained unseen. In 1580, Hatton declared he would not visit his estate until his holy saint, to whom it was dedicated – the

Queen – came to sit in it. Northamptonshire was a step too far for Elizabeth, and she never did visit her shrine. Even more strangely, Hatton rarely travelled northwards to view the developments, although William Cecil went to visit and wrote to him about what he saw. By the time Hatton died in 1591, he was bankrupt, ruined by the expense of building Holdenby and nearby Kirby Hall, and creating their gardens. The queenly saint took broth to his last bedside.

The fourth courtier gardener of this circle was Bess of Hardwick, and she also built a great house and laid out gardens in the hope of a visit from the Queen. Bess was born in late 1527 into an old established Derbyshire family that had fallen into a state of genteel poverty. When she was only a few months old, her father died, leaving her and her three sisters the modest sum of £26 13s 4d apiece, while a few hundred acres and a rather rundown mediaeval manor house went to her only brother, James. But from this unpromising beginning, Bess built up her personal fortune through her four marriages and by her astute and careful husbandry. Like many daughters of gentry, she became an upper servant in another household, that of the Zouche family who divided their year between their Derbyshire home, Codnor Castle, and a house in London. In London Bess became waiting woman to Frances Brandon, Henry VIII's niece, and met her second husband, Sir William Cavendish, Treasurer of the King's Chamber. Cavendish was one of the Tudor 'new men', not from an aristocratic family, but well-educated and able, like his contemporary, Sir William Cecil.

Bess has not enjoyed a good press historically. Her wealth and ambition have rankled and she has been called a harridan, pushy, 'proud, furious, selfish and unfeeling' and 'of masculine understanding'.[24] Yet her last three husbands married her for love, and she was clearly a lady of beauty and charm. Cavendish declared his devotion by selling his various properties and buying estates in her native county, Derbyshire, and together they built a great house at Chatsworth and began to lay out the gardens there. Sir William's death in 1557 did not halt progress, and the house and garden were not complete until the early 1580s, when Bess was married to her fourth husband, George Talbot, Earl of Shrewsbury. An estate map drawn by William Senior, a surveyor who began to work at Chatsworth in 1609 for Bess's son, William Cavendish, first Earl of Devonshire, shows the Tudor house set in extensive parkland.[25] To the south of the house is a terrace with banqueting houses and a formal garden with fountains, obelisks and a turret set on a mount. To the north lies an extensive orchard and seven large ponds. William Cecil took much interest in the creation of Chatsworth, and may have taken note of these water gardens when completing his own pleasure gardens at Theobalds.

All these features have long gone from Chatsworth, with the exception of a rather odd structure with a stepped approach over a gothic arched bridge. It is now known as Queen Mary's Bower, a reminder that in 1569 Shrewsbury was handed the poisoned chalice of acting as custodian of Elizabeth's cousin, Mary Stuart, who had fled over the border to England the previous year. Mary stayed several times at Chatsworth and would have been familiar with the gardens. One theory is that the 'Bower' provided an area for the captive Queen to exercise on horseback. Another is that it served as a prospect place for viewing the surrounding water gardens.

Mary's presence imposed an intolerable strain upon the Shrewsburys' marriage, with Bess suspecting that her husband had fallen under the Scottish queen's thrall, while he developed a form of paranoid illness which made him quarrel with everybody, and nobody more so than his wife. Queen Elizabeth, along with leading courtiers such as Robert Dudley and William Cecil, made attempts to reconcile the warring couple, but in the end nothing could mend matters, save the death of Shrewsbury in 1590.

Bess decamped from Chatsworth in 1584, having acquired her birthplace, Hardwick Hall, from her bankrupt brother James. She began to enlarge the old house, and to refurbish it, but with Shrewsbury's death, she abruptly stopped this work, and with the money now at her disposal, began at once to build a new and ambitious house, the New Hall, just yards from the Old. Bess had a particular agenda in view when creating the New Hall. In 1574 her daughter Elizabeth had met and married Charles Stuart, Earl of Lennox. It was a match that must have thrilled the ambitious Bess, for Charles had a claim to the English throne through his grandmother Margaret Tudor, sister of Henry VIII. A year later, a daughter, Arbella, was born to the couple, but soon afterwards Charles Lennox was dead, followed to the grave by his wife in 1581. Bess took on the responsibility for her orphaned granddaughter, bringing her up in the expectation that she might one day inherit the throne of her cousin, Queen Elizabeth. This, of course, raised the suspicions of the Queen, who would brook no discussion about the succession, and she never took up the invitation to visit Hardwick.

William Senior also made a map of the estate at Hardwick for Lord Devonshire in 1610.[26] This shows in a very sketchy way that the formal gardens and orchards formed an integral part of the design of the New Hall. Four roughly rectangular courtyards were enclosed by high walls to match the façades of the house: an entrance court to the west, an orchard within the court on the north, and to the south gardens for flowers, vegetables and herbs.

Within these spacious Tudor courtyards, covering more than eleven acres, colourful plantings have been made by the National Trust, including an extensive herb garden with culinary plants that would have been familiar to Bess and her household.

Although details of the original gardens at Chatsworth and Hardwick are few, Bess is a significant figure as the one woman in Tudor England who is known to have created great gardens. William Cecil was married to a woman of considerable intellectual and cultural standing, yet we know nothing of her contribution to his prodigy houses and their gardens. The only clue to a possible interest in gardening by Mildred Cecil lies in a presentation copy, now in Cambridge University Library, of Bartholo Sylva's *Il Giardino cosmographico cultivato* dating from 1572, which contains poems by the Cooke sisters. Mildred's poem in Greek describes the transformation of earth from the disorder of the forest, through to the cultivation of a lovely garden. Her sister Anne organised with her husband, Sir Nicholas Bacon, the stencilling of a series of Latin adages, *sententiae*, on the walls of Gorhambury House, but again we do not know whether she helped with the design and layout of the house and garden. A third sister, Catherine, married to Sir Henry Killigrew, was credited by the Flemish botanist Matthias L'Obel with providing information on seeds of Spanish beans probably carried by the Gulf Stream and washed up on the shores of Cornwall. Did Catherine help with the fine gardens that adorned their house of Arennack, overlooking the harbour at Falmouth? With her marriage to the scholar and traveller Sir Thomas Hoby, the fourth sister, Elizabeth, moved to Bisham Abbey in Berkshire, where her husband redesigned the gardens. It seems impossible that the Cooke sisters should not have been involved in some way in the development of these gardens, for this is an area where women played an increasingly important role in the centuries that followed.

As the witness to the royal visit to Theobalds noted in the quotation at the top of this chapter, the Queen compared the house and its gardens to those in Italy. Elizabeth never travelled beyond her realm, and nor did many of her courtiers. William Cecil made only two, brief visits to the Low Countries, and neither Sir Christopher Hatton nor Bess of Hardwick visited Europe. The only person from this group with experience of the Continent was Robert Dudley, but his travels were hardly conducive to studies of the local gardens or plants. His first visit to the Low Countries in the train of Philip II was strictly political, and, on one of his military forays into France in 1557, he witnessed the death of his youngest brother Henry at the Siege of St Quentin.

His final foreign experience was as Governor-General to the Netherlands when he not only lost his favourite nephew, Sir Philip Sidney, at the Battle of Zutphen in 1586, but with his strong Protestant views alienated himself from the plant-loving burghers of Leiden, Middelburg and other Dutch cities by supporting the hard-line Calvinists.

Yet Theobalds and Kenilworth in particular show strong Italian influences. While Cecil's earlier houses, Burghley and the house on the Strand, incorporated individual classical features, when he was creating the Fountain Court at Theobalds he drew his inspiration directly from Renaissance Italian designs. With its four square towers and garden arcades, it bears a strong resemblance to the Poggio Reale near Naples, built for King Alfonso II in the 1480s by the Florentine architect Giuliano da Maiano. Poggio Reale had magnificent views over the bay of Naples, but Cecil went one better and furnished his south front at Theobalds, 330 feet long and three storeys high, with windows that climbed from floor to ceiling. The garden at Theobalds also had echoes of Poggio Reale with the water gardens overlooked by an arcade. The southernmost edge of the Great Garden formed an elaborate complex with a banqueting house and pool: this was modelled on Emperor Hadrian's great outdoor dining room at Tivoli.

Where did Cecil get these ideas? He was an avid book collector, with a library that was exceptionally large for the time, but it has been dispersed and we have to guess at what textual and visual sources he might have possessed. A vital component of a cultured gentleman's library in sixteenth-century England was a collection of architectural treatises. William Harrison provides a clue: 'If ever curious building did flourish in England, it is in these our years, wherein our workmen excel and are in manner comparable in skill with old Vitruvius and Serlo'.[27] These words were written in 1577, and ten years later he added Leon Battista Alberti to his list. The Roman Vitruvius wrote his architectural treatise, *De architectura*, now known as *The Ten Books of Architecture*, in the first century AD. Various editions were published from the late fifteenth century onwards, and the Cecil family owned copies in Italian and French.[28] Alberti in his *De re aedificatoria*, first published in Florence in 1485, stressed the importance of a relationship between house and garden. Although his text was not illustrated, Alberti provided clear advice, including the plants to be used: myrtle, laurel and ivy in shady areas; vines trained over garden walks; rows of trees laid out in a quincunx pattern; hedges of rose entwined with hazel and pomegranate. He also advocated circular and semi-circular arbours 'modeled out of laurel, citrus, and juniper when their branches are bent back and intertwined.'[29] All these elements were present in Cecil's gardens.

The Italian painter and architect Sebastiano Serlio was able to include adaptable, illustrated models in his treatise on architecture, the first two volumes of which were published in Venice in 1537 and 1540. After he went to the French court, Serlio brought out further volumes that were gathered together after his death and published in quarto in Venice in 1566. The impact of these books was profound right across Europe, influencing not only the architecture and layout of houses and gardens, but also, through his images, providing patterns for knot gardens and mazes. In Book III, published in 1540, Serlio shows the elevation of Poggio Reale with its outside arcades and a flat roof to allow views over the gardens and countryside. It is highly probable that Cecil owned a copy, and his attention may have been drawn to Poggio Reale by his brother-in-law, Sir Thomas Hoby, who had visited this famous site in 1550, noting 'where so many gardens of pleasant and sundrie fruit are, with sundry conveyances of water'.[30]

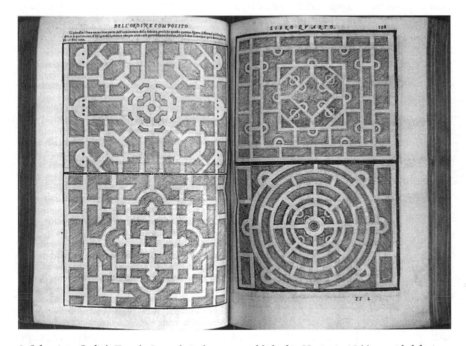

8 Sebastiano Serlio's *Tutte le Opere di Architettura*, published in Venice in 1566, provided designs that could be used both for ceilings inside houses, and labyrinths in gardens. One such design can be seen in the background to the portrait of Sir George Delves (Plate IV).

While Serlio with his images was the exception amongst Italian books, the French made good the deficiency with their highly illustrated works. We know for certain that Cecil owned a copy of Philibert de l'Orme's *Nouvelles Inventions* (1561), which he ordered from Sir Thomas Smith in Paris in 1568. Jacques Androuet du Cerceau with his *Les plus excellents bastiments de France*, published from 1576, provided a generous variety of plans and bird's-eye views of great houses and their surroundings. The details of water in his view of Verneuil, for instance, are reminiscent of the effects achieved in Cecil's garden at Theobalds. Engravings were also provided by the Flemish engraver J. Vredeman de Vries in *Hortorum viridariorumque elegantes … formae*, published in 1583, and it would seem likely that Cecil had access to this through his contacts with the Low Countries, including his great friend Sir Thomas Gresham. One illustration shows little figures of dancers and feasters being soaked by trick fountains – and Cecil certainly had these in his gardens.

Dudley's library has likewise been scattered, and again only a few books can be identified as belonging to him or his family. He gathered around him a circle with particularly strong Italian connections – artists and craftsmen, merchants and engineers, writers and translators. In 1572 his friend Sir Henry Killigrew – who was also William Cecil's brother-in-law – wrote to Dudley reporting that he had commissioned from an Italian craftsmen a fountain, 'a singular piece of work whereof the like was never seen in these parts', for the garden at Kenilworth at the considerable price of £50.[31]

Dudley continued with the Italian theme at Kenilworth, and the gardens and surrounding landscape were developed to echo the estate of Cardinal Gianfrancesco Gambara at the Villa Lante, at Bagnaia in Lazio. The villa and these gardens, which can still be visited, were laid out from 1568, probably by the Bolognese architect Giacomo Vignola, designer of the lower gardens at the Villa Farnese at nearby Caprarola. Gambara's personal emblem was the crayfish, a pun on his name, and this symbol is repeated throughout his garden. Likewise Dudley embellished the gardens at Kenilworth with frequent references to his family's emblem of the bear and ragged staff. But an emblematic programme had enjoyed a long tradition in England, and the striking innovation at Kenilworth was the concept of a single unified landscape. Vignola's design for the Villa Lante brought together the house, garden and park, and Dudley's achievement was to develop a similar concept using the much more difficult ingredients of a mediaeval castle and its surroundings. Robert Laneham, in his letter about the 1575 festivities at Kenilworth, painted a picture of the very diverse landscape of the park, the great pool and the chase for hunting, alluding to the Renaissance ideal of art imitating nature.

Dudley undoubtedly owned or had access to architectural books, including Vignola's rules on the five orders of architecture published in Rome in 1563. He was familiar with John Shute's *First and Chief Grounds of Architecture*, also published in 1563, in London. Shute had been sent out to Italy in 1550 by Robert's father, John Dudley, to meet the leading architects and to look at ancient monuments, and his book was the first Renaissance architectural treatise to be published in English. Members of Dudley's circle would also have provided him with first-hand reports of Italian gardens. For example, the painter Federigo Zuccaro, from whom he commissioned portraits of himself and of the Queen, was associated with the frescoes at Bagnaia.[32]And works of the imagination also had an important influence. The *Metamorphoses* by the Roman writer Ovid, written at about the time of the birth of Jesus Christ, provide all kinds of stories about gardens and flowers. The author set out to provide an account of how, from the beginning of time, bodies could be

9 Ovid's *Metamorphoses* provided an important source for gardens in the sixteenth century. For Kenilworth Robert Dudley commissioned a fountain that depicted scenes connected with water. This illustration from the herbal of Tragus, published in 1552, shows another of Ovid's stories, of how the white fruit of the mulberry turned to red from the blood of the tragic lover, Pyramus. Silkworms would not have appreciated this metamorphosis.

10 The Villa Lante at Bagnaia, a woodcut from *Descrizione di Roma Moderna*, 1697. This shows how the 'house', garden and park are brought together as a unified landscape, a concept that Robert Dudley sought to achieve at Kenilworth Castle.

turned into other bodies by the power of the gods. Thus the beautiful youth Narcissus fell in love with his reflected image and wasted away till death, leaving only a flower with white petals clustered around a cup of gold. Daphne, pursued by Apollo, was turned into a laurel so that the god declared thereafter he would wear her leaves rather than oak, and that all who sought his favour should do likewise. Ovid's stories enjoyed great favour in the Middle Ages and beyond, providing a rich source for both Chaucer and Shakespeare. At Dudley's behest the *Metamorphoses* were rendered into English by Arthur Golding and were used as the source for the decoration of the great fountain at the centre of the formal gardens at Kenilworth.

Another work of 'fiction' that had an influence on gardens was the wonderfully titled *Hypnerotomachia Poliphilli* attributed to the monk Francesco Colonna and published in Italian in 1499. A French edition was produced in 1546 under the title of *Le Songe de Poliphile*, and it was partially translated into English in 1592 as *The Strife of Love in a Dream*. The young hero Poliphilus dreams of his quest for a beautiful nymph, Polia. Beginning in Wilderness, he passes through landscapes populated by classical buildings, coming finally to the circular garden of Cythera. In the book a plan was provided of this garden, along with designs for topiary, knot gardens and practical instructions on what plants to use.

Around two hundred books from Sir Christopher Hatton's library have survived at Holkham Hall in Norfolk, but these represent only a fraction of his collection. Even so, it is clear that Hatton had a considerable library that included books on theology, law and history. From the evidence of books dedicated to him, he had a special interest in Italian literature. The only architectural book that can be firmly identified is an edition of Palladio. However, the evidence of his houses and gardens at Holdenby and Kirby suggest that he was influenced by the ideas of William Harrison's trinity, Vitruvius, Alberti and Serlio.

Hatton at Holdenby created a formal garden consisting of nine compartments, and a sketch of Theobalds made by William Cecil indicates that his great garden was similarly divided into nine squares. Just such an arrangement appears in the background of a portrait of Sir George Delves, a distant kinsman of Mildred Cecil, now in the Walker Art Gallery in Liverpool. Painted by an unknown artist in 1577, this remarkable picture shows Delves hand in hand with a mysterious lady, her face covered by boughs of myrtle, and contains rhyming verses as well as the image of the garden. Sir Roy Strong has deciphered the elements and suggests that the painting represents Delves as a man disappointed by his career at Elizabeth I's court, symbolised by the garden as a world of sensual delights. The garden is large, divided into several compartments by tunnel arbours. In one compartment is a kitchen garden complete with bee skeps and espaliered fruit. Another contains a circular maze, probably of turf or a low-growing herb. A third is laid out in plats with a fountain at its centre. This is certainly not the garden of Delves's home, Doddington Hall in Cheshire. In its scale it resembles the Queen's garden at Hampton Court and Cecil's Theobalds, but the features do not accord with descriptions of these, and it may well be a work of the imagination. However, it is invaluable in giving some idea of the appearance of these gardens (Plate IV).

The structure of a sixteenth-century garden of nine compartments is still to be seen at Godolphin in the far west of Cornwall. Sir Francis Godolphin worked with Sir William Cecil; indeed, he was something of a marcher lord, for the Godolphins were Protestants in a county where many were still wedded to the Roman faith, and as governor of the Scillies Sir Francis was responsible for keeping the Spanish fleet at bay. It would seem natural therefore that his formal garden was inspired by Theobalds, but the arrangement of Godolphin dates back to the previous century when a castle was set in the central compartment of a large rectangle surrounded by walls and a ditch. So, was it Sir Francis Godolphin who inspired Cecil and Hatton? Whatever the chronology, the garden, recently opened to the public by the National Trust, provides a chance to experience the scale of a grand Elizabethan garden. The intricate planting schemes have all vanished and the trees have grown huge, imbuing it with a romantic Sleeping Beauty atmosphere very different from the effect created at Kenilworth. At Godolphin the visitor is overwhelmed by the immensity of the garden and the ambition that went into its creation.

The political rivalry between Robert Dudley and William Cecil has been much discussed by historians. Stephen Alford in his recent biography of Cecil concludes that their feelings were ambivalent, neither friends nor enemies. Cecil had once served Robert's father, John Dudley, and they had many friends in common. Both were determined Protestants, and were often united in their opposition to the interests of the Queen's cousin, Thomas Howard, Duke of Norfolk. Although an entire book has been posited on the rivalry between them in creating their buildings and gardens, there are several examples of how they acted in a spirit of cooperation, not only with each other, but with Hatton, Bess and others in the vanguard of design and development.[33] Designers were exchanged, so that Robert Smythson first worked for John Thynne at Longleat before moving to Wollaton in Nottinghamshire to work for Francis Willoughby and then for Bess at Hardwick. The priest, Hugh Hall, may have worked in the Northamptonshire gardens of William Cecil and Christopher Hatton. Precious and expensive books with the latest Continental designs would have been consulted and borrowed. Plants were swapped and gardens visited. In 1591 Bess, in her late sixties, paid one long, last visit to London and the royal court. When she was given a tour of the gardens at Greenwich Palace, she was presented with strawberries, her favourites, by the gardeners. On her way back northwards, she visited the gardens at Holdenby and at Wollaton.

As the group of gardening courtiers from the first years of Elizabeth's reign withdrew from the scene, so a new generation took their place. One person who created a magnificent garden and built houses that were prodigies of their time could have belonged to the circle around the Queen, but for his devotion to his faith. Thomas Tresham, born in 1543 into one of the prominent families of Northamptonshire, was on familiar terms with his neighbours Cecil and Hatton – he was probably related to the latter. When the Queen visited Kenilworth in 1575 he was knighted alongside Cecil's younger son, Robert. In about 1566 Tresham married Muriel Throckmorton, from the prominent Catholic family of Coughton Court in Warwickshire. Both brought wealth to the marriage, for Tresham was a ruthless exploiter of his large estates, but his conversion to the Roman Church was to cost him dear. Some of his money went into building schemes, including the triangular lodge at Rushton built in the early 1590s, where all the numbers and devices were expressed in threes or multiples of three symbolising his devotion to the Trinity. He also modernised his principal seat of Rushton Hall, laying out the gardens to create a series of large terraces, with a spiral viewing mount surmounted by a statue of Hercules, and an extensive lake.

In 1594 Tresham turned his attention to his estate at Lyveden, where the manor house dating from the fourteenth century stood within a modest enclosed garden. Extending this garden southwards towards the ridge of the valley, he designed a garden lodge, the New Bield or Building. This time he chose the shape of a Greek cross, taking multiples of the number five, symbolising the wounds of Christ, and seven to symbolise the seven stations of the Cross together with the seven instruments of the Passion. For Lyveden New Bield Tresham drew upon his architectural library. While the libraries of Cecil, Dudley and Hatton have been dispersed and details of the books contained within are extremely patchy and prey to chance, we have several catalogues of Tresham's library and many of his books are now in the collection of the Brudenell family at Deene Park in Northamptonshire. The antiquary John Dee was regarded as having the largest private library in England in 1570 with 170 manuscripts and 2,500 books. Few private libraries exceeded 200 books, and many owned just a handful. Therefore Tresham's collection of 2,600 works is outstanding. He owned over twenty architectural books, including three editions of Vitruvius, two of Serlio, Alberti, Vignola, Palladio, Du Cerceau, de L'Orme, Hans Vredeman de Vries and John Shute. In other words, almost the entire corpus of what was available.

It is a fine irony that through Tresham's misfortunes we should know so much about his library, his intentions for his buildings and gardens, and the men who carried them out. Tresham was officially received into the Roman Catholic Church by the prominent Jesuit missionary Robert Parsons in 1580, although this has been described as 'scarcely more than a formality'.[34] From this date Tresham was subject not only to frequent monetary fines but also to periods of imprisonment, obliging him to send to his servants his instructions on the layout, planting and cultivation of his gardens. Some of these, along with notes and accounts, were found in 1832 in the walls of Rushton Hall, where they had been hidden after Tresham's son Francis was identified as a conspirator in the Gunpowder Plot of 1605.

Tresham corresponded regularly with the 'architect freemason' Robert Stickells who was employed by both Cecil and Hatton, although it is not certain how much Stickells worked at Lyveden. The foreman at Lyveden was John Slynn, and the surveyor George Levens, who drew out the plots for both the building and the garden. From prison in Ely, Tresham wrote a long letter in October 1597 to Slynn, in which he recorded directing Levens 'how to draw the perimeter (or circuit) of my garden plot wherein my garden lodge [the New Bield] now standeth'.[35] What Tresham planned was extremely ambitious. Moving upwards and southwards from the manor house in the valley towards the New Bield, he created a series of six terraces, rising approximately 13 metres to a lower orchard, with sycamore and elms providing structural planting. Tresham was particularly interested in fruit trees and his lower orchard was extensive: aerial photographs have shown approximately 300 planting pits. Tresham's correspondence with Slynn and his nurseryman Andrewes mentions the planting of walnut, warden pear, medlar and black cherry, while he also asks them to try to obtain cider apple, crab apple, wheat (white) and horse (small red) plum.

This lower orchard was separated from an upper orchard by a moat and a triple terrace planted with hawthorn, surmounted at each end by stepped pyramidal mounts. The terrace acted as a dam to retain the water of the moated garden, and as a kind of outdoor long gallery so that visitors might look down upon the flowering fruit trees in spring. They could also, in true Renaissance manner, enjoy the landscape beyond, the deer park and the hunting forests.

The moat continued around this upper orchard to encircle it, with two snail mounts at the southern end answering the pyramidal mounts to the north. The water was only about a metre in depth, but that was enough for stocking fish and for floating a boat: the effect would have been like the Flemish garden at Wacquem and William Cecil's water features at Theobalds. Aerial photographs reveal that the centre of this upper orchard was laid out as a series of ten circular rings in the style advocated by the Flemish designer Hans Vredeman de Vries. In the letter of 1597, Tresham asks his staff: 'If my moated orchard could in any part be prepared for receiving of some cherry trees and plum trees, I should like well thereof'.[36] A marginal note referring to circular borders suggests that the outermost two or three of the rings were to be planted with fruit trees, while the remaining inner circles were later to be planted with standard roses and raspberries. Slynn reported in a letter of 12 December 1604: 'I have received from Rushton the plum stocks, raspberries, and 4 Juniper trees. There is 400 raspberries . . . I have set them all in the moated orchard in the circular borders there . . . And whereas your worship mentions in your letter for setting up of some certain circular borders of Roses, we do differ in opinion of your directions.'[37] The singular combination of roses, which are thought to have been eglantine and damask, with raspberries may have been symbolic of Christ's Passion, echoing the theme of the architectural details of the lodge. More formal gardens were to be created around the lodge itself, divided by hedges into eight large arbours, possibly to be laid out in line with the arms of the Greek Cross. The areas between the hedges were to be cobbled, to enable the ladies of the household to walk, sheltered from exposure. Moving away from the lodge, Tresham planned a bowling alley and a parterre of peach trees under-planted by strawberries. And in a third garden area north of the Lodge, which he called 'my warden quincunx hills', he again proposed warden pear and walnut trees planted in patterns of five.

Tresham died before he could complete the New Bield and his remarkably ambitious garden. The lodge survives as a romantic ruin, the bequest of a man who combined the passions of building and gardening with his religious faith. Lyveden New Bield now belongs to the National Trust, who have undertaken substantial research on the garden. The lower orchard is now replanted with 300 fruit trees, using the varieties of apples, pears, plums, damsons, gages and cherries that Tresham listed at the end of his letter of 1597. The moats encircling the upper orchard and the banks and snail mounts have been cleared of undergrowth, and it is planned to recreate the circular rings of the orchard through a cutting regime.

Another committed Catholic gardener was John, first Baron Lumley. He was very rich, deriving his wealth from the coal on his extensive estates in north-east England which he was able to inherit despite his father's execution for his part in the Pilgrimage of Grace in 1537. He married into one of the great Catholic families: his wife was Jane, daughter of Henry Fitzalan, twelfth Earl of Arundel. As an adherent of Arundel, in 1571 Lumley became implicated in the Ridolfi Plot which aimed to marry his brother-in-law the Duke of Norfolk to Mary Queen of Scots, and re-establish Roman Catholicism in England. Recognising his luck in spending time in the Tower of London rather than losing his head on Tower Green, Lumley put away his political ambitions and turned instead to his garden. He had taken over from his father-in-law, Arundel, the keepership of the great Park at Nonesuch in Surrey.

Using the fantastical backdrop of Henry VIII's palace, Lumley created one of the first allegorical gardens in England as an apologia to Elizabeth I for his disloyalty – 'the smitten fisher at length grows wise'. His theme was the story of Diana and Actaeon from Ovid's *Metamorphoses*. Actaeon, a huntsman, came upon Diana, the chaste huntress, as she bathed naked with her nymphs, and was changed by her into a stag, whereupon he was torn to pieces by his own hounds. Diana was particularly associated with Elizabeth I, the Virgin Queen, and Lumley was presumably the hapless Actaeon. A contemporary record made by Anthony Watson, rector of nearby Cheam, combined with a drawing by Joducus Hondius and engravings from a family album known as the Red Velvet Book, show that Lumley reorganised the Privy Garden and created the Grove of Diana, probably in the early 1580s.[38] In both areas the Goddess of the moon dominates: in the centre of the formal Privy Garden was a large fountain surmounted by the figure of Diana; the layout of the Grove of Diana led the visitor past a series of sculptures, fountains and buildings conveying his allegorical message. This was a highly Italianate garden, in the style of the Villa Lante, or the remarkable garden at Bomarzo created by the Orsini family in the mid-sixteenth century with an iconographic programme based on *Orlando Furioso* and the work of Dante (Plate III). Lumley never travelled in Italy, so his inspiration came from his library, for he, like Tresham, owned one of the largest collections of the day, with over 3,000 books.

The person who did make the European tour was Thomas Cecil, William's elder son, who was sent off in 1561 with his tutor to complete his education. William drew the line at Italy, but decided that although France was the enemy, the court offered a wonderful training for young courtiers. The project was not a success, for Thomas used his time in Paris to enjoy himself rather than to be educated, much to his father's chagrin. Thomas did not inherit William's intellectual rigour or his political ambition, but he derived from him his horticultural passion and love of dramatic garden effects. Thus, after persuading William to give him his estate at Wimbledon, he began in 1588 to build a splendid manor house on a hillside site with spectacular views, laying

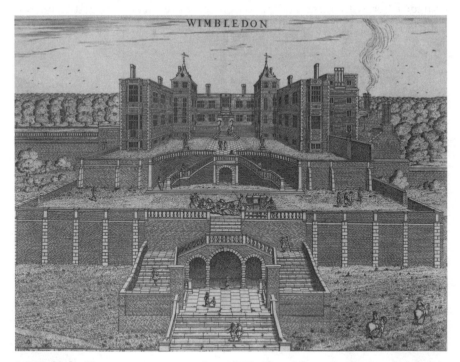

11 Wimbledon House in an engraving made in 1678 by Henry Winstanley, showing the Italianate terraces created by Thomas Cecil at the end of the sixteenth century. The gardens can be seen behind the house.

out magnificent gardens that were inspired by the hillside villas of Renaissance Italy, the Villa d'Este at Tivoli and the Villa Farnese at Caprarola, illustrated in the architectural books in his father's library.

A detailed plan by the architect Robert Smythson, drawn up in 1609, indicates knot gardens to the east of the house, a banqueting house in the form of a Greek cross, orchards at different levels, alternating with walks ornamented by roses, thorn hedges and lime trees.[39] A later engraving, dating from 1678, shows the strong Italian influence of the sophisticated terraced entrance. Indeed, one of the best accounts of the Wimbledon garden comes from an Italian traveller who visited in 1618 and wrote lyrically of the 'extremely delightful situation, with its park, gardens, fountains, covered walks, very lofty hedges . . . and a marvelous orchard surrounded by a wall . . . recreating the eye vastly'.[40]

As the Queen aged, so she restricted her progresses to easy journeys from London. Just as she often visited William Cecil at Theobalds, she paid his son Thomas the signal honour of visiting Wimbledon House at least four times between 1592 and 1602, the year before her death. Perhaps Wimbledon provided her with some compensation for never seeing at first hand the famous Renaissance gardens of Italy.

CHAPTER 2

The Men on the Ground

THE STORY OF AN OVERNIGHT CREATION of a garden below Queen Elizabeth's windows at Kenilworth Castle in 1575 is almost certainly apocryphal, but it shows the expectation at this period that gardeners, through their skills and ingenuity, could perform extraordinary feats.

The gardeners of mediaeval Britain were in the main anonymous figures, but anonymous does not mean they lacked skill. As John Harvey put it in his pioneering work, *Early Nurserymen*, they were 'by no means nameless serfs provided with shovels'.[1] Much gardening lore was held by the religious houses, where monks, nuns and their lay brothers grew flowers to adorn their church or chapel, cultivated fruit trees and kitchen gardens to supply the refectory, and planted herbs to provide physic both for their infirmaries and for the care of the communities beyond their walls.

When the Dissolution of the Monasteries scattered former monks and priests in all directions, some continued their horticultural craft. The unidentified priest mentioned in Chapter 1 working for William Cecil at Burghley House and for Christopher Hatton at Holdenby may have been Hugh Hall, who left a manuscript discourse, 'of gardeninge applied to a spirituall understanding'. This was once in the collection of the Catholic peer John, Lord Lumley, and is now in the British Library.[2] The interconnection between religion and gardening was close at this period, with the Garden of Eden cited constantly, and gardening and botanical books often showed Adam and Eve on their title pages. The Dutch scholar Levinus Leminius compiled a biblical herbal, filled with parables and metaphors borrowed from references to plants, fruits, and trees, which was translated into English in 1587.

In his discourse, Hugh Hall made some delightful sketches of tools, including a watering pot with 'workes of mercy ghostly' on the pot itself, and streams of water inscribed with various aims: 'teach the ignorant'; 'correct the synner'; cowncell the doubtfull'; 'comfort the afflicted'; 'bear the wronge pacyently'; 'foregyve offences'; and 'pray for the quick and the dead'. He also provided two designs for beds, divided into compartments and inscribed with various virtues such as love, fidelity and modesty. The Holdenby priest went on to work in the gardens of Lady Vaux of Harrowden, and possibly for her brother Sir Thomas Tresham at Lyveden New Bield, where the Catholic symbolism of the house and garden would have struck a chord if he was indeed Hugh Hall.[3]

Following the ravages of the Black Death in the fourteenth century and the reduction in the number of lay brothers, some monastic houses abandoned the care of their walled gardens, leasing them out instead to professional gardeners. In Oxford, for instance, the Greyfriars, whose house lay in the western part of the city, below the castle and by the River Thames, rented out their enticingly named Paradise Gardens at some time during the fifteenth

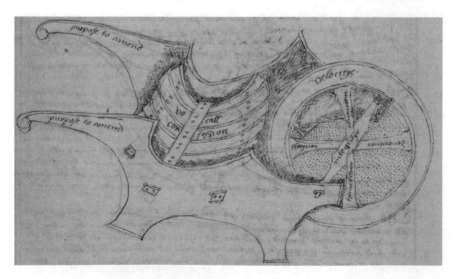

12　A wheelbarrow from 'Discourse of gardeninge applied to a spirituall understanding' by the priest, 'Mr Halle'. He has been identified as Hugh Hall, the mysterious priest-gardener who probably designed the gardens at Holdenby for Hatton, and worked for William Cecil at Burghley.

century. Two centuries later, the gardens were run by the Wrench family, who not only sold seeds and plants, but also provided refreshments for customers as they watched people in boats on the river: the Stuart equivalent of a garden centre.

Unsurprisingly it is the gardeners who worked for Thomas Wolsey and then for Henry VIII who first emerge from the shadows. Not only are their names recorded in the huge volumes of state papers, but they were also important members of the royal household, creating elaborate gardens in the fashionable style of the time and setting the standard for great gardens throughout the sixteenth century. They also provided the King with the luxuries that he loved. Thus John Lovell, who became the gardener at Greenwich in 1519, moved ten years later to Richmond Palace where he was recorded supplying the royal table with fruit, nuts, flowers and sweet waters. At New Hall (Beaulieu) in Essex, Stephen Jasper was rewarded for providing strawberries for the monarch's delectation. When the King acquired Hampton Court from Cardinal Wolsey in 1529, he inherited his gardener, John Chapman from Kingston upon Thames. In addition Chapman looked after Wolsey's garden at York Place in London, which also passed to the King and became known as Whitehall.

Chapman, Lovell and Jasper would all have been what we call head gardeners, with teams of men working for them: in the 1530s, twenty-five garden workers are listed for Whitehall, assisted by nine under-gardeners and fifteen named labourers. Sometimes the regular team would be supplemented by temporary help for short-term projects, so that Chapman prepared for a royal visit to Wolsey's Hampton Court by bringing in local labour and at least six of his senior gardeners from York Place. He also called upon his fellow head gardeners for advice: Stephen Jasper came over from Essex to Hampton Court at least three times between 1529 and 1531, on one occasion delivering artichokes to the King's kitchens.

The schemes that Chapman carried out for Thomas Wolsey were ambitious, but after he passed into the King's service, his job became even more complex. When he was succeeded at Hampton Court by Thomas Alvard, some of the tasks undertaken were noted. Roger Down oversaw the building of terrace walk embankments against the inner sides of the Privy Garden walls, assisted by nine labourers. John Hutton was brought up river from London to work on the design of the Privy Garden's main beds, bringing with him rosemary plants and gillyflowers, mint and other sweet flowers supplied by Agnes Hutton, who was probably his wife. Matthew Garret carried out much of the actual planting in the Privy Garden, with strawberries, violets, primroses and gillyflowers.

Garret was helped in his task of planting by a group of women, while others gathered strawberry and flower roots in the wild at 3d or 4d per bushel.[4] At this time London was a comparatively small city, with fields and pastures beyond its walls and suburbs. Country housewives, sometimes described as herb gatherers, brought their produce into the markets, and a sixteenth-century drawing of Grace Church Market shows them sitting with their baskets.[5] One commentator described how Cheapside in spring turned golden with all the daffodils sold on stalls.

Although this was not a period of specialisation, the highly prized skill of cultivating fruit was attributed to two royal gardeners. Jean le Leu, a priest, is recorded in the last year of Henry's reign bringing apple trees from France. Le Leu, or Le Loup, is most probably John Wolf, a Frenchman who was employed by the King from 1538 principally to design new pleasure gardens, when he was given an annuity for life of 20 marks (£13 6s 8d). In the state papers his versatility is shown in various references, such as 'planter of graffs', 'maker and deviser of King's arbours' and 'confector viridariorum' or layer out of gardens. In 1542, after introducing the apricot into England, he disappears for some years from the records, possibly because he went abroad to seek plants.

Another fruit expert was Richard Harris, an Irishman whose skills were extolled in a book by a Kentish gentleman, William Lambarde. A Perambulation of Kent, written in 1570 and published six years later, has been described as the first ever county history. Lambarde imagines Kent as the garden of England – an epithet which is still used today – but for him it represents a combination of biblical Eden and the classical Hesperides where Hercules found the golden apples. Richard Harris imported from France many apple grafts, especially pippins, and from the Low Countries grafts of cherries and pears, cultivating them on some land at Tenham given to him by Henry VIII. According to Lambarde:

> This Tenham with thirty other parishes . . . be the cherry garden and apple orchard of Kent. . . . In which respect you may fantasy that you now see Hesperidum Hortos, if now where Hercules found the golden apples (which is reckoned for one of his heroical labours), yet where our honest patriot Richard Harris (fruiterer to King Henry the 8) planted by his great cost and rare industry the sweet cherry, the temperate pippin and the golden rennet.[6]

Lambarde also explained that the orchards in Kent were planted to save the nation from dependence on imported fruit.

Harris's 'rare industry' proved very successful, for within half a century orchards were flourishing all over the country. One of the great experts in growing fruit trees was Thomas Tresham: in 1605 Robert Cecil described Lyveden as 'one of the fairest orchards that is in England'.[7] Tresham's nurseryman, Andrewes, was sent westwards from Northamptonshire to Gloucestershire, Worcestershire and Shropshire to acquire pear and cider kernels, and to London for stakes for his plum trees. At the end of the long and detailed letter of instructions written in 1597 from his prison in Ely to his foreman John Slynn, Tresham lists some of the fruit that he suggested should be planted, along with some details of their qualities. Among them is a 'Normandy hawksbyll peare', 'one of petworth rootynge', perhaps obtained from the orchards of the Earl of Northumberland at Petworth in Sussex. This ripened at 'hullontide' (All-hallowtide, 1 November) at the same time as a 'winter queening caterne peare' that grew near Ely and was sold in the market there. Dr Harvey's apple, he noted, kept until Candlemas.[8] The National Trust has found some of these varieties of apples and pears, plums and cherries for the replanting of the lower orchard at Lyveden.

The head gardeners employed by Cardinal Wolsey and the King carried considerable responsibilities with many men working under them. It is very difficult, however, to ascertain just how well they were rewarded for their work, as modern equivalents can be so misleading. Sixteenth-century England, moreover, witnessed a period of considerable fluctuation, given the inflation caused by events at home and internationally. John Harvey attempted to provide some kind of modern comparison in his book, *Early Nurserymen*, reckoning that £12 in Tudor times would be the equivalent of £2,000 in 1973. Three decades on, this sum should be multiplied tenfold. With these calculations, John Lovell, the principal gardener at Greenwich in 1519 on an annual retainer of £3 0s 8d, was receiving today's equivalent of £4,980. Thirty years later when his son, also John, was granted by Mary Tudor the office of his late father as surveyor and keeper of the orchard and garden at Richmond, he received a fee of £6 1s 8d and was given a further grant of £4 per annum for weeding, sanding of the garden and of the orteyard (vegetable garden), today's equivalent of £16,600. These fees, and the annuity of £13 6s 8d paid to Jean le Leu, which might be estimated at around £21,500, do not seem generous. However, they compare favourably with the average annual salary of a schoolmaster of the period at £6 9s, and of a clergyman at between £10 and £20.[9]

13 A gardener with his rake and a basket of vegetables, from a newel post at the top of the stair-case of Hatfield House. It is traditionally identified with John Tradescant the Elder, Robert Cecil's gardener at Hatfield in the early seventeenth century – a likely attribution, for his smart clothes suggest a man of status.

The average wages of the gardeners and labourers working under the head man are even more complex to estimate. In 1563 a Statute of Artificers gave county justices the responsibility to make an annual wage assessment order for every trade. Justices had to decide how the rates should be fixed: 'by the Yere or by the Daye Week Monthe or other-wise, with Meate and Drinck or w[i]thout Meate and Drinck'.[10] Thus Philip Enys, the gardener at Greenwich in 1546, was paid board wages of 4d per day, while the two men he employed to assist him got 7d per day. If these men were paid six days of the week for a year, then Enys received approximately £5 per year, and his assistants £8 15s, assuming that they worked all through the year. Sometimes the head gardener would pay for his assistants out of his own wages. Thus John Gardener, the keeper of the royal garden at West Horsley in Surrey in 1546, took 30s 4d a quarter for his own wages, and to pay four labourers for mowing grass alleys and the orchard in summer. In the quarter leading up to Christmas he employed weeders 'picking and weeding out leaves of the knottes of the privy garden and of the mounte garden, and out of strawberry borders and rose beds'. In addition he took 22s 6d for livery due at Christmas.[11] The weeders mentioned in accounts were often women, whose nimble fingers were valued for the task, although this was not reflected in their remuneration: usually they received half the wages paid to male assistants.

Turning from the royal household accounts to those of noblemen leads the reader into evidence that is much more fragmentary. Some of the accounts of Robert Dudley have survived from the period around the accession of Elizabeth I, and from the mid-1580s. Although Dudley drew his inspiration

14 'Spring' from an engraving by Pieter Brueghel the Elder, published by Hieronymus Cock in 1570. In the foreground men and women are planting up a garden arranged in formal style with raised beds. At the top right, gardeners armed with grafting knives are intertwining a vine over a structure of pliable poles. At top left, diners enjoy a banquet in a galleried arbour.

for the design of his gardens from Italy, several Frenchmen are mentioned as his gardeners. The first reference comes in 1559, for a gardener receiving 20s for expenses incurred at Dudley's house on the river at Kew. Twenty-five years later, Dudley wrote to his secretary, Jean Hotman, Sieur de Villiers St Paul, asking that a gardener might be hired in France to work on his garden at Wanstead in Essex.[12] The man duly arrived but was found to be unsatisfactory and returned to Europe in February 1585, with a blunt message from Dudley to Hotman that 'he hath very little or no skill in that profession, neither do I find him apt to conceive and be instructed in the same.'[13]

While his experiment with this gardener from over the Channel did not work, Dudley was happy with Awdryan, or Adrian, who was paid various sums in 1584 and 1585 for going to Kenilworth. Unfortunately we don't know whether he had been responsible for the ambitious layout and development of the gardens there in the 1570s as the household accounts for this period do not survive. At one stage Awdryan seems to have been sent to see Lord Lumley's French gardener at Nonesuch, one of several examples of owners of great Elizabethan gardens sharing their knowledge and experience. Back in 1558 the accounts mention money being paid to the gardeners 'at Mr Sicells [William Cecil]', probably at Wimbledon Manor, which was close to Dudley's house at Kew.[14] The royal gardeners were also expected to supply plants to favoured subjects. When William Cecil was laying out the gardens at Burghley in 1561, he was assured that Queen Elizabeth's gardener at Greenwich would provide him with herbs such as lavender, rosemary and hyssop. If Greenwich could not oblige, then Hampton Court and Richmond would endeavour to help.[15]

The tantalisingly fragmentary references to Dudley's gardeners are echoed by those in the household accounts of Bess of Hardwick. Her Chatsworth wages book for the years 1577 to 1580 has survived, with the gardeners regularly appearing after the masons, wallers and labourers.[16] The work at this time was under the direction of Robin Gardener. As Bess's long-term head of her kitchens was Henry Cook, we may assume that she named some of her essential servants according to their roles, as was sometimes the custom. At this time, Robin Gardener was laying out the design of the formal gardens with the aid of 'a dozen of packe thread for lynes'. One gardener was paid for mowing the garden and the new orchard, another for bringing bushes of rosemary and fruit grafts, and others for constructing the ponds that were such a feature of Chatsworth. These were one-off payments, but under regular

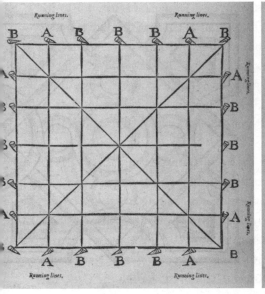

15 Illustrations from *The Countrie Farme*, Richard Surflet's 1600 translation of the sixteenth-century *Maison Rustique* by Charles Estienne and Jean Liebault. These show how gardeners laid out knot gardens, which had become highly intricate by this period. The string and pegs in the diagram on the left are often mentioned in household accounts of garden equipment.

wages comes a team of female workers. Top of the list is Elinor Gardener, who was probably Robin's wife, followed by her sister Margaret Hawthorn and then up to seven others reflecting fluctuations in the amount of work required. Several of the ladies shared their surname with male workers, so came from families on the Chatsworth estate. Weeding was one of their tasks, but also 'bearing earth'. They were paid 1d per day (compared to 1½d for their menfolk). Bess seems to have been frugal with her wages, for ten years later Tresham was paying his labourers 6d per day, his women 4d and his boys 3d. The wages of Bess's head gardener, Robin, are not given, for the surviving ledger was for day labourers, and presumably his remuneration was recorded elsewhere.

Sometimes head gardeners also ran nurseries. Nursery, meaning a seedbed for plants, began to appear in records from 1565, while the term nurseryman came into use a century later. A reference in Wolsey's accounts in 1515 for his London residence, York Place, talks of 'Erbs provided for my lord's garden by John Chapman', which suggests that his head gardener also sourced the plants, possibly with the help of his wife and family, or even of paid assistants. At the end of his reign Henry VIII took over the manor of Chelsea that had formerly belonged to Westminster Abbey, and the accounts include payments to Henry Russell for materials from his nursery: 'To Henry Russell of Westminster, gardener, for two banks of Rosemary by him bought to be set with in the King's Garden at his manor at Chelsea, price 13s 6d; for six borders of lavender price 26s 8d. And to him for three loads of Calesse [Calais?] sand for the great bowling alley . . .'[17]

Seeds were being brought in from the Low Countries, in particular from Antwerp and Bruges, the principal ports of entry for the international trade into Northern Europe. In 1566 a correspondent, writing from Antwerp to Lord Cobham, owner of a particularly fine garden in Kent, promised 'I will bring you seeds'.[18] A port book, recording the ships and their cargoes entering the Port of London, noted in April 1568 the arrival of *Samson* of Bruges with 50lbs of garden seed to the value of 40s, and later in the month the *Cock*, also from Bruges, with 'all manner of seeds' in a barrel valued at 33s.[19] By this time there was clearly an organised trade in London, and probably in the provinces too. It was usually grocers who would supply the seeds; the term seedsmen, like nurserymen, was not used until the late seventeenth century. Thus when Sabine Saunders married a London draper, John Johnson, and moved to Glapthorn Manor, near Oundle in Northamptonshire in the late 1540s, she applied to her brother-in-law in London to get from the grocers the seeds she required to plant out her garden.[20]

The range offered by these grocers was wide. A list providing 'the names of all sortes of sedes which are to be sowen in winter and sommer', dating from the 1570s or 1580s, was discovered in 1989 among the papers of the Randle Home family of Chester and analysed by John Harvey.[21] It includes 122 plants, which suggests that it was drawn up by a supplier of seeds rather than by a gardener considering what to plant in their garden, and begins with vegetables and herbs and ends with flowers planted for ornament rather than practical use. Half a century later Robert Hill, a grocer in Lombard Street in London, drew up a similar list of seeds for John Winthrop, who was about to embark on his voyage across the Atlantic to the New World, but this is a more personal selection, organised in alphabetical order (see p. 239).

Of course, not everybody could afford to apply to a grocer or a nurseryman for seeds for their garden. Thomas Tusser in his *Five Hundreth Pointes of Good Husbandrie*, first published in 1573, provided a list of 'seedes and herbs for the kitchen', forty-three in all. As well as those that we might expect to find in a modern herb catalogue, such as rosemary and thyme, the list includes primroses, 'violets of all sorts' and marigolds, a reminder that these flowers were used in salads. Marigolds not only were used to dress dishes, but to add colour to cheese. Tusser also advised that in August housewives should collect seeds and organise an exchange network within the community:

> Good huswifes in sommer will save their owne seede,
> against the next yeere, as occasion neede.
> One seede for another, to make an exchange,
> With fellowlie neighbourhood seemeth not strange.[22]

In 1538 the establishment of parish registers to record births, marriages and deaths makes it possible to identify all ranks of society. The first London nursery of which we have definite information belonged to the Banbury family. This began with John Banbury, of the parish of St Margaret's Westminster, basket maker, who probably grew his own willows and osiers for his trade. In his will made in 1560, a year before his death, he directed his son Henry 'to plante and grafte for the behalf of his mother (Elizabeth) and he to have the third part of his labour'.[23] The contents of the will show that John enjoyed moderate prosperity. Henry, who was born in 1540 and died in 1610, was described by John Gerard in his herbal of 1597 as 'an excellent graffer and painfull [industrious] planter, Mr Henry Banbury of Touthill [Tothill] street neere unto Westminster', and was praised for his stock of varieties of apples and pears.[24] Westminster was an area with several important nursery gardens in the early seventeenth century, including that of the florist Ralph Tuggie, who was particularly celebrated for his carnations and his auriculas.

As the population of London increased during the seventeenth century, so the nurseries moved further out from the centre, some westwards to Kensington and Chelsea, some to the east, to Old Street and Spitalfields, and others south across the river to Lambeth. These supplied plants, trees and seeds not only to Londoners, but also to gardens and estates all over the country. Oxford and York also had established nurseries. That of the Wrench family in Paradise Gardens on the west side of Oxford has already been noted. Outside Micklegate Bar in York, orchards and gardens were leased to Robert Elden on 25 November 1541 for twenty-one years on condition that 'he promyseth to graft and set fruyt treys of the sayd ground and to leyff them growing of the sayd grownd at the end of the term.'[25] There is evidence of other nurseries and orchards on the sites of former monastic houses in York, including Friars' Gardens which became the first important trade nursery in the city.

***

Whether gardeners worked for the Crown, for private estate owners or were commercial nurserymen, they undoubtedly acquired their horticultural knowledge through hands-on experience rather than studying practical manuals. A handful of mediaeval manuscript treatises have survived but these are descriptions of plants rather than instructional works, and would have been accessible to a very limited number of people. The invention of printing in the mid-fifteenth century offered the opportunity for a market in gardening books, but the English were slow to take this up. The earliest example of a printed gardening manual has been identified as an anonymous treatise entitled *The crafte of graffynge & plantynge of trees*. This was produced *c*. 1520 by Wynkyn de Worde, associate and successor to London's first printer-publisher, William Caxton, and its probable source was the fourth-century Roman author of *De re rustica*. The book was small and fitted in with de Worde's production of relatively inexpensive books for the general public.

The first book in English which dealt with gardening in general, *A most briefe and pleasaunte treatise, teachying how to dresse, sowe and set a garden*, was written by Thomas Hill and printed for him by the bookseller John Day, probably in 1558. On the title page he describes himself as a Londoner, and in a later work he claimed to have received a modest education, though he was acquainted with Latin and Italian and had begun his authorial career as translator of popular books on science and the supernatural. In 1568 he published a second horticultural book, *The Proffitable Arte of Gardening*, which he packed with practical advice, culled from all kinds of sources including French and Flemish, and this proved a winning formula, attracting the burgeoning market of owners of small gardens who did not have the services of an experienced gardener. Hill's third gardening title, *The Gardeners Labyrinth*, was published in 1577, three years after his death, under the pseudonym of Didymus Mountain. This eccentric choice may have been a pun cum joke on his Christian and surnames, for in St John's Epistle 11.16, there is reference to 'Thomas, which is called Didymus [Twin]'. Alternatively it could be a reference to the 'Twin Peaks' in Greek mythology, where Mount Parnassus, home to the Muses, had two summits. Whatever, this play on words would have appealed to Elizabethan audiences who appreciated puzzles, and not least William Cecil, to whom the book is dedicated.

The text for *The Gardeners Labyrinth* was completed by Hill's friend Henry Dethick and printed by Henry Bynneman, an outstanding printer for late sixteenth-century London, whose work was commended for its quality by the Archbishop of Canterbury, Matthew Parker, a connoisseur of books. Indeed, the woodcut illustrations for *The Gardeners Labyrinth* are of significantly higher quality than other practical and cheap books of the period, so that it is possible that Bynneman imported them from the Continent, and Arnaud Nicolai, one of the favourite engravers employed by the Antwerp publisher Christopher Plantin, has been proposed. So popular did the book prove that it was reprinted every six or seven years up to 1608, and a final edition appeared in 1651.

The illustrations show gardeners working in a garden of modest size, like those featured on Tudor maps of London and other cities. Men are depicted digging, raking, training climbers over arbours, and planting flowers in raised beds. These skills would have been used by gardeners across the board, from the elite working in royal and aristocratic gardens to the owners of modest plots, although an engaging picture of workers at rest, enjoying a picnic in an arbour, might have applied only to the last group.

One of Hill's illustrations shows the different implements used by gardeners, and these accord with the tools recorded as belonging to John Chapman, when he was Wolsey's gardener in the early years of the sixteenth century. The Cardinal's clerk not only noted the tools but also their values: wheelbarrow (1s 3d); mattock (1s 7d); hatchet (8d); hedgehook (7d); line (6d); shovel (4d); three sieves (1s); three trays (1s); rake (4d); water-tub (10d); two waterpots (2d); and brooms (1d).[26]

The line would have been used to mark out the design of knots, the ornamental squares with geometric patterns that were a feature of formal gardens right through the sixteenth and early seventeenth centuries. Staked line cords were set onto the soil surface of the bed and the pattern outlined lightly before being cut as trenches. This technique is shown in *La Maison Rustique* by Charles Estienne and Jean Liebault, which was translated into English by Richard Surflet in 1600 (see p. 53). The translator explains: 'to plant within the earth, whether it be roote or slip, you must cast trenches, rather with some short handled handforke, or hand spade, than with a dibble, which you shall finde a great deale more easie'.[27]

The water-tub is described in the Hampton Court records as a 'cole' with metal rimmed wheels or tyres so that it could be rolled around the garden and dispense water where needed. Water pots were usually made in ceramic, and with sprinkling heads like modern watering cans. One example in the Museum of London has neither handle nor rose, but holes in the bottom through which water could be released by control of the thumb held over a small aperture at the pot's neck. Thomas Hill described this type, which has no modern equivalent, as a 'common watering pot for the Garden beddes with … a narrow neck, bigge belly, somewhat large bottome, and ful of little holes, with a proper hole formed on the head, to take in the water, which filled full, and the thombe laide on the hole to keep it in the aire, may on such wise be carried in handsome maner to those places by a better help ayding, in the turning and bearing upright of the bottom of this pot, which needfully require watering'.[28]

To water larger areas of garden, a sprinkling system could be used, with water being forced by a stirrup pump from a large standing tub. Another system used a form of irrigation, with shallow ditches filled by pumping a feeding shaft connected to a standing tub.

A formidable array of tools, including pruning knives, saws and 'graffing chisells', is also on show in another popular manual of the late sixteenth century, Leonard Mascall's *Booke of the Art and Maner, howe to Plante and Graffe All Sortes of Trees*, published in 1569. Leonard Mascall was a kinsman,

16 A watering pot from a mid-seventeenth-century emblem book. Instead of a small sprinkler rose, as in modern watering cans, the entire pot forms the sprinkling device.

17 An illustration from *The Gardeners Labyrinth*, 1577, showing one method of keeping substantial areas of garden well watered. The gardeners are operating a stirrup pump in a tub. Hill explains: 'There be some which use to water their beds with great Squirts, made of Tin, in drawing up the water, and setting the Squirt to the brest, that by force squirted upward, the water in the breaking may fall as drops of raine on the plants, which sundry times like squirted on the beds, doth sufficiently feed the plants with moisture' (p. 83).

possibly the nephew, of the clerk of works at various of Henry VIII's buildings, including Hampton Court Palace. He followed in the family tradition by becoming clerk of the kitchen to Archbishop Parker. His book on the cultivation of trees was partly a compilation from various Dutch and German sources, partly a translation of a French manual.[29] Again Mascall's book proved a great success, going into thirteen editions, the last appearing in 1656. He went on to write books on housekeeping recipes, fishing and on the care of poultry and cattle.

Despite the popularity of both Hill and Mascall's books, they do not appear in the inventories or private collections of books of this period, apart from a reference to Henry Percy, ninth Earl of Northumberland, taking a copy of the 1608 edition of Hill's *The Gardeners Labyrinth* into the Tower of London.[30] Percy, known to posterity as the Wizard Earl because of his interest in science and alchemy, was implicated in the Gunpowder Plot at the time he was

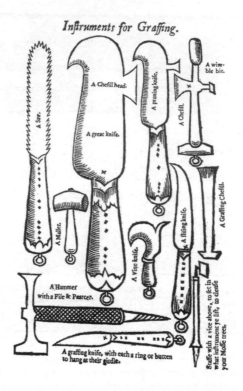

18 Tools for the grafting of fruit trees from Leonard Mascall's *Booke of the Art and Maner, howe to Plante and Graffe All Sortes of Trees*, published in 1569.

planning to rebuild his house and create new gardens at Petworth in Sussex, so this may explain why he might need such a book. Otherwise, such practical books may not have been considered appropriate to grace the shelves of a gentleman's study, but rather to be kept near the entrance to the garden, just as cookery books may have been placed in the kitchen for reference. Both Hill and Mascall are included in the catalogue of available English books compiled in 1599 by a London bookseller, Andrew Maunsell, where Hill is listed among the herbals, while Mascall comes under 'Of gardening, graffing and planting'. They do not appear in the catalogue of the books in the Bodleian Library at Oxford drawn up by its first librarian, Thomas James, in 1620. Nothing can be taken for granted, however, for an author whose name surprisingly does appear in that catalogue is Thomas Tusser.

Tusser was a Suffolk farmer, who developed his manual written in verse over the course of twenty years. His first edition was published in 1557 as *A*

Hundreth Good Pointes of Husbandrie, which by 1573 had expanded to *Five Hundreth Pointes.* Moreover he had by this time added advice for housewives. As he explained:

> For huswifes must husbande, as wel as the man:
> or farewell thy husbandrie, do what thou can.
>
> In Marche, and in Aprill, from morning to night:
> In sowing and seting, good huswives delight.
> To have in their gardein, or some other plot:
> to trim up their house, and to furnish their pot.
>
> Have millons [melons] at Mihelmas, parsneps in lent:
> In June, buttred beans, saveth fish to be spent.
> With those and good pottage inough having than:
> thou winnest the heart of thy labouring man.[31]

Although apparently not a very successful farmer, Thomas Tusser had hit on a winning formula with his books. It is notoriously difficult to assess what the level of literacy was in Tudor England, but it has been estimated that one-third of the population in London could neither read nor write, with a higher proportion in the countryside, and the figure was always higher for women. By using simple verse, Tusser could reach out to those who were not confident about their letters. In the nineteenth century Sir Walter Scott was to compare Tusser's 'homely, pointed and quaint expression' to the old English proverb, 'which the rhyme and alliteration tended to fix on the memory of the reader'.[32] Satire is often an indication of success, and in 1565 the publisher Edward Allde, who specialised in books of practical advice, printed 'An hundredth pyntes of evell huswyfraye'. Tusser's book continued to be bought and read in large quantities, with eighteen editions between 1557 and 1599, making it probably the biggest-selling book of poetry of Elizabethan England. More editions appeared right through to the twentieth century, and John Clare recalled that the bookshelf of an early nineteenth-century cottager included 'old Tusser'.

Husbandry in verse on a rather higher plane appears in Shakespeare's play *Richard II,* which he probably wrote in 1595 although its first performance took place two years later. The gardening theme takes centre stage when the aged John of Gaunt, despairing of the weak governance of his nephew Richard, speaks the famous lines:

> This royal throne of kings, this seat of Mars,
> This other Eden, demi-paradise . . .
> This blessed plot, this earth, this realm, this England. (Act II, Scene 1)

Contemporary accounts make clear that a fruitful orchard was considered the mark of an orderly and prospering household, and the practical tasks involved in the cultivation of fruit an appropriate occupation for gentlemen. Thus the chronicler John Stow said of Sir Thomas Smith, diplomat and scholar friend of William Cecil, 'in the Art of Gardening he was very curious and exact: Employing his own Hands sometime for his version in grafting and planting.'[33]

19 An unusual family portrait: Thomas Wentworth with his wife, his daughter, his gardener and his dog. Wentworth is shown holding a tree-stock with grafts, with another stock by his left foot. His gardener holds a bundle of grafts and a grafting wedge. Behind is the Tudor mansion at Wentworth Woodhouse in Yorkshire. This painting, probably a seventeenth-century copy of an original of *c.* 1575, is attributed to John Lavorgne.

A remarkable painting, probably a seventeenth-century copy of an original made *c.* 1575, has survived of a Yorkshire gentry family. Thomas Wentworth, accompanied by his wife, his daughter, his gardener and his dog, is shown holding a tree-stock with grafts, with another stock at his feet, while his gardener holds a bundle of grafts and a grafting wedge.

Audiences watching a performance of *Richard II* would have made the connection between a fruitful orchard and an ordered family as Shakespeare developed his theme. In the third act Richard's queen, walking in the orchard, overhears a conversation between the gardener and his assistant in which they talk of the overthrow of the king by Gaunt's son, Bolingbroke. The metaphor of England as a garden is here even more clearly drawn. The gardener first instructs his assistant:

> Go bind thou up yond dangling apricocks
> Which, like unruly children, make their sire
> Stoop with oppression of their prodigal weight.

The assistant questions why they should bother:

> When our sea-walled garden; the whole land
> Is full of weeds, her fairest flowers choked up
> Her fruit trees all unpruned, her hedges ruined
> Her knots disordered and her wholesome herbs
> Swarming with caterpillars?

The gardener's response reads almost like a manual for the cultivation of fruit as he regrets the wasteful king:

> O, what pity is it
> That he had not so trimmed and dressed his land
> As we this garden: we at time of year
> Do wound the bark, the skin of our fruit-trees
> Lest, being over-proud with sap and blood
> With too much riches it confounds itself
> Had he done so to great and growing men
> They might have lived to bear and he to taste
> Their fruits of duty. Superfluous branches
> We lop away, that bearing boughs may live
> Had he done so, himself had borne the crown
> Which waste and idle hours hath quite thrown down. (Act III, Scene 4)

At the very time that William Shakespeare was writing and staging *Richard II*, the nation was experiencing famine. Years of plenty were followed in 1595–1597 by a series of disastrous harvests as a result of unceasing rain and tempestuous winds that rotted the corn. This occurred not only in England but throughout Europe, so that it was said that Tartar women in Hungary ate their own children, while in Italy and Germany the poor resorted to whatever was edible, including cats, dogs and even snakes. In London the burial records of some parishes show a doubling in the number of deaths in 1597 which is thought to have been the result of malnutrition.[34] Shakespeare is probably making reference to these terrible visitations in *A Midsummer Night's Dream*, also written at this period, when he has Titania describe the effects of her quarrel with Oberon:

> . . . the winds, piping to us in vain,
> As in revenge, have suck'd up from the sea
> Contagious fogs; which, falling in the land
> Have every pelting river made so proud
> That they have overborne their continents:
> The ox hath therefore stretch'd his yoke in vain,
> The ploughman lost his sweat, and the green corn
> Hath rotted ere his youth attain'd a beard;
> The fold stands empty in the drowned field,
> And crows are fatted with the murrion flock;
> The nine men's morris is fill'd up with mud,
> And the quaint mazes in the wanton green
> For lack of tread are undistinguishable. (Act II, Scene 1)

The population of London had risen sharply during the second half of the sixteenth century from 70,000 in 1550 to 200,000 by 1600. The pressure on land within the city's walls meant that many inhabitants no longer had gardens and were thus dependent on food being brought in. When the famine struck, the Privy Council was obliged to order authorities in the provinces to release grain, and foreign ships were hijacked in the Channel. But given the dearth throughout Europe, other solutions had to be found. All major grains had been affected, as well as peas and beans, so the answer lay in root vegetables.

Root vegetables were not held in high esteem at this period, but one writer who advanced their cause was Hugh Platt. Platt was the son of a rich London brewer, enabling him to devote his time to writing. He began with moralistic

and poetical works but, developing an interest in natural science, he turned his
attention to all kinds of topics, from mechanical inventions to alchemy. With
gardens in St Albans in Hertfordshire, Bethnal Green to the east of the City of
London, and St Martin's Lane to the west, he was able to conduct horticultural
experiments and became fascinated by the cultivation of gardens, orchards
and agriculture. In his treatise, *Sundrie new and Artificiall Remedies against
Famine*, written in 1596 'upon thoccasion of this present Dearth', Platt not
only explored various substitutes for conventional bread flours but also
suggested bread alternatives such as cakes made of parsnip meal.

Richard Gardiner from Shrewsbury combined a career as a linen draper
with an enthusiasm for growing and marketing vegetables. In 1599 he
produced a treatise entitled *Instructions for manuring, sowing and planting of
Kitchin Gardens*, which was printed by Edward Allde for Edward White in
London, with a second edition in 1603. In this octavo book of just thirty
pages, he provided very practical advice on how to raise and save seeds of all
manner of vegetables, from cabbages and lettuce, to beans, artichokes, radishes
and leeks. He was particularly keen on carrots, providing cooking tips, such as
cutting them up and boiling them to a broth with salt beef or pork. Red carrots
could be made into a salad with vinegar and pepper to accompany roast meat.

The second part of Gardiner's book gave advice on how to counter 'the
great dearth and scarcitie last past in the Countie of Salop'. Rather than
planting his own four-acre garden with 'dainty sallets', he turned it over to the
cultivation of 700 close cabbages, thus providing food for hundreds of people.
Again carrots are strongly recommended, for 'in necessitie and dearth, [they]
are eaten of the poore people, after they be well boyled, instead of bread and
meate ... they give good nourishment to all people, and not hurtful to any,
whatsoever infirmities they be diseased of'. He also sold his vegetables and
seeds more cheaply to the poor, thus providing us with a rare record of the
kind of prices commanded at this period. For example, he normally charged a
penny for 5lbs of small yellow carrots, a penny for 2lbs of large close cabbages
and two pence the stone for 'fair and large' turnips. His close cabbage seeds
usually cost four pence per ounce, explaining the high price because the seeds
'are hardly saved in this Countie of Salop, for being devoured with birds'. He
likened dishonest grocers who tried to profit from the famine to 'catterpillers'.

The development of the trade in market gardening reduced the possibility
of future catastrophes when harvests in corn failed. Indeed, the famine of the
1590s acted as a stimulus for an expansion of the trade. In 1655 the great
promoter of husbandry Samuel Hartlib looked back to the beginning of the

century and observed: 'About 50 years ago, about which time Ingenuities first began to flourish in England, the Art of Gardening began to creep into England.'[35] In fact, Dutch and Flemish gardeners had been coming to England since the early 1570s, driven from their homeland by religious persecution, and settled in East Anglian ports such as Norwich, Yarmouth and Colchester. Another important centre was Sandwich in Kent: at the beginning of Elizabeth's reign, Protestants from the Netherlands petitioned to practise their trades, and 400 came over to Sandwich. They were mostly weavers, but gardeners too, appreciating the sandy soil of the area, which heated up quickly and thus was ideal for the cultivation of vegetables, which they sent up in sailing vessels to the markets of London.

Hartlib noted that by 1600 there were Dutch gardeners in Surrey, in places such as Fulham, well placed to supply fresh vegetables to the city, and by 1650 London was ringed by market gardens and orchards. These gardeners were skilled in getting a good yield from the soil by their use of manure, crop rotation and plenty of hoeing and digging. The Thames valley was not naturally good for vegetables as the soil was gravelly. But Busoni, chaplain to the Venetian ambassador, described in 1618 how the market gardeners dug through the gravel layer, selling it for ballast for ships and to repair streets. The holes were filled with nightsoil from London's latrines, 'as rich and black as thick ink'.[36] Once the holes were filled, the land was enclosed by palings, deep ditches or walls of soft mud with rotted straw and thatched on top. These market gardens paid good returns, much better than arable, and farmers further distant from London also turned over some of their fields to vegetable crops.

In time these burgeoning market gardens helped to bring about a revolution in eating habits. In the sixteenth century meat dressed with rich sauces, followed by dishes of sweetmeats, was the desired food of the rich, much to the detriment of their health: Queen Elizabeth was particularly fond of sugar, and her teeth were black and rotten as a result. Vegetables were the diet of the poor, and root vegetables were particularly despised as farmers would feed their cattle with turnips. However, need overcame prejudice, and the poor were saved in times of dearth by the vegetables that were increasingly available. Hartlib spoke to old men in Surrey in the 1650s who remembered how the gardeners began 'to plant Cabages, Colleflowers, and to sow Turneps, Carrets and Parsnips, to sow Raith (or early ripe) Pease, Rape, all which at that time were great rarities, we having few or none in England, but what came from Holland and Flanders'.[37] Again, his time frame is not quite accurate, for

William Harrison back in 1577 in his *Description of England* was reporting how the poor were eating a whole raft of vegetables, including cucumbers, radishes, parsnips, cabbages, and turnips.[38]

Vegetables and salads gradually became fashionable among the higher echelons of society, so that John Parkinson wrote in 1629 how turnips were 'often seene as a dish at good mens tables' though he did go on to point out that 'the greater quantities of them are spent at poor mens feasts'.[39] Asparagus, one of the most fashionable of vegetables in the seventeenth century, was being raised on the former marshlands of Battersea, while Fulham was renowned for its carrots, and Hackney for small turnips. Just as the Wrench family turned their Oxford nurseries into a place of entertainment, so the market gardeners of the Neat Houses, the former pasture lands in Pimlico of the abbots of Westminster, offered food and drink and fun. Samuel Pepys recorded in his diary how he took a boat upriver to the Neat Houses, and bought himself a melon.[40]

Dutch and Flemish gardeners were also skilled in the cultivation of hops. Until the early sixteenth century beer in the southern part of England was made from barley malt. Then hopped beers began to arrive from the Low Countries, although there was strong opposition to this foreign brew. Andrew Boorde in *The Breviary of Helthe* published in 1542 declared: 'Beere is a Dutch boorish liquor, a thing not known in England, till of late days an Alien to our Nation, till such times as Hops and Heresies came against us, it is a saucy intruder in this land'.[41] However, hops had a preservative quality, so that they were widely cultivated in many counties, most intensively in Kent. A small landowner in that county, Reginald Scot, published a book expressly on the culture of hops, *A perfite platforme of a hoppe garden*, in 1574.

Samuel Hartlib could look back at another watershed in the development of the 'Art of Gardening', James I's grant of royal charters in 1605 to gardeners and fruiterers so that they might form their own companies. A 'mystery' or fellowship of gardeners had existed in London from the mid-fourteenth century, ensuring that training took place through an organised apprenticeship system and acting as a benevolent fraternity looking after members and their families, but they did not enjoy the freedom of the City and other privileges accorded to livery companies such as the mercers and the grocers.

The old-established livery companies had shown themselves able to adapt to the development of new trades, and were wary of any proposed new groupings that might challenge their authority or dilute their financial and political powers. The sensible way of gaining independence therefore was to secure the

If you laye fofte græne Ruſhes abꝛoade in the dewe and the Sunne, within twoo oꝛ thꝛæ dayes, they will be lythie, tough, and handſome foꝛ this purpoſe of tying, which may not be foꝛe-

ſowed, foꝛ it is moſt certaine that the Hoppe that lyeth long vpon the grounde befoꝛe he be tyed to the Poale, pꝛoſpereth nothing ſo wel as it, which ſooner attayneth therebnto.

It ſhall not be amiſſe nowe and then to paſſe thꝛough your Garden, hauing in eche hande a foꝛked wande, directing aright ſuch Hoppes as

declyne from the Poales, but ſome in ſteade of the ſayde foꝛked wandes, vſe to ſtande vppon a ſtoole, and doe it with their handes.

Then you may with the foꝛked ende, thꝛuſt vp, oꝛ ſhoue off, all ſuch ſtalkes as remayne vpon eche Hoppe Poale, and carie them to the flooꝛe pꝛepared foꝛ that purpoſe.

The beſt and readyeſt way to take the Hoppes from the Poales.

foꝛ the better dooing hereof, it is very neceſſa-rie that your Poales be ſtreyght without ſcrags oꝛ knobbes.

20 Illustrations from Reginald Scot's *Perfite platforme of a hoppe garden*, published in 1574. These show the hops being tied, trained and stripped from the poles.

support of the City's Court of Aldermen, the route taken by the fruiterers when they began their campaign to secure a royal charter, asking the court to draw up a set of ordinances. The gardeners, however, did not do this. The charter issued by the King to the Company of Gardeners on 18 September 1605 granted them near-exclusive rights over 'gardening, grafting, setting, sowing, cutting, arboring, rocking, mounting, covering, fencing and removing of plants, herbs, seeds, fruits, trees, stocks, sets, and contriving the conveyance to the same'. Moreover, this applied to gardeners within a six-mile compass around the City of London, greater than that which applied to most other companies. Eleven years later, the King further increased the Company's powers and privileges, preventing any person not a member of the Company from selling garden produce except at those places where foreigners (those not freemen of the City) offered their wares. The Company could search out the London markets and confiscate and burn 'any unwholesome dry rotten deceitful and unprofitable wares'.[42]

Historians who have studied the early history of the Company believe that by appealing directly to the King, rather than seeking approval of the Court of Aldermen, the gardeners met resistance, and failed to secure freedom of the City. In the hierarchical list of City companies which began with the Mercers and reached down through fifty trades, the Company of Fruiterers appeared some two-thirds down the list, with Adam and Eve flanking a fruit-laden tree on their coat of arms, but the Gardeners were nowhere to be seen. Only in 1659 did they become freemen of the City, and even then the City Court, still rankled by the Company's earlier behaviour, ruled that it should not be granted livery. This situation continued for another two hundred years to the detriment of their prestige.[43]

Moreover, despite their apparently draconian powers, from the very outset the new Company of Gardeners experienced difficulties in the enforcement and control of their trade. London was expanding rapidly, and the prospect of laying out and working in the gardens of the houses that were being built drew gardeners and labourers from all over the country, and these men had not come up through the Company's apprenticeship scheme. The effect of this was that many gardeners working in and round the City of London did not enrol as members, and even those that did, frequently failed to pay their fees. To make matters worse, the Company in 1633 sought to exclude gardeners in Fulham, Chelsea and Kensington, whom they accused of pretending to be market gardeners when they were really only husbandmen who had not served full apprenticeship. This was a losing battle, for these descendants of Dutch immigrants were skilled men.

In 1659 the Company proposed to incorporate ten garden designers, 150 noblemen's gardeners, 400 gentlemen's gardeners, 100 nurserymen, 150 florists, twenty botanists, and 200 market gardeners. Although this plan was never implemented, the number of gardeners cited shows that the profession was expanding and attaining status. In the 1660s gardeners in Middlesex were paid between £3 and £6 per annum according to skill, with day labourers receiving either 2s 6d or 1s 6d without food, or between one and two shillings with food, again according to skill.

Meanwhile head gardeners of substantial estates could earn more than the butler, one of the most important household officers. Being separate from the rest of the household, in their own domain, they could also maintain some independence. Just as Lord Emsworth went in mortal fear of the disapproval of his gardener, Angus McAllister, in P.G. Wodehouse's novels of Blandings Castle, so references begin to appear to this independence of spirit among some seventeenth-century gardeners. Thus Lady Reresby of Thrybergh in Yorkshire complained that while her husband, Sir John, was in London she could not get the gardener to work to his orders, and resorted to asking for a kinsman's gardener to prune the trees and vines.[44] The concept of nameless serfs provided with shovels had been well and truly laid to rest.

CHAPTER 3

Strange Encounters

B Y THE 1570s THE GARDENS OF WESTERN EUROPE, great and small, were being enriched by the introduction of exotic plants and flowers. As William Harrison exclaimed of England: 'It is a world . . . to see how many strange herbs, plants and unusual fruits are daily brought unto us, from the Indies, Americas, Tabrobane [Ceylon], Canarie Iles and all parts of the world.'[1] The excitement engendered by these new arrivals is palpable and Harrison was echoed by other commentators in late Tudor England. Bulbs and seeds, easily transportable, arrived enclosed with the correspondence of merchants, noblemen and scholars. When ships from far-off lands docked on the Thames, gardeners and botanists, grocers and apothecaries would gather on the quaysides to see what treasures might be unloaded. The London port book for 1567–1568 recorded the arrivals at the wharves on the north bank between Queenhithe and Tower Dock, an area set aside for the overseas trade. Thus the *Prym Rose* from Antwerp brought in spices from the East Indies, such as cloves, peppers, ginger and dates; the *Lawrence* of Plymouth came from Biscay with oranges and lemons; while the *Prymrose* of Harwich arrived from the Barbary coast with sugar and almonds.[2] Harrison makes clear that the strange fruit – apricots, almonds, peaches, figs and capers – were not only being imported, but also cultivated in the orchards of noblemen.[3]

Key players in these introductions to Western Europe were the Ottoman Turks, not only as a source of new plants, but also as controllers of the trade routes of Central Asia. In 1520 Suleyman the Magnificent had succeeded to the throne of the Ottoman Sultans in Constantinople. Thanks to the ruthless culling of all possible heirs to the throne carried out by his father, Selim I, known to posterity by the less flattering name of 'the Grim', Suleyman was able to come to power unopposed. His father had significantly expanded the Ottoman Empire by defeating the Mamelukes and conquering most of modern Syria, Lebanon, Palestine and Egypt. He also very briefly held sway over the Safavid Persians, thus gaining control of the overland routes that had existed for centuries from the Far East, the Silk Road. Cut off from their supplies of silk and spices, Dutch and Portuguese merchants found alternative sea routes eastwards to India, the East Indies and China, and west to the Americas, which they discovered were not the Indies of Columbus's imagination, but a New World.

Suleyman continued his father's conquest of territory, adding Serbia and Hungary to the west and again challenging the Safavids in Persia. But he also began to make diplomatic contacts with the powers of Western Europe. He was a man of wide interests including a love of flowers, something he shared with many of his followers. His great-grandfather, Mehmed II, following his conquest of Constantinople in 1453, had laid out gardens open to the public. In his 'Treatise on Husbandry' (*Irshad az-zara'ah*) written in 1515, Qasim ibn Yusuf of Herat, then part of the Turkish Empire, describes the layout of such gardens and the combinations of flowers within the beds: colchicums with violets, roses with narcissi and saffron crocus, Persian lilac with tulips and stocks. The beds nearest the house might be filled with roses, sacred in Islam as the flower that sprang from Mohammed's sweat.

One of the diplomatic missions to Suleyman on behalf of the French King Henri II included an enthusiastic botanist, Pierre Belon. Born in 1517 near Le Mans, Belon had studied natural history and medicine with the botanist Valerius Cordus and travelled with him in Germany and Bohemia. Returning to Le Mans, he became apothecary to the bishop, who provided him with the means to undertake a scientific expedition. Belon set off with the diplomatic mission, sailing from Venice in 1547, but was robbed by pirates and left alone on an empty ship without food and money. A man of resource, he learnt to sail it, finding harbour in Crete where he saw several new species of garden plants, such as cistus and oleander. His next port of call was Constantinople, where he explored the wonderful spice and food markets, carrying a copy of *al-Qanum fi at-tibb* ('Canon of Medicine') by the eleventh-century Persian physician Avicenna. He noted how a measure of the importance given to medicinal plants was the care with which the camels were guarded – more so than even those who carried the bales of silk. Belon was also the first Westerner to describe the trade in tulips, referring to them as 'Lils rouges' (red lilies).

Belon travelled through Crete, Egypt, Jerusalem and Lebanon before returning home. Again he was attacked by pirates, but allowed to keep his seeds and plants, including the mandrake, the Christmas rose and the Egyptian peony. Back in France, he tried to persuade the King to found a royal botanic garden, but when he refused, the Bishop of Le Mans proved more generous, establishing a garden at the Château de Touvoie in Savigné-l'Evêque. Belon then turned his attention to writing, publishing several influential books of natural history, but his most widely read book was his memoirs of his travels, published in Paris in 1553.[4] Five years later he visited Italy, determined to find out more about how to acclimatise exotic plants to local conditions, and explored the gardens of the Medici villas around Florence. Having survived so many dangerous adventures, he met his death at the hands of assassins in the Bois de Boulogne in 1564.

The next botanist traveller from Western Europe to the Ottoman lands was Leonhard Rauwolff, a physician from Augsburg, who had studied at the medical faculty of the University of Montpellier with the charismatic teacher, Guillaume Rondelet. Rauwollf's expedition was financed by his merchant brother-in-law who already had contacts in the Levant and recognised the lucrative nature of the trade in medicinal plants. He set sail from Marseilles in May 1573, 'chiefly to gain a clear and distinct knowledge of those delicate herbs . . . by viewing them in their proper and native places.' His travels lasted for three years, from Tripoli to Aleppo, on to Baghdad and then back via Jerusalem. When he was staying in Aleppo he collected plants 'not without great danger and trouble, which I glued upon Paper very carefully'. In other words, he was creating a herbarium, an incredible achievement in such conditions.

Like Belon, Rauwolff published an account of his travels. He was the first European to describe the preparation and drinking of coffee: 'A very good drink by them called Chaube that is almost as black as Ink, and very good in illness, chiefly that of the Stomach; of this they drink in the Morning early in the open places before everybody, without any fear or regard, out of China cups, as hot as they can, they put it often to their Lips but drink little at a time.' Physicians and apothecaries were to be fascinated by this exotic beverage, devoting books to its medicinal properties in the seventeenth century. Rauwolff also noted the banana:

These Trees bear their Fruit no more but once, wherefore they are cut down, and so the Root shoots out several other Stalks about a Foot distant from the old one, which grow up again, and bring forth Fruit, which groweth on a thick Stalk in great numbers; they are almost shaped like the Citruls, round and bended, only they are less, smooth without, environed with a thick rind, which is first yellow, but when they are kept a few days it grows black, it is easily separated when they are new, within they are whitish, full of Seeds; sweet and good to eat.

He noted that they fill mightily and are apt to gripe, so that the classical writer Theophrastus recorded how Alexander the Great would not let his men eat them on campaign.

Rauwolff's great interest was in the flowers and how they were regarded by the local population. In Aleppo, he noted, 'In their Gardens the Turks love to raise all sorts of Flowers, wherein they take great delight and use to put them on their turbans, so I could see the fine Plants that blow one after another daily, without trouble. In December I saw Violets, with dark brown and white Flowers . . . . Then came the Tulips, Hyacinths, Narcissies, which they still name by the old name *Nergis*. Before all the others I saw a rare kind with a double yellow flower called *Modaph*.'[5]

Rauwolff's travel memoirs also proved an enormous success, being translated into Dutch and English. His life ended adventurously, killed while fighting for the Emperor against the Turks in Hungary in 1596. His album of dried plants also had many adventures. During Rauwolff's lifetime, it was consulted by botanist authors and their engravers, but eventually was sold to the Duke of Bavaria, who kept it in his *wunderkammer* in Munich. During the Thirty Years War, soldiers carried it off to the Swedish court, and in 1650 Queen Christina gave it to her Dutch librarian, Isaac Vossius, who showed it to botanists and gardeners such as Robert Morison, John Ray and Charles Hatton during a visit to London, before it was bought by the University of Leiden. Rauwolff cleverly used borders of thick paper to frame each page so that the pressed plants have survived in fine condition, and the album is one of the great treasures of the Leiden herbarium (Plate VII).

The Turkish custom of wearing flowers in turbans was also noted by the resplendently named Ogier Ghiselin de Busbecq. From 1554 to 1562, this Flemish aristocrat was the Holy Roman Emperor's ambassador to the court of Suleyman the Magnificent. Busbecq has been credited with introducing the cultivated tulip to Western Europe, though it is almost certain that this had happened earlier. However, we can probably attribute to him the naming of the tulip. The Turkish name for tulip is *lale*, but when an interpreter indicated the flower in his turban, *tulband*, it is thought that Busbecq muddled the words.

Busbecq had been interested in botany from an early age, so that he was particularly observant about the flowers that he saw. He noted how

> There is a great abundance of the narcissus and hyacinth in Greece; their fragrance is perfectly wonderful, so much so, that, when in great profusion, they affect the heads of those who are unaccustomed to the scent. The tulip has little or no smell; its recommendation is the variety and beauty of the colouring. The Turks are passionately fond of flowers, and though somewhat parsimonious in other matters, they do not hesitate to give several aspres for a choice blossom.[6]

In 1572 Busbecq returned to Vienna and, keeping up his Turkish connections, received parcels of tulip bulbs and other rare plants and passed them on to his friend and fellow countryman Carolus Clusius, prefect of Maximilian II's medical garden.

Carolus Clusius occupies such a vital role in the sixteenth-century world of botany, and in particular in the circulation of exotic plants in Western Europe, that his career must be examined in some detail. Clusius, or Charles L'Ecluse, was born in Arras in Artois in 1526, the son of a clerk and receiver of the abbey of Saint Vaast. His maternal uncle was prior of the abbey, so he attended the well-regarded school there before moving on to the Latin school in Ghent and finally the Collegium Trilingue at Louvain. The last was the university for the region, where Hebrew was available along with Latin and Greek. At this time Clusius's focus was on law, but before starting in the profession, he set off on a study trip to the Lutheran university at Marburg. Here he lodged with a local theologian who took him botanising in the woods of Hesse, awakening his lifelong passion for natural history.

One of the great centres for studying natural sciences was in the south of France, at Montpellier. Clusius became one of the star pupils of Guillaume Rondelet, learning from him how to study plants in depth, observing, analysing and writing. During his time at Montpellier, Clusius helped Rondelet write his work on fishes, duly receiving acknowledgement when it was published in 1555. On his return to the Low Countries, he began his own writing career with a translation of the herbal of Rembert Dodoens from Dutch (Flemish) into French. This was published in 1557 by the Antwerp bookseller Jan van der Loe.

The following years were a time of travel for Clusius, acting as a tutor to children of noble families. First he went to France with Thomas Rehdiger, then to the Iberian Peninsula with Jacob Fugger, scion of the very wealthy Catholic merchant house based in Augsburg. With Jacob he travelled all around Spain and Portugal, visiting many of the universities there, in the north Burgos and Salamanca, in the west Toledo and Lisbon, in the south Seville, and in the east Alcala de Henares. As in all his travels, he was invited into the gardens and libraries of scholars and noblemen, investigated the native flora and collected newly published books on the exotic botany of New Spain, the colonies being established in the Americas. In 1561 he paid a visit, his second, to England.

This peripatetic life came to a temporary halt when he helped to lay out and look after the garden at Malines of Jean de Brancion, a member of the Hapsburg court in the Low Countries. It was here that Clusius first came upon the flower with which he is most associated, the tulip. Bulbs had been added to a shipment of cloth from Constantinople, but were mistaken for onions, and most of them eaten. A few were rescued by a merchant, and given to either Clusius or Brancion. The bulbs were of the feathered type, and later were named after Brancion. Two years later Clusius made a significant move, becoming praefectus of Maximilian II's imperial garden in Vienna, with a passport provided by his friend, Ogier Ghiselin de Busbecq. The four years spent in Hapsburg service were possibly the most carefree of his hectic career, with few financial worries, and his own private garden at Schottenberg, where he could cultivate his own bulbs and seeds. He made many botanising expeditions. In the woods around Vienna he first came across the auricula and, noting that this Alpine member of the primula family had leaves shaped like bears' ears, he named it *Auricula ursi*. Further afield he travelled to Moravia, Bohemia and the south-west of Hungary.

In 1577 the respite came to an end with the death of Maximilian and the succession of his son Rudolf II. Life became less conducive and Clusius removed himself from service to the Hapsburgs. Tradition has it that the new Emperor wanted to get rid of part of the botanical garden to build a riding school, but it is more probable that Clusius found Rudolf's hard-line Catholicism the decisive factor in his departure from court. Clusius had been brought up a Catholic, but less than a decade before his birth, Martin Luther, professor of theology at the University of Wittenberg, had issued a challenge to papal authority that reverberated throughout the Continent. On All Saints' Eve, 31 October 1517, he posted on the door of the castle church at Wittenberg his Ninety-Five Theses, arguing against indulgences. This challenge had a relatively slow fuse. Luther was excommunicated by the Pope in 1521, but during the 1540s Clusius was able to study at Lutheran universities such as Marburg and Wittenberg. His personal wish would seem to have been for a broad and traditional church. At some stage he probably became a member of a group known as the Family of Love, interested in inner piety rather than outward show, and believing that no one Church would be supreme at the Second Coming. The best known Familist was the Antwerp bookseller Christopher Plantin, who was to publish many of Clusius's books.

Leaving Vienna, Clusius resumed his travels, visiting England again in 1581, before finally settling down in Leiden in 1593 and becoming director of the newly instituted botanical garden. He remained in the city until his death in 1609, at the advanced age of eighty-three. The very existence of the University of Leiden, and its botanical garden, was a reflection of the political changes taking place in Europe at this time. The nearby universities of Louvain, Cologne and Douai had become bastions of Counter-Reformation Catholicism. William the Silent, Prince of Orange, resolved that a place of learning should be available to educate a new generation of leaders for the developing Dutch nation, as he explained in a letter of 28 December 1574: 'a firm support and sustenance of freedom and good legal administration of the country, not only in matters of religion, but also with regard to the general welfare of the people.'[7] Leiden was chosen as a reward for the city's bravery in resisting a Hapsburg siege in 1572 when it stood in the path of Philip of Spain's conquest of the provinces of Holland and Zeeland. As the food ran out, Prince William ordered the dykes along the River Maas to be cut, flooding the land around Leiden, and when a storm topped up the waters, the Spanish fled and the Dutch Sea Beggars were able to relieve the town. The Dutch Republic had been saved from an early death.

The medical faculty at Leiden represented a bastion for the investigation of nature without concern for religious conformity. One of the advisers on the establishment of the university, Guillaume de Feugeray, felt that if Leiden was to live up to the highest ideals of medical education, then students should attend not only the classroom, the disputation hall and the library, but also the anatomical theatre, the chemistry laboratory and the botanical garden.

The first botanical gardens in Renaissance Europe had been established in Italy.[8] In 1533 the Venetian senate endorsed the appointment of Francesco Buonafede at the University of Padua as the first professor of *simplicia medicamenti* – plants for medicine, or in modern terms, botany. A decade later a botanical garden was founded in Padua, with an *ostensor simplicium* whose job was to lead students on guided tours. These were shrewd steps, for the Venetians dominated the lucrative Mediterranean trade in spices with the east, and wanted to continue to do so, though others were determined to get in on the act.

Under the patronage of the Medicis, the botanical garden at Pisa was developed in 1544 by Luca Ghini after he had been lured from Bologna where he had the reputation of being the best teacher in Europe. He was prepared to go to Pisa because the authorities in Bologna kept delaying the establishment of a garden there. As *prefetto* or director of the Botanical Garden at Pisa, Ghini

21 'Herba croce' from the album of Cibo, a botanist who lived in Rocca Contrada and mostly confined his study of plants to his native Marche. He probably attended the lectures of Luca Ghini in Bologna, an inspirational teacher and the owner of one of the first *hortus siccus*.

held demonstrations for the benefit of students, including two future botanists of distinction, Andrea Cesalpino and Ulisse Aldrovandi, who followed
him from Bologna. By 1548, 620 different kinds of plants were growing in the
garden, flourishing in the warm climate of Italy that enabled cultivation of
exotics such as maize, sweet potatoes, runner beans, pineapples and sunflowers.
Ghini not only created at Pisa an encyclopaedia of growing plants but also
developed the *hortus siccus* by pressing plants and sticking them into a book so
that they might be studied at all seasons.

When the university authorities were searching for a director for their new
botanical garden in Leiden, their original choice was the Louvain physician
Rembert Dodoens, but his death in 1585 dashed this thought. Justus Lipsius,
the professor of law and a keen gardener, approached Clusius, but at first he
felt himself too old at the age of sixty. He also pointed out that he was not a
physician. However, he was eventually won over by Marie de Brimeu, Princess
of Chimay, a wealthy and influential supporter of the university. Clusius had
maintained a long correspondence with her, and may well have designed her
garden when he was working with de Brancion in Malines in the late 1560s.
With the proviso that he would not have to give lectures and could have a
private garden of his own, Clusius accepted the position, but a heavy fall left
him permanently lame, so that the botanical garden was laid out in the
summer of 1594 by a team of gardeners under the day-to-day supervision of
an apothecary from Delft, Dirk Outgers Cluyt.

The botanical gardens at Pisa and Padua had been laid out in complex
geometrical designs. At Padua a circular earthen rampart was thrown up,
penetrated by four tunnels. From the ramparts visitors might look down on
the design, which consisted of enclosed parterres divided into four square
quarters, an elaborate design made by the Venetian cleric Daniele Barbaro
according to architectural and mathematical principles. The taste was exquisite but not easy for study, so that in the 1590s the garden was redesigned on
more utilitarian lines.

For Leiden a much simpler plan was chosen from the start. The square site
was divided into quarters with long, straight beds. These beds, known as
pulvillus or small cushions, contained plantings of eighteen, twenty-six or
thirty-two, organised within particular families. John Prest in *The Garden of
Eden* likens this arrangement to members of a household sitting around a
dining table, with spaces behind for servers to gain access to any part of the
table. An inventory drawn up when the garden was first established records
that it contained 1,060 species, one third of medical interest, the rest exotics

or ornamentals – a proportion that must have been influenced by Clusius, with his passions for botany and horticulture.

An engraving of the garden dating from 1610 shows a gallery with large glass windows on the south side for the over-wintering of delicate plants, for teaching and for the collection of curiosities of natural history. The last is in the tradition of naturalia kept in private museums or cabinets. One of the most famous of these was the *wunderkammer* created by Hans Jacob Fugger in Augsburg, and no doubt familiar to Clusius. Botanical gardens have been likened to encyclopaedias of plants, and, with the discovery of the Americas, they could also reflect the four corners of the earth. There is some evidence that at Padua an effort was made to place plants in their appropriate quarter, so that laurel and myrtle and cedar, coming from the east, were planted in that section of the garden.

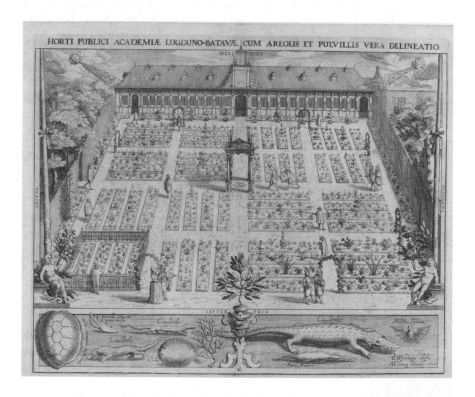

22 The botanical garden at Leiden, from an engraving of 1610, with the beds arranged according to particular families of plants. At the top is the gallery for protecting delicate plants over the winter. Here also were kept curiosities of natural history, and some of these are shown at the bottom of the engraving.

A century before Pierre Belon, Rauwolff and other European travellers were exploring the territories of the Turkish Empire, the Portuguese had developed ocean-going carracks with lateen sails which enabled them to explore lands even further distant within an extraordinarily rapid time-span. Madeira was reached in 1419, the Azores in 1439, Cape Verde in the 1450s and in 1498 Bartholomew Dias rounded the Cape of Good Hope and explored South Africa. On 22 May 1498 Vasco da Gama reached Calicut on the Malabar coast of India, and forts were established within the decade at Cochin and Socatra bringing the Far Eastern spice trade under the control of the Portuguese. At the very centre of disseminating information about the newly discovered plants from these lands was that powerhouse of energy, Carolus Clusius. In 1567 he published his second book, a Latin translation of Garcia ab Orto's account in Portuguese of plants from India, *Coloquios simples, e drogas e cousas medicinais da India.*

The story of Garcia ab Orto serves as a grim reminder that this was not only the age of exploration but also of religious intolerance. He was from a family of 'New Christians' who settled in Portugal after the expulsion of Jews from Spain in 1492. Orto became professor of medicine at Lisbon University in 1530, but four years later the threat of the Inquisition caused him to flee the country and to take the post of personal physician to his friend Martin Alfonso de Sousa, who bore the resplendent title of Captain Major of the Indian Ocean. The headquarters of the Portuguese in India was based in Goa, and here Orto spent the next thirty years in comparative tranquillity, but after his death in 1568 his family once more faced persecution, and his body was exhumed and burnt in an auto-da-fé.

Garcia ab Orto was able to travel extensively with de Sousa on his military campaigns, and thus had a wide knowledge of the natural history of the subcontinent. He wrote his book in the form of a dialogue between himself and a fictional alter ego, Dr Ruana, discussing the medicinal plants, including many spices, and their uses. *Coloquios* was published in Goa in 1563 by a Dutch bookseller, Johannes de Emden, and therefore copies were scarce in Europe. However, Clusius acquired a copy while travelling in the Iberian Peninsula with Jacob Fugger and, teaching himself Portuguese, concentrated in his translation on the botanical aspects, including cloves, cinnamon, manna and pepper. The resulting text was illustrated with sixteen woodcut illustrations by Peter van der Borcht and the first edition was produced by Christopher Plantin in Antwerp in 1567.[9] In one of Clusius's later editions of ab Orto he added a translation of the work of Christavao A Costa. Little is known about

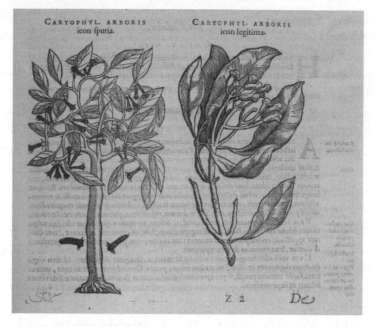

CARYOPHYL. ARBORIS
icon ſpuria.

CARYOPHYL. ARBORIS
icon legitima.

23 Cloves from India, illustrations in Clusius's *Exotica*, published in Leiden in 1605. The picture on the left was originally cut for the Spanish edition of Christavao A Costa's book on Indian plants, and was considered so misleading by Clusius that he included it alongside a much more accurate representation from the treatise by Garcia ab Orto as a warning to the unwary.

Costa apart from the fact that he died in Burgos in 1580, and produced a treatise on the plants of Portuguese India first published in 1578.[10]

Going in the opposite direction, Christopher Columbus, financed by Queen Isabella of Spain, set sail in August 1492 with the objective of finding a westward route to the Indies. Instead he found Cuba, which he thought was the territory of the great khan, and Santo Domingo (Española). On his return to Spain he announced that he had discovered the Indies, but he had instead found a new world. Over the next century the Spaniards established themselves in Central America, conquering the empire of the Aztecs and renaming it New Spain, and in South America the empire of the Incas, renaming it the Vice-Royalty of Peru. Meanwhile the Portuguese established themselves along the Atlantic coast of Brazil.

The Spanish and Portuguese earned themselves reputations as brutal conquerors, but they were fascinated by the flora and fauna of their new colonies. The first Spaniards arriving in Mexico noted that the Aztecs laid out their gardens in regular squares, with intersecting paths, and a scientific arrangement to their planting, giving rise to the theory that they may have inspired the botanical gardens in Italy of the 1540s. One of the early chroniclers of New World plants was the Spanish physician Nicolas Monardes in *Dos Libros* published in Seville in 1569. He described the three plants that were considered effective against the syphilis that the Spaniards had brought back with them to Europe: the guaiacum, the bark of a tree growing around Santo Domingo; china, with a root like ginger; and sarsaparilla. He also devoted considerable space to tobacco, from the Spanish after the island of the same name, which was known to the American Indians as *peciels*.

Clusius came upon Monardes's book on his visit to London in 1571, and made a Latin translation which was published by Plantin in 1574. Three years later an English translation was published by a merchant, John Frampton, who had spent much of his working life in Spain. His title was *Joyfull newes out of the newe-found world*, and he explained how 'there is discovered newe regions, newe kyngdomes and newe Provinces by our Spanyardes, thei have brought unto us newe medicines and newe Remedies.' Frampton noted in his edition that tobacco was known in France as nicotiane, named after the French

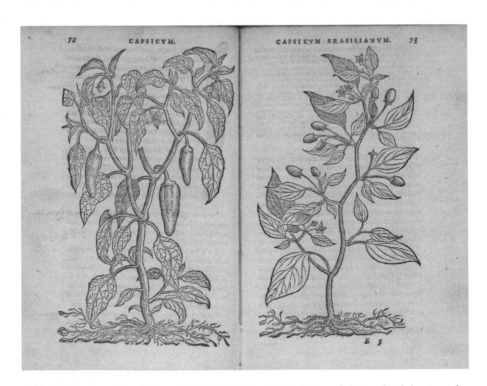

24 Peppers from Brazil, from Clusius's 1574 Latin translation of the work of the Spanish physician, Nicolas Monardes, the sixteenth-century authority on New World plants.

ambassador to the Portuguese court, Jean Nicot, who was presented with the plant in 1559 and grew it in his garden.

Clusius obtained sketches of plants made by a French artist, Jacques le Moyne de Morgues, who went out to the Huguenot settlement in Florida in 1564. When the Spanish overran the settlement the following year, de Morgues made good his escape and returned to France. The one record of the New World that escaped the eagle eye of Clusius was the work of Francisco Hernández de Toledo. Personal physician to Philip II of Spain, he was dispatched to the Americas charged with the mission of collecting and classifying specimens of flora and fauna. Indigenous artists illustrated plants for him, including the 'acocotli' or 'chichipathi', meaning water pipe in the languages of two tribes under the rule of the Aztecs. These were the first pictures of the flower that came to be known as the dahlia, but delay dogged the publication of the book, which only appeared in Mexico in an unillustrated version in 1615, and it was not until 1651 that an illustrated edition was published in Rome.[11] The dahlia, named after the Swedish botanist Andreas Dahl, only burst upon the European floral scene at the end of the eighteenth century.

The English, as in so many endeavours in the sixteenth century, were late on the scene of exploration. The voyage of Jean Cabot, an Italian merchant who had settled in England, to Newfoundland in 1497 proved a false dawn. But by the 1570s, English sea dogs, with the tacit encouragement of Elizabeth I, were in full sail, and among their booty were new plants. When Clusius paid a repeat visit to London in 1581, he met Francis Drake, recently returned from his famous voyage around the world. Taking a route from the South Atlantic through the Straits of Magellan, he had explored the coasts of Chile and Peru, sailing right up to what is now California, before heading across the Pacific to the Moluccas, and returning to England via Java and the Cape of Good Hope. From Drake, Clusius received cocoa beans and sweet potatoes, and he was able to describe these, together with an account of Drake's expedition, in a supplement to his 1582 translation of Garcia ab Orto's book.

Clusius was determined to make accessible information about expeditions to all parts of the known world. Therefore in 1589 he translated into Latin Pierre Belon's account of his travels in the Middle East.[12] The following year he turned to North America, and the description of Virginia written by the English explorer Thomas Harriot, a brilliant mathematician who probably met Walter Raleigh at Oxford. He entered Raleigh's household in 1582, setting a telescope on the roof of Durham House on the Strand in London and

giving lectures on navigation, advocating the idea of an English empire overseas. In 1585 Raleigh sent him off to the Roanoke Island colony in Virginia
with the artist John White. Before the voyage, Harriot had studied the local
language from two Algonquian Indians, brought to England on a reconnais-
sance expedition. Harriot even invented a phonetic alphabet so that when he
was in America, exploring the area north of Chesapeke Bay, he was in an ideal
position to study local customs, together with the flora and fauna. Returning
with Drake in June 1586, he produced a pamphlet, 'A Brief and True Report
of the New Found Land of Virginia', with drawings by White, to encourage
fresh settlers and investors. He mentioned 'operauk' (potatoes), and 'uppowa'
(tobacco) which he recommended smoking for the purging of 'superfluous
phlegm'.

Harriot stands out as a man out of time with his age. As John Aubrey
explained in his *Brief Lives*: 'on the Creation of the World. He could not
believe the old position; he would say *ex nihilio nihil fit* [nothing comes of
nothing] . . . He was a Deist'.[13] His unusual ideas are reflected in the sympathy
that he showed towards Algonquian beliefs and customs at a time of brutal
intolerance of native inhabitants by colonists. The earliest expeditions to the
New World were introduced to Europeans in general in 1590 in an influential
book, *America*, published by the Frankfurt goldsmith Theodor de Bry.
Harriot's text about Virginia was included, in a Latin translation by Clusius. It
is often said that Clusius the multi-linguist had no English, but this showed
that he had some ability with the language, and was able to converse with
many of the leading botanists and explorers in London.

Clusius provided yet one more translation, this time of a journey made in
the very northernmost part of America in search of a passage through to
China. In 1596 Gerrit de Veer, a Dutch carpenter who took part in Willem
Barentsz's voyage, kept a diary that Clusius duly rendered into Latin for publication by an Amsterdam bookseller.[14] It is a bleak tale of snow and ice, of
violent battles with polar bears, and not a sighting of any plant, apart from the
dismissal of the enduring myth that barnacle geese were hatched from a tree.

Clusius truly was a phenomenon: botanist, gardener, scholar, thinker and
indefatigable traveller. Not only did he translate into Latin a series of books on
travel and natural history, but he also wrote several works of his own, which
will be considered in the next chapter. His translations were into the *lingua
franca* of Europe so that they might be read by scholars and interested laymen:
cosmography and travel books feature in many private libraries and catalogues
of the sixteenth century. He was a prodigious correspondent, and it has been

estimated that he wrote over four thousand letters in his lifetime. His publisher, Christopher Plantin, described the letters that he received as arriving like flocks of sparrows, and Clusius's postbag must have been similar. He was generous in giving information, plants and seeds to other botanists and gardeners, feeling that he was part of a club, and thus found irksome the increasing commercialisation of the flower trade, particularly the dealing in tulips.

Thus Clusius stood in the centre of a circle of botanists from all parts of Europe – Alpino from Italy, Gesner from Switzerland, L'Obel from Flanders and Rondelet from France, among many others. Anna Pavord in *The Naming of Names* regards these men as at the cutting edge of the science of their day, comparing them with nuclear physicists and researchers into DNA in modern times.[15]

***

Botanical gardens were an important adjunct to the faculties of medicine in universities, but noblemen and merchants also had similar gardens where they could display their new and strange plants. The Venetian Pietro Antonio Michiel travelled through the whole of Italy in search of rare plants, making a garden of exotics on the island of San Trovaso. One of the earliest private botanical gardens in Europe was created in Antwerp by the apothecary Pieter van Coudenberg. While his pharmacy was in the centre of the city, he bought land in the nearby hamlet of Borgerhout and started to lay out his garden there in 1548. Within twenty years he had 600 thriving exotic plants, including the bead-tree from India, agaves from Mexico, and tulips from the stock originally given to Clusius by Busbecq. Coudenberg tended this garden himself, hibernating plants used to warmer climates by putting them in pots and plunging them into the earth. We know a lot about the plants grown by Coudenberg because in 1557 he sent a catalogue of them to his friend the Swiss naturalist Conrad Gesner, who was compiling his account of the gardens of Northern Europe.[16] Gesner sought advice from other owners of private botanical gardens, including a chemist in Leipzig and a herb trader from Nuremberg. In England in the early 1550s Protector Somerset's garden at Syon on the banks of the Thames, looked after by William Turner, was also sometimes described as a botanical garden, and sometimes as a physic garden.

Unlike university botanical gardens, these private collections rarely survived the death of the owner. In the case of Coudenberg, obliteration occurred in his lifetime during the Siege of Antwerp in 1584–85, when a chronicle recorded

I William Cecil, Lord Burghley, on his mule. This portrait by an unknown artist shows the Queen's Chief Secretary riding in a flowery meadow, carrying a nosegay of pinks and honeysuckle.

II The recreated Elizabethan garden at Kenilworth Castle. An arbour for training roses stands at the top of the staircase on the left, leading down into the privy garden arranged in formal beds of knots, with a 'porphyry' obelisk. The outer beds are bordered by thrift, *Armeria maritima*, and the inner by strawberries, *Frageria vesca*.

III The *Sacro Bosco* at Bomarzo in the lower valley of the Tiber, near Viterbo, was laid out by the Orsini family in the 1550s, adopting as its programme scenes from Ariosto's *Orlando Furioso* and the works of Dante. Take a wrong turning, and the visitor encounters the mouth of Hell, seen here. At Nonesuch in the 1590s, Lord Lumley composed a similar programme, where the visitor might trespass on the realm of Diana, and witness the fate of Actaeon, the hapless hunter from Ovid's *Metamorphoses*.

IV Portrait of Sir George Delves, holding the hand of a mysterious woman, possibly his deceased wife, by an unknown artist, *c.* 1577. An elaborate garden is shown in the background, divided into compartments, including a kitchen garden and a circular maze.

V Miniature portrait of Sir Thomas More and his family, painted by Rowland Lockey in 1593–94. On the left are two arrangements of cut flowers displayed on a buffet. On the right, a garden can be glimpsed in the background, thought to be More's walled garden in Chelsea, with individual beds enclosed by hedges.

VI White hellebore from the album of the botanist, Cibo, showing two botanisers identifying the plant amid the landscape of the Marche. (See also p. 78.)

VII The title page to the fourth volume of Leonhard Rauwolff's *hortus siccus*, in which he put the rare plants that he collected on his travels in the Near East from 1573 to 1575. At the top and bottom of the page, the artist has painted depictions of the Garden of Gethsemane and Jesus entering Jerusalem riding on a mule. On the left a gardener is digging, while on the right stands an apothecary in a black cloak, presumably Rauwolff himself, holding a plant.

VIII Rowland Lockey's portrait of Elizabeth I, commissioned by Bess of Hardwick and still hanging in the Long Gallery at Hardwick New Hall. The Queen's ornate petticoat is decorated with flora and fauna, either painted onto the silk, or embroidered. Centre stage on the hem is an iris, the flower used by Bess to show not only her loyalty to her Queen, but also to her husbands.

how the Duke of Parma ordered all grain and green be pulled by the roots, to remove any notion of hope.[17] Coudenberg, aged sixty-five, could not find the heart to restart his life's work, and even the site of this, once one of Antwerp's great attractions, is unknown.

This passion for plants was also reflected by more modest amateur gardeners. One community existed in the last years of the sixteenth century in the Dutch city of Middelburg. The fall of Antwerp in 1585 caused a mass migration of merchants, many of whom settled in the cities along the Dutch coast, such as Leiden, Amsterdam and Middelburg on one of the islands on the coast of Zeeland. As they prospered, these citizens filled their gardens with rare and expensive plants, and became so passionate about them that they were known as liefhebbers (herb lovers). From Middelburg merchants set off northwards to Archangel and south to the Mediterranean and beyond to the Indies, bringing back exotic plants to the delight of these gardeners. Their pleasure was given visual form by skilled artists such as Ambrosius Bosschaert and Balthasar van der Ast, who created some of the finest flower-pieces ever painted, so that those wealthy enough to purchase them might hang them in their houses and enjoy the glory of the flowers all the year round.

In the tradition of Belon and Rauwolff, a Middelburger decided to visit some of the lands from which these plants had come, and subsequently wrote up his travel memoirs. But Jehan Somer's achievement was even more remarkable than theirs, for he was able to walk only with the aid of a crutch. Somer, the son of a wealthy magistrate, set off in 1590, visiting first Italy and then taking a merchant vessel through the Mediterranean. It seems the inevitable fate of such travellers that they encounter pirates, and Somer was duly captured by Turks and consigned to slavery in their galleys. By incredible luck he was rescued by the French consul in Alexandria and, undaunted by his horrific experience, continued his journeying. He became entranced by the flowers that he saw, recording how even poor Turks had their own gardens and spent much money on strange plants and flowers. In Constantinople, he noted, there was one market given over to the sale of flowers and herbs 'which are brought there from the Black Sea, or Mare Magiore, and from other places, from Egypt to India'.[18]

When Somer made his way back to Middelburg in 1592, he brought with him bulbs and herbs from Constantinople and from Italy, thanks to the generosity of the Dutch herbalist at the Duke of Florence's Pratolino Garden, including dogstooth violets, auriculas, double narcissi, crocuses and small tulips. Perhaps his tulips were not exciting enough, for in May 1597 Somer plucked up courage to 'molest' Clusius in nearby Leiden, asking for one of his tulips, 'since I understand that your honour shares liberally with those who consider themselves connoisseurs of flowers, among whom I consider myself to be the very least . . . for however small it is that comes from your honour's hand I shall receive with the greatest thanks'.[19] For his part, he sent Clusius a painting of a yellow fritillary that had bloomed in his garden that year and 'seeded beautifully', and offered an offset of the martagon lily that he had brought back from Constantinople.[20]

Just as Dutch cities like Middelburg had profited from the sack of Antwerp and the devastation of southern Flanders, so cities in Germany and England gained wealthy refugees. Another community of connoisseurs of flowers has been identified in Lime Street in the City of London.[21] This street, running in a curve between Leadenhall and Fenchurch Street, was a prosperous area in the late sixteenth century with plenty of open spaces at a time when many other parts of the city were losing their gardens as a result of the rapidly rising population.

One of the prominent members of the community was James Cole, a silk merchant, who had taken as his second wife Louisa, the daughter of the Flemish botanist Matthias L'Obel. He too was Flemish in origin, originally Jacob Coels, and had fled Europe to escape religious persecution. His uncle was the Antwerp mapmaker Abraham Ortelius, and he was himself a scholar, the author of several treatises, one in praise of the study of plants.[22] Just as Ortelius tapped into the particular knowledge held by Clusius about the French and Spanish Mediterranean coasts, so he ascertained from his nephew, James Cole, the precise location of 'Widgandecua' or Virginia. In gratitude he sent him valerian and sunflower seeds, gathered from his garden. Given Cole's gardening skills, Ortelius likened his gift to sending owls to Athens, a classical version of coals to Newcastle. These seeds may well have been sent under the auspices of another of Cole's relations, and an inhabitant of Lime Street, Emmanuel van Meteren. He was consul for the Dutch merchants in London, acting as postmaster for the community, and thus able to ensure that seeds and bulbs were safely sent back and forth to Europe through his mail service.

Several members of the Lime Street community were apothecaries. James Garret, who had a garden near the city walls at Aldgate where he was particularly successful in propagating tulips, was well known in London for importing exotic plants. The Queen's cousin, Lord Hunsdon, sent him seeds from the Peruvian balsam tree, while the piratical Earl of Cumberland provided a potted herba mimosa, acquired in Puerto Rico. His brother, Peter Garret, would tip him off when a ship with a potentially interesting cargo of plants and seeds was due in port, often at Sommers Quay adjoining the west side of Billingsgate, where the Flemish merchants did their trading. Clusius described James Garret as 'my dear friend, a man of honour, greatly delighting in the study of herbarism'.[23] Another member of the Lime Street community with an international reputation was the physician Thomas Penny, a friend and pupil of Conrad Gesner in Zurich and a graduate of the University of Montpellier. Yet another was Thomas Moffett, who had studied at Cambridge with Penny before moving on to Basel.

This close-knit, knowledgeable community naturally offered hospitality to eminent colleagues on their visits to London. Clusius stayed in Lime Street during his visits in 1571, 1579, and in 1581 when he came to England to receive strange roots from Francis Drake. Matthias L'Obel paid his first visit to London from 1569 to 1571, when he saw the book that he was writing with Peter Pena, *Stirpium adversaria nova*, through the presses. During this stay he met Clusius, and the two of them went off on a botanical field trip to Bristol to investigate the microclimate of the Avon Gorge which provided the exceptional botanical specimens of St Vincent's Rocks.

Later L'Obel returned permanently to London, taking up residence in Lime Street and becoming supervisor of the garden of Lord Zouche in Hackney. Edward Zouche, a former ward of William Cecil, had used the large fortune inherited from his father for travelling and becoming acquainted with the gardens of Europe. He also acted as the Queen's ambassador in Constantinople, so saw at first hand the gardens of the Ottomans. Returning to England, he set out to create a botanical garden in Hackney, then a country village favoured by courtiers because of its proximity to the capital and its healthy air. Sadly, the only details that survive of this famous garden appear in the writings of L'Obel, who recorded some of the plants that he cultivated for Zouche, including the transplantation of mature fruit trees. The horticultural importance of the garden is vouchsafed by the fact that Zouche could attract a major European figure to act as his supervisor.

It was, however, not always sweetness and light in the communities of plant lovers. The Dutch scholar Justus Lipsius noted that a passion for flowers could bring out a competitive streak, concluding 'What should I call this but a kind of merrie madnesse? not unlike the striving of children about their little puppets and babbies'.[24] It was a conflict of a different kind that broke out among the flower beds of Lime Street in the 1590s.

The London bookseller John Norton decided to publish an English edition of Dodoens's last book, *Stirpium historiae pemptades sex*, that Plantin had published in Antwerp in 1583. The translation, commissioned from Robert Priest, a member of the Royal College of Physicians, was quite a challenge, for Dodoens's book ran to over 800 pages in folio format. How much Priest managed to achieve is a matter of some conjecture, but with his death Norton was obliged to look elsewhere. He turned to John Gerard, the barber surgeon and supervisor of Lord Burghley's gardens. Although Gerard had his garden in Long Acre, he was a friend of James Cole and therefore a frequent visitor to the plantsmen of Lime Street. He went on botanising expeditions to Kent with L'Obel, and, when he published a catalogue of the contents of his Holborn garden in 1596, the Flemish botanist provided him with a letter of attestation. Gerard was also a friend of the tulip expert James Garret, and so it must have been with some consternation that Garret pointed out to Norton

25 John Gerard holding a potato plant from Virginia, from his herbal of 1597.

26 One of the illustrations specially cut for Gerard's herbal was the Virginian potato, *Solanum tuberosum*. In fact, this potato probably originated in South America, and was first brought to Europe in the 1530s or 1540s by Spanish sailors.

that Gerard's text for his ambitious publishing venture was full of mistakes. Garret suggested that L'Obel should go through the text, checking and correcting the placing of the pictures, and undertake editorial revisions. L'Obel later claimed that he corrected more than a thousand mistakes, and would have done more, but Gerard found out what was afoot, and protested that a foreigner should not be interfering with his work, especially as English was not L'Obel's first language.

Apart from being offensive to one of Europe's leading botanists, Gerard was accused of inaccuracies which could be potentially dangerous for the physician or the apothecary. He was also condemned for failing to acknowledge the work of others, offences taken seriously by the world of botanists. Gerard has enjoyed a mixed press over the years. Some of this could be attributed to intellectual snobbery – he was, after all, only a barber surgeon, not a university-trained botanist or physician. He was also a pushy individual, a trait that might be admired at some times in history, but despised at others. Canon Raven condemns him as an ignorant rogue, but others have defended him, maintaining that he was generous in his research and attributions, and that L'Obel only became really angry about the whole matter several years later.[25]

Whatever the rights and wrongs of the quarrel, it is John Gerard who emerges as the author of one of the most famous botanical books. Within a generation he was described as the 'skilful Gerard' in Michael Drayton's remarkable poem *The Poly-Olbion* in praise of the glories and beauties of England. Two generations on, John Milton in *Paradise Lost* copied almost verbatim Gerard's description of the Banyan as the source of the fig-leaves donned by Adam and Eve. Matthias L'Obel, on the other hand, is remembered as a distinguished scholar whose name was given to the lobelia family by the French botanist Charles Plumier in the late seventeenth century, but is hardly a household name. The flower lovers of the Lime Street community are even less known, while their gardens are now subsumed under the towering edifice of Lloyds of London. The message would seem to be: publish and be famous.

CHAPTER 4

Spreading the Word

WHEN GUTENBERG INVENTED THE PRINTING PRESS in the middle of the fifteenth century, botanical books in the form of herbals at last became available to a larger public. Blanche Henrey, author of the monumental work on British botanical and horticultural books, defined a herbal as a book containing the names and descriptions of herbs, or of plants in general, with their properties and virtues. She went on to define the audience for such books as the herbalist, botanist and gardener, physician and apothecary. At a time when only the rich could afford professional medical attendance, she added the housewife, who would find such information useful for her kitchen and stillroom.[1]

The title page of the collected botanical works of Clusius, *Rariorum plantarum historia* published in 1601, has two seated figures, Theophrastus and Dioscorides. It is the writings of these two men from the classical world – along with Pliny the Elder – that formed the foundations on which Renaissance books about botany and horticulture were based. Theophrastus was born *c.* 372 BCE at Ereos on Lesbos. In his youth he was taught both by Plato and Aristotle, and then himself taught at the Lyceum in Athens. His two surviving botanical works, in which he discusses about five hundred plants, read like lecture notes with philosophy underpinning his enquiries, so that he looks to defining a plant, and identifying which are the most useful parts when classifying.[2] The plants that he studied came not only from Greece, but also Egypt, Libya and parts of Asia that had been conquered by Alexander the Great. After his death, Theophrastus was forgotten, and the link with Europe

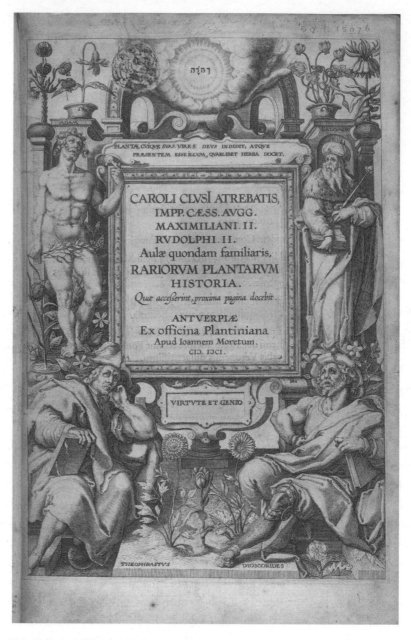

27 The title page of Clusius's book of rare plants published by the house of Plantin in Antwerp in 1601. Not only does it show some of the exciting new plants that were being introduced to Western Europe, such as the Crown Imperial, *Fritillaria imperalis* (top right) and the tulip (bottom, centre stage), but also the two botanical authorities of the classical world, Theophrastus and Dioscorides.

snapped when the famous library at Alexandria was put to the torch in the seventh century. His work, however, lived on through Arab scholars, and was reintroduced to Europe in the fifteenth century, translated into Latin from a manuscript discovered in the Vatican.

Pedanios Dioscorides, born *c.* 40 at Anazarbus in Cilicia, was a Greek physician who studied in Alexandria and Tarsus before joining the Roman army as a doctor, and travelling widely. His *De Materia medica* of CE 77 was a field guide to plants useful for medicine, becoming the ultimate authority for the next 1,500 years, alongside the *Historia Naturalis* compiled by his contemporary, Pliny the Elder. Pliny too was a Roman soldier who provided in his book an amalgam of information on science, art, plants, animals and human inventions and institutions. His quest for information led to his untimely death, as he investigated the eruption of Vesuvius in CE 79.

Anna Pavord in *The Naming of Names* laments the fact that Theophrastus, much the most questioning of the three, was the lost author, for by trying to define the characteristics of plants, he was adopting a 'scientific approach' that was to be taken up by sixteenth-century botanists in their search for classification. It was, however, the texts of Dioscorides, and to a lesser extent Pliny, that became the standard. The sixteenth-century Spanish physician Nicolas Monardes likened the enduring fame and glory that Dioscorides achieved through his writings to a general conquering cities 'with his warlike actes'.[3] One of the reasons why Dioscorides was so much admired was that his descriptions of plants were clear and precise, but not always very accurate.

The search for accurate identification of plant names was a vital one, for mistakes could be fatal. As more and more plants were discovered, and in more and more parts of the world, so this search became increasingly problematic. One way of dealing with this was to introduce illustrations into botanical books. This became possible when, less than thirty years after Dioscorides and Pliny wrote their texts, a technical change in the way paper was made enabled long rolls of papyrus to be replaced by sheets that could be bound into volumes. Before this innovation, readers had to hold the roll in both hands and read a few lines of text at a time, and would therefore find it difficult to take in the whole of an illustration. With bound volumes, artists could illustrate a plant that was integrated with the textual description.

One of the most beautiful illustrated botanical books was made by the townspeople of Honorata, a district of Constantinople, and presented *c.* 512 to their imperial patron, Juliana, in gratitude for giving them a church. The manuscript was derived from Dioscorides, and therefore not a departure from the norm, but the illustrations, showing nearly 400 plants, were startlingly original. These Byzantine citizens had commissioned artists to paint the pictures of cereals, roots, herbs and seeds, and then chose the bits of Dioscorides that matched them. Some of the pictures are schematic, others are very accurate with an exquisite vitality, clearly drawn from life.

This treasured book was still in Constantinople when the city fell to the Ottomans, and came into the possession of Hamon, physician to Suleyman the Magnificent. In 1562 it was seen by Busbecq, who wrote to his friend Nicolas Michault:

> One treasure I left behind in Constantinople, a manuscript of Dioscorides, extremely ancient and written in majuscules, with drawings of the plants . . . It belongs to a Jew, the son of Hamon, who, while he was still alive, was physician to Soleiman. I should like to have bought it, but the price frightened me; for a hundred ducats was named, a sum which would suit the Emperor's purse better than mine. I shall not cease to urge the Emperor to ransom so noble an author from such slavery.[4]

Seven years later, the book was in the Imperial Library in Vienna, and is now known as the Codex Vindobonensis, the Latin name for the city. Either Busbecq bought the book himself, or he persuaded Maximilian II to give him the money.

However, the accuracy and vitality of the illustrations in the Codex Vindobonensis proved a false dawn. Illustrators throughout the Middle Ages again and again made copies of pictures of plants, widening the gap between plant and reality. Even with the invention of printing, botanists turned once more to tired old texts, while the accompanying woodcut illustrations were often crude and schematic. The exception to this was produced by the Mainz printer Peter Schöffer in 1485. Now known as the *German Herbarius*, it was compiled by an anonymous wealthy amateur botanist with the help of a physician, probably Dr Johann von Cube from Frankfurt am Main. When the work was in progress, the compiler, discovering that many of the herbs noted by classical authors were not available in Germany, set off on a hazardous journey to the Near East and North Africa. The woodcuts in the completed book vary in quality, with the finest made from drawings of living plants, but others derived from pure fancy, so that the mandrake, with its forked root, is here given human form. When the publisher Johann Meydenbach came to produce his very popular herbal, *Ortus Sanitatis* (Garden of Health), in 1491, he used many of the illustrations from the *German Herbarius*, recut, reduced in size,

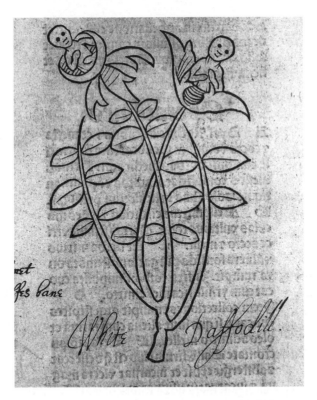

28 The 'white daffodil' or narcissus depicted in *Ortus Sanitatis*, published in Mainz in 1491. The little figures are drawn from the classical legend of Narcissus, which would have been familiar to readers of Ovid's *Metamorphoses*, but not helpful in identifying the plant.

and often misunderstood. While the plants native to Germany were fairly naturalistic, exotic plants were highly fanciful. The narcissus stands out in particular. Two infants emerge from the floral trumpets, recalling Ovid's legend in his *Metamorphoses*, where Narcissus, the beautiful son of the river god and a water nymph, fell in love with his reflected image and wasted away till death, leaving only a flower, white petals clustered round a cup of gold. It is a charming image, but impossible to use for identification by the physician or the apothecary, the botanist or the gardener.

The English were late starters in printing in general, and in botany in particular. In 1495 Wynkyn de Worde published an English version of *De proprietatibus rerum*, a work written in the thirteenth century by Bartholomaeus Anglicus, a Franciscan friar and professor of theology at the University of Paris. One of the nineteen sections dealt with trees, shrubs and herbs. Another thirty years were to pass before a London printer produced a book entirely devoted to herbs, a small quarto from the press of Richard Banckes in 1525. This contained no pictures, but clearly met a market, for it was reprinted many times from several presses with different names attached. Robert Wyer, a printer who recognised the growing demand for small, cheap books of a popular nature, saw that linking the text with a well-known authority made good commercial sense, so in his edition he made the unlikely claim 'as practised by Dr Lynacro', Thomas Linacre, the founder of the Royal College of Physicians.

The first illustrated English herbal – called *The Grete Herbal* – appeared in 1526 from the press of Peter Treveris. The publication of this book is significant in that it marks the beginning of the development of scientific works published in the vernacular as opposed to Latin. As Agnes Arber notes, 'Between 1500 and 1640 a higher proportion of scientific works were printed in the vernacular in England than in any other country except Italy. In regard to a herbal which was aimed mostly at an unlearned public, use of English was almost obligatory.'5 Nevertheless the material was slavishly copied from a second-rate French herbal, *Le grant herbier*, with dim copies of illustrations from the German *Ortus Sanitatis*.

But the gentle rains of the European Renaissance were about to fall upon this unpromising soil. Again there was a trinity of writers, but this time accompanied by artists: Brunfels and Weiditz; Fuchs and Meyer; Mattioli and Liberale. Otto Brunfels was born in 1488 in Braunfels in Germany, the son of a cooper. Despite his father's opposition, he became a Carthusian monk who converted to Lutheranism and escaped to Strasbourg where he was taken in by the bookseller Johannes Schott, combining a career as a schoolmaster with studies in medicine. For Schott he wrote *Herbarum vivae eicones* (Living Portraits of Plants), publishing the first part in 1530. In the book's dedication he explained that he was aiming to revive 'a science almost extinct. And because this has seemed to me only possible by thrusting aside all the old herbals, and publishing new and really lifelike illustrations, and along with them accurate descriptions extracted from ancient and trustworthy authors, I have attempted both; using the greatest care and pains that both should be faithfully done.'6

For his text, Brunfels drew upon no fewer than thirty-seven sources, including Theophrastus, Dioscorides and Pliny, and Islamic physicians such as Avicenna. But he gave credit too to the 'vulgus' as well as the 'docti', paying tribute to herb-women who, for instance, told him about the herb Good King Henry, which resembled spinach. Brunfels also credited the artist who drew the living portraits of the title, likening him to Apelles, the famous Greek

corum, TOMVS Primus. 129

NARCISSVS. A

B

De NARCISSO, & Hermodactylo,
Rhapfodia Vicefima.
NOMENCLATVRÆ.
Græcæ, νάρκισσος, λυχρινίδι, βλέσσε ἡ λυντικός, λιμίᾳ, ἄνθρας.
Latinæ, Narciffus, Hermodactylus.
Germanicç, in Marcio, Hornungs blům. In Septembri, Zeytlōflin.

29 Although Otto Brunfels's *Herbarum vivae eicones* was published only forty years after the *Ortus Sanitatis*, reproduced on p. 97, the quality of the images is in a completely different league, thanks to the skill of the artist, Hans Weiditz. This page shows the daffodil, *Narcissus pseudonarcissus*, alongside a snowflake.

artist, and praising him for producing images that are indistinguishable from the real thing. And indeed so he should, for it was the skill of Hans Weiditz that turned the book into a best-seller and took herbals into a new realm. Weiditz was a pupil of the great German artist Albrecht Dürer, who had advised 'Be guided by nature ... Do not depart from it, thinking that you can do better yourself. You will be misguided, for truly art is hidden in nature and he who can draw it out, possesses it.'[7] Dürer produced a series of watercolours of plants that still astonish us with their beauty and acute observation. Perhaps the most remarkable, *Das grosse Rasenstück*, is a worm's-eye view of a piece of meadow turf with blades of grass and wild flowers. For *Herbarum vivae eicones* Weiditz produced 260 images, including a lovely combination of a daffodil with a snowflake, and another of a pasque flower that Brunfels could not classify, so that he settled rather unhappily for 'herba nuda'.

In some ways Brunfels and Fuchs shared similar backgrounds, having been raised as Catholics before converting to the Lutheran faith. But while Brunfels achieved fame with a book that was in reality a scissors and paste job, Leonhart Fuchs proved the better scholar and plantsman, able to tap into the developing network of scholars throughout Europe to gain knowledge and acquire plants. Born in 1500, he studied at the University of Erfurt before opening a school in his home town of Wemding. With a degree in medicine he began practising medicine at the age of twenty-three, and established his reputation with his success in treating the sweating sickness that swept Germany. In 1535 he accepted the invitation to teach at the University of Tübingen under the patronage of Duke Ulrich of Brandenburg and settled into a comfortable academic life. In his garden he grew sweet galingale and sowed the seeds of the newly introduced 'weed', tobacco. In the summer months he took his students on field trips into the countryside and mountains, a requirement set down by the Duke, so that they might 'carefully observe the appearance of plants, and point out their living characteristics, and not, as many have been doing up to this time, to entrust the knowledge of medicinal herbs to those crude ointment peddlers and simple herb-women.'[8] The arguments about the merits of herb-women ebbed and flowed throughout this period. Women steeped in the lore of the countryside often knew more about the characteristics of plants than the trained apothecaries and physicians, and their treatments were less expensive and drastic. This, of course, did not endear them to the medical experts.

In 1542 Fuchs published his history of plants, De Historia Stirpium, from the press of Isingrin in Basel. On the title page he advertises that he has included information acquired from intrepid travellers to foreign lands who 'at huge cost, with tireless effort, and sometimes not without peril to their lives, in order to acquire intimate knowledge of the substance of simples; all this substance you will be pleased to learn from this book, as in a living pleasure garden, at a great saving of money and time, far from any peril'. Not only was he offering a saving of money and absence of danger, but also an abbreviated explanation of difficult and obscure words, with a four-fold index, of Greek, Latin and German names, along with those used by druggists and gatherers of herbs, to appeal to the widest possible market.

Fuchs included more than five hundred images of plants in De Historia Stirpium, and took the unusual step of not only thanking the craftsmen

30 Leonhart Fuchs acknowledged the contribution made by his artists and engraver in his history of plants, published in Basel in 1542. Top left, Albrecht Meyer draws a corncockle from life, and top right, Heinrich Füllmaurer transfers an illustration onto a woodblock. Below is shown the engraver, Veit Rudolf Speckle.

involved, but also reproducing their portraits at the back of the book. The artist, Albrecht Meyer, was shown making a drawing of a corncockle from life, alongside Heinrich Füllmaurer, depicted transferring an illustration to a woodblock, and below, the engraver, Veit Rudolf Speckle. Meyer's pictures were very accurate, including details of flowers and seeds, and introducing the idea of cross-sections, though they lack some of the drama and immediacy of those produced by Hans Weiditz.

Fuchs's book, like that of Brunfels, proved a great success, going through thirty-nine imprints within his own lifetime, with translations into German, French, Spanish and Dutch. The original book was produced in folio, but in 1545 Isingrin issued a pocket edition, in tiny sextodecimo (16mo) format, so that it could be used for reference in the field, the surgery or the garden.

The third of this herbal trinity was Pier Andrea Mattioli, born in Siena in 1501. After practising as a doctor in Rome, he travelled to Prague as personal physician to the Archduke Ferdinand, who became Emperor in 1564. One of Mattioli's friends was Ogier de Busbecq who, as the Imperial Ambassador in Constantinople, secured for him two manuscript texts of Dioscorides, and on his return to Europe in 1562 noted that he had brought with him drawings of plants and shrubs for Mattioli, and had already supplied him with a scented iris and other specimens. Busbecq's doctor in Constantinople, William Quackelbeen, sent him accounts of several new plant species, including the lilac and the horse-chestnut.

Dioscorides was the great authority for Mattioli. He first published his commentaries on him in Italian, in an edition printed in Venice without illustrations in 1544. This was so successful that a remarkable sixty-one editions followed, with translations into French, Czech, German and Latin. Because of the patronage of the Hapsburgs, he could afford to commission pictures for his 1554 version drawn for him by Giorgio Liberale, and he continued to add images as he introduced new plants, such as the tulip which appeared in the 1565 edition, classified as a narcissus.

Mattioli's text was turgid, sticking to the system adopted by Dioscorides, but adding many of his own mistakes. However, there is no natural justice in the world of publishing: he got himself into print when others were unable to do so. His fellow Italian Luca Ghini, who had developed the botanical garden at Pisa, was renowned as the best teacher in Europe. He was one of the first plantsmen to attempt to put together a local flora, gathering much material that never saw publication. He also intended to compile a herbal, but when Mattioli's commentaries came out in 1544 and were such a success, Ghini gave up the idea, instead generously sending him specimens of dried plants. Likewise one of Ghini's pupils, Andrea Cesalpino, amassed a huge amount of material for a book that would provide a new system for classification, showing the affinity between types of fruit and seeds. This was published in Florence in 1583, under the title of *De plantis libri XVI*, consisting of 600 pages of text with 1,500 plants divided into thirty-two groups, such as *Umbelliferae* and *Compositae*. He wanted to include engravings from drawings that he had gathered, but his patron, Francesco I, Duke of Florence, abandoned a scheme to give him sponsorship. The result was a daunting book that never enjoyed the huge success of the three illustrated herbals, of Brunfels, Fuchs and Mattioli.

The sack in 1462 of the birthplace of European printing, Gutenberg's Mainz, accelerated the spread of printing throughout the Continent. By 1480 it is estimated that there were 110 presses, fifty in Italian towns, with Venice dominating the industry. Italians were the first to establish botanical gardens, in Pisa and Padua, and some of the leading scholars in medicine, botany and horticulture were Italians. Yet the momentum gradually shifted as the sixteenth century progressed, so that Germany and the Low Countries became the dominant forces. Why this should be so has been the subject of some debate. Canon Raven, author of the seminal book *English Naturalists*, published in 1947, looked to religion as the key as befitted the Regius Professor of Divinity at Cambridge. For him there was 'an acknowledged indifference to nature in Catholic countries', and he quoted a twentieth-century Catholic writer who considered that 'for Catholicism nature always remains more or less the enemy'.[9] Thus Raven came to the conclusion that it was the Reformation that allowed Protestantism to recover the delight in nature to be found among the Greeks and Hebrews and in the Gospels. He admitted that there was much scientific botany in sixteenth-century Italy, but believed it was crushed by the Counter-Reformation.

There are others who look more to financial factors. The example of Cesalpino shows how difficult it was for Italian botanists in particular to secure the vital sponsorship that would enable them to publish the results of their research and theories. While Venetian merchants had dominated trade contacts with the East during the early years of the sixteenth century, the Dutch were gaining ground and becoming the dominant trading power that imported new plants from further afield, notably from the East Indies. The Medicis could hardly be described as down to their last florin, nor the Venetian Republic to their last ducat, but the new wealth was flowing into the ports of Northern Europe, Antwerp, Bruges, Amsterdam, and here were the potential patrons for publications and expeditions.

And what of the English? Henry VIII's break with Rome made academic intercourse difficult with European counterparts, and travel impossible for many. But one English botanist was given plenty of opportunity to travel – indeed, his life depended upon it. William Turner was born in Morpeth in Northumberland *c.* 1508, probably the son of a tanner. The family gained the patronage of Thomas, first Baron of Wentworth, and in a dedication in one of his books, Turner recorded that he received from him a yearly exhibition which helped him in his studies at Cambridge. While at the university, he came under the influence of Hugh Latimer, imbibing not only humanist philosophy but also concern for social conditions and sympathy with common folk. In particular he disliked how first Wolsey and then courtiers were growing fat on the spoils of the dissolution of monastic houses. His strong Protestant leanings were only to grow fiercer with the years, and he so disliked bishops in their finery that he taught his dog to snatch their hats off while they were at supper.

Turner held Greek culture in high regard, including the botanical works of Theophrastus and Dioscorides. He was vocal in his criticisms of ignorant modern interpreters, and was sufficiently well versed in the language to discuss variants in translations. When he came to write his herbal, he recorded in the preface:

> Above thirty years ago ... being yet fellow in Pembroke Hall in Cambridge where as I could learn never one Greek, neither Latin, nor English name, even amongst the Physicians of any herb or tree, such was the ignorance in simples at that time, and as yet there was no English herbal but one, all full of unlearned cacographies and falsely naming of herbs [the *Grete Herball*, see p. 98], and as then neither Fuchs nor Mattioli, neither Tragus [Hieronymus Tragus or Jerome Bock, author of the *New Kreüterbuch* of 1539] written of herbs in Latin.

Just as botanists all over Europe were trying to match up and reconcile vernacular names with those mentioned by the classical authors, so Turner sought to cope not only with English equivalents, but local variants too. In *Libellus de re Herbaria novus*, published in London in 1538, Turner took 144 plants and gave their synonyms in Greek and English. On the narcissus, for instance, he wrote:

> For a long time among us Narcissus has concealed itself under foreign names. There was no herb that gave me more trouble. For after I had seen its picture and outline and studied them as carefully as I could, no one could be found to show me the plant, much less tell me its English name. [Here he was probably talking about the images of the daffodil, *Narcissus pseudonarcissus*, and the snowflake, *Leoucoium vernum*, illustrated by Hans Weiditz in Brunfels's

Herbarum vivae eicones.] At last when I was taking a holiday in Norfolk a little girl hardly seven years old met me as I was walking along the road: she was carrying in her right hand a bunch of white flowers; as soon as I saw them I thought to myself 'Those are Narcissi' – for the description of them was still fresh in my mind, and I begged some of them from her. But when I enquired the name no reply was forthcoming. So I asked the folk who lived in the neighbouring cottages and villages, what was the name of the plant. They all answered that it was called 'laus tibi': I could get no other name from them. But when I got home I learnt that asphodel was called by many people 'laus tibi'. Then a little old man, whose name is Guarinus Asshe, a canon of Barnwell Priory and well-skilled in herbalism, told me this plant was called French Gillyflower. We must use that name until a better is found.[10]

Botanists throughout Europe were beset by confusion, and this was only to get worse as new plants were introduced from all parts of the world: a Tower of Babel was being constructed. It not only posed a confusion of classification, but also potential danger to patients who could be treated with the incorrect medicinal plants or suffer from misinformation about dosage. William Turner nearly killed himself with opium: 'I washed an achying tooth with a little opio mixed with water, and a little of the same unawares went down, within an hour after my hands began to swell about the wrestes, and to itch, and my breth was so stopped, that if I had not taken in a pece of the roote of masterwurt . . . with wyne, I thynck that it wold have kylled me.'[11] The gathering of this information in books with pictures to identify the plants was literally vital.

In 1540 Turner was forced into exile, not for his pioneering botanical books but for expressing his disapproval of Henry VIII's treatment of his fourth wife, Anne of Cleves, and for his outspoken preaching. For the next seven years he travelled widely around Europe, making the acquaintance of leading writers and botanists. In Switzerland he met Fuchs, who was preparing his history of plants for publication, as well as the encyclopaedic scholar Conrad Gesner, and in Ferrara Antonio Musa Brasavola, whom he subsequently described as his master. Travelling northwards Turner visited the famous garden of the apothecary Pieter Coudenberg in Antwerp, and in Holland began work on his Latin herbal. Advised to delay publication until he had seen more plants in England, he took his chance when at last news came of the death of Henry VIII in 1547.

Back in London Turner secured the post of physician in the household of Edward Seymour, Lord Protector Somerset, at Syon House where he worked alongside William Cecil. Turner is credited with laying and planting the gardens, and in his writings he mentions studying other private gardens at this time. William Brooke, Lord Cobham, a friend of Cecil, had a garden near Gravesend in Kent famous for the exotic flowers and trees 'from the furthest part of Europe or from other Strange Countries'.[12] As patron of the chronicler William Harrison, he set him up in his rectory in Essex, and Harrison repaid the compliment by listing Cobham Park as one of the great gardens of England, alongside Hampton Court, Nonesuch and Theobalds. The garden's most spectacular feature was a two-storey banqueting house created in a lime tree by training the branches. Whether William Turner saw this phenomenon when he was observing the garden in the late 1540s is not known; his attention would surely have been fixed on the exotic herbs. Another garden he investigated was that of Dr Richard Bartlot, President of the Royal College of Physicians, who lived in Blackfriars. Urged on by physicians such as Bartlot, he made

> a little book, which is no more but a table or register of such books as I intend by the grace of God to set forth hereafter . . . this little book containeth the names of the most part of herbs, that all ancient authors write of both in Greek, Latin, English, Dutch and French. I have set to also the names which be commonly used of the poticaries and common herbaries . . . I have showed in what places of England, Germany and Italy, the herbs grow and may be had for labour and money.[13]

This book, *The Names of Herbes*, which is indeed little and without illustrations, was published in 1548 by John Day and William Seres, forming the condensed first draft of a herbal that began to appear in print three years later.

The first part of *A New Herball* was published by a Dutch bookseller resident in London, Stephen Mierdman, and dedicated to the Duke of Somerset. The author justified using his native tongue by pointing out that many surgeons and apothecaries did not have the skills to understand the Latin of Pliny, let alone the original Greek of Dioscorides, and arguing that at the present time they knew no more of the identity of herbs than the old wives or the grocers who sold to them. The book was small folio in format, with 196 pages running from A to P with headings in English but plants arranged according to the initial of Latin names. Most of the 169 woodcut illustrations were taken from Fuchs's *De Historia Stirpium* that had been published six years earlier. But this, the first truly Renaissance herbal in English, was let down by the quality of its production: many of the pictures were reversed, others had no captions. Moreover, hopes for a speedy production of the second part of the book were dashed by the death of Edward VI and the accession of the Catholic Mary Tudor to the English throne. The uncompromising Turner fled abroad once more, taking refuge along with many other English Protestants in 'High Germany'. The second and third parts of Turner's herbal were published by Arnold Birckmann of Cologne and, although received with respect by botanists throughout Europe, the work was never well known, for it fell between two stools: had he written in Latin it might have enjoyed greater influence; had all three volumes been published in England, more copies might have been sold in his native land.

The references made by Turner in the herbal show that he had excellent contacts among gardeners and herbalists in London. The apothecary Hugh Morgan, for example, had a large garden in Coleman Street, running north from Lothbury to London Wall, where he grew many exotic plants that had been given by sea-captains and Venetian merchants arriving at the Port of London. Other references are made to Turner's botanising expeditions and his interest in English native flowers. In the third volume, dating from 1564, he talked of exotic places such as Ceylon, Java and the East Indies and introduced rhubarb from China and cassia from the West Indies. In 1568 the complete work was updated and reissued by Birckmann, with a dedication to Queen Elizabeth I. In that same year the intransigent Protestant Turner died at his house in Crutched Friars in London, at last in accord with his sovereign.

31 Golden rod from William Turner's *Herbal* published in Cologne in 1568. This copy belonged to the seventeenth-century botanist and gardener, John Goodyer, who has noted in the margin, 'this figure is not so well made as it should be, for it wanteth hidsuted [hirsute] leaves'.

Turner's last publisher, Birckmann of Cologne, was one of the biggest players in the Latin trade – international publishing – with a prominent presence at the Frankfurt Book Fair, and shops in Antwerp and in St Paul's Churchyard in London. Another leading European publisher was Christopher Plantin, based in Antwerp, and he became the leading creator of botanical books in the late sixteenth century. There is much uncertainty about Plantin's early life, but it is known that he was born c. 1520 in Touraine and trained as a bookbinder in Caen. His name was not originally Plantin, and he later claimed that he chose it because of the plantain, the green-skinned banana, while his brother Pierre, who became an apothecary in Paris, chose the leek and was subsequently called Porret. Perhaps we have here the beginning of Plantin's interest in botanical books.

Plantin chose to establish his business in Antwerp in 1548 because he recognised it as an ideal centre for trade, with capital, an excellent communications network, and a skilled pool of craftsmen. As he later explained to Pope Gregory XIII: 'Although I would have been able to secure better conditions for myself in other regions and cities, I still preferred the Low Countries above all the rest, and in particular this city of Antwerp, where I settled, primarily because I believed that there was no city in the world that offered better opportunities for the trade that I had undertaken.'[14] Here Plantin moved from bookbinding to printing in 1555. His original list consisted mainly of classical authors, devotional books and illustrated parables, but he also published medical textbooks by Vesalius and botanical studies by the Flemish botanist Rembert Dodoens. For his illustrated books he used two techniques: woodcuts and engravings. Woodcuts, employing printing in relief, enabled pictures to be on the same page with the text. Intaglio engraving, etched from a metal plate, began to be developed from the 1470s, yet it was not an easy technique to use and could be very costly. From the start of his printing activities Plantin produced individual prints, but his 1566 edition of Vesalius proved a breakthrough in producing an entire book with engraved illustrations.

For his botanical books, however, Plantin always used woodcuts, as he printed long runs and thus needed a medium that could last, and be constantly reused. Rembert Dodoens's Flemish herbal, or *cruydebeock*, was produced in 1554 with 715 illustrations by the Antwerp publisher Jan van der Loe. At van der Loe's death, Plantin bought from his widow the woodcut blocks, thus beginning his collection that built up over the years to create a sixteenth-century version of the modern picture library. The wonderful Plantin Museum in Antwerp contains 3,874 of them. The impact of the lavishly illustrated books with their accurate images that enabled easy identification can scarcely be imagined. For special clients, the illustrations of the plants could be hand coloured by a team of three craftswomen, Myncken Liefrinck, Lyneken Verhoeven and Lisken Zeghers.

Christopher Plantin's star botanical authors constitute yet another three-some: Dodoens, Clusius and L'Obel. Rembert Dodoens, from Malines in the Southern Netherlands, became physician to Maximilian II in Vienna in the 1570s, working alongside Clusius, before being appointed professor of medicine at the young University of Leiden. Dodoens's first publications were on medicine and cosmography, but in 1543 he translated Fuchs's herbal into Flemish and began preparing a herbal of his own by producing booklets on various botanical themes that were brought together in 1563 under the imprint of Jan van der Loe. This was a record of plants native to the Low Countries or cultivated in gardens, although every so often he would venture into the exotic. Van der Loe realised that a much wider audience could be achieved if he also produced a French version, and commissioned Clusius to make the translation, which appeared as *L'Histoire des Plantes*. Dodoens then moved to the publishing house of Plantin, working on the concept of another, much more ambitious herbal. Again he adopted the system of producing a series of smaller booklets leading up to the complete work, which eventually appeared off Plantin's presses in 1583 as *Stirpium historiae pemptades sex*. The six 'pemptades' refer to his system of grouping related plant genuses.

Clusius began his collaboration with Christopher Plantin when he produced a Latin version of Garcia ab Orto's book on Indian plants, published in 1567. A whole series of translations and adaptations followed, as noted in Chapter 3, but he also produced a series of his own botanical works. In 1576 Plantin published the account of the plants that Clusius had observed in his travels in Spain and Portugal, with the addition of bulbs and tuber plants, such as the tulip and the anemone, from Thrace that he had received through the good offices of Ogier de Busbecq.[15] Seven years later, he moved on to a study of plants that he had observed while in the service of the Hapsburg Emperor.[16] These included flowers from botanising expeditions around Vienna, and from further afield into Moravia, Bohemia and Silesia. Clusius's final collaboration with the publishing house of Plantin came in 1601, with his *Rariorum plantarum*. By this time Christopher Plantin was dead, and the publisher was his son-in-law, Jan I Moretus.

The third botanist of the Plantin trinity was Matthias L'Obel, whose first book had been published in 1570 in London, where he had taken refuge with his co-author, Peter Pena (see p. 2). L'Obel subsequently returned to the Low Countries and was personal physician to William the Silent when Plantin produced a second edition of *Stirpium adversaria nova* in 1576. Although Plantin had bought 800 copies of the original, London, edition, it had not proved a commercial success, probably due to the poor quality of the illustrations. Now L'Obel's text could be boosted by Plantin's excellent collection of botanical woodblocks, and the book prospered. Five years later Plantin produced a Flemish edition, at the same time reusing the pictures without text apart from the names of the plants.[17] For this botanical atlas he chose an innovative landscape format, easy to carry as a reference book in the field, the garden and the surgery, and this too proved a financial winner.

Producing large illustrated botanical books was, however, not a simple exercise. At the height of his business, Plantin employed 150 men, including thirty-two printers and twenty typesetters. For his botanical books he used the artist Pieter van der Borcht, who worked alongside the engraver, Arnaud Nicolai. Among the manuscripts given in the mid-seventeenth century by John Goodyer to Magdalen College, Oxford, is the original text of Matthias L'Obel's next book, *Stirpium Illustrationes*, marked up for the typographer but left incomplete at the author's death in 1616. Fragments of pages from his earlier books are pasted alongside his manuscript notes, giving a vivid example of the kind of complex task facing Plantin's typesetters and printers.

The next step towards providing an English audience with botanical information in their native tongue was made by Henry Lyte when he translated Dodoens's herbal, using the French version by Clusius. *A Niewe Herball or Historie of Plants* was printed in Antwerp by Henry Loe, son of Dodoens's original publisher, and sold in London by the English bookseller Gerard Dewe at the sign of the Swan in St Paul's Churchyard in 1578. Lyte was a Somerset knight, Oxford-educated, who had travelled in Europe so that he had an amateur knowledge of plants. He carefully compared the original 'Douch' (Flemish) edition of 1554 with the French edition of 1559, adding his own observations in roman type (white letter) to distinguish them from the prevailing gothic black letter. His original copy of the French version with his notes written in red or black ink is preserved in the British Library.[18] The additions included his notes about the peculiar flora of St Vincent's Rocks outside Bristol, and flowers to be found in the London garden of the apothecary John Rich. Lyte undertook his translation to contribute to the welfare and renown of England, dedicating the book to Queen Elizabeth. His pride in his country, and in particular his native Somerset, can be clearly seen on the reverse of the

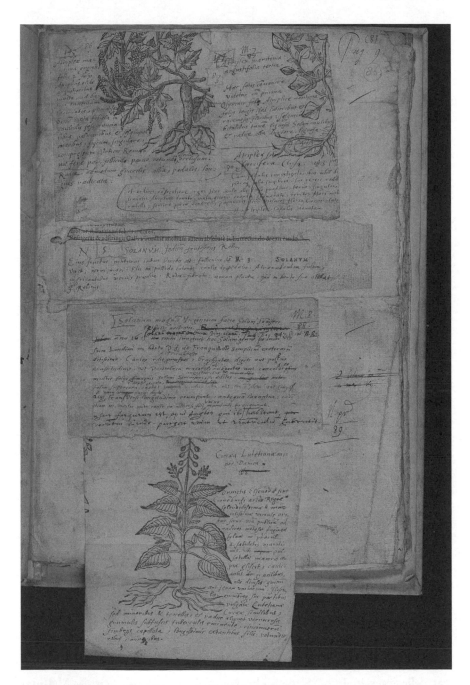

32 The nightmare author: the text that Matthias L'Obel was preparing for the press of his *Stirpium Illustrationes*, still incomplete at his death in 1616. He has cut pages out of his former books and stuck them side by side with his handwritten notes. This very rare example of a 'typescript' of the period shows the interpretive skills required by the printer.

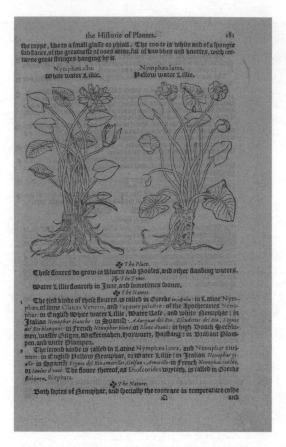

33 Water lilies from Henry Lyte's *Historie of Plants*, published in London in 1578. Lyte based his text on a translation of the herbal of Rembert Dodoens, but used the typography to distinguish between Dodoens's observations, in black letter or Gothic, and his own notes, which are in white letter italics.

title page. Under his coat of arms of three swans runs the verse: 'Liyke as the Swanne doth chaunt his tunes in signe of joyful mynde, So Lyte by learning shewes himself to Prince and Countrie kinde.' His delightful house at Lytes Cary is now looked after by the National Trust.

The punctilious care shown by Lyte stands in marked contrast to the slap-dash approach of John Gerard in his herbal that so raised the ire of his botanical colleagues in Lime Street. The complaints of James Garret, Matthias L'Obel and others must have made the task of publication by John Norton even more complex, but in the end he triumphed. Fortunately Norton, one of the wealthiest booksellers in St Paul's Churchyard, was able to share the considerable costs of producing the very large book with his cousin Bonham, thus spreading the risk. Twice yearly John Norton attended the great book fair in Frankfurt and thus had the appropriate international contacts to obtain the woodcut blocks for the illustrations. Nicolaus Basseus, the Frankfurt book-seller and publisher of the herbal of Bergzabern, better known by the rather indigestible name of Tabernae-montanus, rented to Norton nearly all the 1,800 woodcut blocks required. Gerard was not always able to identify the plants carved on these blocks, causing the mismatch with his descriptions.

A few new illustrations were cut for Gerard's herbal. One was an early picture of the potato which Gerard described as a native of Virginia, 'other-wise called Norembega' (see p. 91). In fact this type of potato was probably from further south, from Cartagena in Colombia, one of the plants brought back to England by Francis Drake in 1586. Gerard reported how it grew and prospered in his garden, and recommended that it be 'boiled and eaten with oile, vinegar and pepper, or dressed any other way by the hand of some cunning in cookerie'.[19]

Despite the mistakes, Gerard's *Herball* proved an enormous success. One of the reasons for this was that although it is called a herbal, John Gerard's skills lay in his gardening, and thus his book was a source of delight for generations of gardeners. Rather than introduce 'any curious discourse upon the generall division of plants' or go into botanical details, he wanted to show the variety and beauty of plants available for English gardens. This he makes clear in his letter of dedication to his patron, William Cecil:

> To the large and singular furniture of this noble iland, I have added from forren places all the varietie of herbes and flowers that I might any way obtaine, I have laboured with the soile to make it fit for the plants, and with the plants to make them to delight in the soile, that so they might live and prosper under our climate, as in their native and proper countrie; what my successe hath beene, and what my furniture is, I leave to the report of them that have seene your Lordships gardens, and the little plot of my speciall care and husbandrie.

And Gerard could write. This is his description of the sunflower, one of the sensational introductions from the New World, which he also called the 'Marigolde of Peru':

> This great flower is in shape like to the Cammomill flower, beset rounde about with a pale or border of goodly yellowe leaves, in shape like the leaves

of the flowers of white Lillies: the middle part whereof is made as it were of unshorne velvet, or some curious cloth wrought with a needle, which brave worke, if you do thoroughly view and marke well, it seemeth to be an innumerable sort of small flowers, resembling the nose or nozell of a candlesticke, broken from the foote thereof.[20]

Of a less exotic but favourite garden flower, the rose, he wrote: 'being not onely esteemed for his beautie, vertues and his fragrant and odiferous smell; but also bicause it is the honor and ornament of our English Scepter, as by the conjunction appeareth in the uniting of those most royall houses of Lancaster and Yorke'. He goes on to provide both medicinal and culinary advice: 'The distilled water of Roses is good for the strengthening of the heart, and refreshing of the spirits, and likewise for all things that require a gentle cooling. The same being put in junketing dishes, cakes, sauces, and many other pleasant things, giveth a fine and delectable taste.'[21]

Norton produced the book in large folio, printed in clear roman type. For the very attractive title page he commissioned a copper-plate engraving, rather than a woodcut, from the artist William Rogers. He also provided a handsome portrait of Gerard, holding in his right hand a book, and in his left a spray of the potato plant (see p. 90). So proud was Norton of his new book that in 1601 he gave a copy to the newly founded Bodleian Library in Oxford. For this copy Gerard's portrait, the engraved title page, the ornamental capitals and woodcuts were all skilfully coloured by artists. One of the great losses of the book world occurred in the late twentieth century when the portrait and title page were stolen from the Bodleian copy, though their beauty can still be appreciated through transparencies taken before their disappearance (Plate XII).

***

These, then, were some of the books for gardeners that were available in sixteenth-century England, along with the titles introduced in previous chapters. But who were the audiences? Titles appear in catalogues of private libraries, in inventories, and in references in correspondence and diaries, but the picture is extremely patchy. It tells us, moreover, about the books of wealthier members of society, but not of the 'common reader' nor, except in rare cases, of women. We know, for instance, that Grace, Lady Mildmay, was given a copy of the herbal of William Turner by her governess because she mentions it in her autobiography; that Lady Anne Clifford owned a copy of

Gerard's herbal because she included it among her books in the Great Portrait detailing her life; and that Bess of Hardwick either owned or had access to the commentaries of Mattioli because she used the book as reference for some of her needlework. But these are just tantalising glimpses.

When looking at audiences, it is important to compare the price of books against the buying power of different levels of society. As noted earlier, in the late sixteenth century the average salary of a schoolmaster was £6, while a clergyman could expect to receive between £10 and £20 per year. In 1560 craftsmen earned between 8d and 10d per day, which had risen to 1 shilling by 1600. Labourers and apprentices earned considerably less. The first factor that determined the price of books was format – the largest being folio, the smallest octavo and duodecimo, with quarto in between. Books were often offered for sale unbound, so that the cost of binding could add up to another third, depending on the quality of the materials. Prices would also depend on whether the book was new or second-hand, whether it had been printed in England or abroad, and whether the book was obtained directly from the originating bookseller or through an intermediary. Architectural treatises and herbals were some of the most lavishly illustrated books of the period, and it has been estimated that their images could double the cost of production, and thus the price.

All these factors have to be taken into account when looking at prices in booksellers' records, and from the notes that owners occasionally made in their books. Lord Herbert of Cherbury was one such book owner and, although his notes date from the early seventeenth century, prices remained remarkably stable so that they provide an invaluable indication of the costs of more expensive titles in Elizabethan England. Thus Lord Cherbury paid £1 13s for an English edition of Serlio, £1 10s for a Venetian edition of Palladio, and £1 7s for Barozzi's book on the rules of perspective.[22] These were all large folio in format, and contained the illustrations required by anybody involved with the layout and design of fashionable gardens of the period.

Quarto format books cost between 2s and 10s bound, with the number of pages and the presence of pictures as determining factors. Practical gardening books such as Thomas Hill's *Gardeners Labyrinth*, Leonard Mascall's *Art of Planting and Graffing* and Reginald Scot's treatise on hop gardening, *Perfite platforme*, were all produced in quarto. Octavo and duodecimo books were priced at around 1s bound, though the botanist John Goodyer noted that his 'field edition' of Fuchs's *Stirpium Icones* cost him almost £2, packed as it was with woodcuts of plants. The cheapest publications were pamphlets, unbound books of just a few pages. Among the accounts of William Cavendish, the son of Bess of Hardwick, is a record of the purchase in October 1600 of five copies of 'the arte of setting of corne' costing 3d apiece. This was a pamphlet written by Hugh Platt, advocating methodical sowing by dropping seeds into the ground at set distances, rather than random broadcasting that was the traditional practice, and the multiple copies were probably intended for the farmers on the Hardwick estates.[23] This kind of publication is the most ephemeral, and so it is surprising that we still have copies of Platt's pamphlet. In it, he made a link with gardening, claiming that he got his idea from 'some silly wench', who accidentally sowed some wheat corn rather than radish or carrot seeds when planting out her kitchen garden, and this suggests that there may have also been pamphlets on more horticultural subjects that have not survived the centuries.

An early sixteenth-century and extremely rare example of a gentleman's library containing books relating to botany, husbandry and horticulture belonged to Henry, tenth Baron Stafford. Born in 1501, he was the sole legitimate heir of Shakespeare's 'mirror of all courtesy', the third Duke of Buckingham. He was probably educated in his father's household, although later tradition has him at both Oxford and Cambridge, and he attended what constituted the 'third English university', the London Inns of Court, where he was a member of Gray's Inn. He would certainly have watched his father building the great mansion of Thornbury Castle, just outside Bristol, but in 1521 all this changed when the Duke was attainted for treason and executed. Buckingham's son was stripped of the earldom of Stafford, but was given some lands, including the castle at Stafford, where he set up his library in a well-lit study on the ground floor, near the garden.

We know of Stafford's collection of books through a catalogue compiled in 1556, seven years before his death, and a letter book which gives fascinating insights into his dealings with his booksellers.[24] By 1556 he had 300 books, mostly religious works, but also a significant collection of botanical and medical books. Thus he owned Dioscorides on plants and animals, almost certainly his *De Materia medica* in a folio edition printed in Marburg in 1543, an *Ortus Sanitatis* and medical works by Otto Brunfels and Leonhart Fuchs, the former in the practical 16mo format. These were all in Latin, but he also owned some in English, *The Grete Herball* published by Peter Treveris in 1526 and two of William Turner's botanical works, his *Names of Herbes* of 1548 and *New Herbal* of 1551.

Details of the gardens at Stafford Castle have not survived, but we have a record of those at Thornbury Castle, where Henry Stafford spent his youth, in

34 The title page of the first illustrated English herbal, published by Peter Treveris in 1526. Gardeners gather fruit in the background, while Adam and Eve appear at the bottom of the page, wearing headdresses of the apple of their downfall.

a commissioners' report drawn up after Buckingham's execution. In the inner ward was a 'proper' garden laid out with knots and a fountain. To the east of the castle was 'a large and goodly garden to walk in' alongside 'a large and goodly orchard'. The orchard was filled with 'newly grafted fruit trees, laden with fruit, many roses and other pleasures', and was surrounded by alleys with 'resting places covered thoroughly with whitethorn and hazel'. Among Henry Stafford's books were two that would have helped him with the maintenance of his orchard. Sir John Fitzherbert's *Boke of Husbandry*, first published in 1533, deals mainly with agricultural subjects such as ploughing, threshing and looking after animals, but it does also cover the care of a fruit garden. Thus it explains: 'It is necessarie, profitable, and also a pleasure to a husband to have pears, wardens, and apples of diverse sorts. And also cherries, filberts, bullaces, damsons, plums, walnuts and such other. And therefore it is convenient to learn how thou shalt graffe.' Fitzherbert then proceeds to explain about the different tools used for 'graffing' such as the saw and the knife. He also advises when to graft fruit: after St Valentine's Day for pears and wardens, because their sap rises first, then, once into March, the gardener should turn his attentions to the apple trees.[25] In addition Stafford owned a second book on the care of fruit trees by the London printer Robert Wyer, who specialised in little, practical books.

Stafford's correspondence with one of his booksellers reveals an unexpected attitude to reading. William Riddell, at the sign of the George in St Paul's Churchyard, the heartland of book publishing and selling in sixteenth-century London, was commissioned to seek out for him a first edition of a well-known fifteenth-century medical textbook.[26] If Riddell was unable to obtain it in London, then he should send to Amsterdam for a copy, or failing that, purchase it second-hand from a stall. Stafford's reason for this particular request was that he wanted Humphrey Llwyd, the scholarly physician to the Earl of Arundel, to translate the book into English so that the information on healing and medicinal herbs would be available for those unlettered in Latin. This desire is in marked contrast to the statute issued by the King in 1543 forbidding the reading of the English version of the Bible by a whole range of people from women to servants, an unsuccessful attempt to prevent knowledge being disseminated amongst what might be thought of as dangerous elements. But William Turner would have approved of Stafford's intention.

This was an aristocrat's library, with books on botany, medicine, and husbandry acquired for practical reasons, along with books of theology and classical texts. The inventory of books owned by a practising physician of the period shows a remarkably similar mix. Dr Thomas Simons was a graduate and fellow of Merton College, Oxford, who died in 1553. Dr Simons left a library of 140 titles, a substantial number for a man of fairly modest means, and the spread was both eclectic and sophisticated. His botanical texts included Dioscorides, Ruellius, Fuchs, and a copy of *Ortus Sanitatis*. Valuations were put on individual titles, which were always much less than the prices paid for new books, but even so his copy of Dioscorides was valued at the substantial sum of 5 shillings. In marked contrast the inventory of John Mitchell, who died in 1572, shows that his total estate was valued at 12s 1d. Mitchell was probably the servant of Walter Bayly, Regius Professor of Medicine at Oxford from 1561 to 1582. Mitchell owned a dozen books, botanical and medical, including two in English, the *Grete Herball* and 'Willelmus Turner to Mr Cicell', the 1568 edition of Turner's herbal that had been dedicated to William Cecil. These two titles must have been well thumbed, for they were valued at two pence each.

The prerequisites of an Elizabethan gentleman are usually described as an ability to sit well on a horse, to use a sword with a flourish, to turn an elegant leg on the dance floor, and to compose a clever verse for the beloved. But contemporary records show that interests in natural science and in gardening were also considered assets. Robert Dudley and Christopher Hatton certainly had these interests, as did later leading members of the Elizabethan court, such as Dudley's favourite nephew, Philip Sidney, and Walter Raleigh. Edward, Lord Herbert of Cherbury, born *c.* 1582, wrote in his autobiography of the ideal education for a young man:

> . . . I conceive it is a fine study, and worthy a gentleman to be a good botanic, that so he may know the nature of all herbs and plants, being our fellow-creatures, and made for the use of man; for which purpose it will be fit for him to cull out of some good herbal all the icones together, with the descriptions of them and to lay by themselves all such as grow in England, and afterwards to select again such as usually grow by the highway-side, in meadows, by rivers, or in marshes, or in cornfields, or in dry and mountainous places, or on rocks, walls, or in shady places, such as grow by the seaside; for this being done, and the said icones being ordinarily carried by themselves, or by their servants, one may presently find out every herb he meets withal, especially if the said flowers be truly coloured. Afterwards it will not be amiss to distinguish by themselves such herbs as are in gardens, and are exotics, and are transplanted hither.[27]

Just such an Elizabethan gentleman was Sir Thomas Knyvett of Ashwellthorpe in Norfolk, born in about 1539. He had close connections with the Tudor court, but chose to pursue a quiet life in Norfolk, building up his library which, by his death in 1618, amounted to a very substantial collection of 1,400 books and 70 manuscripts. His library is well documented as a catalogue was compiled after his death, and correspondence has survived, while some of his books are in the Cambridge University Library.[28] He was interested in architecture and perspective, geography and particularly botany and medicine. Indeed, with his brother Edmund he contributed pioneering research to the botanist Thomas Penny who turned in old age to entomology: Edmund provided drawings of crickets while Thomas sent observations on parasites.

Knyvett owned a whole series of herbals, from a 1517 edition of *Ortus Sanitatis* through Fuchs's *De Historia Stirpium*, 1542, to no fewer than three copies of Mattioli's commentaries, all published in Venice. There are some interesting omissions – no herbals from native authors, Turner, Lyte, or Gerard, presumably because he felt that works in English were less authoritative. Clusius is only represented by his Latin translations of Garcia ab Orto's book on Indian plants and of Nicolas Monardes's account of the plants from the West Indies, both published by Plantin in Antwerp in 1574. Knyvett's architectural books include Alberti, Palladio and Serlio.[29]

With the exception of Stafford's books on cultivation of fruit, none of these libraries include practical gardening manuals. Sir Thomas Tresham, as we have seen, did not include any gardening or plant books in his library list, despite the fact that he was a passionate and knowledgeable gardener. But this must be a distorted picture of what people were reading on gardens. Clearly they were buying in sufficient numbers to encourage booksellers to continue importing books from Europe and bringing out new editions and reprints of books written in England. The evidence for this comes from a list of English printed books compiled by an enterprising bookseller, Andrew Maunsell. This was issued in 1595, and tells us that Maunsell was 'dwelling in Lothbury' in the City of London.[30] Maunsell set out to collect the titles of books 'either written in our owne tongue, or translated out of any other language' on all manner of subjects that he thought would provide a useful guide to customers. The overwhelming proportion are divinity books, but the second part of the catalogue is devoted to 'Mathematics, Physicall and Chirurgicall', with titles that pertain to gardening and husbandry appearing under various categories. The originating bookseller, publication history and format are given, but no prices.

There is one architectural title, eccentrically listed under 'Aphorisms', John Shute's *First and Chief Grounds of Architecture*. Under 'Mathematics, Physics and Chirurgicall' he included *Bulwarke of defence against all sickness soreness and wounds* by the physician William Bullein. This title was almost certainly studied by John Gerard when he was training to be a barber surgeon, with its useful illustrations of medicinal herbs. 'Herbals' contains those of Peter Treveris, William Turner and Henry Lyte and, again eccentrically, Thomas Hill's *Art of Gardening*. 'Of the Globe' includes a book by John Maples about the Green Forest, a compendium of natural history that included herbs, trees and shrubs, along with 'brute beasts, fowls, fishes, creeping worms and serpents'.[31]

A separate category covers 'Gardening, Graffing and Planting', containing four titles. Here Thomas Hill appears under the guise of Didymus Mountain, author of *Gardeners Labyrinth*, alongside Leonard Mascall's *Art of Graffing & Planting*, and Reginald Scot's treatise on the hop garden.[32] The books of Hill, Mascall and Scot, all in the same format, were sometimes bound together to provide a kind of encyclopaedia of gardening. A London bookseller, Thomas Chard, noted in his list of 1583 that he was offering 'Graffing Hoppes Laberinth' at two shillings the set to a bookseller in Cambridge.[33]

Thus Andrew Maunsell lifts the lid a little on the market for gardening and husbandry books in the English language that was gradually developing in London during the later part of the sixteenth century. But this was merely the prelude to what was to become in the seventeenth century a very lively publishing scene, reflecting the growing national passion for gardening.

CHAPTER 5

House and Garden

'THERE SHOULD BE GARDENS FULL OF DELIGHTFUL PLANTS, and a
garden portico where you can enjoy both sun and shade. There
should also be truly festive space.'[1] Thus wrote Alberti in his architectural treatise *De Re Aedificatoria*, first published in 1485, and the idea of the
house being integrated with the garden is repeated by architectural and
gardening writers throughout the sixteenth century. The Elizabethans took
this concept up not only in terms of design but also in a social context: flowers
and plants were used to decorate the house, rooms were created to be like
gardens, furnishings reflected a love of the natural world. The garden was
indeed a festive space, an outside dining room, a place for music and games,
and for entertainments great and small. It was also the source of inspiration for
another kind of flowering, of English poetry. The interconnections were like
threads in an intricate piece of embroidery.

The English were celebrated for their delight in decorating their houses
with flowers. The Dutch scholar and physician Levinus Lemnius, who visited
England in 1560, wrote with enthusiasm: 'their chambers & parlours strawed
over with sweete herbes, refreshed mee, their nosegayes finelye entermingled
with sondry sortes of fragaunte floures in their bedchambers and privie
rooms, with comfortable smell cheered mee up and entirerlye delighted all my
sences'.[2] Robert Dudley liked to have sweet-smelling flowers in his houses,
and a bill for 1559–60 for his London home on the Strand records 'For roses
and other flowers for your Lordship's chamber by the space of twenty-seven
days at 6d the day, 13s 6d'.[3]

Lemnius compared his Dutch compatriots unfavourably with the English in the use of greenery in the house: 'Altho' we do trimme up our parlours with green boughs, fresh herbs or vine leaves, no nation does it more decently, more trimmely, nor more slightly than they do in England.'[4] This is confirmed by Thomas Tusser in his *Five Hundreth Pointes of Good Husbandrie*, who provided a whole list of 'herbes, branches, and flowers for windows and pots'.[5] Cut flowers decorating a house are to be seen in details from a miniature portrait of the family of Sir Thomas More. The original painting, by Hans Holbein the Younger, is lost, but a copy made in the 1590s shows vases filled with a mixture of garden flowers, including roses, irises and carnations (Plate V).[6]

The versatile Sir Hugh Platt – he was knighted by James I in 1605 for his services as an inventor – turned his attention to gardening in *Floraes Paradise*, a little octavo volume published in 1608, the year of his death. This covered every activity of cultivation from orchards to flower gardens, but also included a section entitled 'A garden within doors': 'I hold it for a most delicat & pleasing thing to have a faire gallery, great chamber or other lodging, that openeth fully upon the East or West sun, to be inwardly garnished with sweet hearbs and flowers, yea & fruit if it were possible.' All kinds of ideas emanated from his ingenious brain. First, he suggested pots of marjoram and basil, carnations or rosemary be kept on shelves. By rigging up a pulley system the pots could be lowered through the windows and into the garden to enjoy the sunshine and temperate rain. Next he suggested square frames of wood or lead in each window, filled with earth and planted with herbs and flowers. For shady parts of the room he proposed plants such as sweetbriar, bay and germander, although he did warn to set these by open casements at certain times of the day so that they could take their fill of fresh air. He also described how Italians hung up cucumbers and pumpkins 'pricked full of Barlie' to keep away flies. He even proposed a kind of sprinkler system to keep window boxes well watered.

During the summer, when the fireplaces were not in use, he recommended filling the empty spaces 'with a fine banke of moss, which may be wrought in works being placed in earth, or with Orpin [*sedum telephium*, popularly known as 'Live-long' because of its lasting qualities], or the white flower called Everlasting. And at either end, and in the middest, place one of your flower or Rosemarie pottes, which you may once a week, or once every fortnight, expose now and then to the sun and rain, if they will not grow by watering them by rain water.'

For the winter months Platt gave advice on how to grow roses and carnations indoors: 'Place them in a roome that may som way be kept warm either with a dry fire, or with the steame of hot water conveyed by a pipe fastened to the cover of a pot, that is kept seething over som idle fire, now and then exposing them in a warme day, from 12 to two, in the sunne, or to the raine if it happen to raine; or if it raine not in convenient time, sette your pottes having holes in the bottom in panes of raine water, and so moisten the rootes'.[7] Platt acknowledged the advice of others, and in this case he credited Maister Jacob of the Glass-house, who used his fire to keep carnations throughout the winter. This was almost certainly Jacob Verzelini, a native of Murano who worked in Antwerp before coming to London in the early 1570s. He was in charge of the glass house at the Crutched Friars, manufacturing crystal for the table and window glass. His furnaces would have enabled him to indulge his carnations. Platt also described having plants climbing up inside windows, over the walls and even over the ceiling, and a veritable shrub appears at a window in a painting by an unknown artist of the conference held at Somerset House to negotiate peace between Spain and England in 1604.[8] In front of the unidentified greenery are assembled various dignitaries, including the gardening enthusiast Robert Cecil, Earl of Salisbury, and Thomas Sackville, Earl of Dorset.

When Sackville came to refurbish the mediaeval palace at Knole in Kent in the first years of the seventeenth century, he built no less than three long galleries. As Platt pointed out, galleries were very covetable rooms to have. They were built on the top floor of houses so that the family might take exercise there during the winter months or in inclement weather, when walking in the gardens was not possible. Even in fine weather they might look down upon the intricate patterns of their gardens. One of Sackville's galleries, now known as the Cartoon Gallery, was decorated with a series of paintings of flowers and plants in vases. Twelve are still in place, some simple mixtures of flowers, others showing single flower types, which is unusual for this period. As some flower arrangements are in maiolica vases, it is thought that the paintings may have been imported from Spain. The panels are set high up on the walls so that visitors to the gallery could look up at them, and then down through the windows to the garden. This idea is reflected too in the plasterwork ceiling, where botanical emblems from a herbal are set in the spaces between the ribs.

A generation earlier, William Cecil and Bess of Hardwick created what might be called 'garden rooms' in their houses. Jacob Rathgeb, in the entourage of the Duke of Württemberg, visited Theobalds in 1592 and left a description of a remarkable chamber:

On each side of the hall are six trees, having the natural bark so artfully joined, with birds' nests and leaves as well as fruit upon them, all managed in such a manner that you could not distinguish between the natural and these artificial trees; and as far as I could see, there was no difference at all, for when the steward of the house opened the windows, which looked upon the beautiful pleasure-garden, birds flew into the hall, perched themselves upon the trees and began to sing.[9]

In his translation of a book of husbandry published in 1577, Barnaby Googe explained why Cecil and others should create such rooms: 'Your parlers, and your banketting houses, both within and without, as all bedecked with pictures of beautiful Flowres and Trees, that you may not only feede your eyes with the beholding of the true and lively flowres, but also delight your selfe with the counterfaite in the middest of winter.'[10] Googe talks of the middle of winter, but it must be remembered that the growing season in gardens at this time was much shorter than today, when we have the benefit of plants introduced from the Far East. When the courtiers entertained Queen Elizabeth during her progresses, they were taking advantage of the climax of the flowering season in high summer. It was the orchard, rather than the pleasure gardens, that provided autumnal beauty.

At Hardwick New Hall, the detailed plantings have long vanished, and only Bess's walled enclosures remain, but a remarkable amount of her furnishings for the house survive, including her spectacular textile hangings and embroideries. Many of these show her love of flowers, creating another kind of garden within the house. At the top of the New Hall, Bess built a series of state apartments, partly as her granddaughter, Arbella Stuart, had a claim to the English throne so that these rooms were appropriate to her status, and partly because she maintained the fond hope that Elizabeth I would make a state visit. The huge long gallery, the largest surviving from the sixteenth century, is lit by the great windows that gave the house its rhyme, 'more glass than wall'. It is still hung with the tapestries that Bess bought in 1592 from Sir Christopher Hatton's bankrupt estate. At the far end of the gallery is a portrait of Elizabeth I, showing her wearing a rich gown, probably one given to her by Bess as a New Year's gift. The white petticoat is decorated with a wealth of flowers, birds and beasts – it could have been embroidered by Bess, a skilled needlewoman, or painted onto the silk. Among the flowers featured is the pansy or heartsease, one of the Queen's favourite flowers (Plate VIII).

The flower motifs in the Queen's portrait may have been derived from *La Clef des Champs* published in 1586 by the artist Jacques le Moyne. Le Moyne, who also called himself de Morgues, was a French Huguenot who escaped to London, settling in Blackfriars some time after 1580. Some of his exquisite drawings of flowers are now in the British Museum and the Victoria and Albert Museum. The published woodcuts derived from them are very crude in comparison, but their bold forms would be ideal for embroiderers, and pinpricks have been detected around the images in a copy of *La Clef*, now in the British Library, an indication that they were used for tracing. The link between embroidery and gardens is again made in the books of Thomas Trevelyon. A shadowy figure of Cornish origin, he combined the skills of embroiderer and drawing master, trading from a shop in Blackfriars. His *Miscellany*, published in 1608, announced that it contained designs for joiners, scriveners, gardeners and embroiderers. Some of the designs for knot gardens were taken straight from Thomas Hill's *Gardeners Labyrinth*.

One of the Queen's favourite flowers, the eglantine rose, was shared by Bess, who adopted it as part of her coat of arms. Standing in the Long Gallery at Hardwick is the 'Eglantine Table', elaborately inlaid with musical instruments, sheets of music, playing cards and boards for chess and backgammon. The eglantine roses are rather lost in the complexity of the decoration, but they appear around the collars of two stags in the centre of the table, supporting the motto: 'The redolent smele of Aeglantyne/ We stagges exault to the deveyne'. The table was made in 1567 to celebrate the triple union of Bess and her fourth husband, George Talbot, Earl of Shrewsbury, and those of her eldest son Henry to Grace Talbot, and of her eldest daughter, Mary, to Shrewsbury's heir, Gilbert Talbot, producing the most complex of family trees.

If the Long Gallery at Hardwick is breathtaking in its scale and richness of decoration, so too is the High Great Chamber next door. In 1579 when he visited Holdenby, William Cecil had written to Hatton 'I found no one thing of greater grace than your stately ascent from your hall to your great chamber'.[11] Bess may well have taken note of this, for she produced the most stately ascent up flights of stairs that wound their way around the New Hall, with visitors arriving at last in a room hung with tapestries, surmounted by a dramatic frieze of painted plaster. The latter shows a forest, the domain of Diana, the virgin goddess and huntress. She is depicted, with her entourage, just above the throne and canopy of state where Bess of Hardwick would sit to receive her visitors. Men are shown hunting deer and boar but their forest surroundings are more like a garden cum menagerie. Exotic animals such as an elephant, an ostrich and a porcupine wander amid garden flowers such as the iris. The iris, which appears again and again in the furnishings of Hardwick, was associated with fidelity. This was one of Bess's favourite themes – the story of Penelope, the faithful wife of Ulysses, also crops up repeatedly. The Eglantine marriage between Bess and the Earl of Shrewsbury that had begun in such high expectation deteriorated into acrimony in the 1580s, so that Bess wished to signal her desire to be a good and loving wife, even if sorely tried.

There is a much-used saying, 'books do furnish a room', but it is entirely justified as far as Bess's decorative schemes were concerned. At Chatsworth in the 1560s and 1570s, at Hardwick Old Hall in the 1580s, and at the New Hall in the 1590s she drew upon literary sources to furnish her rooms. Bess spent many hours working with another superb needlewoman, Mary Stuart, for Lord Shrewsbury had been given the unwelcome role of custodian of the Scottish Queen. Among the pieces that they worked together was a series of octagonal panels in tent stitch, each depicting a plant surrounded by a Latin saying. The images of the plants were taken from the commentary on Dioscorides by Mattioli.[12] The Latin sayings were drawn from the *Adages* of the humanist philosopher Erasmus, and may have been taken from the schoolbooks of Bess's sons. The sayings have no bearing on the subject of the central octagon: for example, a lily of the valley is surrounded by *per publicam viam ne ambules* ('stray not upon the highway').

Embroidered pieces throng the rooms at Hardwick, some of them created by Bess herself, others made for her by professional needlewomen who formed part of her household. Flowers are a dominant theme and reinforce the close interconnection between horticulture and embroidery. Gardeners still refer to cuttings as slips, and this term is also used to describe flowers made up in tent stitch. The records of Mary Queen of Scots show that her slips were outlined with black stitches before the colours were filled in. Bess and her ladies followed drawn outlines provided for them by the professional needlewomen, gradually accumulating enough slips to be applied on a plain background to decorate an item of furnishing. One of Bess's embroidered panels is decorated with sprays of eglantine and strawberry, marigolds, honeysuckle, thistle, coltsfoot, borage and iris, with the leaves, fruit and flowers cut from cloths of gold and silver. A long cushion of crimson velvet is decorated with applied floral motifs, such as lilies, peonies and pomegranate, with ES for Elizabeth Shrewsbury adorning the centre.[13]

35 & 36 An octagonal piece of canvas work stitched by Bess of Hardwick, with an image of the lily of the valley derived from Pier Andrea Mattioli's commentary on Dioscorides, published in Lyons in 1572.

Privileged visitors to Hardwick New Hall would have been welcomed into the state apartments on the second floor. Perhaps even more privileged would have been the diners who climbed still further, up into one of the towers that dominate the skyline, where a little banqueting house had been installed. Access was via the leads of the roof, allowing guests not troubled by vertigo to view the formal gardens laid out below. Bess built more banqueting houses at ground level in the gardens.

These banqueting houses were very much a feature of Elizabethan and Jacobean houses and gardens. They came in different shapes and sizes, although a favourite form was the octagon. Robert Dudley had an octagonal tower built in stone overlooking the lake at Kenilworth, and this may have accommodated a set of four handsome tapestries woven by the Midlands factory of William Sheldon. The one surviving tapestry, now in the Victoria and Albert Museum, shows ornate gardens, probably imaginary, flanking the arms of Dudley as Earl of Leicester (Plate IX). Bess's garden banqueting houses are still to be seen at Hardwick, lozenge in shape with strapwork cresting and obelisks on their roofs, echoing the roofline of the main house. Another favoured shape was the Greek cross, as in Thomas Tresham's Lyveden New Bield, which is in fact a very grand banqueting house. Much more modest are two delightful early seventeenth-century buildings in the gardens at Montacute in Somerset, Greek crosses superimposed on squares. Not all these structures were permanent. When Elizabeth I entertained a French embassy at Greenwich Palace in 1560, a banqueting house was fashioned out of fir poles decorated with branches of birch and flowers from the garden and the meadow, including roses, carnations, lavender, marigolds and strewing herbs.

William Lawson, in his book *A New Orchard and Garden*, published in 1618, shows a suggested layout of a garden for a moderately sized household that includes two small houses. Although they are both captioned as still-rooms, one could be used as a banqueting house, where the products of the still-room might be served. The banquet was a special, final course that had developed from the custom of eating sweet food and drink at the end of a mediaeval meal. Sugar, at this time brought to England from North Africa in the spice ships of Venetian and Genoan merchants, was the luxury item to be incorporated in pastes, jellies, cakes and distilled drinks, known as 'banquetting stuffe'. While the cook might rule supreme in his or her kitchen attended by boys who turned the spit and carried out the routine tasks, the still-room was the domain of the lady of the house, assisted by her daughters and maids. As well as producing dishes for banquets, medicines were also prepared here. The inventory for

Northaw in Hertfordshire, one of the houses owned by Sir William Cavendish, has survived. It was probably drawn up in 1547 and was annotated by Bess, then just twenty years old. 'In a little coffer within my mistress's closet' are listed various utensils connected with the preparation of 'banquetting stuffe', including square dishes for suckets (fruits candied in syrup), saucers for caraways and biscuits, basins for possets and perfume pans.[14]

The raw ingredients came from the garden, as can be seen in the manuscript household books that have come down from this period. Grace, Lady Mildmay, who was born c. 1550, had an extensive still-room at her home at Apethorpe in Northamptonshire. Thirty-one large bottles of cordials and oils, shelves of powders and pills, and a chest full of medical papers and books were used to dispense medicines to the local community. In her autobiography she recorded how her governess gave her the herbal of William Turner and an English translation of a book on physick. When she died in 1620, Grace Mildmay left her daughter a list of the flowers, roots and herbs to be grown in her garden along with her books and papers.[15]

Margaret, Lady Hoby, was one generation younger than Grace Mildmay, born c. 1570. She was brought up in the household of the Earl of Huntingdon, where she learnt the Puritan habits of self-examination and regular religious exercise, and these are both evident in the diary that she kept between 1599 and 1605. By this time she was living in Yorkshire, married to her third husband, Thomas Posthumous, the son born to Elizabeth Hoby after the death of her husband, the translator and diplomat, also called Thomas. Life could not have been easy for Margaret Hoby, for her husband apparently was humourless and cantankerous, while her mother-in-law was one of the formidable Cooke sisters. However, amongst the constant reiteration of prayers and readings of the bible recorded in Margaret's diary are scattered details of her household routine, including gardening and giving medical advice and treatment to neighbours and tenants. On 5 October 1603, for instance, she records an Indian summer, with second blooming of white, red and musk roses, as well as artichokes. Her entry for 17 September 1599 notes that 'after private prayer, I saw a mans Legg dressed'. Often entries tell of working in the afternoon in her still-room, preserving fruit and making sweetmeats. But such was her religious devotion that she frets over horticultural distractions. On 6 April 1605 she laments 'this day I bestowed too much time in the Garden, and thereby was worse able to performe sperituall duties'.[16]

Elinor, Lady Fettiplace, was an exact contemporary of Margaret Hoby, and may well have known her, for she was related to the Cooke sisters. Her household book, dated 1604 on the flyleaf, gives the kind of recipes and remedies produced by well-born ladies. From her garden at Appleton Manor in Berkshire Elinor gathered her flowers to be dried, powdered and distilled. Her syrup of violets was highly labour-intensive, requiring between 4 and 6 pints of petals: 'First take a thick syrup of sugar and clarify it well, then take blue violets and pick them well from the whites [base of petals] then put them in the syrup, let them lie in it 24 hours keeping it warm in the mean time, then strain these violets out and put in fresh, so do 4 times then set them on the fire, let them simmer a good while but not boil fast, put in some Juice of lemons in the boiling, then strain it and keep it to your use.' The syrup could be used as the basis of a refreshing drink, or to cool fever.

One of the great treats of the banquet course was what was known as wet suckets, which we would think of as crystallised fruit in syrup. From the orchard Elinor Fettiplace gathered apricots and what she called pearplums and noted this recipe:

Take your apricocks or pearplums, & let them boil one walme [warming] in as much clarified sugar as will cover them, so let them lie infused in an earthen pan three dayes, then take out your fruits, & boile your syrupe againe, when you have thus used them three times then put half a pound of drie sugar into your syrupe, & so let it boile till it comes to a verie thick syrup, wherein let your fruits boile leysurelie 3 or 4 walmes, then take them foorth of the syrup, then plant them on a lattice of rods or wyer, & so put them into yor stewe, & every second day turne them & when they bee through dry, you may box them & keep them all the yeare; before you set them to drying, you must wash them in a little warme water, when they are half drie you must dust a little sugar upon them throw a fine Lawne [muslin].[17]

Sugar plate, a kind of uncooked fondant, was another staple of the still-room, as well as appealing to Elizabethan and Jacobean ingenuity. Elinor Fettiplace coloured some of her sugar plate blue with the juice of violets, some yellow with cowslips, and some she left white, and she would then make layers and roll it into various marbled shapes. Sir Hugh Platt, in his *Delightes for Ladies*, published in 1602, described how to make a complete sugar-plate dinner service of saucers, bowls, and so on, as a spectacular feature of the banquet. This he complemented with a suggestion in *Floraes Paradise* that guests at a banquet should go into the garden and pick the flowers that had been candied as they grew. The flowers were to be dipped in gum water 'as strong as for Inke, but made with Rose-water' at around ten o'clock in the morning on a hot summer's day, and then shaken. An alternative was to use a soft pencil and shake over a sugar powder using a box with a sieve of fine lawn. After three hours, the candy would have hardened on the flowers, 'so you may bid your friends after dinner to a growing banquet'.[18]

For those who had smaller gardens, or did not want to go to the expense of building a banqueting house, an arbour could be constructed to shelter a table for outdoor meals. In his *Gardeners Labyrinth* Thomas Hill illustrated the erection of one such arbour or 'herber' made from juniper or willow, as advocated by Alberti in his treatise. Such structures could make excellent hiding places, as shown in a painting from a 'friendship album' compiled by Gervasius Fabricius of Salzburg in the early seventeenth century. A meal is laid out in the middle of the garden, while figures lurk in an arbour, close to a courting couple (Plate X). This scenario was evoked by Shakespeare in *Much Ado about Nothing*, when Hero and Ursula walked up and down garden paths, talking loudly so that Beatrice might overhear them from her bower, 'Where honeysuckles, ripened by the sun/Forbid the sun to enter' (Act III, Scene 2).

Little wonder then that the Puritan Philip Stubbes regarded outdoor eating with such suspicion. In his *Anatomy of Abuses*, published in 1583, he fulminated:

37 A woodcut from Thomas Hill's *Gardeners Labyrinth*, published in 1571, showing an arbour or herber being erected around a table for outdoor meals. Hill explains how 'the herber in the garden may be framed with Juniper poles, or the willow, either to stretch, or to be bound together with Osiers . . . that the branches of Vine, Melone, or Cucumber, running and spreading all over might so shadow and keep both the heat & sun from the walkers and sitters there under' (pp. 22–3).

In the Fieldes and Suburbes of the Cities, thei have Gardens, either palled, or walled round about very high, with their Harbers and Bowers fit for the purpose. And least thei might be espied in these open places, thei have their Banquetting Houses with Galleries, Turrettes, and what not els therin sumpteuously erected; wherein thei maie (and doubtlesse doe) many of them plaie the filthie persons. These Gardens are exelent places, and for the purpose, for if thei can speak with their dearlynges no where els, yet there thei maie be sure to meete. And truly I think some of these places are little better than the Stewes and Brothell Houses were in tymes past.[19]

Eating in the garden was just one of many activities enjoyed by the Tudors. As the observer noted of the gardens of Richmond Palace in 1501, there were 'pleasant galleries and houses of pleasure to disport in, at chess, tables, dice, cards, billiards; bowling alleys, butts for archers, and goodly tennis plays – as well to use the said plays and disports as to behold them so disporting.'[20] In midsummer, when the interior of houses could be hot and the closeness unpleasant, playing bowls or merely walking in the cool of the evening in the garden must have been a very welcome relief for every level of society. Another painting from Fabricius's album depicts a group of ladies hard at work at their embroidery and lace-making in a garden, being entertained by a lady at a virginal accompanying a singer (Plate XI).[21]

Most of these entertainments have passed unrecorded. However, details of some of the festivities held for Elizabeth I during her progresses have survived, and, although on a grand scale, they give an idea of some of the enjoyments on offer in more modest gardens. One of the most famous examples took place at Kenilworth in July 1575 when the Queen stayed for nineteen days with Robert Dudley. A feature of Kenilworth was the huge lake, more than one hundred acres in dimension, constituting the largest artificial stretch of water in England. Dudley was able to use this to provide a dramatic setting for his festivities, with the water enhancing the light from torches, and from the candle-lit house: 'In day-time on every side so glittering by glass; at nights, by continual brightness of candle, fire and torch-light, transparent thro' the light-some windows, as it were the Egyptian Pharos relucent unto all the Alexandrian Coast.'[22] Sir Henry Killigrew had acquired for Dudley an Italian expert in pyrotechnics and, once he had been persuaded not to use live animals, he produced spectacular displays of fireworks with fighting cats and dogs, along with dragons and birds exploding over the lake.

As the Queen approached the inner gate of the castle in the early evening of 9 July, she was met by the Lady of the Lake accompanied by nymphs floating on a torchlit island, for Dudley was planning a masque where, as the Queen's knight, he would rescue the Lady from an unwanted suitor. The formal entertainments were in the charge of the poet George Gascoigne. Faced with severe financial difficulties, Gascoigne had served as a soldier in the Netherlands, spending several months as a prisoner of the Spanish. In his absence friends published some of his poetry, which was criticised as being lascivious. In the year of the Kenilworth festivities, he had published an anthology of verses using his nickname as a soldier, the Green Knight, claiming to have turned over a new leaf. In 'Farewell to Fancy', the Green Knight bids goodbye to life's vanities, including gardening:

> To plant strange country fruits, to sow such seeds likewise,
> To dig and delve for new found roots, where old might well suffice;
> To prune the water boughs, to pick the mossy trees,
> Oh how it pleased my fancy once to kneel upon my knees,
> To griff [graft] a pippin stock, when sap begins to swell;
> But since the gains scarce quit the cost, *Fancy* (quoth he) *farewell*.

It is a source of wonder that Gascoigne had time to indulge in gardening as well as soldiering and getting into various financial scrapes. Only two years after the Kenilworth festivities, he died at the age of forty-three.

On 11 July as the Queen returned from hunting, she was greeted by Gascoigne dressed as a wild man, covered in moss and ivy, carrying a young oak tree. A dialogue ensued between the wild man and Echo. We know about the entertainments as Gascoigne subsequently published *The Princely Pleasures of the Court at Kenilworth* in which he included transcripts of the masques. It has been assumed that there was a person playing Echo, but it is also possible that Gascoigne used the water and buildings to project his own voice which came back as an echo. Six days later, comic relief was provided by a mock wedding, with Morris dancers and Maid Marion. This may not have seemed amusing to Elizabeth, for the bride was old and the groom lame, a possible allusion to the courtship that she was conducting with the Duc d'Alençon, youngest son of Henri II of France and Catherine de' Medici, who was many years the Queen's junior. Robert Dudley was trying to do everything in his power to prevent the match.

The following day, the Queen was once more returning in early evening from the hunt, when she encountered an 18-foot mermaid swimming with

Triton on her back, who explained that the Lady of the Lake had been taken prisoner by Sir Bruce Sans Pitié because she refused to marry him. Neptune had therefore sent his son Triton to ask the Queen to free her by the force of her magical presence. With the Lady duly freed, Arion arrived on a dolphin, 24 feet in length to accommodate an orchestra. In classical mythology Arion was a musician threatened with murder by the sailors who were carrying him on a voyage to Corinth. Leaping into the sea, he was rescued by a dolphin which carried him safely to land. Elizabeth's Arion began to sing but, growing hoarse, pulled off his mask and declared that he was really 'honest Henry Goldingham', a well-known singer, much to the Queen's delight.

However, the relaxed atmosphere disappeared two days later, when Elizabeth threatened to leave Kenilworth precipitately. The most likely cause was that she had discovered the affair between Dudley and Lettice Knollys. The Queen was always possessive of her favourites, but this relationship must have particularly riled as Lettice, her cousin, was a red-haired beauty some ten years her junior, married to Walter Devereux, Earl of Essex, who was fighting in Ireland. Essex did not survive long among the Hibernian bogs, and died a year later of dysentery, whereupon Dudley married Lettice to the fury of the Queen, who would never receive her at court thereafter. But somehow matters were patched up at Kenilworth in 1575. Although the projected masque was cancelled, Gascoigne steered the Queen towards a holly-bush arbour where he told her of Zabeta, one of Diana's favourite nymphs, who turned her suitors to beasts, birds and plants. Dudley, hidden in the bush, managed to persuade the Queen to stay another week.

The entertainments for the Queen at Kenilworth were open to all, and it was estimated that between three and four thousand people came each day. Among them, surely, was the eleven-year-old William Shakespeare from nearby Stratford on Avon. Some of the events echo elements in *A Midsummer Night's Dream*, written twenty years later: the tactless mock wedding could have inspired the play performed by the 'rude mechanicals'; Goldingham's declaration that he was not Arion is reflected in Snug the joiner's reassurance to his audience that he was not a lion; the appearance of the dolphin and fireworks are evoked by Oberon's description of a water pageant:

And heard a mermaid on a dolphin's back
Uttering such dulcet and harmonious breath,
That the rude sea grew civil at her song,
And certain stars shot madly from their spheres
To hear the sea-maid's music.

Oberon goes on to tell Puck how Cupid's arrow

> ... fell upon a little western flower,
> Before milk-white, now purple with love's wound
> And maidens call it, Love-in-idleness. (Act II, Scene 1)

This was one of the names given to heartsease, the wild pansy, a favourite flower of Queen Elizabeth.

Shakespeare's presence at Kenilworth in July 1575 remains conjectural, but Philip Sidney, Robert Dudley's favourite nephew, was definitely there. Despite the fact that eight sons had been born to John and Jane Dudley, not one had produced a legitimate child, so that Sidney, the eldest son of Robert's sister, Mary, was his heir presumptive. He was, however, not smiled upon by the Queen or Cecil, who felt that he had learnt from his uncle inflated ideas of his own importance, and were later to worry that both men, strongly Protestant, might lead England into religious wars against Catholics in Europe. Despairing of preferment at court, Sidney turned to poetry and romance, joining the circle of poets and scholars that his sister Mary created around her after her marriage to the Earl of Pembroke. At her house at Wilton in Wiltshire, Sidney began to compose *The Countesse of Pembroke's Arcadia*, responding to his sister's challenge to write a romance in English to match the *Arcadia* written a century earlier by the Neapolitan Jacopo Sannazaro.

Sidney's original version, now known as the *Old Arcadia*, depicts a realm of great princes and poor shepherds, and includes a melancholy gentleman-poet, a version of himself. Revisions were made first by him, and then by his sister after Sidney's early death at the Battle of Zutphen in the Netherlands in 1586. Thus when 'New Arcadia' appeared in print in 1590 the romantic adventures had developed into an epic poem. The figure of Kalander was introduced, with his house and garden. Sidney characterises the house as 'not affecting so much any extraordinary kind of fineness as an honourable representing of a firm stateliness'. In his youth, he had travelled in Italy and particularly admired the Palladian villas of the Veneto with their combination of beauty and practicality as working estates. Kenilworth could in no measure resemble a Palladian villa, but the garden that Sidney evokes in 'New Arcadia' has some echoes of his uncle's pleasure grounds. As Kalander leads his guests down behind his house 'they came into a place cunningly set with trees of the most taste-pleasing fruits', and beyond 'into a delicate green, of each side of the green a thicket bend, behind the thickets again new beds of flowers, which being under the trees, a mosaical floor, so that it seemed that art therein would needs be delightful by counterfeiting his enemy, error, and making order in confusion'.[23]

Another soldier poet, Edmund Spenser, was not present at Kenilworth but he must have become familiar with the entertainments presented there, for in 1579 he became Dudley's secretary, and his pastoral poem, *The Shepheardes Calender*, published that year, was dedicated to Sidney. This was divided into twelve eclogues, and the one for April celebrated the Queen as 'fayre Elisa, Queene of shepheardes all'. Elizabeth is represented wearing a coronet of damask roses and daffodils interleaved with bay, primroses and violets. Spenser evokes a heady mixture of spring and summer flowers, from the garden and the hedgerow:

> Bring hither the pink and purple columbine,
> With gillyflowers;
> Bring coronations [carnations] and sops-in-wine [pinks],
> Worn of Paramours
> Strew me the ground with daffadowndillies,
> And cowslips, and kingcups, and loved lilies
> The pretty paunce [pansy]
> And the chevisance [wallflower],
> Shall match with the fair flower de lis [iris].[24]

Clearly Spenser knew his flowers, and it has been suggested that he used as his reference Henry Lyte's herbal, which appeared in 1578, the year before *The Shepheardes Calender*.

Spenser began at the same time his greatest work, *The Faerie Queene*, the first three books of which were published eleven years later, in 1590. Gardens play an important part. One of the knights serving Gloriana, the Faerie Queene, is Sir Guyon, the knight of Temperance. When he visits the Bower of Bliss belonging to Acrasia, the personification of Intemperance, he halts at different points, just as Queen Elizabeth had done at Kenilworth, and each time he has to read, judge and make his decisions. At the heart of the Bower lies a secret garden with a sorceress:

> Upon a bed of Roses she was layd,
> As faint through heat, or dight to pleasant sin,
> And was arayd, or rather disarayd,
> All in a vele of silk and silver thin.[25]

Guyon, seeing her victim, a sleeping youth, lying next to her, decides to destroy the Bower. Like so many Elizabethan entertainments and High Renaissance gardens, Spenser's *Faerie Queene* is replete with symbolism. The Bower of Bliss is beguilingly deceptive while other gardens in the work, notably that of Adonis, reflect more harmoniously the collaboration between art and nature. As Protestants, Spenser and Sidney would reject the hothouse luxury of the gardens of Rome, while admiring the 'firm stateliness' of those of Venice.[26] Stubbes had already made clear that gardens can be places of innocent activities but also of sensual temptation, Eden but also the Fall.

Kenilworth was to prove the climax of Dudley's tributes to the Queen, but others took up the challenge and magnificent entertainments continued right through to the end of her reign. Lord Hertford presented an elaborate water pageant and firework display in his garden at Elvetham in Hampshire in 1591. For the occasion he had a lake created in the shape of a crescent with three islands capped by buildings representing a fort, a ship and a snail. On this he staged a sea battle with a great display of fireworks. The Queen was provided with a withdrawing room in the form of a bower, with walls covered in boughs and decorated with ripe hazelnuts. This structure can be seen in an engraving that was made of the occasion, set behind the Queen, who is shown enthroned under a silver and green canopy watching the entertainment on the lake. A tract describing the entertainment was published that year and sold by a London bookseller.

The following year an intriguing entertainment was presented to the Queen at Bisham Abbey in Berkshire. This was the home of Elizabeth Cooke, Margaret Hoby's mother-in-law. After Sir Thomas Hoby's early death she had married John, Lord Russell, the second son of the Earl of Bedford. Widowed a second time, she was determined that her two young daughters, Elizabeth and Anne, should become maids of honour to the Queen, thus improving their chances of a good marriage. Lady Russell decided to present a quasi-dramatic performance featuring her daughters as 'two Virgins keeping Sheepe' who were being harassed by the god Pan. It is thought that this was the first occasion that English noblewomen had speaking parts in such an entertainment.[27] But she also unusually and ingeniously linked gardens and needlework. When the Queen approached Bisham Abbey, she was met by Pan and the Russell daughters as Sybilla and Isabella, sewing samplers. Sybilla opened the dialogue by declaring 'Mens tongues, wrought all with double stitch but not one true', whereupon Pan asked what then were the 'true' stitches. Her reply was 'Roses, Eglentine, harts-ease, wrought with Queene's stitch, and all

38 Memories of the defeat of the Spanish Armada were recalled for Elizabeth I at an elaborate sea battle held at Elvetham in Hampshire in 1591. For the occasion, Lord Hertford created a lake in the shape of a crescent, the symbol of Diana, the goddess associated with the Queen, with three little islands. Elizabeth is shown sitting under a canopy of state in the top left corner of the engraving.

right'. The flowers were all known to be the Queen's favourites, while Queen stitch was a kind of counted thread, not appropriate apart from the name. Double stitch stood for men's perfidy.

Skill in embroidery was an important attainment for upper-class ladies in Elizabethan times, and an area where women could be creative, as the needle-work of Mary Queen of Scots and Bess of Hardwick has shown. Another area where the skills of women were admired was managing a household, be it great or small, and this was the theme that was adopted in the last great enter-tainment for Elizabeth I. In August 1602, she was the guest of Lord Keeper Egerton and his wife, the Dowager Countess of Derby, at Harefield Place in Middlesex. On entering the garden the Queen was met by two 'rustics', the Bailiff and Joan the Dairymaid, who welcomed her with a garden rake and fork in the form of jewels, declaring her to be 'the best housewife of all this company'.

Six months later, this supreme housewife had become very frail and descended into melancholy. She chose as her last progress to go to Richmond Palace, a 'warm winter box to shelter her old age' and, unable to think of going to bed, snatched at sleep from her chair, or on cushions on the floor. In the early hours of 24 March 1603 the Queen died, and the Tudor age was at an end.

CHAPTER 6

Court and Country

E LIZABETH I's DEATH IN MARCH 1603 did not bring about a complete change of scene, least of all in the dynamic world of horticulture. However, it is possible to see in the passing of the Queen a watershed as far as the impetus for creating great gardens was concerned. James, King of the Scots, now also James I of England, brought down from Edinburgh his consort, Anne of Denmark, and three children; Henry, born in 1594; Elizabeth, born in 1596; and Charles, born in 1600. James was not particularly interested in gardens, but was content to let his Queen and his first-born son create some of the most spectacular gardens of early seventeenth-century England.

The turn of the century also brought about a time of peace in Europe, beginning with the Treaty of Vervins concluded in 1598 between Spain and France. Just as William Cecil was Elizabeth's secretary, so his younger son Robert fulfilled that role for James I, negotiating in 1604 a skilful peace with Spain and avoiding concessions that included contentious issues of trade with the New World. Five years later a lull came in the long struggle in the Low Countries with the signing of the Twelve Years Truce. It was also much easier for Englishmen and women to travel in Europe, and in particular in Italy, for in the very last years of Elizabeth's reign diplomatic relations were re-established with the Venetian Republic, and these were extended to the courts of Savoy and Tuscany under James.

Somerset House in London was given to Anne by the King and in 1606 she began elaborate changes, spending the huge sum of £34,500 on the house and garden. The privy garden was raised and levelled, and paths of black and white stone were introduced. The lower half of the garden, separated from the upper by terraces, was divided into quarters. But the most dramatic addition came in a part of the garden to the east, where a huge octagonal basin was created, on which was raised a Mount Parnassus accompanied by four reclining river gods representing the principal rivers of Britain, headed by the Thames. On the mount itself, on the side facing the house, sat the Nine Muses, probably accompanied by Apollo, with a golden Pegasus at the top. A visitor to London in 1613 described how the mount was made of 'sea-stones, all sorts of mussels, snails and other curious plants'.[1]

This massive garden structure was the work of a French Huguenot engineer, Salomon de Caus. He had travelled to Italy in the late 1590s and visited amongst other gardens Pratolino outside the city of Florence, where Bernardo

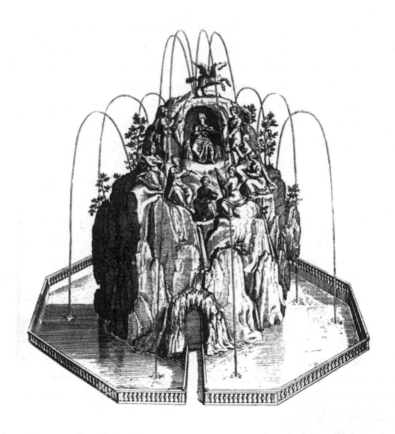

39 Mount Parnassus, with the Nine Muses, Apollo and, atop, Pegasus, from Salomon de Caus's *Les Raisons des forces mouvantes*, published in 1615.

Buontalenti worked on the palace and its gardens for Francesco I de' Medici, the Grand Duke of Tuscany, from 1569 until 1584. At the very time that de Caus may have visited Pratolino, an English traveller was also there. Fynes Moryson wrote a detailed description of the wonders that he beheld: 'This garden is divided into two inclosures, compassed with stone walls. In the upper inclosure is a statua of a Giant, with a curled beard, like a Monster, some forty-six els [approximately 172 feet, or 53 metres] high, whose great belly will receive many men at one, and by the same are the Images of many Nimphes, all which cast out water abundantly'. Although the sixteenth-century garden at Pratolino has been swept away, this giant survives, a mournful reminder.

Moryson went on to describe many other features of the garden at Pratolino, including fountains that were 'wrought with little houses, which house is vulgarly called grotto, that is Cave (or Den) yet they are not built under the earth but above in the manner of a Cave'. Grottoes had become the fashion-able feature of late sixteenth-century Italian gardens, echoing the Mannerist style in the architecture of buildings, where the bizarre and the exotic were extolled. The Grand Duke's interest in scientific experiment was reflected in the automata contained in the grottoes. In one instance Moryson noted that 'Duckes dabble in the water, and then looke around them', and in another 'the Image of Fame doth loudly sound a Trumpet, while the Image of a Clowne putteth a dish into the water, and taking up water, presents it to the Image of a Tyger, which drinketh the same up, and then moves his head and looks around about with his eyes'.[2] And Pratolino was also intended to be read as an alle-gory. In 1586 Francesco de' Vieri published his interpretation of the meaning of the gardens.[3] Thus the Giant described by Moryson represented Mount Apennine, one of the fallen Titans who had tried to overthrow Jove, a reminder that without God's aid the outcome would be disastrous.

Pratolino featured a Mount Parnassus which became famous throughout Europe. De' Vieri's interpretation was that it symbolised celebrated men whose lives were dedicated to the pursuit of virtues by service to the Muses. When de Caus came to build his Mount Parnassus by the Thames, which the 1613 visitor described as surpassing Pratolino, his iconographic programme was to celebrate Anne of Denmark as 'Tethys, Queen of Nymphs and Rivers'. The Queen loved elaborate court masques, not only commissioning them but often also partici-pating. In 1610, to mark the creation of her son Henry as Prince of Wales, she commissioned the poet Samuel Daniel to write a masque in which she was Tethys, wife to Neptune, James I. Rivers of the newly created Empire of Great Britain were represented by her ladies, so that two of Bess of Hardwick's granddaughters symbolised the rivers appropriate to their titles: Elizabeth Grey, Countess of Kent, was the Medway; Alethea Howard, Countess of Arundel, was the Arun. A grotto in the style of Salomon de Caus was used as one of the backdrops.

In 1610 de Caus became 'Ingenieur du Serenissime' to the Prince of Wales, and gave him lessons on perspective, as indicated in the dedication in his book, *La Perspective avec lae raison des ombres et miroirs*, published in London two years later. The concept of Renaissance man is usually associated with gentlemen scholars, but it equally applies to the men whom they employed to design and build for them. Engineers were expected to double up as artists, artisans, military designers and organisers of court festivities – the most famous example being Leonardo da Vinci. De Caus was just such a polymath, laying out gardens for the Queen and her family, studying perspective, and designing all kinds of devices such as speaking statues and water organs. For his automata he drew upon the works of the School of Alexandria that flourished in the first century CE, and in particular *Pneumatica*, the writings of Hero. This key text was known in the fifteenth century through translations into Latin and Arabic, and in the sixteenth century it was published in Latin, and later, in Italian by Aleotti.[4]

40 A speaking statue from John Evelyn's unpublished work on gardens, *Elysium Britannicum*. Evelyn takes as his example a statue of Memnon from Thebes in Egypt, showing the mechanism hidden in the base of the statue, which was activated when the sun rose above the horizon.

In his book Aleotti provided illustrations which showed how some of the automata worked. In one, he depicted Hercules slaying the dragon and seizing the golden apple of Hesperides. The pedestal was made up of two sections, the upper filled with water so that when the apple was lifted, it raised a cone within the upper section, and this, by means of a pulley, raised Hercules's bow. Water passed via a cone to the lower part of the pedestal, creating a noise of hissing air, which came up into the mouth of the dragon via a tube. In 1615 de Caus wrote his own book on mechanical devices, *Les Raisons des forces mouvantes*, first published in Frankfurt in 1615. In this work he reproduced some of the garden devices that he had created for the Stuart court circle, including the Mount Parnassus from Somerset House. Such was his ingenuity, that the book also contained the earliest exposition of a steam engine. Later he turned his attention to treatises on music and on sundials.[5]

De Caus acted not only as tutor to the Prince of Wales, but also participated in the layout of his gardens at Richmond. His contribution here is not easy to define because others were also involved. Robert Cecil's gardener, Mountain Jennings, prepared drawings of certain features, and the architect Inigo Jones, acting as the Prince of Wales's surveyor, was also doing some work on the garden. This scenario became even more overcrowded when the Florentine architect Constantino de' Servi was acquired from the Medici court with an annuity of £200, almost four times Jones's salary, and twice that paid to de Caus. This may explain why, when the Prince suddenly died in November 1612, both Inigo Jones and de Caus decamped to Europe. De' Servi produced an elaborately worked plan for alterations to both the palace and the gardens at Richmond, now in the state archives in Florence. This included a huge figure 'three times as large as the one at Pratolino, with rooms inside, a dovecot in the head and grottoes in the base'.[6] This giant was another representation of Mount Apennine, a man-made landscape of stone and earth moulded and planted to produce a fantastic image. However, this probably was never built because of the Prince's untimely death.

In 1613 when James I's daughter, Princess Elizabeth, married Frederick, the Elector Palatine, and left England for a new life in Heidelberg, Salomon de Caus was appointed their engineer and architect. Drawing on his knowledge of the Villa d'Este at Tivoli, de Caus produced a garden in the Italian style, complete with a water parterre, orangery, grotto, and speaking statue of Hercules in the style of Hero of Alexandria. The non-water parterres were in the new embroidered, curving fashion, which had come to eclipse the geometric patterns of earlier decades. The Heidelberg garden was never

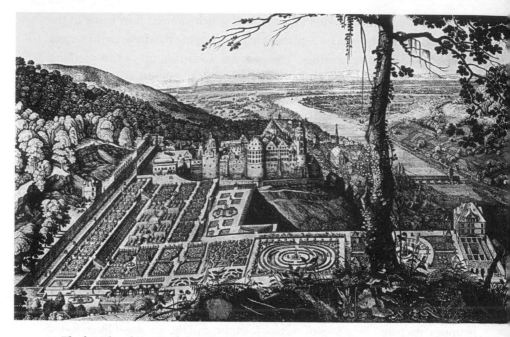

41 The formal garden at Heidelberg, laid out by Salomon de Caus following the marriage in 1613 of Elizabeth Stuart and Frederick, the Elector Palatine.

completed, for the outbreak of the Thirty Years War in 1619 only too soon doomed it to extinction, but a book published by de Caus, *Hortus Palatinus*, shows its appearance, and probably that of Prince Henry's garden at Richmond.

It is striking how the children and grandchildren of Elizabeth I's courtier gardeners continued the tradition – they could be said to have inherited 'green genes'. Robert Cecil received Theobalds at his father's death, but when James I made clear how much he coveted the property for its hunting, he was obliged in 1607 to render it up to his sovereign in exchange for the old Tudor palace of Hatfield. A new house at Hatfield was built under his supervision by the architect Robert Lyming with help from the King's surveyor, Simon Basil, and Inigo Jones. The main formal gardens went through a series of designs by different hands, with Cecil probably acting as the final arbiter. In 1611 Salomon de Caus was brought in to provide plots or plans, as well as models of individual features. Among the fountains he created was one with a reclining river god and the figure of Fame that sounded a trumpet by means of a hydraulic organ. It was ornamented by leaves, snakes, fishes and shells that had been brought back from France by Cecil's gardener, John Tradescant.

Although John Tradescant became one of England's most famous gardeners, his origins remain obscure. He was born some time during the 1570s, probably in Corton in Suffolk. Some accounts describe him as a Dutchman, but he was more likely to have been of Dutch descent. He started work at Hatfield on the first day of 1610, at an annual salary of £50, five times the money paid to John Gerard by William Cecil. Where he had worked previously is also not known, but the fact that he was paid a substantial sum and that within a year he had been sent to Europe to buy plants and fruit trees suggests that he had already built up a reputation.

Tradescant's first European foray lasted for only a few weeks, when he was sent off by Cecil with an advance of £10 to buy plants. The second trip was much more elaborate and longer lasting. Disembarking at Flushing, he travelled to Middelburg, Rotterdam and Delft, where he bought cherry and quince trees from a nurseryman, Dirryk Hevesson. Moving on to Leiden he visited the famous botanical garden, and thus must have also seen the 'museum of curiosities' housed there. In the archives at Hatfield are the bills for plants purchased: from a Leiden nurseryman, Falkener, one headed 'roots of flowers and Roasses and shrubs of Strang and Rare'; from a Haarlem nurseryman Cornelis Helin 'for flowers called anemones at 5s; for the Province [Provins] Rosses at 8s' and 'for two arborvitae trees at 1s'. The last is the Tree of Life, *Thuja occidentalis*, which had been introduced from Canada in the early sixteenth century.[7]

Tradescant had earlier written to William Trumbull, James I's chargé d'affaires in Brussels, giving him a shopping list. From Pierre, the kitchen gardener of the Archduke Albert and his duchess, Isabella, he wanted vines, especially 'the blewe muskadell, the Russet grape', along with a 'specled anemone', and several roses. From Mr John Joket, probably a well-known Brussels nurseryman, he requested a whole series of white flowers, and two or three small grafted orange trees. He went on to give Trumbull clear instructions on how the plants were to be packed ready for transport: the trees, shrubs and vines in baskets planted about with the young roots of rare varieties of pinks. The other flower roots were to be sealed up in a basket or box covered with dry moss or sand, and secured with padlocks. All plants, and especially the vines, were to be labelled with their names, so that when they reached Hatfield they should be identifiable. Tradescant then set off for Brussels to collect his treasures.

Next Tradescant moved on to Paris. Henri IV, who was known as 'the gardener king', had brought prosperity to France, and in particular to his capital. The palace of the Tuileries had been restored, and a team of skilled gardeners installed that included Claude Mollet, supervising the design, Pierre le Nôtre, in charge of the parterres, and Jean Robin looking after the plants. Robin also had his own garden on the western end of the Ile Notre Dame in the Seine, where Tradescant visited him. For the next eighteen years, until Robin's death in 1629, the two gardeners exchanged plants, and it may have been Tradescant who gave Robin the tree that is named after him, *Robinia pseudoacacia*, the black locust or false acacia. In Paris Tradescant acquired yet more exotic plants, including pomegranates, myrtles, oleanders and fig trees given to him by Robin. The King's gardener helped him to pack up his acquisitions and send them downriver to Rouen. Here Tradescant made his purchases for the fountain being created at Hatfield: 'one chest of Shells with eyght boxes of Shells, £12 . . . for an artyfyshall bird, 2s 6d'.[8]

Back at Hatfield, Tradescant worked alongside Mountain Jennings, who had been Robert Cecil's chief gardener for many years. How they apportioned their areas of responsibility is not known, but as Mountain Jennings had produced designs for the gardens of the Prince of Wales at Richmond, presumably this was his expertise, while Tradescant's strengths lay in his plantsmanship. By 1612 two ornamental gardens had been laid out in front of the principal apartments of the house, above a great water parterre. Also part of the garden was a kitchen garden, a huge orchard, and a vineyard. As secretary of state, Robert Cecil was a man of influence, and so received many plants as gifts. From Madame de la Broderie, the wife of the French ambassador, came 30,000 vines. From the French Queen, Marie de' Medici, 500 fruit trees along with two experts to supervise the planting. And from the widowed Lady Tresham at Lyveden New Bield, fifty orchard trees: not the huge number provided by Queen Marie, but no doubt greatly valued by Cecil, who had earlier sent Jennings over to Lyveden to view 'one of the fairest Orchards that is in England . . . to pick some such observations as may enable him to spend my money to better purpose'.[9] Lady Tresham in her turn wrote: 'I think no one can furnish you with more and better trees and of fitter growth than this ground, for my late husband, as he did take great delight, so did he come to great experience and judgement therein.'[10] Robert Cecil died on 24 May 1612, so never lived to enjoy his magnificent new garden.

Like his cousin Robert Cecil, Francis Bacon combined statesmanship with an enthusiasm for gardening – but in addition he was an eminent lawyer, eventually becoming Lord Chancellor, and natural philosopher, regarded as the pioneer of empirical science in England. For the Christmas and New Year festivities of Gray's Inn in 1594–95, Bacon wrote a series of six speeches on the choices of life. One of these pleaded the cause of philosophy, urging: 'the collecting of a most perfect and general library, wherein whatsoever the wit of man hath heretofore committed to books of worth, be they ancient or modern'; 'a spacious wonderful garden wherein whatsoever plant the sun of diverse climates, out of the earth of divers moulds, either wild or by the culture of man brought forth'; 'a goodly huge cabinet wherein whatsoever the hand of man by exquisite art or engine hath made rare in stuff, form or motion'; and lastly a still-house or laboratory 'so furnished with mills, instruments, furnaces, and vessels, as may be a palace fit for a philosopher's stone'.[11] Although this was not the choice that carried the day, it is revealing of the interests and attitudes of Bacon.

Gray's Inn, where he had lodgings, provided the setting for an early gardening venture for Francis Bacon. In 1597 he began to create walks in one of the enclosures just north of the buildings of the inn, planting them with trees, particularly birch, cherry and elm, and flowers such as eglantine, pinks, violets and primroses. In 1608 the gardener Richard Brookes was paid £2 'towards the makinge of the mount', and later payments refer to a banqueting house built on top of it. A bowling alley was then added, along with a second banqueting house, providing the lawyers of Gray's Inn with an area in which to promenade, an early example in London of a kind of public park.

In 1595, from his half brother, Edward, Francis bought the lease of Twickenham Park, a suburban retreat just over the river from Richmond Palace, and here he proceeded to create an extraordinary garden. A plan of this was drawn by the architect Robert Smythson, c. 1609, a year after Bacon had sold the house to Lucy Harington, Countess of Bedford. Lucy was one of Queen Anne's closest friends, and like her combined cultivation with extravagance, presiding over a brilliant circle of poets and men of letters, so that the Twickenham garden is often attributed to her. However, she would have been unlikely to have created such a complex design in so short a time, and it is probable that this was Bacon's work.[12] According to Smythson, the garden was laid out in a series of concentric circles based on a plan of the pre-Copernican universe. In each corner steps led down to viewpoints that enabled the visitor to see Earth in the centre, with Luna, Mercury and Venus in circles of birch, lime circles for Sol and Mars, and a fruit circle for Jove, with Saturn on the outside. The layout of the garden at Chastleton in Oxfordshire is believed to be a nineteenth-century version of this concept. The planting at Twickenham would appear to be dense, with many hedges and no flowers, and recalls the labyrinth garden at Castello, just outside Florence, created for Cosimo de' Medici in the mid-sixteenth century.

If Twickenham is indeed Bacon's creation, his gardening activities were intense in the first years of the seventeenth century. In 1602 his mother, Anne Bacon, gave him the house and garden at Gorhambury that had been created half a century earlier by his father Nicholas. Francis began to build an elaborate water garden, and according to his journal in 1608 he devised a plan for an island in a lake, making a note to remind himself to ask his cousin Robert Cecil for advice.[13] This concept sounds as if it harked back to the complex water gardens of the previous decade, such as Thomas Tresham's creation at Lyveden New Bield, although Bacon was also drawing on the gardens he had seen at Gaillon and Fontainebleau during a stay in France in the 1570s. The lake at Gorhambury sat in a square walled enclosure which was bordered on the exterior by birch and lime trees. Within this was a walk 25 feet (7.5 metres) in width, and within again was a stream enclosing yet another walk of the same width, bordered by lilies. These all enclosed a second square lake enclosed by gilt balustrading underplanted with flowers and strawberry plants. A bridge led to a large central island, 100 feet (30 metres) in breadth, on which stood a house 'with an upper galery open upon the water, a tarace above that, and a supping roome open under that; a dyning roome, a bedd chamber, a Cabanett, and a Roome for Musike'.[14] More islands were planned for the lake, accessible only by boat. One was to be planted with hornbeam, another with 'flowres in ascents'; another 'with an arbour of Musk roses sett with double violets for scent in Autumn'; another was to have a grotto; another a treehouse. Each island was to be adorned with the statue of an appropriate nymph or triton.

The writer and biographer John Aubrey visited Bacon's garden at Gorhambury in 1656 when its glory had rather faded and the island building was about to be sold to two carpenters at a knock-down price. He drew a sketch of it, describing it as a 'curious banqueting-house of Roman architecture with a pavement in black and white diamonds'. Aubrey was astonished by the lakes, which he reckoned covered at least four acres, their bottoms lined with coloured pebbles.[15]

In 1625 Bacon published his third set of essays which included one devoted to gardens. Both his language and his opinions are powerful, with his stirring opening: 'God Almighty first planted a garden. And indeed, it is the purest of human pleasures. It is the greatest refreshment in the spirits of man; without which, buildings and palaces are but gross handy-works'.[16] He then goes on to

IX One of a set of tapestries commissioned by Robert Dudley for a banqueting house. In the centre is his coat of arms, topped by a bear with a ragged staff, and flanked by scenes from gardens with elaborate fountains.

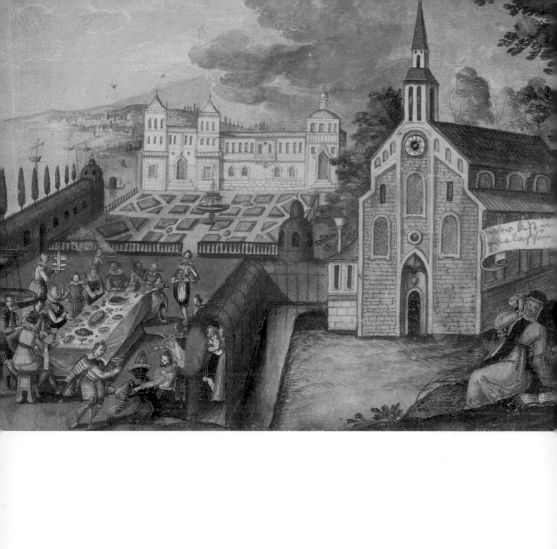

X & XI Favourite activities in the garden are shown in these paintings from the 'friendship album' of Gervasius Fabricius of Salzburg, dating from the early seventeenth century. Left: dining alfresco in an arbour. Below: ladies at their embroidery listening to a singer accompanied on the virginal.

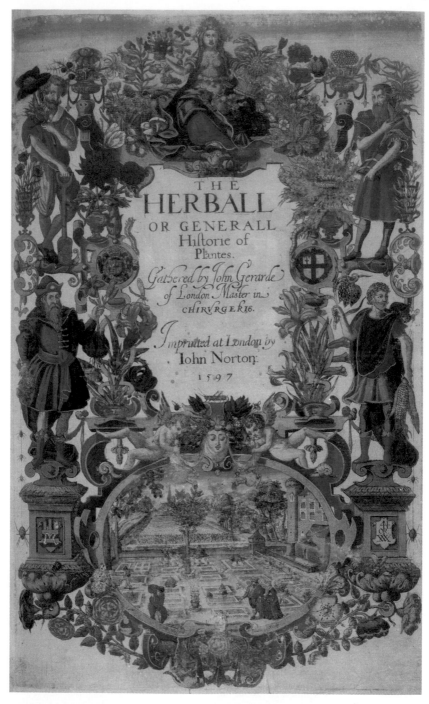

THE
HERBALL
OR GENERALL
Historie of
Plantes.

Gathered by John Gerarde
of London Master in
CHIRVRGERIE.

Imprinted at London by
Iohn Norton.
1597

XII The elaborate title page of John Gerard's herbal published in London in 1597. Flora presides over a group of gardeners carrying a variety of plants and vegetables. Among the flowers depicted are pinks, sunflowers and Crown Imperials. At the foot of the page is a garden with raised beds, probably based on a Continental engraving. This coloured edition of the herbal was presented to the newly established Bodleian Library in Oxford by the publisher, John Norton.

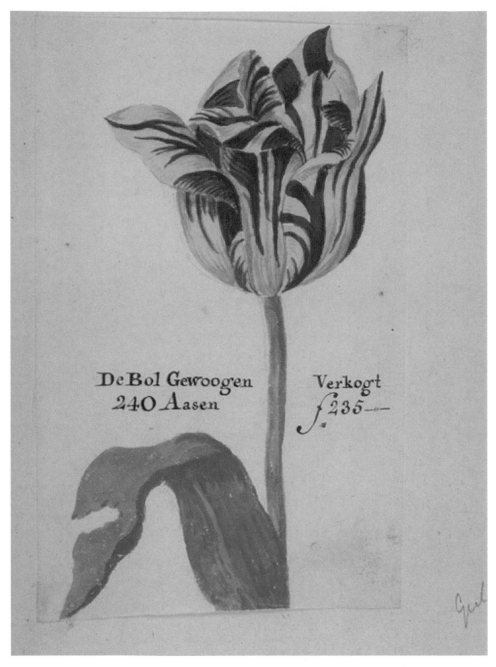

De Bol Gewoogen
240 Aasen

Verkogt
ƒ 235—

XIII A page from the tulip book of Pieter Cos, 1637. This tulip, 'Gel en Rot van Leijen' (Yellow and Red from Leiden), is accompanied by the weight of the bulb and the price achieved at sale.

XIV A mid-seventeenth-century painting by an unknown artist of Massey's Court at Llanerch, Denbighshire. The land, arranged in two terraced gardens, falls steeply from the manor house towards the

river. Experts think that Robert Cecil's garden at Hatfield House would have had a similar arrangement.

XV Painting by an unknown artist of the south front of Newburgh Priory, Yorkshire, showing the development in formal gardens. Next to the house is the earlier garden, laid out in symmetrical patterns of grass plats and beds, probably *c.* 1600. In the foreground the gardens are still formal, but the patterns are much more fluid, using box to surround flower beds and clipped trees in the mid-seventeenth-century style.

list the flowers and trees that should be grown in the garden at various times in the year, showing in the range of plants yet another facet of his encyclo-paedic mind. He starts off with evergreens that will provide a show throughout winter: holly, bay, juniper, pineapple trees and 'mirtles if they be stooved'. In spring he celebrates the blossoms of the cherry, damson, plum, and lilac. In high summer he advises the gillyflowers, musk roses, and the early fruits. These he explains are based on the climate of London, but he leaves the reader to work out what adjustments to make for their area of the country. He goes on to note the flowers that can provide scent, or breath as he puts it. Thus he commends wallflowers to be set under a ground-floor window, and the 'cordial smell' of strawberry leaves as they die off. But above all he favours the violet, especially the double-white that flowered twice a year, and which he had chosen for autumn scent on his island garden at Gorhambury.

Bacon, born into a world of privilege and wealth, recommended that a garden should be no less than thirty acres in dimension, and divided into three parts: green (four acres); main garden (twelve acres); and heath around it (nineteen acres). The green should consist of short grass with covered, pleached alleys. The main should be square, surrounded with a hedge upon a bank of flowers six feet high, supported by arches of carpentry work, set with tiny aviaries and turrets, or 'some other little figure, with broad plates of round coloured glass, gilt, for the sun to play upon'.

Some gardens of this period used coloured earth for knots rather than herbs and flowers. Bacon did not approve of this, saying they reminded him of the ornate patterned tarts that were the gastronomic fashion. Nor did he like topiary work of animals and symbols, which he thought were best left to chil-dren. Rather he advised broad walks, low hedges, pyramids, decorative wooden columns, and a mount in the middle of the garden with a banqueting house atop, as he had created at Gray's Inn. Despite his own water garden, he declared that pools would 'mar all, and make the garden unwholesome, and full of flies and frogs'. The bottom and sides of pools should be lined with images, embellished with coloured glass, the style he had adopted at Gorhambury. Hero of Alexandria and his waterworks were dismissed as 'pretty things to look on, but nothing to health and sweetness'. Bacon, hurt by the treachery of James I and his favourite, Buckingham, that had allowed him as Lord Chancellor to be impeached for taking bribes, was looking back nostalgically to the gardens of his youth, to Theobalds and Kenilworth.

Within a year of the publication of the essays, Bacon was dead. Legend has it that he was killed by his own scientific empiricism, stuffing a chicken with

snow to test its preservative properties and dying from a chill. His servant
Thomas Bushell, however, 'in obedience to my dead lord's philosophical
advice' resolved to follow his precepts as laid out in *New Atlantis*, published in
1627, the year after Bacon's death. Here Bacon wrote an account of a visit to
an imaginary Pacific island and of the social conditions prevailing there, along
with 'Solomon's House', a college of natural philosophy 'dedicated to the study
of the works and creatures of God'. Bushell thus first retired to live as a hermit
on Lundy in the Bristol Channel, and on his return created a garden on a little
estate he had inherited at Enstone in Oxfordshire. This was completed for the
visit of Charles I and his Queen, Henrietta Maria, in August 1636. The royal
couple were shown how Bushell had harnessed natural springs by means of
pipes and conduits to create a grotto complete with elaborate water effects, in
contravention of Bacon's disapproval of such 'pretty things'.

Another visitor described some of the effects on display: 'many strange
forms of Beasts, Fishes and Fowles doth appear; and with the pretty

42 The grotto at Enstone in
Oxfordshire, created between
1628 and 1635 by Thomas
Bushell, was built into the
basement of his hermitage. It
offered spectacular effects,
including a water curtain over
the entrance, far right.

murmuring of the Springs; the gentle running, falling and playing of the water; the beating of a Drum; the chirping of a Nightingale, and many other strange, rare and audible sounds and noyses doth highly worke upon any Mans fancy'. The garden did not consist solely of water effects, for the approach to Bushell's little house, where he lived in three cells like a hermit, was by terraces interconnected with flights of steps and planted with fruit trees, while flower gardens lay on the other side. But the overall effect was one of strangeness, and the visitor finished his account by describing Bushell as: 'A mad gim-crack yet heriditary to these Hermeticall and Proiecticall Undertakers'.[17] As Roy Strong observes, Bushell was behaving like a magus, a Prospero figure, harnessing the magic properties of water and leading a life of solitude and religious contemplation which brought him closer to the studies of Elizabeth I's astrologer Dr John Dee than the practical exploration of the physical world as expounded by Francis Bacon.[18]

Just as Robert Cecil and Francis Bacon inherited the enthusiasm for creating fine gardens from their fathers, so Bess of Hardwick seems to have bequeathed her passion for building to her youngest son, Charles. In 1608 he acquired the mediaeval ruined fortress of Bolsover in Derbyshire from his close friend Gilbert Talbot, seventh Earl of Shrewsbury, who was also his step-brother through the triple Eglantine wedding of 1567. On the dramatic hill-side site, he began to create a little Gothic keep, with turrets, battlements and arrow-loops. This was not a castle built for defence, but rather for pleasure, a retreat from the great house of Welbeck Abbey that Charles Cavendish had also bought from Gilbert Talbot. Bolsover resembled in purpose, though not in form, the pavilions of pleasure often known as *casini* built by Italian prelates such as Cardinal Gambara at the Villa Lante, and Thomas Tresham's garden lodge at Lyveden New Bield, where normal life could be set aside to study, to enjoy music and to eat banquets. The little castle at Bolsover was designed for Charles Cavendish by his surveyor, John Smythson, and bears a close resemblance to one of the backdrops designed by Inigo Jones for the masque, *Oberon*, performed in honour of Prince Henry of Wales in 1611.

When Charles Cavendish died in 1617 the development of Bolsover passed to his elder son, William. Although Charles once declared in a letter to his sister that Italian houses had draughty halls and dining rooms, and that the diet was 'but salads and frogs', he was happy to send William to Italy.[19] In 1612 he travelled with the diplomat Sir Henry Wotton to the court of Savoy to carry out the tricky diplomatic task of informing the Duke that the Prince of Wales did not wish to marry his daughter. William Cavendish's interest in architecture would have been nurtured by Wotton, later the author of *Elements of Architecture*. While Charles Cavendish wished to evoke Gothic chivalry, his son was firmly of the classical persuasion, and furnished Bolsover Castle with features such as the highly inventive fireplaces that were probably based on engravings by Serlio.

He also laid out a small garden in the Italian style, with paths and grass in simple patterns around a large, elaborate fountain of Venus. The goddess of love, shown rising from her bath, was based upon a sculpture by Giambologna, but the local carver produced a rather more wholesome girl with feet that squirted water into the basin. Below her, four little boys in dark marble also squirted jets of water, as if urinating, while a set of Roman Emperors in the circular basin that formed the base of the fountain peered up at the naked goddess. Interspersed with these lascivious figures were heraldic beasts with enlarged genitals, along with horned satyrs and griffins. This wonderful ensemble, combining refined learning with coarse humour, must have come as rather a surprise to Charles I and Henrietta Maria when they visited Bolsover in 1634 to watch a masque, *Love's Welcome*, that William Cavendish commissioned from Ben Jonson. The Venus Fountain has been recreated from fragments and documentary records by English Heritage.

As part of his education as a young gentleman, William Cavendish had been brought up in the household of Gilbert Talbot alongside Shrewsbury's three clever daughters: Mary, who became Countess of Pembroke and presided over the garden at Wilton; Elizabeth, who became Countess of Kent; and Alethea, who married another of the Earl's friends, Thomas Howard, Earl of Arundel. Gilbert Talbot became a great support for Howard, whose early life had been blighted by his patrimony. Thomas Howard's father, Philip, first Earl of Arundel, was sent to the Tower of London for his Catholic sympathies shortly before his son's birth in 1585. This was a time of high tension, with Elizabeth I under pressure to rid herself of her troublesome cousin, Mary Queen of Scots, and the increasing threat of a Spanish invasion. Arundel died in the Tower ten years later, never having seen his son and heir, who was brought up by his embittered mother, Anne Dacre. Recognising that Thomas Howard, now Lord Arundel, had an interest in gardens, the Earl of Essex described him as a 'winter pear', a late developer, and his judgement proved a shrewd one. Howard blossomed under the influence of Gilbert Talbot, a man of culture, especially interested in architecture, and in 1606 he married Talbot's youngest daughter, Alethea.

In 1612 Arundel paid his first visit to Italy, arriving in Padua in September, but this was cut short when he learnt of the sudden death of Prince Henry.

The following year Princess Elizabeth married Frederick, Elector Palatine, and Arundel, together with his Countess and Inigo Jones, formerly Prince Henry's surveyor, were part of the entourage that accompanied the royal couple to Heidelberg. En route they visited nurseries in the Low Countries, and the English agent in Brussels, William Trumbull, who had helped Tradescant with his purchases, arranged for the Arundel plants to be transported back to their villa in Highgate, just north of London. This garden was organised by Alethea, who clearly had an interest in horticulture, for John Aubrey attributes to her the introduction into England of the cherry laurel. Despite the fact that she was an extremely strong-minded woman – the marriage turned out to be a stormy one – Alethea's role in the creation of the Arundel gardens remains tantalisingly unclear.

This was also the second Italian visit for Inigo Jones, who had travelled here some time between 1597 and 1603, although he seems on that occasion to have concentrated on looking at paintings rather than garden design. Like Tradescant, Jones's early life is obscure, but he was probably the son of a debt-ridden cloth worker from St Benet's, Paul's Wharf, and started his career as a scene painter, before joining the design team who created the house and gardens for Robert Cecil at Hatfield House. For both Arundel and Jones the twenty-one months that they spent in Italy from 1613 came as a revelation. The Earl acquired chests of architectural drawings by Andrea Palladio and Scamozzi. In Rome he began to develop his collection of statuary, supervising excavations and buying from dealers, commissioning the English ambassador in Constantinople, Sir Thomas Roe, and sending his own chaplain, William Petty, to search out more in Greece and Asia.

Returning to England, Arundel set about reorganising the garden of his London home, Arundel House, which stood on the north bank of the Thames. The layout of the garden echoed that of next-door Somerset House, with rectangles of grass planted with trees along the edges to form walks. But in the east garden some of the statuary collected during the Arundels' European tour was placed along a wide terrace that ran parallel with the river. This collection continued to grow through the years, so that by the 1630s, there were 32 statues, 128 busts, 250 inscriptions, sarcophagi and altars. One of the 'eye-catchers' was a giant head of Jove that Arundel was given by the diplomat Dudley Carleton, which the Earl placed in the garden so that it could be glimpsed by visitors entering his sculpture gallery within the house. Howard also acquired land on the south bank of the river, in Lambeth, and placed more of his collection there, using the Thames as a kind of water feature. In the following century, this area became a pleasure garden, Cupid's Garden. At the end of his essay on gardens, Francis Bacon expressed his disapproval of 'great princes' sometimes adding 'Statuas, and such Things for State and Magnificence, but nothing to the true Pleasure of a Garden'.[20] Little wonder, then, that on arriving in Arundel's garden 'where there were a great number of Ancient Statues of naked men and women', Francis Bacon is reputed to have cried out 'The Resurrection!'[21] Londoners must have been equally astonished when floating past a gigantic god's head sitting cheek by jowl with the Mount Parnassus of Somerset House.

Inigo Jones's contribution to the garden at Arundel House was to design a charming garden gate in the Italian style. However, as with gardens of the previous half century, the Italian style was being applied through features rather than imbuing the garden as a whole. The Arundels were trying to create a Renaissance garden on a cramped riverside site, next to a rambling Elizabethan house. John Aubrey had no doubt that it was his kinsman, Sir John Danvers, who was the 'first who taught us the way of Italian Gardens' in his relatively small garden in Chelsea.[22] Danvers had travelled extensively in France and Italy before creating his garden in 1622, at the very time that his older brother Henry, later Earl of Danby, was establishing the first botanical garden in Britain by donating land and a site to Oxford University. The two brothers, however, had fallen out over John's marriage to Lady Magdalen Herbert, a widow twenty years his senior with ten children, including Lord Herbert of Cherbury and the poet George Herbert. Although Henry Danvers may have disapproved of her, Magdalen was much beloved by Donne, who composed an elegy to her with the opening lines:

No spring, nor summer beauty hath such grace,
As I have seen in one autumnal face.[23]

John Aubrey was so excited by the garden in Chelsea that he made a rough sketch of it, and wrote a detailed description. From the outset the garden and house had been conceived as one entity, so that 'As you sitt at Dinner in the Hall you are entertaind with two delightfull Visto's: one southward over the Thames & to Surrey: the other northward into that curious Garden'. Visitors entering the garden from the *piano nobile* did so by a double flight of steps, with a wall 'to hinder the immediate pleasure and totall view'.[24] This idea echoes the advice given by Sir Henry Wotton in his treatise *Elements of Architecture*, published in 1624, that not all should be revealed at once from the terrace, but that there should be 'a delightfull confusion'.[25]

Centred axially to the house, Danvers's garden was divided into three, alternately open and hidden spaces. On arriving at the bottom of the steps from the house, there lay a wilderness of sweetbriars, lilac, syringas, holly and juniper, intermingled with apple and pear trees divided into walks. In the middle of these stood polychrome statues of a gardener and his wife by the sculptor Nicholas Stone. Emerging from the east and west sides of the garden were two wide gravel walks, each terminated at the end nearest the house by statues – Hercules and Antaeus, Cain and Abel. The walks were bordered with hyssop backed by more than twenty-four varieties of thyme and, according to Aubrey, on a fine summer morning John Danvers would brush his beaver hat on the herbs to acquire their scent. Between the walks was a huge oval bowling green, surrounded by a walk, with access on four sides. Statues of shepherds and shepherdesses flanked three of the entrances, while a fourth was guarded by sphinxes. All this was surrounded by a wall of cypress trees and spandrels. At the far end of the garden Danvers dug a deep trench to form a terrace walk, and in the centre of the dip was a grotto with a banqueting house, lit by stained glass. This northern terrace was terminated at each end by summer houses.

With his statues of shepherds and shepherdesses Danvers was making his garden Arcady. Aubrey praised the sculptor for 'expressing Love-passions in the very freestone: where you read rustic beauty mixt with antique innocent simplicitie'.[26] The sphinxes were the symbols of ancient wisdom, complementing the allusions of Golden Age pastoral innocence of shepherds. So the visitor entering the garden was acting out the search for ancient wisdom, a return to the Eden before Man's fall.

Danvers's garden, with its novel ideas, represented the prototype from which the Italian garden style spread through England during the next decades. One such garden can be glimpsed in the background of the portrait of the Capel family by Cornelius Johnson. It shows Hadham Hall in Hertfordshire, which was inherited by Arthur, first Baron Capel, in 1632. Although opposed to Charles I's attempt to extort Ship Money from his subjects, Lord Capel was very much part of the court, and was executed by the Parliamentarians during the Civil War. Johnson's portrait of the family echoes the famous Van Dyck depiction of Charles I with Henrietta Maria and their children. Capel was able to embark on his ambitious garden because in 1627 he married Elizabeth Morrison, a rich heiress who came from a gardening family. Her grandfather, Sir Baptist Hickes, had laid out a major garden at Chipping Campden in Gloucestershire, the bones of which are still to be seen, along with his delightful banqueting houses. The horticultural genes continued

43 Cornelius Johnson's portrait of the Capel family, painted *c.* 1639. Sir Arthur created the fine Italianate garden at Little Hadham in Hertfordshire, which can be seen in the background. His eldest daughter, Mary, on the right, became one of the great gardeners of the late seventeenth century as Duchess of Beaufort, while Elizabeth, the child offering a rose to the baby, was a skilled flower painter. Two of their brothers also had fine gardens, Arthur at Cassiobury Park and Henry at Kew.

in the Capel family, for Lord Capel's two sons both created fine gardens, his daughter Elizabeth, Lady Carnarvon, was a skilled flower painter, and his other daughter, Mary, as Duchess of Beaufort at Badminton collected exotics from all over the world.

If Johnson's depiction of the garden at Hadham is accurate, the garden had terraces on two levels looking down onto the parterre. A central broad path cut through the compartments of the parterre, to a grotto house with a garden gate leading out into the countryside beyond. This gate was one of three at Hadham, all in the style that Inigo Jones had adopted at Arundel House. This suggests that Jones may have had a hand in the creation of Capel's garden, possibly in conjunction with Isaac de Caus, Salomon's younger brother, and Nicholas Stone.[27]

The combination of de Caus, Stone and Jones worked on one of the grandest gardens of the Caroline period, Wilton House. In 1630 Philip Herbert, fourth Earl of Pembroke, inherited the estate from his older brother, William, and set out on an ambitious modernisation scheme. The house where in the 1580s and 1590s Mary Sidney had gathered round her a circle of poets, thinkers and scientists was demolished and a new mansion, designed in the Palladian style by Inigo Jones, was begun. At the same time Herbert swept away a garden symbolic of the trinity that Adrian Gilbert, half-brother to Sir Walter Raleigh, had created for his sister-in-law, Mary Talbot. We know a lot about the new garden from a book of engraved views and plans published in the mid-1640s. Aligned to the proposed central portico of the south front of the new house, it was divided into three parts. Nearest the house was a formal area of four compartments in the fashionable broderie style with hedges of clipped box, and at the centre of each stood a fountain with a statue of a female deity by Nicholas Stone. Next came a wilderness, densely planted, through which flowed the River Nadder. Finally there was an oval circus, similar in style to the one in Sir John Danvers's Chelsea garden. In the centre stood a copy of the famous Borghese gladiator by Le Sueur, surrounded by cherry trees. Behind him was a vaulted grotto, probably by de Caus, with water pipes imitating the singing of nightingales.

44 An engraving by Isaac de Caus of the garden that he helped to lay out at Wilton in the 1630s for the fourth Earl of Pembroke. He has taken his viewpoint from the south front of the house, showing the three parts of the garden: the formal garden with the scrolling broderie parterres; the wilderness with the River Nadder flowing through; and the oval circus in front of a grotto.

Philip Herbert was Charles I's Lord Chamberlain, and presided over the entertainments of his court. One of the most expensive masques ever staged was *The Shepherd's Paradise*, designed by Inigo Jones, and performed on Twelfth Night 1633 at Somerset House. Lasting over seven hours, and largely inaudible, it was not a great dramatic success, but two of the drawings by Jones survive at Chatsworth. These show a remarkable relationship to Wilton, with a colonnade of trees looking towards a great house, which in reality was still only on the drawing board: a glimpse of Arcadia from the very park where Philip Sidney had created his masterpiece.

The broderie compartments at Wilton were of a fashion that originated in France around 1614, when Claude Mollet laid out the spectacular gardens at St Germain en Laye and Fontainebleau for Henri IV. The style may have been introduced to England by Henrietta Maria when she married Charles I in 1625, for the French princess had inherited from both her father, Henri IV, and her mother, Marie de' Medici, an interest in gardens, and in court masques she often appeared in horticultural guise, symbolising the springtime goddess bringing peace after the storms. When Charles gave her the gardens of Anne of Denmark at Oatlands, Somerset House and Greenwich, she employed

45 'A simple parterre of embroidery': this style of parterre may have been introduced to England by Henrietta Maria when she married Charles I in 1625.

André Mollet, son of Claude, to modernise the parterres in the new style. And when the Queen bought Thomas Cecil's Wimbledon House in 1639, Mollet designed new formal parterres there for her too.

Henrietta's role as the bringer of peace after the storms proved a false one. Even as she and Mollet were embarking on the garden at Wimbledon, the quarrel between the King and Parliament was edging towards crisis. In 1642 Charles I raised his standard at Nottingham, signalling the beginning of the Civil War. Looking back at these times, Clarendon described the 1630s as 'the garden of the world', a time of 'the greatest calm and the fullest measure of felicity that any people of any age, for so long time together, have been blessed with'.[28] Now this world was falling apart, and the creating of great gardens had drawn to a close.

***

The creators of the gardens described above were all part of the Stuart court circle, wealthy and high in status. They were able to gain information and ideas from the architectural treatises in their family libraries, or increasingly available through the developing book trade. In addition, there was Sir Henry Wotton's *Elements of Architecture*. This was not a practical book, containing neither plans nor elevations, but more a reassurance of what a gentleman should be thinking about when planning to build his house or lay out his garden.

Another publication that was not practical in any way, but could be used as a source for both house and garden, was the emblem book. This had proved one of the most popular genres since Andrea Alciati produced his *Emblemata* in 1531. The best early English examples were Geoffrey Whitney's *A Choice of Emblems* of 1586, and Henry Peacham's *Minerva Britanna* of 1612. Peacham, who became tutor to the children of Thomas Howard, Lord Arundel, sub-titled his book 'a garden of Heroical Devises, furnished and adorned with Emblemes and Impresa's of sundry natures', and went on to explain in his preface that the true use of emblems was 'to feede at once both the minde, and eie, by expressing mistically and doubtfully, our disposition, either to Love, Hatred, Clemencie, Iustice, Pietie, our Victories, Misfortunes, Griefes, and the like'.

Sir Henry Hobart clearly had a copy of Peacham's *Britanna* in his collection, for it was used in the decoration of both his new house and garden at Blickling Hall in Norfolk, completed in 1627. In the magnificent long gallery, the plasterwork ceiling contains twenty-one emblems copied from Peacham expressing, among other subjects, womanly beauty and the power of love, kingly majesty and kingly cares, divine wisdom and pity. On a wet day, the visitor might peruse the ceiling to improve their mind, but on a warm summer's morning, they could descend into the garden and view one of the pavilions, where a tree rose through a dome as in one of Peacham's garden emblems. The seventeenth century formal gardens have long gone, but the pavilion can be glimpsed in the background of a portrait dating from the 1620s, which Sir Roy Strong has linked with Blickling.[29]

Such books were for those with time and money to spend on their gardens. But advice was on hand for those with more modest aspirations. In 1613 Gervase Markham published the first part of his *English Husbandman*. Of gentry stock from Nottinghamshire, he described himself as 'onley a horseman', but his book on the care of horses, *A Discource of Horsemanshippe*, proved very successful, and in its various guises appears in many gentlemen's libraries of the period. The range of his writings was wide, including poetry and the completion of a prose version of Sir Philip Sidney's *Arcadia*. The *English Husbandman* begins with practical information on 'the Knowledge of the true Nature of every soyle within that kingdome, how to Plow it and the manner of the plough, and other instruments belonging thereto'. It then passes on to 'the Art of Planting, Grafting and Gardening after our latest and rarest fashion', including how to lay out knot gardens. The reference to 'that kingdome' is significant, for Markham disapproved of the tendency among English writers on husbandry to translate and paraphrase works from classical times, such as Virgil's *Georgics*, and from modern European authors, for they were 'all forrainers and utterly unacquainted with our climbes'.[30]

Markham considered the arrangement of the gardens, orchards and service areas in relation to the house, recommending 'You shall place the upper or best end of your house, as namely where your dining parlor and cheifest roomes are, which ever would have their prospect into your garden, to the South'.[31] The orchard should be an area that combined pleasure and profit, and he advised a simple layout divided into quarters in which a wide range of fruit and nut trees might be cultivated.

Although he refers to the practices and designs to be seen in great gardens, Markham claims that he is aiming his book at the 'plaine russet honest Husbandman'. For instance, he provides a table to give the meaning of hard words, thus defining the chive as 'a small rounde hearbe growing in Gardens, like little young onions or Scullions not above a weeke old'. When looking at designs for knots, he disdains the desire for novelties, choosing rather simple, traditional layouts. Nevertheless, the concept of the plain russet husbandman has to be taken with a pinch of salt, for the garden would have to be of some size in order to accommodate a flower garden, an orchard, and also possibly an area for the cultivation of hops. The market at which he is aiming is that of the small landowner, and one man who may well have taken his advice was Sir John Oglander.

Sir John lived at Nunwell near Brading on the Isle of Wight, and kept a commonplace book in the 1630s. He was an enthusiastic gardener, recording in 1632:

> I have with my own hands planted two orchards at Nunwell: the Lower with pippins, pearmains, puttes, hornies and other good apples and all sorts of good pears: in the other, cherries, damsons and plums. In the upper garden, apricocks, mellacatoons [melons] and figs. In the Parlour Garden, in one knot, all sorts of French flowers and tulips of all sorts: some roots cost me 10d a root. In the Court, vines and apricocks: in the Bowling Green, the vine and an infinity of raspberries. Insomuch as ... I have now made it a fit place for any gent.

He also planted a hop garden, and set out to make it a profitable enterprise: 'My hop-garden was the first in the Island that was made according to art. I brought 2 men from Farnham to plant mine and I have had in it 1000lbs in a year being not full an acre of ground. A hop garden, if it be in good ground, well-ordered and dunged, will return a great profit. I have often made £50 on an acre of ground according to the proportion.'[32]

Markham was a canny operator, protecting his own book with his concern about the work of 'forrainers'. He was referring specifically to *La Maison Rustique*, which, despite its 'infinite excellency', was 'proper and natural to France'.[33] It didn't stop him publishing an edition of the book in 1616 as *The Country Farm* 'augmented by GM'. *La Maison Rustique* was first produced by the physician publisher Charles Estienne in Paris in 1554, with an augmented edition appearing sixteen years later when fellow physician Jean Liebault joined forces with him. An English translation by Richard Surflet first appeared in 1600. This is an encyclopaedic work of nearly 1,000 pages in quarto. The breadth of the subject matter is demonstrated in the reverse of the title page to the English edition:

> There is contained in this last edition whatsoever can be required for the building or good ordering of a husbandmans house or countrie Farme: as

namely to foresee the charge and alteration of the times, to know the motions, and powers of the Sunne and Moone, upon the things about which husbandrie is occupied, as to cure the sicke labouring man, and to cure beasts and flying fowls of all sorts, to dresse, plante or make gardens as well for the kitchen and phisicke use.

After this ambitious start the book proceeds to offer help on all kinds of herbs, including tobacco and quinine, the planting of trees, including oranges and lemons, the keeping of bees, recipes for the still-room and the brewery, the care of silkworms, the organisation and stocking of fishponds, the baking of bread, the trimming of vines and the running of a rabbit warren. It was the Mrs Beeton of its day, commemorated in our times by the Maison Rustique book-shop in Paris, where all kinds of gardening books may be purchased.

A book of this size must have been beyond the price range of many 'russet husbandmen'; French editions were owned by John Evelyn and his friends, Sir Henry and Elizabeth Puckering. The English edition is listed in the library catalogues of William Cavendish, Earl of Devonshire, and of Robert Cecil. Sir Henry Danvers gave a copy to Elinor Fettiplace to help her with her garden and still-room, and the Virginia Company dispatched a copy across the Atlantic, making it one of the key books in the establishment of the colony in New England. The section on tobacco must have proved useful to the colonists, for John Rolfe had begun to plant seed of the sweeter kind, imported from Trinidad and South America.

Both Markham's *English Husbandman* and *La Maison Rustique* contained no illustrations beyond suggested designs for knots and labyrinths. However, William Lawson in his *New Orchard and Garden*, published in 1618, includes a plan for an ideal garden providing on a small scale the fashionable layouts of the time. Paula Henderson suggests that Lawson may have taken a simplified form of the garden created for Robert Cecil at Hatfield.[34] The house is shown at the top with access to the garden by a bridge over a moat. The garden itself is divided into three parts, flanked by tree-lined walks. A mount at each corner supports four little houses; the two nearest the house are indicated as still-houses, although one was probably for banqueting; the other two are designated as standings for bees. Six square compartments include an orchard arranged in quincunxes, a knot garden, kitchen gardens and possibly a horse and swordsman as topiary.

William Lawson was a clergyman who became vicar of Ormesby in the North Riding of Yorkshire in 1583, and his book refers many times to his

46 William Lawson's ideal layout for the garden of a moderate-sized household from his *New Orchard and Garden*, published in 1618.

own experience of gardening on the banks of the River Tees. He was Puritan in his attitudes, a friend of the pious Lady Margaret Hoby. However, while she frets in her diary about her gardening rendering her neglectful of her devotional reading, Lawson shows a delight in flowers, makes jokes about knots and knotty problems, and gives away his fruit to stop his neighbours from pilfering, advising 'For as liberality will save it best from noisome neighbours, (Liberability I say is the best fence) so justice must restrain Rioters.' It has been suggested that the mention of rioters could refer to disturbances in the 1590s when there was such a dearth of food, as described in Chapter 2.[35]

Lawson's table of contents on the title page of *A New Orchard* lays out three sections. First, the 'Best way of planting and grafting, and to make ground good, for a rich orchard, particularly in the north parts of England, generally for the whole kingdome'. Secondly he provides a garden for the 'country

26 *Of Grafting.* *An Orchard.* Chap.10.

CHAP. X.

47 Gardeners at work in an orchard from William Lawson's *New Orchard*, illustrating how to make and plant grafts.

housewife', following the lead of Thomas Tusser in recognising the important role that women played in gardening. He promises to look at the 'vertues' and 'seasons' for herbs, along with a variety of knots and models for trees. Thirdly he looks at the husbandry of bees, 'with their severall uses and annoyances, all grounded as the Principles of Art, and precepts of experience, being the Labours of forty-eight years of William Lawson'.

Lawson specified the best uses for the different fruit trees, with plum, cherry and damson for borders or to cover a mount. Orchard squares were reserved for quince, apple and pear. Another illustration shows the ideal shape of an apple tree to ensure health, strength and productivity. Apple trees were to be planted about 24 feet (7.5 metres) apart to allow sufficient room for growth over thirty or forty years, while the spaces in between could be used as a nursery for the cultivation of saffron, liquorice, roots, flowers and herbs – all invaluable for the still-room and kitchen.

Lawson and Markham knew each other: for instance, Markham refers to Lawson when talking about bee-keeping in his subsequent book *The Country*

Housewife's Garden of 1626.[36] Constantly reissuing his own books and borrowing from others, Markham absorbed Lawson's texts into a compilation, *A Way to get Wealth*, first published in 1623, with no less than fourteen further editions up to 1695.

A contentious question at this time was whether a garden should provide profit as well as pleasure. As the market for gardening and husbandry books widened in the late sixteenth and early seventeenth centuries, so thrift and profit became important selling points. However, some conservative commentators felt that this attitude posed a threat to the order of society. Estienne, the physician publisher, talked of the menace of the 'saving' tenant. Peacham, who wrote a book entitled *The Complete Gentleman*, combined social prejudice with the observation that Thomas Tusser was not a successful farmer when he included him in *Minerva Britanna*:

> They tell me *Tusser*, when thou wert alive,
> And hadst for profit, turned every stone,
> Where ere thou cammest, thou couldst never thrive.[37]

Gervase Markham had no doubts on the subject, as he demonstrated by choosing the title *A Way to Get Wealth*, a clever and successful move to entice yeomen, country gentlemen and wealthier townsmen – and, of course, their wives – to profitable enterprise as well as the 'purest of human pleasures'.

CHAPTER 7

Curious Gardeners

I N THE SEVENTEENTH CENTURY THE TERM 'CURIOUS' was a mark of intellectual distinction, and in the horticultural world it indicated the collecting and growing of rare and unusual plants. New varieties were being produced from the flowers that had been introduced into Western Europe in the second half of the sixteenth century. For instance, John Gerard in his *Herball* in 1597 grouped tulips into fourteen categories, protesting that to try to describe all the varieties was like trying to 'number the sands'. Thirty years later, John Parkinson outlined sixteen major forms with forty-nine cultivars of *T. praecox* (early flowering), seventy of *media* (mid-season), and five *serotina* (late). Another twenty years, and John Evelyn was told by the French gardener Pierre Morin that there were no fewer than 10,000 kinds of tulip.[1] In particular, gardeners were fascinated by streaks and speckles in petals, and by multiple colours and double varieties. In a remarkable speech in *The Winter's Tale*, written in 1610 or 1611, Shakespeare has Perdita explaining to Polixenes:

> . . . the fairest flowers o' th' season
> Are our carnations and streak'd gillyvors
> Which some call nature's bastards: of that kind
> Our rustic garden's barren, and I care not
> To get slips of them . . .
> For I have heard it said
> There is an art which in their piedness shares
> With great creating nature . . . (Act IV, Scene 3)

Gardeners did not yet realise that plants had sexuality just as much as animals: this only began to be established in the late seventeenth century, when Nehemiah Grew, a Coventry physician, published his *Anatomy of Plants*. In his use of the term 'nature's bastards' Shakespeare is hinting at the possibility of such sexuality, but he is also reflecting the fear that gardeners and botanists had that they might be tampering with God's work. Even in the early eighteenth century, Thomas Fairchild, a nurseryman in Hoxton, finessed the account of his discovery that a carnation might be mated with a Sweet William to create a plant of a 'middle nature', which he called Fairchild's Mule. For extra insurance, at his death he left his parish church the sum of £25 for the preaching of an annual sermon on 'the wonderful works of God in creation', signifying that man could never have been able to produce a new species.

Some 'curious' gardeners came to be known as florists. The horticultural equivalent of bird fanciers, these were the people who developed new varieties of certain plants. The first time the term was used in English was in 1623 when Sir Henry Wotton referred to making the acquaintance of 'some excellent Florists (as they are stiled)'.[2] Half a century later, Samuel Gilbert wrote of 'trifles adorned amongst country women, but of no esteem to a Florist, who is taken up with things of more value'.[3] But the eighteenth-century creator of the modern plant classification system, Carl Linnaeus, was to take a very different view. The multi-coloured and double varieties of flowers developed by florists he called 'monsters', strongly protesting about the pompous names attached to them, and warning, 'These men cultivate a science peculiar to themselves, the mysteries of which are only known to the adepts; nor can knowledge be worth the attention of the botanist, *whereof let no sound botanist ever enter into their societies*'.[4]

The flowers that particularly attracted these 'curious' men were the carnation, anemone, ranunculus and tulip. Later in the seventeenth century they were joined by the auricula and the hyacinth. The tulip was particularly responsive to the selective process: the Turks in the sixteenth century had taken wild species from different parts of the Ottoman Empire, including the Siberian steppes, Afghanistan and the Caucasus, and applied targeted breeding. In Constantinople florists' councils adjudicated admission of new varieties to the official tulip list, according them exquisite names such as 'Delicate Coquette', 'Slim One of the Rose Garden' and 'Beloved's Face'. Prize flowers were displayed singly in narrow-necked vases, *laledan*, from the Turkish for tulip, *lale*. On the tiled walls of mosques and palaces, Iznik artists painted the tulip in the shape favoured by the Turks, with thin waists and pointed petals fanning out like needles.

When the cultivated tulip travelled westwards from the Sublime Porte in the bags of Ogier de Busbecq and other travellers, so too did the passion for the flower, and none took this up more fervently than the Dutch. The Cornish traveller Peter Mundy noted in his journeys through Holland how difficult it was to walk in the countryside, so that the Dutch indulged in 'home delights, as in their streets, houses, roomes, ornamentt [ornaments], Furniture, little gardeins, Flower Potts, in which latter very curious off rare rootes, plantts, Flowers, etts [etc]'; and also how people were paying 'incredible prices For tulip rootes'.[5] Mundy was writing in the 1640s when what the Dutch called 'the wind trade' and we now term 'tulipomania' had passed its peak, but the effects were still very strong.

What particularly attracted Dutch florists was the rich variety in colour and pattern of tulips. All kinds of methods were employed to try to change the colour. Gervase Markham suggested that purple could be achieved by steeping seeds in red wine and then watering the plants with the same. For other colours, he recommended making an insertion between the 'rinde' and the little bulbets that grew on the main bulb. Scarlet could thus be obtained by adding vermillion or cinnabar, dissolved azure for blue, orpiment for yellow and verdigris for green.[6] In an attempt to get stripes, some growers cut the bulbs of red-flowered tulips in half and bound them with halves of bulbs of white-flowered. But all to no avail, for the fantastic variety of breaks that made the tulip so fascinating and dangerously unpredictable was caused by a virus carried by aphids that was only identified in the 1920s. Three categories became particularly sought after: the Rosen or Roses – scarlet, pink or crimson streaks on white; the Violeteen or Bylbloemen – mauve, purple or black on white; and the Bizarden or Bizarres – any colour of flame or feathers on a yellow ground. Of these, the Rosen was the rarest, and by the 1620s 'Semper Augustus' had emerged as the most expensive.

Just as we name new varieties of flowers after celebrities, so the Dutch called their tulips after generals and admirals, though as republicans, they tended to avoid kings and princes. To underline the status of the flower, the Dutch also commissioned portraits of them. These were not the same as the paintings or flowerpieces, for they were generally presented alone on a page, executed in watercolour or gouache, sometimes as single sheets, sometimes bound into tulip albums. Nearly fifty albums have survived, produced by highly skilled artists. One album was compiled by Jacob van Swanenburch of Leiden, who was Rembrandt's master. Another contains two illustrations of tulips by Judith Leyster, a rare example of a female artist. Unusually an album belonging to Pieter Cos and illustrated by Pieter Holsteijn the Younger, dating from 1637, includes information on the price and weight of each bulb, suggesting that it was used as a sales catalogue (Plate XIII).[7]

Tulip sales initially took place in summer, after flowering and the lifting of the bulbs, and before replanting. However, the trade was becoming speculative, with bulbs sold in anticipation before lifting, by middlemen who held auctions in taverns. Tulipomania reached its climax during the winter of 1636–7 when a 'Semper Augustus' fetched 10,000 guilders. An estimate of what this meant in terms of a total of other commodities has become legendary: eight pigs, four oxen, twelve sheep, twenty-four tons of wheat, forty-eight tons of rye, two barrels of wine, four barrels of superior beer, two barrels of butter, 1,000 lbs of cheese, a silver cup, garments, a wardrobe of clothes, a bed complete with bedding and mattress, and a salt cellar in the shape of a ship. Perhaps even more telling is that the tulip trade was valued at about three times that of the Dutch East India Company, then Europe's leading trading organisation.

Then, just like Britain's South Sea Bubble in the early eighteenth century, came the spectacular crash, with the state of Holland attempting to intervene to cancel debts and calm the situation. Further bouts of tulipomania were to occur in France and Turkey in the eighteenth century, while England contracted a bout of mania over hyacinths in the late seventeenth century, but these were all mild in comparison.

Florists began to form themselves into the societies that were later so condemned by Linnaeus. In Holland and the Low Countries these had religious affiliations and were often dedicated to St Dorothy, the patron of flower lovers. In Bruges, for instance, the society had eighteen members, wealthy landowners and high-ranking clergymen, who met on St Dorothy's Day, 6 February, to celebrate Mass and to hold a banquet. In England these societies were secular in style and activities. Detailed evidence is scanty, but a play written by Ralph Knevet has survived in printed form in the Bodleian Library in Oxford. Entitled *Rhodon and Iris*, it was performed at a feast held by the Norwich Florist Society on 3 May 1631. Since the 1570s, Norwich had become home to many 'strangers', Protestant refugees from the Low Countries and France who brought with them their love of flowers and skill in cultivating them. The preface to the play refers to a feast 'celebrated by such a conflux of Gentlemen of birth and quality in whose presence and commerce (I thinke) your cities welfare partly consists', suggesting that merchants were among the members.[8]

Two poems connected with Norwich feasts have also survived in the Bodleian. The first appears in a volume of the poems of William Strode, chaplain to the Bishop of Norwich between 1632 and 1635. Strode was at pains to counter accusations levelled by Puritans in Norwich that such feasts were dedicated to a pagan deity, Flora:

> . . . Our feast we call
> Only with Flowres, from Flora not at all,
> The Springs Returne, the Earths new Livery
> Inheaven'd with aemulous Light of starry Flowres,
> The woodes shrill Chanters singing short the howres
> And all the Ayre thick fill'd with double sweete
> Of Sound and Odour . . .

Only one flower is mentioned by name, the tulip, right at the end of the poem.[9]

The second poem, entitled 'At the Florists Feast in Norwich, Flora wearing a Crown', was published in 1645 in a collection by Matthew Stevenson, *Poems upon Several Occasions*. Stevenson was happy to introduce Flora, who explains that the feast is not for 'rustic fopperies', nor even for 'the lilly and the rose . . . though of flowers the King and Queen'. Carousing and flagons of beer are mentioned, along with a whole list of named carnations, which Stevenson calls 'The Spanish, French and Welch infants' that were commended for 'their unmatch't variety'.[10]

The infants were probably seedlings, new varieties being brought in from the Spanish Netherlands, but the mention of Wales points to the florist Sir Thomas Hanmer, whose estate was at Bettisfield in Flintshire. Hanmer was born in 1612, inheriting the baronetcy ten years later. He married one of Queen Henrietta Maria's ladies in waiting, and served as a cup-bearer to King Charles I, so he was very much part of the court circle. However, his passion was for horticulture, and he must have become familiar with many florists' flowers while travelling on the Continent. Systematically he kept notes about plants, trees and fruit that he compiled into a 'Garden Book' completed in 1659. This was probably intended for publication, as he frequently addressed the 'reader', but it did not appear in printed form until 1933.[11] This horticultural treasure gives a wonderful insight into the world of the gentleman gardener of the mid-seventeenth century.

Several carnations from Stevenson's poem are mentioned in Hanmer's *Garden Book*, including 'Grey Halo', which he calls 'murrey', indicating that it is purple-red, and 'Philomell or the Nightingale', which he describes as 'gride-line', a grey-purple. In fact, Hanmer had difficulty growing his carnations at Bettisfield. In a letter to John Evelyn, he explained: 'I thought once to have ventur'd some gillyflowers, having two years since raised some very good ones from seed (which I never did before, nor I thinke never shall againe, because the wett of England hinders the ripening of the seed more than in Holland and Flanders) but there is such store of excellent ones all about London that I had not the confidence to adventure any to your view.'[12]

As in so many areas of gardening at this time, female florists usually go unrecorded, though it is impossible to believe that they did not exist. One reference has survived, however, in a letter written c. 1629 to Jane, wife of Sir Nathaniel Bacon of Brome Hall in Suffolk. Sir Nathaniel, a nephew of Sir Francis Bacon, shared his kinsman's interest in horticulture, and one of his paintings, now in the Tate Britain, depicts a cookmaid amid a plethora of fruit and vegetables, and a garland of wild flowers (Plate XIX).[13] Lady Bacon's letter was from an English clergyman based in Holland, who begins by reporting 'with much difficulty I have got the box of flowers at last, being once out of hope for the report was that the ships were cast away or taken by the Dunkirkers'. An enclosed letter from the florist supplier, Alexander van Eyndem, explains that the colours of some of the flowers are faded but assures Lady Bacon that she has been given 'the rarest flowers that can be had'. The florist also supplied two tulip bulbs for 10s – a considerable sum – which the Reverend Greenhill tells Lady Bacon to 'bestow upon Miss Anne for the increase of her garden and inducement for her to love flowers'. Her daughter, Anne Bacon, would have been aged around fifteen at this time, a florist in the making.[14]

An increasing number of books were available to these curious gardeners to help them in their accurate identification of plants. These books were also increasing in bulk as more new plants were discovered and varieties created. One of the largest was the *Hortus Eystettensis*, compiled by Basil Besler and published in Nuremberg in 1613. The apothecary Besler was fortunate to have as his patron the Prince-Bishop of Eichstatt, a keen lover of flowers and creator of the famous garden around his residence, the Wilibaldsburg. The herbal of his garden took sixteen years to compile, with a team of six metal engravers for the 374 plates that illustrated more than a thousand flowers. The book is arranged according to the seasons, no doubt because chests of fresh specimens were sent weekly during their flowering period from Eichstatt to Nuremberg. The resulting two parts were sometimes bound into one volume that was so huge and heavy that a wheelbarrow was said to be required to transport it.

A much more manageable reference book was the *Hortus Floridus* produced by the de Passe family, with the first edition printed in Arnhem in 1614. This project had begun life two decades earlier when Hans Woutneel, a Protestant refugee living in Blackfriars, acquired the watercolours of his neighbour, Jacques Le Moyne. Le Moyne had published them as *La Clef des Champs* in 1586, but with limited success because of the crudity of the woodcut engravings. The development of engraving on metal gave very different results, however. Woutneel sent the watercolours to the Flemish artist Crispijn de Passe, who engraved them in his workshop in Cologne in the relatively new landscape format, with two numbered flowers on each sheet, and identifying labels. At this period, sets of prints were published without a proper title page, so this new book of sixty-three plates, published *c.* 1604, carried only the imprint of de Passe and Woutneel. After Woutneel's death, the plates remained with the de Passe family, and were reprinted as an appendix, described as *Altera Pars* ('other part'), in the *Hortus Floridus*.

The production of *Hortus Floridus* marks an interesting development in botanical publishing. Most of the plates in the main part of the book were engraved by Crispijn the Younger, then aged twenty but already a highly talented artist, helped by his younger brothers. Their father organised the preparation of the text, production of the plates, printing and distribution. This was a complex venture for the first edition was published in Latin with Dutch labels, aiming for the traditional market of botanists and scholars. Subsequent editions added French and English labels and, instead of scientific descriptions, instructions were given for colouring the plates. The flowers were depicted in a highly naturalistic way, with perspective detail giving the viewer the impression of being in an actual garden.

Engraving on metal was also used to great effect for Giovanni Battista Ferrari's *Flora, overo cultura di fiori*, published in Rome in 1638. A man of many parts, Ferrari combined the professorship of Hebrew and rhetoric at the Jesuit College in Rome with advising the Pope on horticultural matters. Among the artists that he employed to work on the copper-plate illustration was Anna Maria Variana, thought to be the first female engraver. Not only did Ferrari reproduce illustrations of individual flowers, but also designs for gardens and equipment. Gardens, he advocated, should be laid out like drawers in a cabinet, and the flowers planted should be carefully recorded in an index book, so that the garden echoed the cabinets of curiosity that were popular among gentlemen

48 When Crispijn de Passe illustrated the *Hortus Floridus*, first published in 1614, he adopted a highly naturalistic approach, as in this charming illustration of the saffron crocus with a mouse nibbling at its bulb.

scholars of the time. He also considered how flowers might be arranged indoors, providing elaborate illustrations of vases with lids through which the stems might be inserted. The lid could then be removed to change the water with the flowers still in place. He stipulated that the most beautiful flower should crown the vase, just as a beautiful head of hair crowns a body. Ferrari's *Flora* proved highly influential, not only in Italy, but throughout Europe.

These three books were illustrated with engravings on metal, a process that was superseding woodcut images. But when the London apothecary John Parkinson came to produce his first book, his choice, whether by inclination or necessity, was to illustrate it with woodcuts, albeit of high quality. *Paradisi in Sole, paradisus terrestris*, a pun on his own name, was published in London in 1629, and from it we know a lot about his life and the details of his gardening.

John Parkinson was born in 1567 in Whalley in Lancashire. His family were of farming stock, and Catholic, so that he was brought up amid plants and had a good knowledge of Latin. One of his cousins was a steward in William Cecil's household and through this connection he travelled to London to be apprenticed to Francis Slater, grocer, at a shop near St Mary Colechurch. When

49 A flower arrangement, engraved by Anna Maria Variana, from Giovanni Battista Ferrari's *Flora, overo cultura di fiori*, published in Rome in 1638.

Parkinson was duly inducted into the Grocers' Company, the master was Hugh Morgan, apothecary to the Queen, whose botanical garden was near Coleman Street by London Wall. In Morgan's garden, the young apothecary met the skilled plantsmen of Lime Street, including James Garret, John de Franqueville and Matthias L'Obel. Parkinson had read L'Obel's second book, *Stirpium Observationes* ('Observations on the History of Plants'), where the Flemish botanist devoted attention to garden plants, including those cultivated solely for their decorative value. This struck a chord with him, and in 1589 he started to create his own garden in Cripplegate, moving westwards eight years later to Long Acre to avoid the pollution that was beginning to affect the City.

The Long Acre garden was about two acres in area. Originally he enclosed it with a hedge of whitethorn interlaced with dog roses, but later used walls of brick and stone. Planting beds were separated from the orchard by household shrubs such as lavender, rosemary, and plashed cornelian cherry trees.

Parkinson observed the sophistication of the manures used by Flemish gardeners, distinguishing between cattle manure for dry, loose and dusty soil, where it was dug in and left to go rotten, and horse manure, which could be used for clayey soil. The results were often spectacular, with the 'great white Spanish daffodil' from the Pyrenees growing to two feet, a 'radiant lily', which was probably the Madonna lily that he had seen in Lord Zouche's garden in Hackney, and a whole variety of fritillaries.

Parkinson strove to find the best plants to create knots, trying thrift and germander, both of which had drawbacks, and juniper and yew, which both grew too big, but he did well with lavender cotton, a recent introduction that was 'for the most part in the gardens of great persons'. His Flemish friends taught him how to manage the 'small, lowe or dwarfe kinde [of shrub], called French or Dutch Boxe', which he found the best for outlining knots, even though there was 'the want of a good sweet scent with his fresh verdure'.[15]

From Garret and de Franqueville, Parkinson learned how to grow tulips from seed, taking five years to produce tulips of spectacular variety and colour from the mother flower. The seeds were sown at the end of October, 'after they be thorough ripe and dry'. In the following years an ever thicker leaf would appear from the seed until in the fourth or fifth year a second leaf broke out from the first, 'a certain sign that it will bear a flower'. Tulips do not grow true from seed, so the excitement was engendered in seeing just how the blooms would appear. Parkinson noted that writers like Markham sought to change the colour by adding pigments, but was sceptical of this. As an experienced and observant gardener, he noted that streaking and striping happened as the bulb grew older and decayed, likening the resultant flare of colour to the brightness of a light 'bidding a good night' just before being extinguished.[16]

Parkinson also worked on extending the flowering season of anemones, a complicated operation involving planting some 'roots' in February rather than August, so that he had continuous flowering for months before the usual season. He then selected the seeds to acquire a range of colours 'that can hardly be expressed', advising that the best results came from the broad-leaved varieties of anemones. His delight in these varied hues is obvious: one 'of a pale whitish colour tending to gray, such as the monks and Friars were wont to wear with us, and this we call A Monk's Grey', another 'of a lively flesh colour, shadowed with yellow, and may be called The Spanish Incarnate Anemone'. Parkinson was frustrated by the lack of interest shown by English florists in raising anemones from seed, comparing them unfavourably with gardeners in the Low Countries, where 'their industry hath bred and nourished up such diversities and varieties, that they have valued some Anemones at such high rates as most would wonder at, and none of our Nation would purchase, I think'.[17]

Parkinson somehow managed to combine the cultivation of his garden with his work as an apothecary. He also began to gather notes to write an encyclopaedia of plants, writing by candlelight late into the night, according to his neighbour, Sir Theodore de Mayerne, physician to James I, who reassured him 'It is difficult things that are beautiful. May the sweetness of due praise soften the harshness of the wakeful hours.'[18] In this enterprise he was also encouraged by the King himself, who wanted to be remembered for initiating a project for the well-being of his subjects. Perpetually short of money, James could provide no financial support, but did give Parkinson a lease on land in St Martin's Lane and a coat of arms. Events moved on with the arrival in England of Henrietta Maria in 1625. The encyclopaedia was put on hold, and instead Parkinson produced for the Queen a 'garden of pleasant and delightfull flowers', selecting plants that were 'the chiefest for choice, and fairest for shew, from among all the Tribes and Kindreds of Natures beauty'.[19]

The book is large, folio in format, with over 600 pages. Dedicated to Henrietta Maria, 'a feminine of flowers', *Paradisus* begins with tips on the secrets of horticulture, followed by the ordering of the kitchen garden and the orchard, and ends with an index to plants in English and Latin and a table of the medicinal properties of herbs. Although sometimes described as a herbal, this is very much a gardening book, in which Parkinson shares with the general public his professional knowledge both as an apothecary and as a practising gardener.

Because the book contained many new introductions, and varieties of plants, Parkinson could not easily draw upon existing illustrations. Therefore he commissioned from the German engraver Albert Switzer woodcuts taken from drawings in other books. In all there are 612 illustrations, many of them full-page, sometimes with twelve different varieties shown. Despite the lack of finesse of woodcuts compared to engravings on metal, Switzer has managed to convey the stripes and featherings that made the tulip such a source of fascination, and to capture the delicate fringing of pinks and carnations. However, the paper used by the printers, Humfrey Lownes and Robert Young, was rather thin, so that the 'see-through' from the next page sometimes mars the impact of the illustrations. Switzer also engraved a portrait of the author, proudly holding a sprig of armeria, or 'Sweet John', and a title page that shows Adam and Eve in the Garden of Eden surrounded by some of the florists' favourite flowers, such as the tulip, fritillary, lilies and, rather incongruously, a pineapple.

50 The title page of John Parkinson's *Paradisi in Sole*, a pun on his name in Latin, published in 1629. Adam and Eve are depicted tending plants in the Garden of Eden, including the Turk's cap lily, a cactus, cyclamen, fritillaries, tulips and a pineapple. In the middle distance can be seen the vegetable or Scythian lamb, which, it was believed, grew on a stalk and died once it had exhausted the grass around it.

In his text, Parkinson follows the usual convention of referring to botanical authorities, both from classical times, and from the sixteenth century, but in his 'Epistle to the Reader' he explains that he has perused many herbals in Latin and found that many flowers and rare fruits have been omitted because they have only recently become known. 'Gerard, who is the last, hath no doubt given us the knowledge of as many as be attained unto his time, but since his daies we have had many more varieties then he or they ever heard of'. He also cited his own personal connections, giving us a glimpse into the networks of florists in early seventeenth-century England. After leaving Hatfield, John Tradescant had become head gardener first to Edward Wotton, half-brother of Sir Henry, at St Augustine's Abbey in Canterbury, and then to the King's favourite, George Villiers, Duke of Buckingham, at his various properties, including York House in London. The year before the publication of *Paradisus*, the Duke was assassinated by a disaffected soldier following the disastrous expedition to La Rochelle to help the Huguenots. Tradescant retired to his own garden in South Lambeth and worked on his collection of plants. Parkinson describes him as 'my very good friend and often remembered', who drew his attention to 'the Italian tulipa'. He also includes in *Paradisus* 'the soon fading spider-wort of Virginia, or Tradescant his spider-wort', which we know today as *Tradescantia Virginiana*. Parkinson explains that 'the Christian world is indebted unto that painfull [careful] industrious searcher and lover of all natural varieties ... who first received it of a friend, that brought it out of Virginia'. Another professional gardener mentioned is Ralph Tuggie, whose nursery was in Westminster. Tuggie was celebrated for his colchicums and auriculas, but perhaps his greatest speciality was the cultivation of carnations. Parkinson chose to illustrate two of his varieties of tawny carnations, which he describes as 'marbled types', 'Princess' and 'Rose Gillyvor'.[20]

In his preface to *Paradisus* Parkinson talked of 'Out-landish flowers' that were being introduced into the country. Too busy to be able to travel and seek out plants for himself, he employed plant-gatherers to collect unusual bulbs and plants for him. One of these was a Frenchman, Francis le Veau, who brought him mountain daffodils from the Pyrenees. Parkinson describes him as 'the honestest roote-gatherer that ever came over to us'. He also commissioned the Flemish Dr William Boel to collect plants for him in the Iberian Peninsula. One of these was the 'starry Iacinth of Peru', which Parkinson noted 'doe naturally grow in Spaine, in the Medowes, a little off from the Sea, as well in the Island Gades, usually called Cales [Cadiz] ...

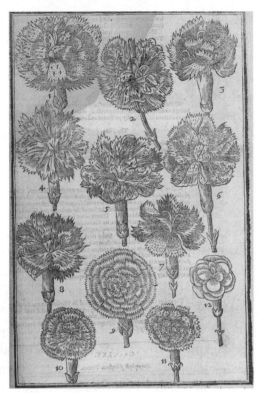

51 Carnations from Parkinson's *Paradisus*, including the tawnies raised by the Westminster nurseryman, Ralph Tuggie: his 'Princess' (no. 1); and 'Rose Gillyvor', (no. 12)

which when they be in flower, growing so thick together, seem to cover the ground like unto a tapestry of divers colours, as I have been reliably informed by Guillaume Boel'. Boel brought him seeds of the South American Marvel of Peru. The name had first been used by Gerard translating from the Spanish, *Maravilla del Peru*, probably a reference to the fact that these remarkable flowers, that open at night to enable pollination by moths, came in a variety of colours and produced a wonderful evening scent. Parkinson noted, 'You shall hardly find two or three flowers in a hundred, that will be alike spotted and marked, without some diversitie'.[21] To keep these exotic plants alive through the winter, he dried the roots in autumn, wrapping them in brown paper and laying them in a chest through the coldest months.

More plants came to Parkinson through his friends in the merchant community, including Nicholas Leate, 'a worthy merchant, and a lover of faire flowers' who obtained for him the Persian Lily via the Turkey merchants in

Constantinople.[22] Appropriately Leate was a member of the Ironmongers' Company, for he had many irons in the fire. He invested or participated in twelve trading companies, more than any other contemporary merchant or member of the gentry. These included the Merchant Adventurers, the Eastland Company that traded to the Baltic ports, and further afield the Russia and Levant Companies, and Leate was a founding member in 1600 of the East India Company. As he combined all this with an interest in horticulture, he was able to use his contacts to great effect, introducing not only the Persian Lily, but also the Syrian double yellow rose and, more prosaically, beet seeds from Poland.

Other contacts included a member of the College of Physicians, Dr Fludd, from whom Parkinson received the seeds of the Great White Sea Daffodil, brought back from the botanical garden in Pisa. From Richard Barnesley, who gardened in Lambeth, he was given information about the intriguingly named Woolly Hyacinth that had only flowered once, back in 1606. From Humfrey Packington, Esquire, of Harvington in Worcestershire, he received the double purple velvet anemone. The description of Packington as an Esquire would indicate that he was a member of the county gentry, for there were aristocratic Packingtons in Worcestershire at this period. Parkinson frequently refers to gentlewomen in his text, when giving the common names that they applied to flowers. In one case he identifies the gentlewoman, a fellow Lancastrian with whom he was in regular correspondence, Mistress Thomasin Tunstall, who lived at Bull Bank near Hornby Castle. She explored the dales and crags around her home, sending roots of flowers by messenger to Parkinson in London, together with written descriptions. These included a pale yellow orchid found in a wood 'called the Helkes, which is three miles from Ingleborough, the highest Hill in England'. One of Parkinson's neighbours in Covent Garden was Sir John Danvers, who was in the process of making his radical Italian garden in Chelsea. Parkinson would travel westwards out of London to visit him there, identifying plants on his journey. Thus he describes finding 'Clownes wound-wort ... by the path ... in the fields going to Chelsea'.[23] The florists of Parkinson's acquaintance therefore present an interesting mix of different levels of society at a time of acute consciousness of status.

Parkinson intended to add to *Paradisus* an account of simples, medicinal plants, but he was obliged to put his authorial career on hold when a new, emended edition of Gerard's *Herball* was published. This was revised by the ambitious and intellectually curious apothecary Thomas Johnson, who had contributed a verse of commendation in Latin at the beginning of *Paradisus*. Johnson was born in Selby in Yorkshire *c.* 1600 and, after serving his apprenticeship, set up his apothecary's shop in Snow Hill in London. In 1629 he had joined nine like-minded botanists to form a club of travellers, *socii itinerantes*, and to explore the flora of Britain. Their first foray was into Kent, where they found not only new native varieties of flowers, but various adventures, including being taken in front of the Mayor of Queenborough on the Isle of Sheppey on suspicion of being spies, all recorded and published by Johnson in a witty account in Latin. These adventures may sound rather like those of Dickens's Pickwick Club, but the *socii itinerantes* included Hugh Morgan, sometime Master of the Society of Apothecaries, and Sir Henry Wotton, then the Provost of Eton, and had a serious scientific purpose.

The book trade took notice of Johnson's little book, and the Norton family asked him to correct and update Gerard's work. In a remarkably brief period of time, he had completed the task, and the herbal duly appeared as Johnson's Gerard in November 1633. Johnson not only corrected some of Gerard's mistakes, in a manner that could not be described as self-effacing, but also added more than 1,000 plants that had been introduced since the 1590s.

John Parkinson realised that there was not room for two extensive herbals to be published at the same time, so delayed the production of his next book. Letting go of his apothecary's shop, he concentrated on his garden at Long Acre,

52 Illustration of bananas that Thomas Johnson included in his emended edition of Gerard's *Herball*, published in 1633. He drew the image from the bunch of a plant imported from the Bermudas, which he hung up in his apothecary's shop in Snow Hill in London, noting that the fruit became ripe at the beginning of May.

and made his project a theatre of plants, including all those known from the New World and the Far East, giving their medicinal properties along with their histories. The result was *Theatrum Botanicum* that finally reached the press in 1640.

Theatrum was a monumental book, a large folio of 1,755 pages, arranged in the traditional herbal style as an encyclopaedia. The woodcut illustrations were borrowed from previous herbals, so lacked the charm of those in *Paradisus*. Parkinson appears on the title page, looking very much his seventy years, clutching a thistle. He is styled Apothecary of London and the King's Herbarist, a title bestowed on him by Charles I, to whom he dedicated 'this manlike worke of herbes and plants'. Many of the gardeners and botanists acknowledged in the text had already appeared in *Paradisus* – Sir John Danvers, Mistress Tunstall, John Tradescant, and so on – but others had joined the circle, including John Morris, whose Dutch father, Peter, had made his fortune building watermills on the Thames near London Bridge. Returning from a tour of Italy, John Morris bought a copy of *Paradisus* for his library, and acted as an intermediary between Parkinson and Johannes de Laet, a merchant and director of the Dutch West Indies Company based in Leiden. Morris obtained tulip bulbs from Parkinson for de Laet, and in return Parkinson drew up lists of plants he would like Morris to get him from Jamaica and Virginia.

Despite being honoured by the King, and enjoying an elevated network of contacts, Parkinson felt betrayed by some whom he had regarded as his friends. At the beginning of *Theatrum* he admitted how difficult the task of writing it had proved, contrasting his own advanced age with the youth of Thomas Johnson that had enabled the latter to produce so quickly and easily the emendation of Gerard. However, Parkinson also pointed out that speed can bring with it carelessness, '*Canis festinans coecos parit catullos*' (the hurrying dog produces blind puppies). Later in the book he criticised his root gatherer, William Boel, for giving seeds and plants to another florist, William Coys, when Parkinson had paid for him to go to Spain, noting ruefully, 'hee brought mee little else for my money, but while I beate the bush another catcheth and eateth the bird'.[24]

On his title page for *Theatrum Botanicum* Parkinson chose to show representations of the four continents known at the time. Top left comes Asia riding on a rhinoceros, with palm trees and an iris. Top right is Europe in a horse-drawn chariot with oranges, tulips, pomegranates and carnations. Bottom left is Africa upon a rather pallid zebra with palms and agaves. And last comes America on a lop-eared llama, with cacti, sunflowers and a pineapple. Many of the plants that Parkinson included in the book were the curiosities being introduced into the country and taken up with great excitement and

53 The title page of John Parkinson's *Theatrum Botanicum*, published in 1640. The four known continents are shown with their appropriate forms of transport and plants. Parkinson, who was appointed the King's Herbarist a few months before the book's publication, is portrayed at the bottom of the page, holding a thistle in honour of Charles I's Scottish ancestry.

enthusiasm by gardeners. Some curiosities were just not possible to introduce to the English climate – the cocoa and coffee plants, for instance. Others, such as citrus trees, could be cultivated only in the hothouses that were being developed by very wealthy gardeners like William Cecil. Others, such as the potato and tobacco, acclimatised themselves well.

Exactly when the potato first arrived in England is the subject of debate, not helped by the fact that there were two kinds of potato, quite separate botanically. The tubers of the sweet potato (*Ipomea batata*) were probably introduced to England by John Hawkins from his voyage to the coast of Guinea, and 'the Indies of Nova Hispania' in 1564. Richard Hakluyt described them as 'the most delicate rootes that may bee eaten, and doe farre exceed our passeneps or carets. Their pines be of the bignesse of two fists ... and the inside eateth like an apple, but it is more delicious than any sweet apple sugred.'[25] The common, or Virginia potato (*Solanum tuberosum*) came originally from Peru, brought to Europe by the Spanish in the 1530s or 1540s. Exotic fruits and vegetables were often credited with aphrodisiac powers, so that the tomato from Mexico, which arrived in England in 1596, was known as the 'love apple'. The potato is similarly honoured in Shakespeare's *Merry Wives of Windsor*, with Falstaff calling upon the sky to rain potatoes as he prepares for a romantic assignation in Windsor Great Park (Act V, Scene 5). John Gerard grew both kinds of potato in his Holborn garden: the sweet potato he described as 'skirrets of Peru', while the Virginia potato was probably given to him by John White. Both potatoes are illustrated in his herbal, and Gerard is portrayed holding a sprig of *Solanum tuberosum*.

The first record of tobacco was made by Christopher Columbus's sailors on his expedition of 1492, when they observed Cubans and Haitians burning the leaves and inhaling the smoke through a *tobacco*, a device shaped like a catapult with two arms that fitted the nostrils.

Spanish merchants introduced the plants to Europe some time in the 1540s, and the first illustration of the wild tobacco plant from North or Central America appeared in Rembert Dodoens's herbal of 1554, identified as henbane. The German botanist Leonhart Fuchs was having none of this, naming the plant *Nicotiana* in honour of Jean Nicot, the French Ambassador to Portugal, who around the year 1559 sent tobacco seeds to the French Queen and other members of the court. The Queen at that time was Mary Stuart, also Queen of the Scots, which may partly explain why her son, James I, took such a violent dislike to tobacco.

54 The tobacco plant reproduced in L'Obel and Pena's *Stirpium adversaria nova,* published in London in 1570. The artist has added his idea of how the Indians of South America smoked the plant.

In 1585 Thomas Harriot sailed to Virginia on behalf of Sir Walter Raleigh to establish a colony on Roanoke Island, returning with Drake to England the following year. In his pamphlet, *A Brief and True Report of the New Found Land of Virginia,* issued three years later, he described the cultivation and smoking of tobacco by the native Indians. Hariot and Raleigh are thus traditionally credited with the introduction of tobacco smoking in England, but the honour of introducing the noxious weed should probably go to John Frampton with the publication of *Joyfull newes out of the newe-founde worlde* in 1577. This was a translation of the work of the Spanish physician Nicolas Monardes, *Primera y segunda tercara partes de la historia medicinal,* in which he listed the medicinal virtues of tobacco in the treatment of headaches, chest complaints and worms, but also provided a detailed description of the narcotic effects of smoking or chewing tobacco.

The Roanoke colony proved short-lived, but a settlement was established on the Jamestown River in Virginia in 1607. Gardeners in the early American colonies assumed that the plants cultivated in English gardens would also thrive in the New World, but this turned out to be a miscalculation. However, the growing of tobacco flourished in Virginia, and after the colonist John Rolfe, who was to marry Princess Pocahontas, introduced new, sweeter strains from the Caribbean rather than the bitter-tasting kind cultivated by the local Indians, it became the principal export from the colony. This development was viewed with horror by James I, who loathed the smoking of tobacco, recognising its toxic effects. After only a year on the English throne he published his *Counterblaste to Tobacco* condemning the 'manifold abuses of this vile custom'. The King also had a long-held dislike of Raleigh, so he wrote of the Roanoke expedition 'With the report of a great discovery for a Conquest, some two or three Savage men were brought in together with this Savage custom. But the pity is, the poor wild barbarous men died, but that vile barbarous custom is yet alive, yea in fresh vigour.'

'O omnipotent power of tobacco!' he declaimed, 'And if it could by the smoke thereof chase out devils ... it would serve for a precious relic, both for the superstitious priests, and the insolent Puritans, to cast out Devils withall.'[26] James was fighting on two fronts, for not only was tobacco being grown in Virginia but also at home. John Gerard in his herbal noted how easy it was to cultivate: 'being now planted in the gardens of Europe, it prospereth very well and commeth from seede in one year to bear both flowers and seede .... Tobacco must be sowen in the most fruitfull grounde that may be founde, carelessly cast abroade in the sowing, without taking it into the ground or any such pain or industrie taken, as is requisite in the sowing of other seedes.'[27]

The royal disapproval, however, went for naught, and imports from Virginia to England rose dramatically and remorselessly. In the end James's need for money overcame his objections and heavy customs duties were imposed upon imported tobacco, while the Virginian trade was protected by a ban on cultivation in England. In 1619 a proclamation was issued to this effect, on the grounds that 'Inland plantation' had allowed tobacco to 'become promiscuous and begun to be taken in every mean Village even among the basest people'. Moreover the King claimed that he had been advised by experts that the English variety was cruder and more poisonous than the Virginian. All this came as a blow to the botanist John Goodyer, who had cultivated the plant in his garden at Droxford in Hampshire. He had acquired his seeds of two kinds of tobacco from the Governor of Winchester Gaol 'who ... intended to plante greate store thereof, and was hindered of his purpose by a proclamation sette forth by Authoritie'.[28]

On the other hand, James I was determined to promote another gardening curiosity, the mulberry tree. When Henri IV came to the throne in France in 1594 he began to restore the gardens of the Tuileries that had been devastated by civil wars. Inspired by the publication of a treatise on the culture of silkworms written by a Huguenot, Olivier de Serres, he ordered mulberry trees to be installed in the royal parks, including the Tuileries, where more than 15,000 white mulberry trees were planted to provide leaves for the rearing of silkworms to create a French silk industry. James, who was also keen to promote new commercial activities for Britain, encouraged the publication in 1607 of an English version of de Serres's treatise, *The perfect use of Silk-wormes, and their benefit*. The book, dedicated to the King, had an additional English gloss from the translator, Nicholas Geffe. In the same year James wrote to the deputy lieutenants in all the counties, requiring each landowner to buy and plant 10,000 trees, to be delivered between March and April of the following year at the price of 6s per hundred. William Stallenge, 'the Comptroller of the custome house', was charged with providing a 'plaine instruction and direction' for the growing of the trees and the breeding of worms, and granted a patent for seven years to bring in seed.[29] He was also in charge of the King's garden of four acres in Westminster which had been given over specially to the growing of the mulberry trees.

James went further, and commissioned from Inigo Jones a house for the silkworms in the gardens of Anne of Denmark's palace at Oatlands. The creatures were to be accommodated in style, for the royal accounts refer to the joiner being paid for wainscoting with a wrought frieze and portals. The carpenter built shelves for the worms, while the glazier primed and painted the stairs and doors. In 1618 Mountain Jennings was paid an extra £50 for looking after the silkworms: he was succeeded by Jean Bonoeil, an expert in their culture, and in 1630 by John Tradescant.

Yet, despite all this royal support and expertise the silk industry did not take off in Britain. There was debate over which sort of mulberry trees to plant. The delicate white mulberry was known to be preferred by the worms, but the black mulberry was hardier and more suited to the climate. Geffe in his translation of de Serres intimated that the two varieties of tree produced different kinds of silk, 'grosse, strong, and heavie' from the black, 'fine, weake and light' from the white.[30] He felt either sort was acceptable, though preferred the white. John Parkinson would not commit himself, but referred his readers back to de Serres.

55 Silkworms in their luxurious living quarters, from William Stallenge's *Instructions for the increasing of mulberie trees*, printed in 1609.

But the answer may lie in the different attitudes of French and English gardeners. *The Countrie Farme*, Surflet's translation of *La Maison Rustique*, contained much information originally from Olivier de Serres, and goes into detail about how the housewife should look after 'these prettie creatures' with the same care as lavished on their bees. Their houses should be well ventilated, with careful temperature control and strict hygiene. The care of the worms began as soon as spring approached. Mulberry trees should be dunged 'during the new Moone of March', with the eggs chosen by bathing them in wine, and selecting the heavier ones that sank to the bottom. The selected eggs should be warmed near a fire and then either between two feather pillows or 'betwixt the breasts of women (provided that they have not their termes at the time)'. The silkworm house should be perfumed with 'Frankincense, Garlicke, Onions, Larde, or broiled Sawsages', and the floor sprinkled with vinegar and sweet herbs. Once the silkworms were ready to spin their silk, the shelves should be furnished with arched branches of rosemary, lavender, oak, chestnut or broom to give them a resting place. The pictures in the 1609 edition of *Instructions for the increasing of mulberie trees* show some of these worms in their luxury apartments. Jennifer Potter in her biography of the Tradescants points out that it would be hard to imagine the practical John paying heed to this expensive and exhausting regime.[31] And no doubt his fellow countrymen felt the same, which may explain why a silk industry was established in France, but not in Britain.

John Tradescant was able to do much travelling, beginning with journeys to the Low Countries and France to buy plants for his patrons. In 1618 he sailed to Archangel as part of a mission to persuade the Tsar to allow English merchants to cross Russian soil to reach Persia, two years later he took part in a naval attempt to crush the activities of Barbary pirates of Algiers, and in 1627 he accompanied the Duke of Buckingham on his attempt to help the Huguenots of La Rochelle. All three missions ended in failure, but in each case Tradescant got his plants, including the Muscovy rose, pomegranates and the *artemesia maritima*. He was able to enhance his horticultural collection from further afield through his excellent contacts. The Duke of Buckingham was Lord Admiral of England, so Tradescant could call upon the Secretary of the Navy, Edward Nicholas, to write to merchants to supply him with rare plants from all over the known world. As Parkinson noted in *Paradisus*, one of his contacts in the new American colony provided him with spider-wort, which was named after Tradescant. In turn, Tradescant in the back of his own copy of *Paradisus* noted several American specimens among his list of eighty-seven newly acquired plants.[32] And in 1637 his own son, also called John, set off on a plant-hunting expedition to Virginia, a curious gardener on the trail of curiosities.

John Tradescant the Younger, born in 1608, received his education at King's School Canterbury when his father was working for Edward Wotton at St Augustine's Abbey. Unlike his father, he therefore had a good working knowledge of Latin, although contemporaries regarded him as the lesser horticulturalist, and he certainly felt himself in his father's shadow. However, with his journey to the New World he travelled much further than his father had ever done. Since the establishment of the settlement on the Jamestown River by the Virginia Company in 1607 several towns and plantations had grown up, although the interior of the country was still largely unexplored.

We do not know for certain where the younger Tradescant travelled in Virginia, but he was able to bring back to England about two hundred

56 Spider-worts in Parkinson's *Paradisus*. The three-petalled flowers from Virginia were introduced into English gardens by John Tradescant the Elder, and were thus named *Tradescantia
Virginiana* in his honour by Carl Linnaeus.

introductions, some of which were included by Parkinson in *Theatrum*. These
included the swamp or bald cypress (*Taxodium distichum*), which he must
have found in the waters upriver from Jamestown.[33] Tradescant was later credited with the introduction of two more trees, the red maple, *Acer rubrum*, and
the tulip tree, *Linodendron tulipifera*. The first was attributed to him in the
eighteenth century by Philip Miller, the director of the Chelsea Physic
Garden.[34] The second was included by John Evelyn in his treatise on forest
trees. John Tradescant the Younger was back in England by early June 1638,

possibly cutting short his New World travels on hearing of his father's approaching death, and he took over his post in charge of the gardens, vines and silkworms at Oatlands. Tradescant is supposed to have made two more journeys to Virginia, in 1642 and 1654, but there is no evidence to support this.

When John Tradescant the Elder was asking for plants, he also enlisted the help of merchants travelling to the Americas and to the East to bring back 'all manner of beasts and fowls and birds alive or if not with heads, horns, beaks, claws, skins, feathers ... and also from the East Indies with shells, stones, bones, egg-shells with what cannot come alive'.[35] Just as the botanical garden in the University of Leiden had a building where natural history specimens were kept, so the Tradescants created at Lambeth both a garden and a collection of curiosities known as the 'Ark'. By 1634 the collection had grown to the extent that it took a full day to tour, open to visitors for a fee of 6d. The traveller Peter Mundy went to see the Ark on his return in 1634 from India, where he had worked for the East India Company. He noted 'beasts, fowle, fishes, serpents, wormes (reall, although dead and dryed), pretious stones and other Armes, Coines, shells, fethers etts. of sundrey Nations, Countries, forme, Coullours. ... Moreover, a little garden with divers outlandish herbes and flowers, whereof some that I had not seene elsewhere but in India, being supplied by Noblemen, Gentlemen, Sea Commanders, etts. with such Toyes as they could bringe or procure from other parts'.[36]

The Tradescants also began to produce catalogues of their collections. The idea of printing such a publication was introduced by John Gerard when he compiled in 1596 a catalogue of trees, fruit and plants, both exotic and native, in his garden in Holborn. It was issued in small quarto by a local printer, possibly for circulation amongst his friends, and the only known copy is in the Sloane collection in the British Library. Three years later he produced a second edition in English and Latin in a folio format, printed by John Norton and dedicated to Sir Walter Raleigh. John Tradescant the Elder had begun listing plants in 1629 after he acquired a copy of Parkinson's *Paradisus*, but his first printed list was proofed up in 1634 as the 'Plantarum in Horto Johannen Tradescanti'. This booklet disappeared from view until the 1920s, when the librarian at Magdalen College, Oxford, R.W. Gunther, was cataloguing the library of the gardener and botanist John Goodyer. It is rather crude in style, and may only be a proof that was never published. Nevertheless it lists 634 specimens in the garden at Lambeth, divided into plants and fruit trees. Twenty-two years later a much more professional catalogue was produced of the whole of the *Musaeum Tradescantium*, where the list had increased to 1,701 plants. John Tradescant the Younger had added to his father's collection with his introductions from North America, and also expanded his collection of plants that would be useful to physicians and apothecaries – it is thought that he might have offered these for sale in the London herb markets. He also showed skill in keeping and supplementing his father's tender plants.

Another book that is probably associated with the garden at Lambeth is now in the Bodleian Library and known as 'Tradescant's Orchard'.[37] This album, with watercolours of various fruits, is surrounded by mystery. It is known that the paintings were acquired by Elias Ashmole, who cut down their size to have them bound into a book, adding a table of contents. Another hand applied captions to the pictures, including the note 'the Amber plum which JT [John Tradescant the Elder] as I take it brought out of France and groweth at Hatfield, ripe September 8th' (Plate XVII). This suggests that the writer is not either of the Tradescants but that somehow the album came into their possession. The fruits are ordered according to their ripening times, which seem to be three weeks earlier than now, but this may be due to differences in climate in the seventeenth century. The watercolours glow with colour, giving the texture of nectarines, pears, cherries and others, along with caterpillars, butterflies, and even an owl and a frog. It is possible that the Tradescants used the drawings as a marketing tool for potential buyers of their fruit trees, in the same way that the Dutch bulb merchants sometimes used albums to market their tulips.

At one time it was thought that 'Tradescant's Orchard' could be the work of the artist Alexander Marshall, though this has been discounted by comparison with his other paintings. Marshall certainly stayed with John Tradescant the Younger at South Lambeth in 1641, and worked on paintings on vellum of the plant collection for a flower book or florilegium, which has disappeared.[38] We get some idea of what these pictures might have looked like from his flower album in the Royal Collection – the only one of its kind to have survived from seventeenth-century England – and from individual paintings in the British Museum (Plate XVIII).

The catalogue of the *Musaeum Tradescantium* was compiled by John Tradescant the Younger with the help of Elias Ashmole, a lawyer and translator of alchemical texts, whose first known visit to South Lambeth was in

June 1650. Two years later he offered to help with the cataloguing and, given that Ashmole was adept and energetic, Tradescant no doubt accepted with relief, because he had been attempting the task for several years. He was also in financial difficulties, so that Ashmole's offer to pay for the publication was again probably welcome.

But as Jennifer Potter aptly describes him, this snake in the Garden of Eden had put Tradescant into his debt. With Tradescant's death in 1662 a legal wrangle arose between Ashmole and his widow, Hester, and the lawyer's cunning carried the day: he became the owner of the Ark. Thus when the first institution in England to be described as a museum was opened in Oxford in 1683, it bore the name of Ashmole rather than Tradescant. The curious gardener had been no match for the wily lawyer.

CHAPTER 8

The Sun and the Moon

IN 1621 HENRY, LORD DANVERS, who later became the Earl of Danby, arranged that Oxford University should lease five acres of meadow from Magdalen College to establish a botanical garden. The first botanical gardens of the Renaissance had been founded eighty years earlier at Padua and Pisa, and gradually other European cities followed suit, notably Leiden in the Netherlands in 1593. In these gardens, all attached to universities, it was hoped that the sun, the clear light of science, would not only shine upon the plants, but also enlighten the students of medicine and botany. John Gerard, who looked after the specialist garden for the College of Physicians in London, urged his patron, William Cecil, to establish a garden in Cambridge, even writing a letter for him to sign, but this came to nothing. It comes as rather a surprise that Oxford should be ahead of the game, given that Cambridge is now famous for its natural sciences. However, a botanical garden was extremely expensive to found and maintain – Danby donated £5,000 in all – so the key lay in the fact that Oxford enjoyed royal and court patronage.

To prevent the low-lying land along the River Cherwell from flooding, Danby arranged for 4,000 loads of 'mucke and dunge' to be laid by the University Scavenger, and had walls built around the garden. A rusticated gateway was commissioned in the style of Inigo Jones, although that architect distanced himself from it, complaining that it had been designed 'lamly' by 'sum mathematitians of Oxford' who had misunderstood architecture as a disciplined art.[1] Crowning the portico was a bust of the Earl atop a dedication 'to Charles I and to the glory of God for the benefit of the university and the nation'. The garden was often described as 'the Public Garden', echoing the foundation in 1602 of 'the Publique Librarie in the Universitie of Oxford', the Bodleian. The 'dining table' layout today of the Oxford Botanic Garden was created in the nineteenth century, but the original, four-square plan containing complex geometric designs can be seen in an engraving published in 1675 by David Loggan, which also shows conservatories built of brick.

According to the Oxford historian Anthony à Wood, Danby wanted John Tradescant the Elder to tend the new garden, but deferred appointing a professor of botany because 'The Garden could not be soon enough furnished with Simples, and they with a maturity'.[2] The ageing Tradescant only confirmed his acceptance as gardener in 1636, and two years later he was dead, so that it has long been thought that he had no part in creating the garden. Evidence, however, has recently been found showing that Tradescant had a servant in Oxford in 1637, which suggests that he may have cultivated the garden for one season.[3] His successor was Jacob Bobart, a soldier from Brunswick who had settled in Oxford as an innkeeper, or possibly a tea merchant. In 1641 Danby granted him a ninety-nine-year lease of the site, with benefit of fees and fruits, subject to good behaviour, promising him an annuity of £40 for life for caring for the garden. The timing was disastrous, for the following year civil war broke out in England and Danby's estates were sequestrated. Fortunately for the university and for English botany, whichever part of the catering trade Bobart pursued gave him sufficient income on which to live, together with the sales of fruit cultivated in the garden.

Bobart cut a singular figure with his large girth and his flowing hair. On high days and holidays he tagged his beard with silver, and was invariably followed round the garden by his pet goat which, as the present-day gardeners point out, was the most inappropriate animal to keep.[4] Bobart is sometimes given faint praise for the range of the plants he grew in the garden during the 1640s and 1650s. John Evelyn, for instance, noted in his diary during his visit to Oxford in 1654: 'they grow canes, olive trees, rhubarb, but no extraordinary curiosities besides very good fruit'.[5] But this is surely unfair; obtaining plants during the Civil War cannot have been easy and William Coles acknowledged his debt to Bobart in Adam in Eden, published in 1657. In his epistle to the reader he records 'the best hours of my life being spent in the fields and in physic gardens, more especially in that famous one at Oxford, where I made it a great part of my study to be experienced in this laudable art of sampling [simpling]'. Moreover, a catalogue of the Botanic Garden drawn up in 1648

57 Jacob Bobart the Elder, Superintendent of the Oxford Botanic Garden, from 'Vertumnus – an Epistle to Mr Bobart', 1713. Bobart is shown standing in front of the gateway to the garden, holding a cane entwined by a serpent, the symbol of herbal knowledge, and accompanied by his pet goat. A stork flies above the gateway as a reminder that Bobart came originally from Northern Europe, from Brunswick.

and published by the university printer lists in Latin and English more than 1,600 plants, a remarkable achievement in just six years.

Jacob Bobart began a herbarium of pressed flowers, a *hortus siccus*, which was continued by his son, also Jacob, born in Oxford in 1641. A much less flamboyant character, the younger Jacob was scholarly by inclination, adding twelve folio volumes to the herbarium, with some two thousand named specimens, and on his father's death in 1680, he too became superintendent of the garden. The Bobarts' herbaria are treasures of the Plant Sciences Department at Oxford, containing specimens of vanished cultivars. In the 1648 list of plants grown in the Botanic Garden, auriculas for example, are classified according to colour: 'Beares eare white', 'Strip'd Beares eare', 'Brimstone colour'd Beares eare', 'Sky-colour'd Beares eare', and so on. But in the herbarium compiled by Bobart the Elder, evocative names were applied – 'Bugs Purple and Yellow', 'Plumpton Duchess of Cleveland', 'Roses Morning Star'.

The decline of the nation into civil war was described by the wonderfully named President of Magdalen College, Accepted Frewen, as 'this busy and inquisitive time'. Charles I left London in January 1642, 'driven away by shame more than fear, to see the barbarous rudeness' of the opposition to his rule.[6] The first major engagement of the war came at Edgehill in October of that year. Although the King claimed victory, it was a bloody affair with gain for neither side. The royal army retreated to Oxford, where Charles and his two sons set up headquarters in Christ Church. The Queen was given the warden's lodgings just down the road in Merton College and the garden belonging to one of the canons of Christ Church provided access between the two royal households. The court was to remain here for more than two and a half years.

Jacob Bobart's achievements in the Botanic Garden are all the more remarkable when the conditions in Civil War Oxford are considered. The calm groves of academe were rudely shattered, with the city overcrowded, insanitary and lawless. Pig sties blocked the road, streams were clogged with dead horses and offal, typhoid and smallpox were rampant. Perhaps it was just as well that many physicians were part of the royal entourage, including William Harvey, the discoverer of the circulation of blood. Other migrants included heralds, astrologers, booksellers, botanists, stage players and musicians. The number of undergraduates and fellows fell sharply away and the colleges filled up with these 'strangers'. One Londoner, Thomas Fuller, reported that the 'second cockloft' in Lincoln College cost him more in seventeen weeks than had seventeen years in Cambridge before the war.[7] Perhaps for the only time until the late twentieth century, the city became notably feminine, as the women and children of Royalist families were also poured into the colleges. John Aubrey with great relish told how Ralph Kettell, the elderly President of Trinity, met two aristocratic ladies 'halfe dressed like Angells' in Trinity Grove, a favourite rendezvous for the fashionable. Kettell declared to one, 'Madam, your husband and father I bred up here, and I knew your grandfather. I know you to be a gentlewoman, I will not say you are a Whore; but get you gonne for a very woman.'[8]

With his characteristic ability to cause dissension, the King gave out degrees wholesale. The university tried to rein him in, but he could not resist the temptation to reward his followers cheaply. Among the recipients of royal largesse was the apothecary and emender of Gerard's herbal, Thomas Johnson, who received a doctorate of physic on 9 May 1643. He was not able to enjoy for long his enhanced status; at the siege of Basing House he received a bullet wound in the shoulder that became infected, and he died two weeks later. At that same siege, Inigo Jones, creator of court masques and exquisite buildings, had to be rescued wrapped only in a blanket. The world was indeed being turned upside down.

Oxford in the early 1640s, then, was not a place conducive to the development of scientific knowledge. However, in London from 1644 the first weekly meetings of the 'invisible college' began to be held at Gresham College. At his death in 1596 the Elizabethan financier Sir Thomas Gresham bequeathed his house in Broad Street and an endowment for seven professors to lecture publicly in the English tongue. In addition to the traditional arts subjects of divinity, music, law and rhetoric there were to be professors of astronomy, geometry and physic. The 'invisible college' was influenced by the writings of Francis Bacon, in which he had expressed his dissatisfaction with the theories of the past, arguing instead for the pursuit of knowledge through inquiry and experiment. In 1648 the group divided, with some staying in London, others going to Oxford.

Charles I had slipped out of Oxford on 27 April 1646, wearing a false beard, and accompanied only by his chaplain and a manservant, leaving his supporters to face the besieging Parliamentarian army under the command of Sir Thomas Fairfax. These were miserable times, with the city more crowded than ever as disbanded troops arrived from fallen strongholds, and an enormous sense of relief was felt when the Royalist troops were allowed to leave. College libraries had been plundered, buildings ruined, gardens dug up, yet Jacob Bobart carried on with his Botanic Garden, helping to feed the population with his fruit and vegetables, along with the nurseries at the Paradise Gardens to the west of the city. Cardinal Mazarin was said to have set aside £40,000 to buy up the Bodleian, but Fairfax, declaring his care for learning, set a guard on the library. However, the university, which had identified itself with the Royalist cause and the Laudian Church, inevitably faced severe repercussions. Over 300 university members were expelled along with all but three heads of colleges during 'visitations', to be replaced by men more sympathetic to Puritanism and the Parliamentarian cause. John Fell, son of the expelled Dean of Christ Church, lamented: 'Within the compass of a few weeks an almost general riddance was made of the loyal University of Oxford, in whose rooms succeeded an illiterate rabble, swept up from the plough-tail, from shops and grammar schools, and the dregs of the neighbour university'.[9]

Despite the affliction of plough-boys, shopkeepers, grammar-school men, and, perhaps worst of all, fellows from Cambridge, Oxford became a crucible for the development of knowledge in the various sciences, including botany. Three colleges in particular developed into centres for exploration into the sciences: Christ Church through the new dean, John Owen; Wadham, where the warden was Dr John Wilkins; and Magdalen under the presidency of Thomas Goodwin. Wilkins became the brother-in-law of Oliver Cromwell, and all three men served on a select committee when Cromwell was appointed chancellor of the university. One of the Students (fellows) appointed by the Parliamentary Visitors to Christ Church in 1649 was John Ward whose first degree was in divinity, but increasingly he became interested in medicine and botany, becoming a 'student of medicine', a status only abolished in Oxford in the late nineteenth century. In his diary cum commonplace book which he kept from 1658 Ward noted how he learned about plants at the Botanic Garden from Jacob Bobart, who directed him to what might be found on simpling expeditions to Shotover Hill and Forest Hill, just outside the city. Bobart also discussed with Ward the comparative merits of the herbals of Gerard and Parkinson, shrewdly pointing out that the paper and 'cuts' in Gerard were superior, and recommended to him authors on the subjects of grafting and gardening.

John Ward was a member of the club for experimental philosophy that was formed in Oxford following the division of the 'invisible college' in London in 1648. It was founded by the Parliamentarian physician William Petty, together with Thomas Willis, a Royalist soldier who stayed in Oxford after the city fell to Fairfax, and began to study medicine. Other members later included non-medical scholars such as Robert Boyle, Robert Hooke and Christopher Wren. Boyle, 'the father of chemistry', was persuaded in 1654 to settle in Oxford by John Wilkins, and began to work on his famous experiments with an air-pump in his High Street lodgings, where he was joined four years later by Robert Hooke. The club met in the neighbouring lodgings of William Petty, conveniently over an apothecary's shop, from which materials could be acquired. When Petty left Oxford for Ireland as the physician to Cromwell's army, it moved to the lodgings of Dr Wilkins in Wadham College. The rules that were then drawn up in October 1651, stipulating weekly meetings to take place every Thursday 'before two of the clock', have been preserved in the Bodleian Library.[10] The ambitious aims of the club were set out soon after by the astronomer Seth Ward – to equip a laboratory and observatory, to make chemical experiments, and to examine and index all the scientific books in 'our public library'.

Dr Wilkins combined theology with his scientific interests, wielding considerable influence over the undergraduates in his college, including Christopher Wren, who went up to Wadham as a gentleman commoner in 1649. The warden's garden at Wadham was turned over to experiments in horticulture and in the improvement of fruit trees and flowering plants. In 1654 when John Evelyn was beginning to lay out his own gardens, he visited both the university's Botanic Garden, and the college garden at Wadham. In his diary he noted how he met 'that miracle of a youth Mr Christopher Wren', and after dinner was taken into the Wadham gardens where John Wilkins showed him 'the Transparent Apiaries, which he had built like Castles & Palaces, and so order'd them one upon another, as to take the Hony without destroying the Bees. These were adorn'd with a variety of dials, little statues, vanes, &c'. Evelyn goes on to describe a statue that could be made to speak through a 'long conceal'd pipe' and a gallery full of 'Magical curiosities, a Way-Wiser, a Thermometer, a monstrous Magnes, Conic and other Sections, a Balance on a demie-Circle, most of them of his owne & that prodigious young scholar, Mr. Chr: Wren'.[11] The young Wren was fascinated by sundials and 'magical curiosities', but perhaps it is the ingenious beehives that presage his future career as one of England's most famous architects.

A circle of enthusiastic horticulturalists also formed in Magdalen College, conveniently close to the Botanic Garden. William Hooper, who specialised in arboriculture, was ousted from his college fellowship, but retained his house in the Gravel Walk. According to the diarist Thomas Hearne: 'After he left the college he went without a gown, and wore constantly a very long coat, like your frocks worn by wagoners, and applied himself to gardening with wonderful success, digging himself with a man he constantly hired. He would carry his spade upon his shoulders, and work hard every working day. He would likewise prune, engraft, and do other things of that kind himself. He raised several nurseries and planted many orchards'.[12] The foundation scholars at Magdalen were known as 'demys' and William Browne, a Demy of 1644, played an important role in compiling the 1658 catalogue of the Botanic Garden. One year behind him came Francis Drope, author of *A short and sure Guide in the practice of raising and ordering Fruit-trees*, which eventually saw the light of publication in 1672.

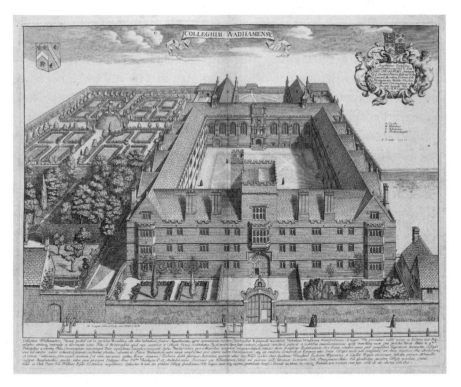

58 David Loggan's engraving of Wadham College, Oxford, 1677. The elaborate garden created by the college's warden, John Wilkins, during the Civil War, is to be seen on the left. The beds are laid out in hedged compartments, with as a centrepiece a mount topped by a statue of Atlas.

Another Magdalen horticulturalist was Walter Stonehouse. He had taken part in Thomas Johnson's botanical tours of North Wales and Kent before becoming rector of Darfield in Yorkshire. Here he became a devoted gardener and drew up a catalogue of the plants that he was cultivating, together with detailed plans of his garden, which was divided into three parts. The 'best garden', 34 yards by 30 yards (31 metres by 27.5 metres) with fruit trees such as peaches and apricots trained on the walls, was laid out with five knots in different geometric patterns. These were not in the fashionable, scrolling form of the seventeenth century, so it has been suggested that Stonehouse inherited them from a previous incumbent. The detailed drawings of them were used as the basis for the National Trust's recreation of a seventeenth-century garden at Moseley Old Hall in Staffordshire (Plate XX). The second part of the garden at Darfield was planted as an orchard, and Stonehouse made a long list of the contents, which included fruit trees from his neighbour, Sir John Reresby of

Thrybergh, and from John Tradescant's nursery in South Lambeth. The third part, a long rectangle, was set aside as a Saffron Garth. Saffron was probably the crop that yielded the best return if the flowers could flourish, and the rector of Darfield in the early twentieth century reported that he still had a border of crocuses, 170 yards (157 metres) in length.[13] Forcibly ejected from Darfield rectory by Parliamentarian commissioners, and imprisoned c. 1648, Stonehouse probably then retired to Oxford. When he got back to Darfield in 1652, he found that few of his plants had survived, poignantly making a note in his catalogue 'Novamque despero coloniam' (I have no hope of a new colony).

Life in Oxford had changed radically since the fall of the city to Fairfax and his troops in 1646. Henry Oldenburg, an itinerant German scholar, who was taken on as tutor to Robert Boyle's nephew, wrote to a medical friend early in 1657: 'Oxford is indeed a city very well furnished with all the things needed for the grounding and cultivation of learning: among which rich libraries, fat revenues, convenient houses, and healthy air easily hold first place.'[14] At the Restoration of Charles II many of the men involved in the Oxford scientific groups joined with their friends in London to form a society to which the King gave a royal charter on 15 July 1662, to become the Royal Society of London for Improving of Natural Knowledge.

***

Charles I's wholesale creation of new doctors of physic during his stay in Oxford resurrected the long-standing quarrels over the status of various sections of the medical community – the physicians, apothecaries and barber surgeons and, at the bottom of the pecking order, women herb-gatherers. This was partly a matter of class. Whereas in some parts of Europe apothecaries and physicians trained together, in England the majority of physicians trained at Oxford and Cambridge, and came mostly from the wealthier ranks of society. The universities insisted on testing for knowledge of the classical physician Galen, penalising anybody who cut short their education. This was an insistence opposed by Francis Bacon, for instance, who felt that the universities of Europe did little to advance wisdom, refusing to have confidence in their own empiricism. Apothecaries and barber surgeons, on the other hand, were members of London companies. The former belonged to the Company of Grocers, who dealt with spices and drugs, while the barber surgeons had their own Company, amalgamated in 1540.

In 1518 Henry VIII had granted a charter for the foundation of the Royal College of Physicians at the instigation of his physician, Thomas Linacre, who became the first president. This elite group of university-trained doctors was given wide discretionary powers over practitioners within a seven-mile radius of the City of London. Although Linacre had based the college on Italian institutions, his successors disapproved of the University of Padua, for example, where students learned about anatomy and the chemical theories of Paracelsus that were not included in Galen's canonical works. The college acted as a watchdog of standards, coming down on apothecaries who prescribed drugs for private customers, many of whom preferred dealing with them because they were less expensive, and their cures often more effective and less drastic than those of physicians.

Despite their royal charter, the college did not always prevail. An act passed in 1542 allowed those experienced in the nature of herbs, roots and waters to practise and use them as a gesture of Christian charity. Thus when a quarrel arose in 1581 between the physicians and a poor woman, Margaret Kennix, who had been supplying her friends and neighbours with herbal remedies, Elizabeth I intervened. In a letter sent to the college via Secretary Walsingham, the Queen declared:

> It is her Majesty's pleasure that the poor woman should be permitted by you quietly to practise and minister to the curing of diseases and wounds, by the means of certain simples, in the application whereof it seems God hath given her an especial knowledge. I shall therefore desire you to take order amongst yourselves for the readmitting of her into the quiet exercise of her small talent, lest by the renewing of her complaint to her Majesty through your hard dealing towards her, you procure further inconvenience thereby to yourselves.[15]

Of course the concerns about unlicensed practitioners were not simply matters of intellectual snobbery. Apothecaries and physicians were dealing with plants which were often unknown in their effects and at times dangerous, and fear of poisoning rendered them vulnerable.

The *cause célèbre* of James I's reign was the trial of Lady Frances Howard and the King's favourite, Robert Carr, Earl of Somerset, for the murder of Sir Thomas Overbury, who died of poison in the Tower of London in September 1613. Although Lady Frances and Somerset were found guilty and sentenced to death, their powerful position at court ensured they were pardoned by the King. Their servants, however, were not so fortunate, and the apothecary James Franklin, and Lady Frances's maid, Mrs Turner, were hanged, which 'the common people did not take to be good payment'. Also implicated in this unsavoury episode was the apothecary grandson of the great botanist Matthias, William L'Obel, who had mixed and delivered medicines to Overbury in the Tower.

In 1589 the *Comitia* of the College of Physicians resolved to publish a uniform 'Pharmacopoeia or Dispensary of Prescriptions to be followed by shops'. The whole range of medicines was divided into groups, such as 'Syrups, Juleps and decoctions', 'Oils', 'Distilled waters', 'Liniments, Ointments, Plasters & Cerates', 'Opiates', with named physicians in charge of each.[16] In order to keep this knowledge from the public, the committee decided to produce the list in Latin. Apothecaries refused to cooperate, partly because they were not necessarily firmly grounded in Latin, but also because they felt they knew more about the ingredients of many medicines than did the physicians. They also began to rebel against the Grocers. By 1605 an energetic reformer, Dr Henry Atkins, who had the ear of James I, persuaded him that apothecaries should form a separate section within the Company of Grocers. Soon after, the radical suggestion of a new and independent Society of Apothecaries arose, led by a Huguenot, Gideon de Laune, who was astonished that in England grocers could dominate the apothecary trade. With the support of influential men such as Francis Bacon and the royal physician, Sir Theodore de Mayerne, the Society was duly created in 1617.

The College of Physicians meanwhile was still working on its *Pharmacopoeia*, but when this finally appeared a year later it was found to be out of date and inconsistent in its information. The college tried to place the blame for this inadequacy on their publisher. John Marriot, but he was having none of this and defiantly produced several 'new' editions without their authority. A corrected edition, excluding Marriot, was produced by the college in 1649, but at the same time a radical bookseller, Peter Cole, decided to produce an English version, commissioning the apothecary Nicholas Culpeper to compile it.

Like William Turner a hundred years earlier, Culpeper combined a fervent interest in herbalism with rebellious nonconformity. Born in Ockley in Surrey on 18 October 1616, he was the posthumous son of a clergyman. After his birth, his mother returned to live with her father, also a clergyman, who inclined firmly towards Puritanism. A clever child, Nicholas Culpeper went up to Cambridge, but left prematurely when an heiress with whom he was planning to elope was struck by lightning on her way to meet him. Perhaps as a result of this extraordinary experience, he became convinced that our lives are heavily influenced by celestial phenomena. Turning his back on Cambridge, he became apprentice to Simon White, an apothecary with a shop at Temple Bar, and began to study herbal medicine.

Culpeper once declared that 'he had courted two mistresses that had cost him dear, but it was not the wealth of kingdoms should buy them from him'.[17] These ladies were physic and astrology. Luckily for him he also married Alice Ford, the daughter of a wealthy merchant. In 1640 they set up home in the precincts of the old hospital of St Mary in what is now known as Spitalfields. This was a good place for an unlicensed medical practice as it lay just outside the City of London, in an area that had been associated with healing since the Middle Ages. Recent excavations of the drains of St Mary's have yielded seeds of medicinal plants such as vervain, hemlock, henbane and mallow, and all around London in the seventeenth century there were places to find wild flowers and herbs. Culpeper had joined the Puritan community of John Goodwin in Coleman Street, expressing views that were radical even by the standards of the day. When Charles I was executed in 1649, he saw it as a portent of the millenarian rule by Christ on earth, and even wrote of the ascendancy of Oliver Cromwell as a leap from the frying pan into the fire. He took the radical step of offering help to all, however poor: 'Jupiter delights in equality, and so do I.'[18] And, 'I wish from my heart our present State would ... take a little care for the lives of the poor Commonalty, that a poor man that wants money to buy his wife and children bread, may not perish for want of an angel to see a proud insulting domineering Physician, to give him a Visit.'[19]

The reference to Jupiter shows Culpeper's fascination with planetary influences, while that to the domineering physician reflects his outspoken dislike of the medical profession. Thus when Peter Cole asked him to compile an English pharmacopoeia, he set about the task with a will. It was duly issued in August 1649, entitled *A Physical Directory*. On the title page Culpeper noted that he had included hundreds of additions to the *Pharmacopoeia* of the College of Physicians, marking them with an 'A' to provide information about how ingredients and recipes should be used. This was revolutionary stuff, for it was putting the power to heal and treat into the hands of ordinary men and women. Little wonder that it proved highly popular, going into eighty editions, including pirated ones. The backlash from the authorities was equally outspoken, with William Johnson, the college's chemist, asking whether the book was 'fit to wipe ones breeches withall'.[20]

Culpeper continued to publish unabashed, including two works in 1651 alone, a directory for midwives and *Semeiotica uranica*, or *An Astrological Judgement of Diseases from the Decumbiture of the Sick*. By 'decumbiture' he indicated his method of getting the patient to lie down and drawing up a chart for the time that the illness had manifested itself. He thus used astrology to provide a prognosis, followed by treatment through medical principles. Culpeper had long courted his mistress, astrology, and on 14 February 1647 attended the 'Feast of Mathematicians' inaugurated by the Society of Astrologers at Gresham College. This society mirrored the 'invisible college' of more mainstream sciences, enjoying the degree of organisation later achieved by the Royal Society. Its first steward was Elias Ashmole, the cunning lawyer who was to acquire the 'Ark' of the Tradescants.

In 1652 Culpeper published his master work, *The English Physitian*, later known as *Culpeper's Complete Herbal*. This proved to be one of the most successful books ever published in the English language, and probably the non-religious book in English to remain longest in continuous print. The main section was a directory of native medicinal herbs, from Adders' Tongue to Yarrow, with their appearance, location, time of picking, medicinal virtues and use, plus their astrological influences. Directions on application and preparation then followed. It was written in accessible language and was aimed particularly at women. Half a century after Culpeper's death, a biography was written of him, in which the writer paid tribute to his achievement: 'To the poor he prescribed cheap, but wholesome Medicines; not removing, as many in our times do, the Consumption out of their Bodies into their Purses; not sending them to the *East Indies* for Drugs, when they may fetch better out of their own Gardens'.[21] On the title page of *The English Physitian* Culpeper threw down the gauntlet to booksellers by prominently displaying the price of three pence, to prevent anybody charging more. There have been over a hundred subsequent editions, including one printed in Boston in 1708, the first medical book to be published in North America.

In his preface to a revised edition of *A Physical Directory* dated 30 December 1653, Culpeper described himself as 'sick and weak, no way fit for study or writing'. Two weeks later he died, aged only thirty-eight. His heavy smoking at Cambridge had been legendary, and his addiction to tobacco continued unabated. Thus after he was badly wounded in the chest while fighting on the Parliamentarian side at the Battle of Newbury in 1643, he never fully recovered, and it was consumption that finally caused his untimely death. In his relatively short life he achieved an astonishingly large amount, introducing a system of remedies that was relatively sophisticated and cheap, and within the reach of the majority of the population.

Despite the popularity of Culpeper's books, he received heavy criticism, not only for his radical ideas but also his astrological beliefs, the realm of the moon rather than the sun. Francis Bacon and Sir Thomas Browne had both ridiculed the idea of astrology affecting science, and William Coles in particular criticised Culpeper in *The Art of Simpling*, published in 1655. However, he was not alone in his attachment to the idea of planetary influences, and astrology was often applied to gardening. Thomas Hill in his *Proffitable Arte of Gardening*, published in 1568, advised his readers to consult almanacs to determine astrological positions for sowing, planting and grafting. This was countered by a pamphlet written three years later by William Fulke, castigating Hill: 'Good days to sowe and plante, I thinke be when the earth is moderately moystened and gentilly warmed with the heat of the sonne'. If these conditions were met, then the position of the constellations were as much help to seeds 'as it was ease for the Camell whenne the Flye leapt of from his backe'.[22]

Others looked to the cycles of the moon. The highly practical Hugh Platt in his *Floraes Paradise* recommended sowing and gathering plants according to this method, including the idea that tulips would produce their highly desirable double form, 'Some think by cutting them at every full Moon before they bear, to make them at length to beare double.'[23] Sir Thomas Hanmer was undecided on the subject. At one stage in his *Garden Book* he dismisses the idea that 'by observing the Moone or heavens to make flowers larger or more double, or to worke such wonders as are both sayd and written to amuse and deceave the unexperienced and credulous'.[24] But in another manuscript he writes of planting tulips: 'Set them in the ground about the full moon in September...'[25]

John Parkinson applied the Galenic theories of medicine to his gardening. Galen was a Greek physician who looked after the Roman Emperor Marcus Aurelius in the second century CE. He took Aristotle's theory that the universe was made up of four elements, fire, air, water and earth, and that each element had two of four primary qualities, so that the possible combinations were hot and dry (fire), hot and moist (air), cold and moist (water), and cold and dry (earth). One quality dominated each combination, giving the four cardinal humours associated with the body's four principal fluids, blood, phlegm, choler and melancholy. By their proportions could be deduced the physical and mental qualities of an individual. A firm proponent of botanical remedies,

Galen dominated medical practices throughout the Middle Ages through Arabic translations, and the European Renaissance through contemporary interpretations. In *Paradisi in Sole* Parkinson maintained that the earth could be treated like a patient, with opposing feeds applied once the temperature of the soil had been assessed. For gardens with cold 'grounds', the 'stable soyle of horses is best and more proper', while for hot, sandy or gravelly grounds he recommended 'the stable soyle of Cattell' being 'of a colder and moister nature'.[26]

Along with these theories, there were botanical myths. Witchcraft, for instance, might be avoided if rowan, vervain, mistletoe or angelica were worn on the person or hung up in the house. If a woman stepped over a cyclamen, then she would miscarry, so as prevention John Gerard put sticks over those growing in his garden. One extraordinary myth was the vegetable lamb from Tartary which features on the title pages of both Parkinson's books. In *Paradisus* this fabulous animal is to be seen in the Garden of Eden, and in *Theatrum* it peeps out from behind the representation of Asia. Known also as the borametz or Scythian lamb, it was believed to grow like a plant with a stalk attached to its belly. Reproduced by a seed like other plants, it died after it had grazed all the grass around it. This link between the plant and animal kingdoms was accepted by the Tradescants, who featured its 'skin' among the wonders of their Ark. To make matters more remarkable, there is a real plant, *Cibotium barometz*, a fern with a furry rhizome, that grows the opposite way from the lamb, with its 'feet' in the air.

Another myth was that a plant produced the barnacle goose. Gerard wrote in his herbal:

> There is a smalle Ilande in Lancashire called the Pile of Foulders, wherein are found the broken peeces of old and brused ships, some whereof have beene cast thither by shipwracke ... whereon is found a certain spume or froth that in time breedeth unto certain sheels, in shape like those of the muscle ... wherein is contained a thing in forme like a lace of silke finely woven ... which in time commeth into the shape and forme of a Bird; ... bigger than a Mallard, lesser than a Goose.[27]

Thomas Johnson in his 1633 emendation of Gerard was scornful of many of his botanical judgements, but retained the story despite the fact that Dutch sailors in search of the North East Passage had observed these geese sitting on their eggs (see p. 85). As late as 1678 the Royal Society published an eye-witness

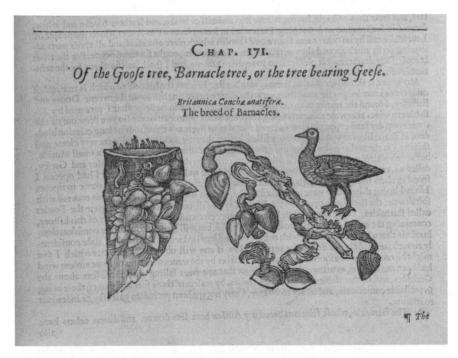

CHAP. 171.

Of the Goofe tree, Barnacle tree, or the tree bearing Geefe.

Britannicæ Conchæ anatiferæ.
The breed of Barnacles.

¶ The

59 The barnacle goose, an enduring botanical myth, as shown in Thomas Johnson's emended version of Gerard's *Herball*. It was believed that the geese hatched out of barnacles attached to driftwood.

account of the barnacle goose emerging from its shell attached to driftwood from a Scottish island. The report stated that within the shells were 'little birds perfectly shap'd'.[28]

Another theory, promulgated by the sixteenth-century Italian botanist Giovanni Battisti Porta, was that of signatures. This held that God had left clues in the leaves of plants, flowers, roots and juice to suggest the disease of an organ. Thus lungwort had spots on the leaves that were reminiscent of lungs, poppies were linked with haemorrhages, agrimony was associated with jaundice, and the mandrake root with sterility. Yet another theory was of propinquity where the remedy could be found nearby, so that both Gerard and Culpeper maintained that in order to deal with afflictions with bad odours, unsavoury plants should be eaten.

It is the astrological section of Culpeper's *English Physitian* that has also caused modern scepticism, with the doyenne of writers on herbals, Agnes Arber, condemning his work as mystical. Yet we have the benefit of hindsight, of enormous developments in the knowledge of botany, horticulture and medicine. Alchemy and science in the seventeenth century were not complete opposites – alchemy after all means 'the chemistry' – and nor were astronomy and astrology. And we should treat our scepticism with caution. One of the remedies recommended by propinquity was willow bark for rheumatism engendered by damp conditions. Now the salix in willow is a basic ingredient of aspirin. Moon gardening is espoused by some modern gardeners as part of biodynamic gardening, where the approach is that plant life benefits from soil that is fully alive and in tune with cosmic forces. Thus the moon, sun, stars and planets influence plants in regular rhythms, offering ideal days or periods to sow, weed and gather plants.[29]

The biographer of Culpeper, Benjamin Woolley, has pointed out that he disapproved of fortune-telling from horary charts, preferring rather to use astrology to provide a prognosis before using medical principles to treat the patient. It is important to remember that Culpeper was a rebel, and it was the unauthorised character of astrology that attracted him, the 'knowledge system of outcasts'.[30]

Not such a rebel as Nicholas Culpeper, but a man with a similar outlook, was Antoine Mizalde, personal physician and astrologer to Marguerite de Valois, daughter of Henri II and Catherine de' Medici. He too sought to put medicine within the reach of all, liberating poor patients from dependence on unscrupulous apothecaries and physicians, and offering effective remedies that could be gathered from a domestic garden. Three of his works, bound in one volume and published in Cologne in 1576, are to be found amongst the books of Lord Herbert of Cherbury.[31]

Edward, first Baron Herbert of Cherbury, at his death in 1648 bequeathed his Latin and Greek books to Jesus College, Oxford. He was not a member of the college, but came from the powerful Welsh family of Herberts, and Jesus was very much a Welsh foundation. It was not a rich college, so Herbert stipulated that the books should be 'for the inception of the library there'. His manuscripts and English books were left to his family, much to the chagrin of the fellows of Jesus, who would have liked the lot. John Aubrey noted in his *Brief Lives* that Herbert had two libraries, one in London and the other at Montgomery Castle, indicating that this was out of the ordinary, and the bequest to Jesus College numbered 900 books.[32]

The collection covers a range of subjects, including astronomy, astrology, philosophy, but in particular Herbert acquired a large number of medical books. These include botanical works, but not gardening. Yet Herbert came from a gardening family – his stepfather, Sir John Danvers, had a garden in

Covent Garden and his famous Italian garden in Chelsea. His step-uncle was Sir Henry Danvers, the founder of the Oxford Botanic Garden, although family quarrels may have made contact between them remote. Possibly any gardening books that Herbert owned were in English, therefore went to the family and are now dispersed. Many of the books at Jesus are marked with his initials and the prices paid.

In his autobiography, Herbert explained not only how important it was for a gentleman to undertake botanising expeditions (see p. 119) but also how he 'delighted over the knowledge of herbs, plants and gums, and in a few words, the history of nature, insomuch that, coming to apothecaries' shops, it was my ordinary manner, when I looked upon the bills filed up, containing the physicians' prescriptions, to tell every man's disease'.[33] He also felt that he should learn about medicines, and make them himself, rather than trust to apothecaries who might provide drugs that were rotten, had lost their natural force, or be missing a vital, rare element in order to avoid expense. He even listed the medical books that he had in his library, including the pharmacopoeia of the London College of Physicians, and those issued by various European university medical faculties, such as Paris, Amsterdam, and Venice. Herbert's library at Jesus contains several herbals, including a folio version of Dioscorides published in Frankfurt in 1581, for which he paid the considerable sum of £1 10s. Some of the botanical books reflect the fascination for exotic plants, such as Johann Vesling's treatise on Egyptian plants, published in Padua in 1638.[34]

Presumably if Herbert had owned the herbals of William Turner, John Gerard or John Parkinson, these too would have remained in the family after his death. His copy of one of Thomas Johnson's botanical expeditions to North Wales, *Mercurii botanici pars altera*, published in London in 1641, however, went to Jesus College. In addition there are some books in English, which may have been a mistake on the part of his clerk. They are a mixed group that include Henry Peacham's *Complete Gentleman* and John Bate's *Mysteryes of Nature and Art*. Bate's book, published in 1634, was a compendium that offered information on subjects such as fireworks, drawing and perspective. In 'Of Water-workes', he described the principles of hydraulics and provided instructions on how to make the kinds of machines proposed by Hero of Alexandria, which Herbert may have used to help him with any that he installed in his garden. Another English title in the collection is William Stallenge's *Instructions for the increasing of mulberie trees*. This was the book produced by James I's 'Comptroller of the custome house', charged

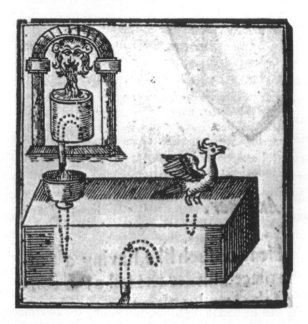

60 'How to make that a bird sitting on a basis, shall make a noise, and drink out of a cup of water, being held to the mouth of it', an illustration from John Bate's *Mysteryes of Nature and Art*, published in London in 1634.

by the King with encouraging the drive to cultivate a native silk industry (see p. 189). The mulberry trees cost 6s per hundred, so the accompanying instruction book represented a bargain at 8d as noted by Herbert.

The books given to Jesus College by Lord Herbert of Cherbury reflect the collection of a gentleman scholar with an amateur interest in medicine and botany – indeed, his autobiography suggests that he was something of a hypochondriac. Somebody with a more professional interest in medicine was Henry Pierrepont, Marquess of Dorchester, whose books are now in the Royal College of Physicians in London. Born in 1607, Dorchester was related to both the Cavendish and Talbot families – his great-grandmother was Bess of Hardwick. According to the physician and natural philosopher Walter Charleton, he established a botanical garden where he grew more than 2,600 plants, 'Each of them being, according to admirable method dispos'd into a particular Classis conteining all the Species referable to their proper Genus or Tribe'.[35] Charleton reckoned that the garden was scarcely inferior to the acme of private botanical gardens of the time, the 'famous Seminary of Vegetables' of Louis XIV's uncle, Gaston, Duc d'Orléans, at Blois.

XVI Portrait of John Tradescant the Elder, attributed to the artist Emanuel de Critz, who was related to Hester, wife of John Tradescant the Younger. Painted after Tradescant's death, it shows him garlanded with flowers, shells, fruit and vegetables.

XVII Illustration from 'Tradescant's Orchard', showing the Amber Plum with the mysterious note 'which JT [John Tradescant the Elder] as I take it brought out of France and groweth at Hatfield, ripe September 8th'.

XVIII Watercolour from an album of Alexander Marshall's paintings, showing white, crimson and purple anemones.

XIX *Cookmaid with Still Life of Vegetables and Fruit*, painted by Sir Nathaniel Bacon, *c.* 1620–25. The artist was a keen gardener, and clearly knew his vegetables: several of those depicted had been introduced into Europe from the New World in the sixteenth century, such as marrows, squashes and pumpkins. The turnips shown at the right elbow of the cookmaid are *Brassica rapa*, a sophisticated variety imported

from the Low Countries. Above the maid is a garland, mostly of meadow flowers, but with some garden cultivars. In the background is the kitchen garden where the gardener is shown carrying his produce in a basket on his back.

XX Topiary bushes and hedges in box at Moseley Old Hall in Staffordshire. The knot designs are based on the drawings made by the rector of Darfield in Yorkshire, Walter Stonehouse, in 1640, although the National Trust has filled the spaces with gravel and stone rather than flowering plants.

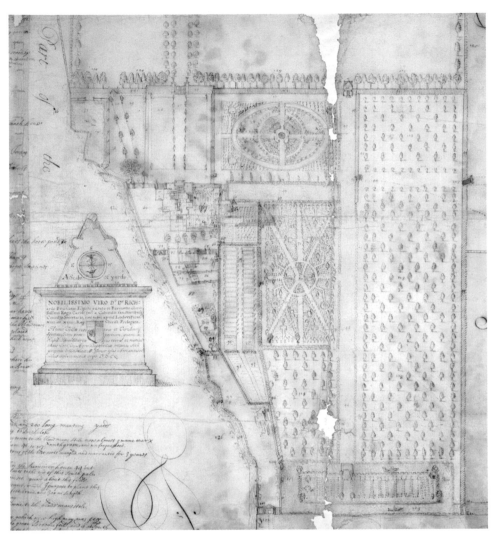

XXI John Evelyn's drawing of the layout of his garden at Sayes Court in Deptford, showing the awkward, triangular site. At the top is his oval parterre, based on that of Pierre Morin in Paris. Below this is the kitchen garden and the grove, and below again, the great orchard. At the bottom are rectangular beds built on an island in the Thames.

XXII Hepaticas from the florilegium of Emanuel Sweerts. This illustration is from a copy owned by John Goodyer, who coloured in some of the examples to help him with his identifications.

Dorchester was reputed to read for ten or twelve hours a day in his substantial library, and this devotion to study proved beneficial during the difficult years of civil war for, although he was a Royalist, the Parliamentarians compounded with him because he did not take part in any fighting, and he was left in peace. He was regarded as the best unqualified practitioner in medicine in England – William Harvey, for instance, thought highly of him – and he was made an honorary fellow of the Royal College of Physicians, the first to be so. He was also a founder member of the Royal Society.

Despite his reputation as a medical practitioner, Dorchester nearly poisoned himself with his own treatment, under the influence of opium muddling two pots of medicine, and in 1680 died of gangrene as a result of rubbing his legs with a bag of salt and breaking the skin. His bequest of his library to the College made up for severe losses suffered as a result of the Great Fire of London in 1666, when books belonging to distinguished physicians such as Thomas Linacre and William Harvey perished in the flames. Over two thousand titles were transferred to the College, along with a catalogue that had been drawn up in 1664.[36] The largest section of the library was made up of science books, including mathematics, architecture, medicine and botany.

Dorchester's substantial collection of herbals included the works of all the major European botanists – Brunfels, Fuchs, Camerarius, Clusius, L'Obel, and so on. His two English herbals were Johnson's emendation of Gerard and Parkinson's *Theatrum*. As he cultivated his own botanical garden, it is not surprising that he had several works that focused on individual European gardens. These include Besler's monumental *Hortus Eystettensis*, showing the plants cultivated by the Prince-Bishop of Eichstatt at his famous garden at Wilibaldsburg, near Nuremberg. He also owned a copy of the *Hortus Farnesianus*, published in Rome in 1625. The Farnese garden had been laid out by Vignola on the northern part of the Palatine Hill in Rome for Cardinal Alessandro Farnese in the 1530s and represented one of the most important botanical collections in early seventeenth-century Italy. The beautiful catalogue, compiled by Tobias Aldinus, director of the garden, with illustrations by the Sicilian botanist Pietro Castelli, depicts rare exotics from India, Mexico, Canada and Florida.

Other books of exotic plants in the collection include a study of the natural history and medicine of both the East and West Indies, *De Indiae utriusque re naturali et medica libri*. This was published in Amsterdam in 1658 under the name of Willem Piso, who had worked as a physician to the Dutch settlement in Brazil for six years from 1636. In fact, it also contains much of the work on the natural history of Java by the Dutch physician Jan Bontius, and the

61 The ornate title page of Willem Piso's book of the flora and fauna of the West and East Indies, published in Amsterdam in 1658. An eclectic mix of plants and creatures are on display, including the dodo from Mauritius, which was facing imminent extinction.

research of another physician in Brazil, Georg Marcgraf, so that, like John Gerard fifty years before, Piso was criticised by contemporaries for taking credit for the work of others.[37] His spectacular title page shows two Indians with the rich flora and fauna that were being discovered from the very opposite sides of the world.

A handsome book in Dorchester's collection is Emanuel Sweerts's *Florilegium*. Florilegia were collections of flower plates, usually engraved on copper, and often without much text. One of the first was produced in Paris in 1608 by the gardener artist Pierre Vallet, *Jardin du Roy très Chrestien Henry IV*, recording plants from the royal gardens as a source of embroidery patterns for the French Queen, Marie de' Medici. Another was a series of plant illustrations, *Icones Plantarum*, begun in 1611 by Johann Theodor de Bry, which moved the focus from the botanist's collecting case to the garden, and this too was the intention of Emanuel Sweerts.

Sweerts was a Dutchman, a minor artist, proprietor of a commercial museum in Amsterdam, and purveyor of novelties to rich men of taste, or as they came to be called, virtuosi. John Evelyn, during his travels in France, recorded how he visited one such virtuoso, the gardener Pierre Morin in Paris and saw his collection of 'pictures, achates, medals and flowers, especially tulips & anemones'.[38] In his museum shop Sweerts offered an extraordinary range: stuffed birds, mineral specimens and floral stock. Twice a year he would attend the Frankfurt Book Fair, then, as now, the greatest trade fair of its kind, and here he would also offer bulbs that he had imported from all parts of the known world. To give his customers some idea of the blooms that might emanate from his bulbs, he decided to produce an illustrated catalogue, and the first edition appeared in 1612 (Plate XXII). An astute businessman, he persuaded his most distinguished customer, the Emperor Rudolph II, to pay for the printing. Sweerts's *Florilegium* was published at about the time of his death, but his family produced five more editions of the book between 1612 and 1647. Dorchester's copy was from the last printing.

The standard of the engravings was uneven, for Sweerts was obliged to employ engravers of varying skills. Not all the plates were original – he used engravings from both Vallet and de Bry – but it may well be that the sharing of engravings among artists was a willing one, for there was a general feeling that botanists did not hold proprietary rights. Clusius and L'Obel certainly subscribed to this system. The overall result was a handsome catalogue with reliable descriptions that proved invaluable to gardeners for nearly half a century.

Conspicuously missing from Dorchester's library are practical gardening books, which he probably did not consider scholarly enough. There are also very few titles in English, and he may have shared Sir Thomas Bodley's view that works in English were 'idle books and riffe-raffes'.[39] However, the tide of general opinion was flowing in a different direction.

CHAPTER 9

Secrets Revealed

T HE LANDSCAPE HISTORIAN W.G. HOSKINS described the seventy
years between 1570 and 1640 as the great age of rebuilding in
England. For two generations of yeomen, farmers, husbandmen and
even prosperous cottagers in the country, and merchants and craftsmen in
towns, there was the wherewithal to build new dwelling houses.[1] And with
these houses came new gardens. This development is reflected in the growing
demand in this period for practical books on a whole range of domestic
subjects. In 1573, for example, John Partridge published the first edition of his
Treasurie of commodious conceits and hidden secrets, with its title page
announcing 'this may be called the huswives closet of healthfull provision'. In
addition to providing his housewife with advice on how to run her home,
Partridge gave instructions on various aspects of gardening, such as when to
gather herbs and flowers, and on a more unpleasant note in a later edition,
how to make 'Oyle of Earth-wormes ... for the sinews that are cold and
helpeth the paine in the joynts'.[2]

The style of the title became fashionable: by the beginning of the seventeenth century secrets were being revealed in books on gardening, medicine,
cooking and general management. These books were in English for a new
audience. Records of book collections in Tudor England indicate that the
overwhelming proportion of titles were in Latin, and this is also shown in the
catalogues and trade lists provided by London booksellers. The principal
market for their wares was monied, male and educated, the culture club of
gentlemen and the republic of letters of scholars – both groups who had

received grounding in the classics. But some writers had written in English for a more modest market. Thomas Hill with his gardening books found a profitable vein, for his books were reprinted again and again. The mystery is why they never feature in the libraries of enthusiastic gardeners, and it must be assumed that in grander establishments copies of Hill and other authors writing in the vernacular stood by the door to the garden, for discussion with the head gardener or estate manager, while more modest homes kept their books on a shelf in the kitchen.

Thomas Tusser had been shrewd when he aimed his books at a female audience. His exhortation, 'Wife, to thy garden', was an early recognition of the growing market for books among women. It was only a privileged few that had command of Latin, especially those born after the English Reformation. Elizabeth I was fluent in languages both dead and alive, so too were the Cooke sisters, but many high-born women did not have benefit of tutors, being trained rather in the skills of household management, embroidery, and music. This distinction continued for centuries. In 1842 the gardening writer Jane Loudon wrote in the introduction to her *Botany for Ladies*: 'It is so difficult for men whose knowledge has grown with their growth, and strengthened with their strength, to imagine the state of profound ignorance in which a beginner is, that even their elementary books are like the Old Eton Grammar, when it was written in Latin'.

By the end of the sixteenth century, however, the book trade in English was growing, taking advantage of the development of literacy, especially among women of the expanding middle class. Household management and gardening in particular were the gainers by this development. The secrets revealed were double: they were being revealed to women as well as men, and they were being revealed in the vernacular. Latin remained the principal language for books on botany, scarcely surprising as it was the international language for plant identification, as it remains today. Thus when the Cambridge botanist John Ray published his works, their titles and their texts were both in Latin. John Parkinson gave both his books Latin titles, *Paradisi in Sole* and *Theatrum Botanicum*, but his texts were in English. Perhaps an even more significant sign of the times was that Sir Hugh Platt entitled his gardening treatise *Floraes Paradise*, although the text was in English when it was first published in 1608. When a revised edition was issued in 1653 by his kinsman, Charles Bellingham, he gave the book an English title, *Garden of Eden*.

In the sixteenth century, when printed works in English on domestic matters were not readily available, many ladies kept their own books of recipes and horticultural information, as shown in Chapter 5, and the practice continued into the seventeenth century. Bess of Hardwick had clearly been a very successful manager of her household, and this skill she passed on through her daughter, Mary Talbot, to her granddaughters, Alethea, Countess of Arundel, and Elizabeth Grey, Countess of Kent. The household book belonging to Alethea, now in the Wellcome Institute Library, includes recipes attributed to her sister, Elizabeth.

Elinor Fettiplace's receipt book of 1604 unusually not only contains her notes for the still-room but also on maintaining the kitchen garden. For example, she writes:

> at Midsummer in the wane of the moon sow all manner of potherbs, & they will be green for winter; Also Lettuce seeds sown at this time and removed when they be of a pretty bigness at the full will be good and hard Lettuce at Michaelmas. . . . Sow red Cabbage seed after Allhallowentide [1 November], two days after the moon is at the full, & in March take up the plants & set from four foot each from other, you shall have fair Cabbages for the Summer; then sow some Cabbage seeds a day after the full moon in March, then remove your plants about Midsummer, & they will be good for winter.[3]

The close relationship between the garden and the house is evident from Elinor's recipes. Thus she explains how to preserve gillyflowers: 'Take Red gillowflowers and cut off all the white from them [the base of the petals] so let them stand all night'. She then took strong wine vinegar sweetened with sugar, and after boiling the mixture two or three times, she allowed it to become completely cold, and then added the flowers. This method could be used for all kinds of different flowers.[4]

By the 1580s printed books on household management were being published with the selling point that they were derived from these manuscripts belonging to ladies of society. In 1585 John Partridge produced *The Widowes Treasure* in which he claimed that he had borrowed from a friend a copy of a household book for the private use of a 'gentlewoman in the country', and decided to publish. This ploy was also adopted by Gervase Markham when he dedicated the 1631 edition of his *English Housewife* to Thomas Cecil's widow, Frances, Countess of Exeter, claiming that much of it was a manuscript which 'many years agon' had belonged 'to the Honourable Countesse'. The most ambitious name dropping was adopted by W.M. when he produced in 1658 *The Queens Closet Open'd*. Identifying himself as 'one of

62 An illustration from Nicolas de Bonnefons's *Jardinier francois*, first published in Paris in 1651, and translated seven years later as *The French Gardiner* by John Evelyn. This engraving accompanied the description of preserving fruit and shows women at work in the still-room.

her late servants,' he claimed that the 'incomparable secrets in physic, chirugery, preserving and candying' had been collected by no lesser personage than Henrietta Maria herself.

Blanche Henrey estimated that roughly five times as many books on botany and horticulture were published in England in the seventeenth century compared to the sixteenth. Although the numbers rapidly rose after the Restoration of Charles II in 1660, a significant number of titles were published during the Commonwealth period of the 1650s. Add to this books on design, perspective, husbandry, medicine, emblems, and the choice available to households from every social level was expanding. In 1657 William London, a bookseller in Newcastle upon Tyne, produced a catalogue 'of the most vendible Books in England'. Although London remained the centre of the book trade, booksellers were opening up shops throughout the provinces, and William explained at the beginning of this catalogue that he was reaching out to 'the Wise, Learned and Studious in the northern Counties of Northumberland, the bishopric of Durham, Westmorland and Cumberland'.

In his very long introduction William London expands on the use of books from various categories. Thus he recommends in his section on physick, 'a well cut [illustrated] Herball, flourishing with all sorts of forreign and Domestick Plants, Flowers, Herbs: with the Virtues of each Vegetable'. Under husbandry and gardening, he talks of 'an Art so courted with delightfull contemplation, that though a man be in willful sweat, he shall not feel it; the recreation sweetens all his labour, like Adam's first task, who is observed to have delight in the greatest toyl'. He argues that reading these books is a rewarding social activity: 'Many by reading Books of this Art, may advance their Knowledg very much, when they walk into a Garden, discoursing fully, freely, and skilfully of any Plant or Flower, more than a Gardener himself, who in a manner grows there, and dwells night and day.'[5] Nine gardening titles are listed, along with eight works on related subjects, such as simpling and herbals, and these seventeen may be compared with the eleven that Andrew Maunsell recorded in his catalogue compiled sixty-three years earlier, in 1595.

The prices of books remained stable, very similar to those quoted in Chapter 4, while wages rose, so that a craftsmen earning one shilling a day in 1600 could expect 16d per day by 1640. This would not have afforded opportunity for 'ordinary readers' to acquire the largest and most expensive books, for folios still commanded a price of around £1, rising significantly if the book was illustrated. In 1640 a copy of John Parkinson's *Theatrum Botanicum* cost the botanist John Goodyer nearly £2, including 3s for the binding. In the Huntington Library in California, a copy of Johnson's amended herbal of Gerard, published in 1633, has a note inside the cover that the price was £1 17s 6d unbound, £2 8s bound. While most quarto books cost around 5s, John Goodyer bought a copy of Crispijn de Passe's *Hortus Floridus* for double that price, but again, this is a highly illustrated book. Octavos were usually priced at around 1s, pamphlets from 1d to 6d.

One of the key factors evident from the prices cited is that illustrations made a great deal of difference to costs. Most botanical and horticultural books published in England were illustrated by woodcuts. Engravings in copper plate became popular from the end of the sixteenth century, but, with the exception of title pages and portraits of the authors, were not used in

Flos Solisprolifer.

63 The generous size of Besler's *Hortus Eystettensis* shows the sunflower in its full magnificence. When the flower from Peru first arrived in Europe, it caused a sensation, and would have been given pride of place in the garden of Besler's patron, the Prince-Bishop of Eichstatt.

gardening books until 1658 when John Evelyn's *French Gardiner* appeared. For his first edition he used only one engraving as the title page, but later added three others from the original French edition, adapted by a Dutch artist living in London. Book buyers were obliged to get their books from Europe if they wanted lots of copper-plate illustrations. Basil Besler's *Hortus Eystettensis* from Nuremberg, and Ferrari's *Flore* from Rome were both supported by generous patrons.

The Puritan Ralph Austen, when he issued the second edition of his book on the cultivation of fruit trees in 1665, advocated that this kind of book should be 'small of bulk and price, because great volumes ... are too great a price for mean husbandmen to buy'.[6] Even an octavo at around 1s would be beyond the purse of most mean husbandmen, who would have probably spent their pence on chapbooks and ballad sheets. Chapbooks usually consisted of between four and twenty-four pages, roughly printed on cheap paper and sold at under 6d. Because of their cheapness, and the value that even their rough paper provided for pastry cooks to line their pie dishes, or to wrap cheese, or to light pipes, or to use in the privy, few have survived. One of the best collections of chapbooks was made by the diarist Samuel Pepys, who was interested in the technological changes taking place in the seventeenth century whereby black-letter (Gothic) printing with woodcut pictures was giving way to white letter (Roman) without pictures. Some of Pepys's chapbooks are practical in nature, such as *The Compleat Cook or the accomplished servant-maids necessary companion* and *The gentlewoman's delight in cookery*, but he was very much an urban man and, unlike his diarist contemporary and friend John Evelyn, not a gardening enthusiast, so there are no gardening manuals. It may be that no such things existed, and that most people of straitened means would have learnt their gardening and husbandry 'on the job' without the benefit of any kind of publication.

One low-priced book with a bearing on gardening is *A Book of Fruits & Flowers* published in 1653: a rare copy is now in the Brotherton Library in Leeds.[7] It could be described as a 'super chap-book' for it was produced in quarto format with forty-nine pages, and what makes it very unusual is that it is illustrated with woodcuts of various fruit, vegetables and flowers. The food historian C. Anne Wilson points out that the compiler was forward-thinking in classifying his recipes under the headings of particular flowers, fruit or vegetables, an arrangement that we are familiar with, but not adopted by seventeenth-century cookery books, which tended to set down cookery recipes at the beginning and medical ones at the end, or jumbled up, like handwritten recipe books. The model for the layout of *A Book of Fruits and Flowers* came from herbals such as Gerard and Parkinson. The book was published by Thomas Jenner, a London printer and bookseller, using text and illustrations from other books that he may have offered for sale in his shop. Thus some of the recipes are drawn from John Dawson's *Good Huswives Jewell*, published in 1596, while many of the images are lifted from John Payne's *Flowers, Fruits, Beasts, Birds and Flies exactly drawne*, published in 1630. The latter was produced in an oblong format derived from the shape of prints, as with Crispijn de Passe's *Hortus Floridus*. If Jenner pirated Payne, Payne had pirated images from the master of botanical illustrations, Joris Hoefnagel.[8] These highly illustrated books, which could be used as references for gardening, natural history, and a decorative source for embroidery, were often bound as multi-volumes in a gentleman's library. John Goodyer had such a multi-volume, including John Payne, in his library.

John Goodyer's library in Magdalen College, Oxford, represents probably the most comprehensive collection of botanical books that has survived from the seventeenth century. He was born *c.* 1592 in Alton in Hampshire, into a yeoman family. His later knowledge of Latin and Greek suggests that he attended the grammar school in Alton before becoming an agent looking after estates. Alton is in Selborne country, and Goodyer represents a worthy fore-runner of the eighteenth-century naturalist Gilbert White, for he was fascinated by the local wild and garden flowers, scribbling botanical details on pieces of paper as he rode around the countryside on estate business. Among his manuscripts is a home-made chart of watercolours, showing that he also drew and painted records of flowers.

Goodyer's practice of dating and pricing books suggests that his first major botanical book was acquired on 31 January 1615, when he bought Caspar Bauhin's 1598 edition of the works of Mattioli in folio for the handsome sum of 20s. Thereafter his purchases came thick and fast, enabling him to build up a fine collection of herbals from sixteenth-century Europe and an entire range of English herbals from Peter Treveris's *Grete Herball* of 1526, through William Turner to John Gerard and, right up to date, John Ray's catalogue of the plants growing around Cambridge, published in 1657.

Within months of acquiring his first recorded books, Goodyer began to make the acquaintance of London apothecaries. His visit to John Parkinson's garden in Long Acre in 1616 resulted in the acquisition of new plants from the Iberian peninsula, probably brought to England by the plant hunter William

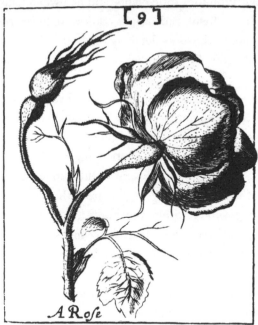

64 & 65 Above, a page from John Payne's *Flowers, Fruits . . . exactly drawne*, published in 1630. The rose, which was no doubt copied from an earlier book, is crudely copied yet again thirteen years later, in *A Book of Fruits and Flowers*, below, a collection of recipes using produce from the kitchen garden, published by Thomas Jenner.

Boel, and these subsequently were grown in Goodyer's own garden. A brief note of 'de Laune in ye black friers' suggests that he knew Paul, the brother of Gideon de Laune who gave land to the infant Society of Apothecaries to establish their hall and garden. Another note refers to 'Mr Cole yt married Mr Lobel's daughter in Lyne Street', showing that he was in touch with the Lime Street community of plantsmen and apothecaries.[9]

Visiting the garden of the merchant John de Franqueville, he saw the newly introduced Jerusalem artichoke, writing: 'Where this plant growth naturallie I knowe not. In Anno 1617 I received two small rootes thereof from Master Franqueville of London, no bigger than hens eggs, the one I planted, the other I gave to a friend, mine brought me a peck of rootes, wherewith I stored Hampshire'.[10] In fact, the artichoke had been imported from North America and was often described as the Canadian potato. The friend to whom he referred was William Coys at Stubbers, near Romford in Essex, whose garden had long been known for its rare plants. After his visit to Coys, Goodyer compiled a list of 126 of the rarities, including the potato, the cherry and the vine from Virginia. Goodyer must have particularly admired Clusius, sharing with him his fascination for exotic plants, and he owned Clusius's translation of the travels of Pierre Belon and various editions of his works on rare plants. His library was filled with works detailing the botany of the different parts of the known world, from Egypt, India, the West Indies, Brazil, Mexico and Canada.[11]

Goodyer established his own garden at Droxford in Hampshire, and here he planted his artichokes, noting how the vegetable could be cooked: 'Their rootes are dressed divers waies; some boile them in water, and after stewe them with sack and butter, addinge a little Ginger: others bake them in pies, puttinge Marrow, Dates, Ginger, Reasons of the Sunne, Sack etc.' but he adds a health warning that however they are prepared, 'they stirre and cause a filthie loathsome stinking winde within the bodie … and are a meat more fit for swine than men'.[12] Later he added water-melon from Virginia and two kinds of tobacco from seeds given to him by the Governor of Winchester Gaol.

Despite the fact that John Goodyer was a gardener, his collection contains no practical manuals, no arkham, Lawson, Estienne and Liebault, although he did own John Parkinson's *Paradisi in Sole* and, patriotically, *Instructions for the increasing of mulberie trees*. It may be that when he decided to leave his library to an Oxford college, he considered practical titles were not appropriate for a scholarly establishment and disposed of any that he owned. His horticultural interest is, however, reflected in his collection of books on specific gardens. Thus he acquired Basil Besler's monumental work on the garden at Eichstatt, Peter Paaw's record of the botanical garden in Leiden, Guy de la Brosse's description of the Jardin Royale in Paris, and the catalogue of the Oxford Botanic Garden compiled in 1658 by William Browne and Philip Stephens.[13] He also owned the 1612 edition of Emanuel Sweerts's *Florilegium*, the catalogue of his Frankfurt nursery, and the unique copy of the list of plants in the nursery at South Lambeth compiled by John Tradescant in 1634.

As Goodyer's knowledge of botany developed, so he became a generous contributor to the work of others, and this too is reflected in his collection. When Thomas Johnson was commissioned to produce an emended edition of the herbal of John Gerard, Goodyer furnished him with 27 manuscript sheets of notes, drawing upon his own observations of native plants, and infor-mation that he had gathered from his friends and merchants commissioned to bring him seeds from their foreign travels. Johnson duly gave Goodyer credit when the herbal was published in 1633 as 'the onely Assistant I had in the Worke'. The herbal, along with accounts of Johnson's botanising expeditions to Kent and Wales, are in the Goodyer collection, and it is possible that he may have been one of the *socii itinerantes*, although there is no firm evidence for this. Goodyer certainly went on expeditions, including the classic site for botanists of St Vincent's Rocks just outside Bristol. Among his books is a work on British flora, *Phytologia Britannica*, compiled byWilliam How, a twenty-year-old physician, which was published in 1650. How intended to revise and update it, so it is interleaved with his notes, but he died before he could complete the work.

Goodyer applied the last years of his life to providing medicines for his ailing neighbours in Hampshire, and his book collection contains a series of the latest medical books that were published in English during the Commonwealth period. Nicholas Culpeper's *English Physitian* is here, along with *The Art of Simpling*, produced in 1656 by Culpeper's stern critic William Coles, who so objected to his astrological beliefs. In 1651 Goodyer was visited by Elias Ashmole, who described him as a practitioner of physic, though one using only 'simple' medicines. As his death approached, Goodyer decided to leave his library and papers to Magdalen College, where his nephew, Edmund Yalden, was a fellow. This important donation, made in 1664 and consisting of 239 books and many manuscripts, was catalogued and given historical context in 1922 by the college librarian, R.T. Gunther, himself a knowledgeable natural historian.[14] John Goodyer emerges as one of England's first amateur botanists of stature, as well as providing us with valuable information about the collection and purchase of books in the early Stuart period.

If John Goodyer was a botanist who gardened, John Evelyn was a gardener who studied botany amongst a whole range of other interests. His gardening, practical and philosophical, will be considered in Chapter 10, but his library is the focus here. John Evelyn's library survived almost intact until 1977, when it went to auction in a series of sales. The loss of such an important seventeenth-century collection was huge, but it was also very well documented, from Evelyn's own catalogue, compiled in 1687, through to the records made at the dispersal.[15] John Evelyn was born at Wotton House near Dorking in Surrey in 1620, into a family that had made its money from introducing gunpowder into England. He was extremely long-lived, dying in 1706, and began buying books in earnest in the 1640s, in England and during visits to the Continent. Thus while some of his books date from the prolific period of publishing after the Restoration, he possessed many works from the sixteenth and early seventeenth centuries. In all, it is estimated that Evelyn owned around five thousand books, many of which were on theology, history and philosophy, as befitted the library of a gentleman scholar. However, he also owned a large proportion of the works that have been mentioned in the earlier pages of this book: herbals, husbandry manuals, gardening titles, medical and culinary books, works on architecture and design.

What distinguishes Evelyn's library from those of John Goodyer and Lord Dorchester, for instance, is the comprehensive collection of manuals on husbandry and horticulture. He owned the classical works on husbandry by the Roman authors Columella and Varro, two editions of John Fitzherbert's early sixteenth-century *Boke of Husbandry*, and a work he described in his catalogue as 'Heresbackius his Husbandry english'd by Barnaby Googe'. This last was Conrad Heresbach's *Four Bookes of Husbandry*, translated from the Latin by Barnaby Googe, a Lincolnshire landowner, a work that was highly esteemed and ran into many editions through the seventeenth century. Another influential book was Olivier de Serres's *Théâtre d'agriculture et mesnage des champs* ('Theatre of agriculture and land management'), first published in Paris in 1600. De Serres dedicated his book to Henri IV, with a frontispiece that linked king and gardener, and suggested that the realm is fertilised by the wise administration of the monarch and by the labour of all his subjects. According to de Serres, agriculture restored to the kingdom the peace and plenty which had been destroyed by the religious wars that had scarred France during the last decades of the sixteenth century. For Evelyn, living through the Civil Wars in England, this message would have found resonance.

John Evelyn's husbandry books include a series of works published in London and Oxford in the 1650s. Like de Serres, the authors of these publications sought to associate government with husbandry, but in their case the government was a commonwealth rather than a monarchy. The leading member of this group was Samuel Hartlib, born at the turn of the century in Elbing, a Baltic town that was then part of Poland. His Polish father was a factor for one of the English companies involved in the Baltic trade, his mother an Englishwoman. In 1628, when the trade in Elbing was imperilled by the arrival of the armies of the Hapsburgs, Hartlib retreated to London, where his marriage is recorded the following January at St Dionis Backchurch, hard by Lime Street and the community of apothecaries and gardeners. During the 1640s Hartlib remained in London, acting as an unofficial agent for the Parliamentarian cause and, following its victory in the Civil War, turned to establishing an 'Office of Address', modelled on the Bureau d'Adresse set up in Paris. This had two offices: the first, a kind of labour exchange in London to deal with the economic dislocations caused by the war; the second, based in Oxford, was to keep registers of information on 'Matters of Religion, of Learning and Ingenuities' and to act as a 'Center and Meeting-place of Advices, of Proposalls, of Treaties and all Manner of Intellectual Rarieites'.[16] Although the proposal created interest, it was never officially instituted, but instead Hartlib became what he called a conduit pipe, employing scribes and translators to copy portions of letters and treatises for circulation to others on a diverse range of practical scientific matters, including horticulture, medicine, and land improvement. Although he held very different political views, Evelyn became a friend, correspondent and a member of Hartlib's circle.

Samuel Hartlib was the author of more than 65 publications, most of them pamphlets. More substantial was *Samuel Hartlib, His Legacy*, first published in 1651, with subsequent editions: he presented Evelyn with the one issued in 1655. The book took the form of letters, a familiar medium for Hartlib, and dealt with a whole range of subjects, from orchards, vines and fruits, to the cultivation of silkworms and bees. Practical matters such as digging and manuring, smut and mildew were considered. Hartlib had no reservations about the importance of profitability in gardening. On the title page he quotes Psalm 144: 'That our garners may be full, affording all manner of Store, that our sheep may bring forth thousands and tens of thousands in our street'. He was frustrated by the fact that the British were still importing flowers, herbs and vegetables from Europe that he felt could grow very well in most parts of the country, and advised that those with two or three acres could maintain themselves and their families by gardening. But profit was not his only motive: 'I could instance ... places, both in the north and west of England, where the name of Gardening, and Howing is scarcely known, in which places a few Gardeners might have served the lives of many poor people, who have starved these dear years.'[17]

One of the authors Hartlib helped financially and encouraged to publish was Adolphus Speed, who finally managed to appear in print in 1659, the year of his death. Speed's title, *Adam out of Eden*, reflects the combination of practical husbandry and religious idealism of the Hartlib circle. The prospect of endless prosperity was Speed's message, a Virginia transported to England by the planting of root crops, new kinds of grasses, and the development of cash crops such as hops, liquorice, saffron and mustard. In fact, Speed had taken many of the ideas from Walter Blith, another member of the circle, much to his annoyance. Blith was a practising farmer in Warwickshire who wrote two books on husbandry described by the agricultural historian Joan Thirsk as surpassing 'all others of their time for their practical good sense'.[18] Blith published his first book, *The English Improver, or, a New Survey of Husbandry*, in 1649, completely revising it three years later as *The English Improver Improved*. The latter was dedicated to Oliver Cromwell, the council of state, nobility, gentry, soldiers, husbandmen, cottagers, labourers and the meanest commoner, in other words, the commonwealth. Among the innovations he proposed was the hops and liquorice taken up by Speed, but also woad and orchard and garden fruits.

Another member of the circle, Robert Sharrock, concentrated on the growing of vegetables. A clergyman and fellow of New College, Oxford, Sharrock also belonged to the circle of botanists who frequented the Oxford Botanic Garden and met in the lodgings of Robert Boyle to discuss scientific ideas. Sharrock published his *History and Propagation and Improvement of Vegetables* in Oxford in 1660, probably with financial help from Boyle, to whom he dedicated the book. He set out to provide a practical text for husbandmen and gardeners, including methods for propagating, layering, grafting and the taking of cuttings, drawing on the expertise of authorities such as Blith on the culture of hops, John Parkinson on the blanching of endive, and Jacob Bobart, keeper of the Botanic Garden, 'a very experienced person'. He also emphasised his own experience in gardening, to explode 'the multitude of monstrous untruths and prodigies of lies in both Latin and English, old and new Writers'. The book not only looked at vegetables, but also the propagation of flowers such as the tulip and the anemone.

John Evelyn's library boasted a significant range of practical gardening manuals, including a 1652 edition of Thomas Hill's vintage *Gardeners Labyrinth*, along with three sixteenth-century editions of his *Proffitable Arte of Gardening*, Gervase Markham's *Way to Get Wealth*, which incorporated William Lawson's *New Orchard and Garden*, and Leonard Mascall's *Art of Planting and Grafting*. He also bought John Parkinson's *Paradisi in Sole*, which he described in his catalogue as 'Parkinson's Flower Garden, Kitchin Garden and Orchard', recognising its value as a practical gardening book, as shown by the many notes that he made in it.

Evelyn also owned more specialised gardening titles on growing fruit trees, on the cultivation of silkworms, on keeping bees, and a little book devoted to the tulip, *Le Floriste François traittant de l'origine de Tulipes*, published in 1658 in Rouen by the resplendently named Charles de la Chesnée-Monstereul. Although monographs on particular plants had been produced in the sixteenth century, they focused on species that were of medicinal value such as the hellebore or balsam. So popular was the tulip, following its introduction to Western Europe, that a treatise on its different varieties was published anony-mously in Paris in 1617, and others followed, often plagiarisms of this first book.[19] Indeed, Paris witnessed a sort of mania for the tulip in the early seven-teenth century: at the wedding of Louis XIII in 1615 ladies of the court wore blooms in their cleavage rather than the customary rose. This enthusiasm was of style rather than the financial madness that later gripped Holland. Monstereul, like florists throughout Europe, was mystified by the tulip's ability to develop into feathered and flamed forms in brilliant colour, but concluded that those seeds that received the most air would produce blue tulips, those that had most weather would be white, and those that got the most sun would be red. He had stern words to say about tulip growers, distin-guishing the true florist from the ignorant pretenders who, like swine, 'love to scuffle through our Flower-Gardens, to carry off their Riches by their Greatness and Impudence. . . . To hear them speak of Tulips is a murdering Noise.'[20]

As the man who became famous for writing about trees, John Evelyn appropriately had a copy of Francis Bacon's *Sylva Sylvarum*, the histories of natural phenomena, first published in 1627. In 1680 Evelyn recorded in his diary that the book had formed the basis for experiments made by the

Royal Society, and he certainly studied it when drawing up plans for his own gardens. Evelyn's *Sylva*, like most of his books on horticulture, was not published until after the Restoration, but he began his authorial gardening career by translating *Le Jardinier François* from a treatise first published in Paris in 1651. No name had appeared on this work, but it was generally known to be the work of Nicolas de Bonnefons, valet de chambre du Roi. In his diary in December 1658 Evelyn recorded 'Now was published my French gardiner the first and best of that kind that introduced the olitorie [kitchen] garden'.[21]

The French edition was little and fat, over 400 pages. Evelyn reduced this and, although Bonnefons dedicated his book to women and particularly household managers, made his version more masculine and practical. Bonnefons had explained that he chose the format 'so that you could carry it without inconvenience, to compare the work of your gardeners with this small book, and judge their capacity or negligence'.[22] Evelyn may have felt that gardeners in England would not appreciate such interference.

66 & 67 Engravings from John Evelyn's *The French Gardiner*: left, laying out a walled garden, with trellis being erected; right, the kitchen garden, with raised beds for melons and cucumbers. Behind these can be seen a broderie parterre.

Although Evelyn was part of the Hartlib circle, he also set himself apart from it: he was, after all, a royalist in his sympathies, while Hartlib and many of his friends supported the Parliamentarian cause. This difference is reflected in the draft of Evelyn's *Elysium Britannicum*, the great gardening book that he never completed, where he explained that he addressed himself not to 'Cabbage-planters; but to the best refined of our nation who delight in Gardens and aspire to the perfections of the Arte'.[23]

Sir Henry and Lady Puckering were precisely the kind of gardeners to whom Evelyn was referring. For some time they were neighbours and later regular correspondents: the discussions on gardening will be considered in Chapter 10. At Henry Puckering's death in 1701, most of the books that he and his wife had collected were presented to the library of Trinity College, Cambridge. A significant proportion of the hundred or so titles is related to gardening and husbandry, almost all in English. These include Thomas Hill's *Art of Gardening*, John Parkinson's *Paradisus* and Hugh Platt's *Garden of Eden*. The Hartlib circle of writers is represented by Walter Blith's *English Improver Improved* and Ralph Austen's *Treatise of Fruit-trees*. There are two titles in French, Estienne and Liebault's *Maison Rustique* and de Bonnefons's *Le Jardinier François*, probably recommended to them by John Evelyn. His own *Sylva* is in the collection. We know that the books were used by both husband and wife, as Elizabeth Puckering has inscribed her name in some of them, one of the first examples we have in England.[24]

There is evidence, however, that one book in particular was valued by women: the herbal of John Gerard. At her death in 1647 Dame Margaret Heath left eighty-two titles in her library as recorded in an inventory.[25] Margaret was the widow of Sir Robert Heath, Attorney-General to Charles I. Most of the books listed are religious in subject, but she also owned John Parkinson's 'Garden of Flowers' (*Paradisus*), 'Concerning Gardening and orchard' (probably Markham's *Way to Get Wealth* incorporating William Lawson's text on orchards) and two copies of Gerard, one uncoloured, the second coloured. This last must have been very valuable, for hand colouring, which was usually undertaken by women and children, was laborious and Gerard's herbal is very extensive. The herbal also features in two portraits. In Lady Anne Clifford's Great Portrait of her life, where she shows the important books of her youth, Gerard is depicted alongside Sidney's *Arcadia*, the poems of Edmund Spenser, and Camden's *Britannia*. In a portrait of Susan, the second wife of Sir Thomas Hanmer, she is shown at her reading desk, splendidly dressed in Van Dyck lace, with a copy of the herbal open

68 Although ownership of gardening books by women is difficult to gauge as there are so few specific references, it is clear from records that they particularly valued the herbal of John Gerard. Susan, the second wife of the florist Sir Thomas Hanmer, chose to be depicted in her portrait reading a copy of the herbal.

before her, an indication that theirs was a marriage made in horticultural heaven.

Gardening books, herbals and husbandry manuals were an important, indeed a vital, part of the possessions that crossed the Atlantic with the colonists to North America. These intrepid travellers set out to observe the native flora and collect plants in the hope that they could be a valuable crop not only for themselves but for dispatch to England. French explorers and missionaries were sending back medicinal plants to the Jardin Royale in Paris, where they were recorded and named by the Parisian physician Jacques Cornut in his *Canadensium Plantarum*, first published in 1635. The English colonists' hope of commercial traffic was not to be fulfilled, although the introduction of sweet tobacco from South America to Virginia proved extremely valuable,

69 Spring-flowering columbine from Jacques Cornut's *Canudensium Plantarum* published in Paris in 1635. Cornut was a physician who studied the plants sent by early French explorers and missionaries from North America and grown in the Jardin des Plantes.

providing the staple crop on which the colony existed. Pomegranate seeds, grapes and mulberries for silkworms were dispatched to New England, but the climate proved too inhospitable.

One of the first descriptions of flowers and trees of Virginia was made by George Percy, son of the Wizard Earl of Northumberland. A member of the expedition that arrived in Chesapeake Bay in April 1607, he noted how the ground was 'all flowing over with faire flowers of sundry colours and kindes, as though it had been in any Garden or Orchard in England'.[26]Another member of that expedition, Captain John Smith, was more practical, noting 'Many hearbes in the spring time there are commonly dispersed throughout the woods, good for brothes and sallets, as violets, Purslin, Sorrell, etc. Besides many we used whose names we know not'.[27] These observers arriving in the 'brave new world' were trying to match up the plants they found with the familiar. Thus when John Josselin published in 1674 *An Account of Two Voyages to New England*, in which he looked back to the journeys he made in 1638 and 1663, he wrote how American plants:

> for their variety, number, beauty, style and vertues, may stand in Competition with the plants of any Countrey in Europe. Johnson hath added to Gerard's *Herbal* 300, and Parkinson mentioneth many more; had they been in New England they might have found 1000 at least never heard of nor seen by any Englishman before: 'Tis true, the Countrie hath no Bonerets [barometz], or Tartar-lambs, no glittering coloured Tuleps; but here you have the American Mary-Gold, the Earth-nut [ground nut] bearing a princely Flower, the beautiful leaved Pirola, the honied Colibry &c. They are generally of (somewhat) a more masculine vertue than any of the same species, but not in so terrible a degree to be mischievous or ineffectual to our English bodies.[28]

Josselin here talks of two of the most important botanical references for the colonists, John Parkinson's *Paradisi in Sole* and Thomas Johnson's emended edition of Gerard's herbal, which appear again and again in inventories and the lists of Boston bookstores. Records also show that William Brewster, one of the founders of the Plymouth Colony, carried a copy of Dodoens's herbal with him on his voyage aboard the *Mayflower* in 1620. With these books, colonists began to create gardens on the European model. The earliest of these was established by Champlain on an island in the St Croix River, in the colony of New France that is now the state of Maine. An early engraving shows how it was laid out in parterres, and clearly the colonists sought to retain the idea of the formality of the gardens that they had left behind, although it was important that these should also be practical. In *New England's Prospect*, published in London in 1634, William Wood gives a glimpse of a kitchen garden 'for Turneps, Parsnips, Carrots, Radishes and Pompions. Muskmillions, Squonterquashes, Coucumbers, Onyons, and whatsoever growes well in England growes as well there, many things being better and larger. . . . In other seasons there bee Gooseberries, Bilberries, Treackleberries, Hurtleberries, Currants, which being dryed in the Sunne are little inferior to those that our Grocers sell in England.'[29]

Enthusiastic early gardeners in North America included the Winthrops, father and son, both called John and both born in Suffolk. John Senior sailed

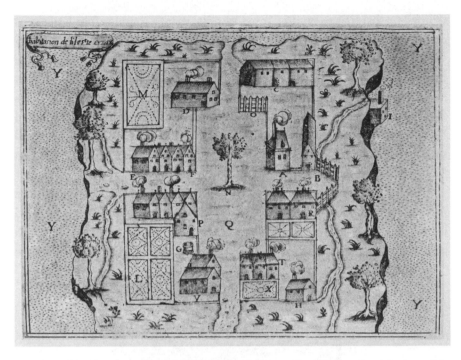

70 The earliest illustration of North American gardens, reproduced from a sketch by Samuel de Champlain in a book published in 1619. Champlain and his men had established a settlement on an island in the St Croix River in New France, and the gardens echo the parterres of Old France.

to America in April 1630, becoming the first governor of Massachusetts-Bay. As he reached the end of his journey, he recorded in his journal that the fragrance of the air blowing towards him from the New England coast was like the smell of a garden.[30] He created the Governor's Garden on a rocky island in Boston Harbour, and this became the port of call for many arrivals, where they were given their first taste of New England apples.

John Junior joined his father the following year, after accompanying the Duke of Buckingham on the unsuccessful attempt to relieve La Rochelle, where he must have made the acquaintance of John Tradescant the Elder. With him on his voyage across the Atlantic the younger Winthrop took a substantial supply of seeds that he had purchased from Robert Hill, grocer, who traded from the Three Angels in Lombard Street. These included seeds for vegetables, herbs, and flowers such as marigolds, monkshood, stock gilli-flowers and wallflowers. Soon he was being supplied with plants and trees from England. His uncle Joseph Downing wrote to him on 28 February 1633 telling him that he was sending some 'quodlin plants' – apples. The letter goes on to explain how these young plants might be kept alive during the sea voyage by being housed in an oyster barrel, but the ship's master must 'see them taken up out of the hold and sett up upon the upper decke 2 or 3 dayes in the weeke to take freshe ayre'. Downing was also offering him pear trees from his 'nourcerie' in his garden at Layer Marney in Essex, and asked Winthrop to let him know whether he had roses in New England. If not, 'I will send you over some damaske, red, white and province rose plants, of all these 3 or 4 a peece or more, if neede be.'[31]

One of Winthrop's most assiduous correspondents was the lawyer Edward Howes who supplied him with books as well as plants. A box that he planned to dispatch to Winthrop in 1634 contained more quodling slips along with books that included *Country Farme*.[32] Howes also sent him the works of

71 Fritillaries from Parkinson's *Paradisus*, including the Crown Imperial that was often planted as the centrepiece of beds. With its clear, practical instructions, *Paradisus* was one of the key reference books for early American gardens.

Sir Hugh Platt: the combination of books on science, husbandry, and gardening would have been very useful in establishing the Massachusetts Colony.[33] A recipe for a cordial for 'the sick, weak or cannot drinke water' consisting of water, white wine and 'a pretty quantitie of potatoe rootes' was dispatched in June 1632. This was apparently a mixture that Francis Drake used to drink during his voyage round the world, and Howes shrewdly realised that Winthrop would have plenty of potatoes for the purpose.[34]

In 1641 Winthrop came back temporarily to England, joining the circle of natural scientists around Samuel Hartlib and Robert Boyle, and taking the opportunity to add the latest books to his library, which constituted one of the largest collections in North America at that time, with more than a thousand volumes. On his return to New England, he exchanged information about gardening and plants and seeds with Robert Child, one of Hartlib's friends. In a letter of 1 March 1645, Child wrote to thank him for the delivery of seeds 'which I have delivered to the Gardiner of Yorke garden and Mr Tredeschan [John Tradescant the Younger], who are very thankfull to you for them and have returned diverse sorts which you shall Receive by the hands of Mr Willoughby.' In return Dr Child sent Winthrop five or six sorts of vine in a cask, 'with some prun grafts, some pyrocanthus trees, and very many sor[ts] of our Common plants and seeds, and I am confident in 3 yeares wine may be made as good as any in France'.[35] John Junior went on to become Governor of Connecticut, establishing his house and garden in New London, and a founding member of the Royal Society at its institution in 1662.

In 1715 Stephen Switzer pronounced that 'gardening can speak proper English'.[36] Although he was referring in particular to John Evelyn's translations of French gardening titles, the process was well under way by the time Charles II was restored to his throne. The secrets of the garden were being revealed to a growing market of readers on both sides of the Atlantic.

CHAPTER 10

The Long Winter

THE FLORIST JOHN REA DESCRIBED THE COMMONWEALTH of the 1650s as 'our long winter': he could equally have included the 1640s, the years of civil war that tore the country apart.[1] These turbulent decades were tragic and unproductive on both collective and personal levels, yet from a horticultural point of view they were far from fallow.

For young men with sufficient funds, a European tour held particular attractions at this period. John Evelyn in all made three visits to Europe, the first in 1641 when he spent two and a half months in Holland and the Spanish Netherlands, and his diary reflects his interest in gardens. When he visited the Hague, he went to see the garden of the Binnenhof belonging to the Prince of Orange, recording that it was 'full of ornament, close-Walkes, Statues, Marbles, Grotts, Fountaines, and artificiall Musique'.[2] On that same tour he visited the famous botanical garden of the university at Leiden, receiving a catalogue of the exotic plants and enjoying the cabinet of natural curiosities attached to the garden. When he returned to England he found the country teetering on the brink of war, and in November 1642 took part in the Battle of Brentford, just to the west of London, fighting for the King. Although the Royalists won this encounter, Charles I failed to push his advantage and march on to the capital. Instead his troops sacked Brentford, encouraging Londoners who feared for their property to come out in support of the Parliamentarians. When the Royalists set off westwards to Oxford, Evelyn felt that he could do no more for the King, and instead made arrangements to travel again in Europe.

Arriving in France in November 1643, Evelyn luxuriated in the great gardens to be seen in Paris and its environs: the Tuileries; the Jardin du Roi; St Cloud; the enormous gardens of Cardinal Richelieu at Rueil; and St Germain-en-Laye with its elaborate mechanical water devices. On the first day of April 1644 he paid a visit to the gardens of the Luxembourg Palace, originally laid out for Marie de' Medici, but now owned by King Louis XIV's uncle, Gaston, Duc d'Orléans, a passionate botanist. Evelyn described in his diary the formal gardens with their parterres marked out in box, 'but so rarely designd and accurately kept cut; that the (e)mbrodery makes a stupendious effect'. He also noted 'an enclosure for a Garden of simples, rarely entertaind, and here the Duke keeps Tortoises in greate number who use the pole [pool] of Water at one side of the Garden; here is also a Conservatory for Snow [an icehouse]'.[3]

The tortoises were part of Orléans's outdoor collection of curiosities, echoing his cabinet of treasures as a virtuoso. But such collections were no longer the preserve of the rich and the aristocrat. Within days of visiting the Luxembourg Evelyn went to see the gardens of Pierre Morin in the Faubourg St Germain, noting in his diary 'from an ordinary Gardner [he] is arriv'd to be

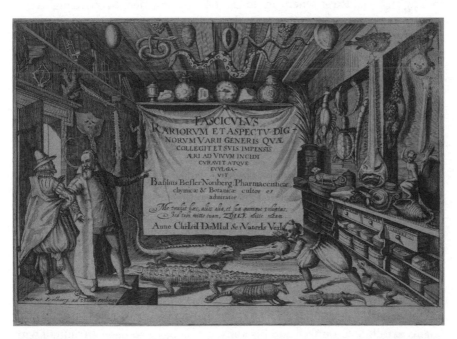

72 The title page of Basil Besler's *Fasciculus rariorum*, published in Nuremberg in 1616. This shows the interior of a cabinet of curiosities, with its eclectic collection of animals, shells, stones and botanical specimens.

one of the most skillfull and Curious Persons of France for his rare collection of Shells, Flowers & Insects'. Morin lived in a kind of hermitage surrounded by his collections of porcelain, prints and his butterfly display. Evelyn was particularly taken by the set piece in Morin's garden, 'an exact Oval figure planted with Cypresse, cutt flat & set as even as a Wall could have form'd it'.[4] Evelyn was to create just such an oval parterre in his own garden.

In October 1644 John Evelyn moved on to Italy, visiting the gardens outside Rome, including the Villa Medici, the Villa Borghese, the Villa Aldobrandi at Frascati and the Villa d'Este at Tivoli. Again he admired the sophisticated constructions of cascades, grottos and automata. At the papal garden on the Quirinale he 'observ'd the glorious hedges of myrtle above a mans height; others of Laurell, Oranges, nay of Ivy, & Juniper'.[5] In Padua he visited the botanical garden that had been founded a century earlier. The chair of anatomy at Padua was at this time held by a German professor, Johann Vesling, who gave him permission to take a representative sample of medicinal plants to dry and to paste into an album. This was in effect a *hortus siccus*, but Evelyn, who loved to use elaborate words, called it his *hortus hyemalis*, winter garden. This prized possession is now in the British Library.[6] Evelyn returned to England via Paris where in June 1647 he married Mary, daughter of Sir Richard Browne, the English Resident to the French court. The Brownes were also keen horticulturalists, with a garden laid out in the sixteenth century at Sayes Court in Deptford, downstream from London on the Thames.

We know many details about Evelyn's journeys in Europe, and particularly of his visits to gardens, from the diary that he kept. The travels of the poet Andrew Marvell, on the other hand, are known to us only through a reference made by John Milton in a letter, written in 1652 noting that he had spent four years abroad in Holland, France, Italy and Spain. Marvell is a man of mysteries and paradoxes. He was born in 1621 at Winestead in the East Riding of Yorkshire, the son of a minister. While his father was educated at Emmanuel College in Cambridge, an enclave of Puritanism, Andrew went to Trinity College, and family tradition has it that there he came under the influence of Jesuits who, 'seeing in him a Genius beyond his Years', enticed him from the university so that his father was obliged to travel to London in search of him, finding him in a bookshop and prevailing on him to return home.[7] His political views were also complex – he became Latin secretary to Milton and wrote poems extolling Cromwell and his aims, yet he has also been attributed with Royalist sympathies. Given his interest in horticulture that emerges from some of his finest verses, it must also be assumed that Marvell visited and enjoyed the gardens of Europe during a tour that lasted for four years from 1642, probably acting as tutor to an unknown pupil. In his biography of Marvell, John Dixon Hunt assumes that he followed a route similar to that taken by Evelyn, apart from a visit to Spain, where he certainly saw Aranjuez and Bel Retiro near Madrid, and probably others too.[8]

A second poet who made a European tour at this period was Edmund Waller. Unlike most poets, Waller was a very wealthy man with large estates in Buckinghamshire and a seat in the House of Commons. His comfortable lifestyle came to an abrupt end in 1643, however, when he was implicated in a political fiasco known as Waller's Plot, which called for an armed rising and seizure of key points in the City of London to let in the King's army. After eighteen months in prison without trial, he was fined a massive £10,000 and permitted to go into exile in November 1644, having managed to alienate all parties by his implication of others in the plot. During his stay abroad, Waller met up with John Evelyn who recorded in his diary that he travelled from Venice 'accompanied with Mr Waller (the celebrated poet) now newly gotten out of England, after the Parliament had extreamely worried him, for attempting to put in execution the commission of Aray, & for which the rest of his collegues were hanged by the Rebells.'[9] Eventually he set up in Paris, living there in considerable style, and, like Evelyn, was able to observe the magnificent gardens in and around the capital. In 1651 he received a pardon from Parliament and returned to his estate at Hall Barn near Beaconsfield.

The last of a gardening quartet that used these years to learn of European gardens and gardening was Robert Morison, born in Aberdeen in 1620. He attended Marischal College, founded in 1593 in Aberdeen for the training of ministers. Morison's abiding interest, however, was in botany, and in particular the flowers of his own country. With the outbreak of the Civil War he fought for the Royalists against the Covenanters, receiving a wound in the head at the Battle of the Bridge of Dee in 1644. Once he had recovered from this serious wound, he fled to France, became a tutor, and studied anatomy, zoology and botany, taking a degree in medicine at Angers. The royal botanist, Vespasian Robin, recommended him for service in the household of the Duc d'Orléans, and throughout the 1650s he worked in his garden at Blois, where he was encouraged to develop his ideas on the classification of plants. Such was his reputation as a gardener and a botanist that Jacob Bobart, the keeper of the Oxford Botanic Garden, considered him without equal. When his ducal patron died in 1660, his services were sought by both Nicholas Fouquet, the French minister of finance, and Charles Stuart, newly restored to the English throne.

By 1652, apart from Morison, all were back in England, with Marvell taking up the post of tutor to Mary, daughter of General Sir Thomas Fairfax, and Evelyn and Waller beginning to apply to their gardens some of the ideas that they had imbibed on their travels. This was the England of the Commonwealth, a republican form of government, though in reality power lay with Oliver Cromwell and his army. It was also an England aflame with ideas and philosophies, including those of a hortulane nature, as John Evelyn inimitably put it.

One man bursting with ideas was Samuel Hartlib, who, as we have seen, enjoyed a reputation as an imparter of scientific ideas and information, acting as an 'intelligencer' for the dissemination of news, books and manuscripts. He believed that God had given Man a talent that should be placed at the disposal of the common weal, encouraged by the establishment of a model college of learning, a 'Solomon's House' as envisaged in 1627 by Francis Bacon in his *New Atlantis*. One of Hartlib's interests was the keeping of bees, and in 1655 he published *The Reformed Common-wealth of Bees*.

Honey was particularly desired at this time, for the trade in sugar from Barbados had been disrupted by the Civil War. It was argued by some that, as a spiritual product, honey was healthier than sugar, and the patriotic drum was also sounded, with the view that mead was infinitely superior to fancy sweet wines from Spain and Portugal. Hartlib suggested new techniques for hives, including in his book one with multi-storeys from a drawing by Christopher Wren, an adaptation of the design that had been used in the garden at Wadham College. The study of bees was a particularly appropriate area, for it combined religious connotations with practical economy. Bees were the natural source of divine wisdom for both classical and Christian traditions, and Hartlib believed nature contained evidence of God's laws which, if understood, would dispel religious controversy. They were, moreover, sound economists, clean, chaste and industrious with a rational social structure that ensured strict division of labour and property. This kind of commonwealth he would have liked to have applied to the nation, and to its leaders.

Hartlib was interested in all aspects of husbandry, and when writing the preface for an anonymous pamphlet, *A Designe for Plentie, by an Universall Planting of Fruit Trees*, published in 1652, he suggested that all waste ground should be planted with apples, pears, quinces and walnuts 'for the relief of the poor, the benefit of the rich, and the delight of all'. England should thus become 'The Garden of God'. The association of gardens with Eden were frequently made at this time. Robert Crab, a Cromwellian trooper, wrote a pamphlet in 1657, in which, between diatribes about steeple-houses

(churches) and starched ruffs, he declared: 'Reader, this is to let the understand, when I was in my Earthly Garden adigging with my Spade, with my face
to the East side of the Garden, I saw into the Paradise of God from whence my
Father Adam was cast forth.'[10]

This idea was given a further spiritual twist by Ralph Austen, a Calvinist
divine who spent much of his life in Oxford. In his *Treatise of Fruit-trees*,
published in 1657, he advances the theory that when Adam and Eve were
expelled from the Garden of Eden, mankind was cut off from the good apples,
and left in a world of bitter crab apples. With the coming of Christ 'God the
great husbandman of his orchard the church, began to plant the vast waste
grounds, the wilderness of the idolatrous nations, the Gentiles'. However, he
also 'upon his own free will and pleasure, without any foresight of faith,
repentance, good works or any thing in us' had 'from all eternity made choice
of what Spiritual Plants he pleased to plant in his Garden, the Church, and
refused others'. As John Prest notes, this is the gardening of the elect.[11] The
treatise was divided into two parts, the first on the cultivation of fruit trees, the
second on the spiritual use of orchards. Hartlib and Robert Boyle tried to
persuade Austen to omit the second part in any reprints, and when a new
edition was issued in 1665, their arguments prevailed.

If Austen reflected the Calvinist doctrine of the elect, his contemporary
John Beale held visionary ideas that could have emanated from William Blake.
Beale was a native of Herefordshire who, after studying at Cambridge and
travelling in France, became rector of Sock in Somerset. In 1657 he published
a small volume, *Herefordshire orchards, a pattern for all England*, which consisted
of two letters written the previous year to his friend Samuel Hartlib. Although
the book contains practical advice on looking after fruit trees, Beale combines
this with spiritual thoughts. In another letter to Hartlib he talks about all kinds
of spirits '(whether they may all at all times bee properly called Angels or not)
that run parallel & have their offices in & over every part of the creation. ....
Some to Mineralls, some to Vegetables, some to Animalls, To severall
Elements, & to several Orbes, or Planets'.[12] This animist theology was highly
unorthodox if not heretical for the seventeenth century.

Beale was fascinated by Britain's ancient past. Antiquarian studies were just
beginning (the term archaeology was not coined until the nineteenth century).
James I commissioned his Royal Surveyor, Inigo Jones, to write a report on
Stonehenge, which eventually was published in 1655 as *Stone-Heng Restored*.
Meanwhile John Aubrey had come upon the prehistoric stone circle that
interweaved with the village of Avebury during a hunting expedition in

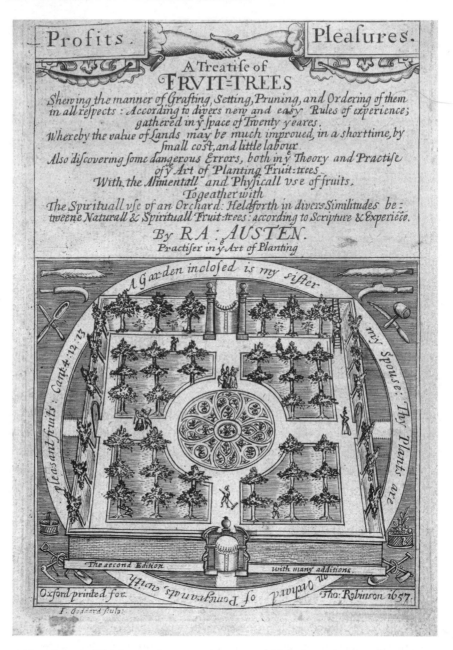

73 The title page of Ralph Austen's *Treatise of Fruit-trees*, published in Oxford in 1657. The theme taken here, reflecting the contents of the book, is that profit should be combined with pleasure, the practical with the spiritual, quoting from Song of Solomon 4:12–13, 'A garden enclosed is my sister, my spouse … Thy plants are an orchard of pomegranates with pleasant fruits'.

January 1649, recording that nobody had taken notice of it before, 'though obvious enough'.[13] More antiquarian investigations followed with much debate about the age and purpose of these sites. In a letter to Hartlib, Beale revealed that he had spent a night on Backbury Hill near Ledbury in Herefordshire, and had there a prophetic dream of a perfect English garden. This vision was included in an edited form by John Evelyn in his compilation of gardening lore, *Elysium Britannicum*, when he described a lofty hill associated with ancient British tribes, with path in trenches winding their way to the top. Here an area, roughly square, was naturally cleared like a garden, looking down on precipices and desolate countryside. This was 'a place so blessed by Naturall situation ... it were capable of being made one of the most august and magnificent Gardens in the World, as far exceeding those of Italy and France, so prodigall of Arte and full of Ornament, as they surpasse our best in England by superlative degrees'.[14] In this extraordinary passage, John Beale speaking through Evelyn is proposing to situate his Eden in England, superimposing the image of the garden on the ancient hill fort.[15]

The circle around Samuel Hartlib adopted the widely held belief of millenarism, that God was intervening in history, purifying religion, fulfilling many of the prophecies of the Old Testament and preparing the way for the Second Coming and the establishment of the rule of the saints under Christ for a thousand years in the earthly paradise. Man would then be restored to his original perfection, enjoying the paradisial state that Adam had forfeited. John Evelyn too was affected by these beliefs, combining them with his great interest in gardens. Writing to the physician and philosopher Sir Thomas Browne in January 1660 he suggested that the air and genius of gardens could operate 'upon humane spirits towards virtue and sanctitie' and 'prepare them for converse with good Angells'.[16]

In this same letter he referred to his intention to write about different aspects of gardening, an early proposal for his book *Elysium Britannicum* which was never completed or published, although a thousand pages survived amongst his papers in the library of Christ Church in Oxford. In this book he set out to describe the skills and knowledge necessary to planting what he describes in his letter as a 'noble, princely and universall Elysium', but digressed into a discourse on the pleasures and virtues of gardens, and eventually it became a plan for life lived entirely on the 'hortulan mode'. Browne not only received his long and complex letter, but also a list of legendary and historical gardens that have influenced man's imagination, from Paradise and the Elysian Fields, through to the gardens of Renaissance Italy which could be emulated or even surpassed by his English design.

Five months earlier, Evelyn had written an equally remarkable letter to Robert Boyle announcing his intention to make a major change in life by withdrawing from the world to a small community of natural philosophers which he was hoping to establish: 'why might not some gents, whose geniuses are greatly suitable, & who desire nothing more than to give a good example, preserve science, & cultivate themselves, join together in society...'. To carry this very Baconian concept forward he proposed 'the purchasing of thirty or forty acres of land, in some healthy place, not above twenty-five miles from London; of which a good part should be tall wood, & the rest upland pastures or downs, sweetly irrigated. If there were not already a house which might be converted, &c. We would erect upon the most convenient site of this, near the wood, our building, viz. one handsome pavilion, containing a refectory, library, withdrawing-room, & a closet.' The house would be a communal centre, with lodgings for guests and apartments or cells 'somewhat after the manner of the Carthusians' for the fellows. 'There should likewise be one laboratory, with a repository for rarities & things of nature; aviary, dovehouse, physic garden, kitchen garden, & a plantation for orchard fruit,

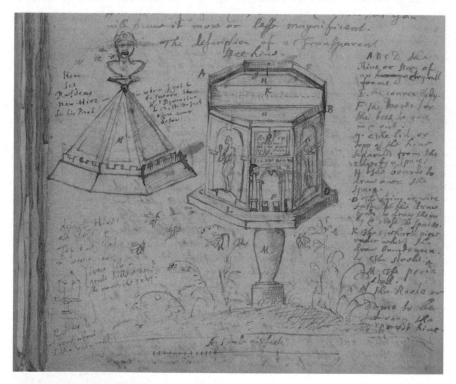

74 John Evelyn was a keen keeper of bees. Here he adopts a whimsical approach, providing them with hives in the form of Gothic church fonts, in drawings from his *Elysium Britannicum*.

&c'. Servants were to be kept at a 'convenient distance', and he expressed the wish to bring his wife, but apparently not offering this luxury to the others.[17]

Evelyn's elaborate ideas reflect his disillusionment with the Commonwealth, which he likened to the Gothic invasions when saints retired from the world, and his frustration in being excluded as a Royalist from public office. In an earlier letter to a friend, he had reflected sadly, 'I might have one day hoped to have bin considerable in my Country. A Friend, a Booke, and a Garden shall for the future perfectly circumscribe my utmost designs'.[18] But within months of his letter to Thomas Browne, Charles II was restored to the throne, and a new era of opportunity opened up for John Evelyn.

Nevertheless the 1650s had also been a period of intense horticultural activity for Evelyn. In 1652, following his return to England, he retrieved the sequestered estate of his wife's family, Sayes Court in Deptford, noting in his diary that it was 'very much suffering, for want of some friend, to rescue it out of the power of the Usurpers'.[19] The task before him as far as the garden was concerned was challenging: the layout and details were very old-fashioned, and the setting, by the Thames, was bleak. Evelyn was determined, however, to turn Sayes Court into the Italian villa of his imagination, flattening the Tudor mount and filling in the moat to provide a platform for a parterre and fountain. At the centre he placed the oval garden based on Pierre Morin's garden in Paris. Determined to get as close to the original as possible, he wrote to his father-in-law in France to ask him to convert the French measurements into English. By the autumn of 1652 he had transplanted 'my Glorious Nursery of neere 800 plantes (two foote high & as fayre as I ever saw any in France) about our Court, and as farr as they will reach (at a foot distance) in our Oval-Garden'.[20] However, he was to find that the exposed site caused almost half of them to perish, so that he was obliged to experiment and to adapt.

North of this garden he created a terrace walk, one bank lined with a holly hedge and the other with a hedge of berberis. Between it and his orchard he planted a grove of mixed deciduous trees with thickets of 'thorne, wild fruites, greenes, &c'. The grove was crossed by walks leading to a central point planted with bays and a small circular walk edged with laurel. To the east of the grove, separated by a lilac hedge, was a kitchen garden with thirty-eight beds for pot herbs, plots of melons, peas and beans. In the private garden near the house, where he grew 'choice flowers and simples', he placed one of the glass apiaries that he had acquired from John Wilkins after dining with him at Wadham College in 1654. Looking out onto this private garden he built a portico and an 'elaboratorie', a laboratory cum still-room, where he could conduct chemical experiments and his wife could apply her skills to distilling essences and plant oils. All the elements of the garden can be seen in a detailed plan that Evelyn drew of Sayes Court (Plate XXI). So detailed is it that, for instance, the centre of the Oval Garden is laid out like a daisy, each petal edged in box.[21]

Not only has Evelyn left us much detail about his life from his diary, but also about how he gardened from the various manuscripts that he was preparing for publication. Apart from his translation of *The French Gardiner*, which first appeared in 1658, his gardening books were produced after the Restoration, and some, like *Elysium Britannicum*, never appeared in print during his lifetime. Nevertheless they show us how he went about creating and developing his gardens. Even *Fumifugium*, a proposal issued in 1661 to solve the problem of London's obnoxious smoke, includes a section on how plantations could be set around the city, 'supplied with such *Shrubs* as yield the most fragrant and odoriferous *Flowers*, and are aptest to tinge the *Aer* upon every gentle emission at a great distance'.[22]

Evelyn's major published work appeared in 1664: *Sylva or a Discourse of Forest-Trees* was full of practical information, some of it acquired while planting his grove and orchards at Sayes Court. At the end of the book are 'Aphorisms concerning Cider' contributed by John Beale. Evelyn, ever the patriot, points out in his preface to *Pomona*: 'It is little more than an Age, since Hopps (rather a Medical, than Alimental Vegetable) transformed our wholesome Ale into Beer; which doubtless much alter'd our Constitutions', inducing 'tormenting Diseases, and a shorter life'. Instead he recommends the planting of apple orchards to 'present us with one of the most delicious and wholesome Beverages in the world'.

A second appendix to *Sylva* was Evelyn's *Kalendarium Hortense*, one of the earliest gardening calendars. Arranged according to the months, it even provides the number of hours between sunrise and sunset. Instructions are given for what the gardener should be doing each month in the orchard, the 'Olitary-garden' (kitchen garden), the parterre and the flower garden. For example, in January with eight hours of daylight he recommends digging over the ground ready for spring, and pruning the branches of mature fruit trees, even providing the reference to the appropriate section of his *French Gardiner*. A list of the apples and pears that are in their prime also indicates which are good for cooking, such as the Winter Musk and Winter Norwich pears that both bake well. Flowers in their prime include the winter aconite, anemones, cyclamen, hyacinths, black hellebore and the early (praecox) tulip. Even the flowers for eating are noted, a reminder that Evelyn was also the author of the first book on salads, *Acetaria*, which was eventually published in 1699.

The entry for June, naturally, is much more extensive, with sixteen hours to undertake tasks such as the sowing of salads like lettuce, chervil and radish, the propagation of fruit trees and the care of vines. Evelyn warns to 'begin to destroy *Insects with Hoofs*'. This strange instruction refers to pushing the hooves of sheep onto sticks placed close to pinks and carnations which are particularly prone to earwigs. The insects would feed at night, then take shelter in the hollows of the hooves, so that they could be collected and killed in the morning, a forerunner of using jam jars as earwig traps.[23] Evelyn also advises to 'Look to your *Bees* for *Swarms*' and 'Look now to your *Aviary*; for now the birds grow sick of their *Feathers*'. For the latter he recommends emulsions made up of bird seed soaked in water.

In September he is preparing for the winter, planting anemones, tulips, daffodils and colchicum. Auricula seeds he sows in cases that he has placed to face the sun through the following months. Tuberoses are taken out of the garden and put into the conservatory, where they are to be preserved in dry sand, or wrapped in paper in a box near the chimney. After Michaelmas, 25 September, these are joined in the conservatory by his 'Greens' and exotic trees such as oranges, Spanish jasmine, oleanders and aloes. More hardy plants are put in pots, two or three inches below the surface of a bed, covered in moss, and then covered by glass. Autumnal plants are staked, 'to prevent sudden Gusts which will else prostrate all you have so industriously rais'd'. Meanwhile he continues his war on wasps and 'other robbing Insects', and gets on with making his cider.[24]

Another text that reflects in detail Evelyn's work in the garden is a manuscript giving 'Directions for the Gardiner at Says-Court: But which may be of Use for other Gardens'. This he compiled in June 1686 for his apprentice gardener, Jonathan Mosse. Evelyn was now in his late sixties and wanted gradually to hand over the running of the garden to his assistant. It must have been daunting for the young man to take over from such a distinguished and experienced horticulturalist, and Evelyn was leaving nothing to chance. He begins the manuscript with 'Termes of Art used by Learned Gardeners', defining different techniques such as lætation (dunging), repastination (a slight digging), semination (sowing) and plushing (cutting a branch nearly half through, to make it bendable for layering). He gives the various terms for season: vernal (spring), estival (summer), autumnal, and hyemal or brumal (winter), præcoce (early blossoming flowers and ripening fruit), median

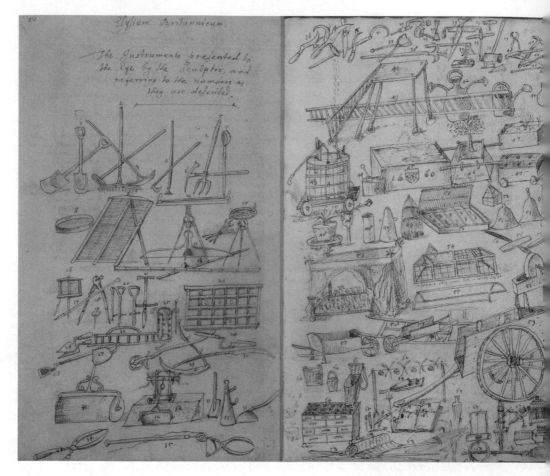

75 John Evelyn's 'advent calendar' of tools and equipment from his *Elysium Britannicum*. He shows the basic assortment of gardening tools such as forks and spades, but also a knife-grinder and a book in which to write the names of plants. The most extraordinary object is no. 53, 'a Bed-stead furnished with a tester and Curtaines of Green' to protect tender flowers from 'the parching beames of the Sunn'.

(middle term, applied particularly to tulips), and serotine (late flowering and ripening). This is followed by long lists of the different fruit trees, when they were planted and where, followed by notes for the kitchen garden and appropriate plants.

He advises Jonathan Mosse to set the plants for the physic garden in alphabetical order, 'for the better retaining them in memorie'. One garden is set aside for coronary flowers – crown-like as in coronation. These could be used for garlands and wreaths, and for flower arrangements for the house, where

76 In his advice to his apprentice, Jonathan Mosse, Evelyn emphasised the damage that could be wrought by vermin. In the kitchen garden, he destroyed slugs by 'strewing lime dry upon the plants'. Giovanni Battista Ferrari, in his *Flora Overo*, provides a more baroque approach to the fight against slugs.

the desired effect was to be crown-like with the most dramatic flowers at the top. Echoing the marketing of books at this period, Evelyn explains that the seeds of stock gillyflowers should be saved and sown in a hot-bed in February and planted out at Michaelmas: 'This is a precious seacret'. Under his notes for 'Ever-greenes' he warns 'Never expose your Oranges, Limons, & like tender Trees, whatever season flatter; 'til the Mulbery puts-forth its leafe, then bring them boldly out of the Greene-house; but for a fortnight, let them stand in the shade of an hedge, where the sun may glimmer onely upon them.' He also includes a 'Complete Culture of the Orange &c. after the Holland way'.

The gardener is given a full weekly regime, beginning with a walk 'aboute the whole Gardens every Monday-morning duely, not omitting the least corner, and so observe what Flowers or Trees & plants want staking, binding and redressing, watering, or are in danger; especially after greate stormes, & high winds and then immediately to reforme, establish, shade, water &c what he finds amisse, before he go about any other work'. Useful measurements and lists of tools complete the manuscript. John Evelyn was clearly no armchair gardener, and provides here a guide to gardening that could form the basis for any horticultural student.

Evelyn was generous in his advice on gardening to his friends. Among his papers is his correspondence with Elizabeth Puckering, whose gardening books are discussed in Chapter 9. Elizabeth was born in 1621, the elder daughter of Thomas Murray, who had been tutor to the future Charles I. With her sister Anne, who wrote a memoir of her life, she was brought up by her mother to play the lute and virginals, to be proficient in French, dancing, needlework and writing. This last accomplishment was not entirely mastered, for her letters are scrawling, difficult to read and spelt phonetically. In the early 1640s she married Henry Newton from Charlton House in Kent but, at the death of his uncle, her husband took the name of Puckering and inherited his estate in Warwick. John Evelyn met the Puckerings through friends in Greenwich in August 1653, and in their subsequent correspondence Elizabeth and Evelyn refer to each other as 'best neighbours', for Charlton was not far from Sayes Court.

In a letter written to Evelyn on 30 October 1654 Elizabeth Puckering explained why she has been 'so great a stranger to Sayes Court'. She had been enriching Charlton with 'tres of hard names wich possibly you may find for their rarity to deserve a place in your Garden'. One of these was cherry laurel, a relatively recent introduction into England, and in a postscript to her letter she offers to send a cutting from her gardener to Evelyn.[25] Two years later the Puckerings moved to Warwick, much to Elizabeth's sadness, for she missed the company of Evelyn, writing to him that she could think of nothing but Deptford and what she had lost by being at so great a distance. Her garden at Warwick, moreover, did not prosper. Evelyn sent her a design for it which he hoped might 'contribute to your wonted passion for the Horticultural entertainments'.[26]

Another of his gardening correspondents was the florist Sir Thomas Hanmer, who contributed a chapter to Evelyn's *Elysium Britannicum*. At the beginning of the Civil War Hanmer raised a band of archers and a dragoon regiment for the King, but in 1644 he obtained leave to go to France with his family where it would seem that he supplied information to Parliament about Charles I's negotiations with France and the Scots. This 'signal service to the commonwealth' enabled him to return home with a comparatively light fine, and to turn his attentions to cultivating his garden at Bettisfield in Flintshire. We have detailed information about how he gardened in his *Garden Book* completed by 1659.

Hanmer's pleasure gardens were laid out in rectangular beds, slightly raised and supported by coloured boards, tiles or stones, planted with flowers and divided by well-kept gravelled or sanded plants. Beyond lay the wilderness with walks set between hedges. The flower beds were filled with the favourite florists' flowers of the period: anemones on the outsides, tulips and narcissi in the middle. He notes gillyflowers at the ends of some beds, cyclamen at the corners. In the centre of one bed he planted his 'coronary feature', a double Crown Imperial, the spectacular fritillary that arrived in Western Europe via Constantinople around the year 1570. A native of the Holy Land, its flowers are said to hang their heads in shame because they stared boldly at Christ on his way to the Crucifixion. Although he accorded the Crown Imperial central stage at Bettisfield, Hanmer was not a great admirer, finding its orange colour 'ill dead'. He also planted a more delicate cousin, the grey fritillary, *Fritillaria persica*, which again came to England from Turkey.

Hanmer's most favoured flowers were his tulips, which he described as 'the Queene of Bulbous plants'. He loved their huge range of colours and their markings, noting 'wee did value in England only such as were well stript with purples and other redds, and pure white; but now, within a yeare or two, we esteeme (as the French doe) any mixtures of odde colours . . . and such as are markt with any yellowes or Isabellas [greyish yellow].'[27] He advised that tulip beds should be about four feet wide, raised in the centre so that 'all the flowers may bee seene the better'. A bewilderingly long list of different tulips is then provided, placing them in ranks for their positioning in the beds.

These gardening plans give us some idea of how the beds would have looked. But one unknown factor is the density of the planting. It has been argued that to modern eyes the planting would seem sparse, and this is borne out by representations of gardens by artists. Crispijn de Passe, for instance, in the garden scenes in his *Hortus Floridus*, shows plants individually with lots of room between them. Of course, botanical gardens had to be like this so that the students might observe closely the plants. However, there is some evidence that artists were following convention rather than strict accuracy. Sir Henry Wotton in *Elements of Architecture*, published in 1624, singles out one garden in particular for praise, that of Sir Henry Fanshawe at Ware Park in Hertfordshire: 'hee did so precisely examine the *tinctures*, and *seasons* of his

77 In his *Hortus Floridus*, Crispijn de Passe not only depicted individual plants but also views of a garden at different seasons. This engraving, of spring, shows formal beds divided by paths, and surrounded by arbour tunnels. The planting is sparse, but this may reflect the artist's wish to delineate individual flowers.

floweres that in their *setting*, the *inwardest* of those which were to come up at the same time, should be always a little *darker* than the *outmost*, and to serve them for a kinde of gentle *shadow*, like a piece not of *Nature*, but of *Arte*.'[28] This suggests that the grouping of the flowers was important, though never like the carpet bedding so fashionable in the nineteenth century, or the swathes of colour of our modern summer borders.

Like Evelyn, Hanmer went into great detail in his *Garden Book*. Indeed, it is probable that Evelyn learnt much of his horticultural expertise from him, for Hanmer was an old friend of Sir Richard Browne. He was also part of the circle of enthusiastic florists who exchanged plants and information, and some of them are acknowleged in his book. John Rea, who was to dedicate his *Flora, seu de Florum Cultura* to Sir Thomas and members of his family when he published it in 1665, is recorded as having presented him with two roots of the daffodil of Constantinople and three apricot trees from London. John Rose, gardener to the Earl of Essex during the Commonwealth period, sent Hanmer auriculas and two of his favourite vines. Rose was particularly interested in viticulture, writing *The English Vineyard Vindicated*, which was incorporated into John Evelyn's *French Gardiner* in 1666, by which time Rose had become Charles II's gardener at St James's.

John Rose may also have supplied plants to the Hatton family. Although the family tree of the Hattons had zigzagged sideways since the time of Elizabeth I's favourite, Sir Christopher Hatton, interest in gardens passed seamlessly through the generations. As Christopher remained a family name, for ease of identification the first is known as Chancellor Hatton, as he had held that office. He died in 1591 leaving huge debts, which were shouldered by his nephew, Sir William, and his cousin and heir, Sir Christopher II. Holdenby was sold in 1608 and Kirby Hall became the family's main seat. Christopher II married Alice, sister of Sir Henry Fanshawe, the man singled out for his garden by Wotton in *Elements of Architecture*, thus reinforcing the interest in gardening. Their son, Christopher III, served as Comptroller of the Household of King Charles I, going into exile in 1648 and leaving his wife to look after their Northamptonshire and London estates. His two sons, Christopher IV and Charles, were both keen gardeners, and it is their correspondence and notes, begun during the 1650s, that have survived in the family archives.[29]

Charles Hatton was a particularly knowledgeable plantsman, with a wide circle of botanist friends, including Robert Morison, who called him 'a curious person and a great lover of flowers', and John Ray, who was to dedicate his very important work, *Historia Plantarum*, to him in 1686. Evelyn also knew him, praising him in his particular convoluted style as 'the honourable and learned Charles Hatton Esq (to whom all our phytologists and lovers of horticulture are obliged and myself in particular for many favours)'.[30] One of those favours was that Hatton presented Mrs Evelyn with the slender native asparagus, which Evelyn found superior to the fat stalks imported from Holland.

In July 1656 Charles was in Paris, presumably seeking out plants for his brother, for tree pruning knives and a copy of 'Tradescants Rarities' (*Museaeum Tradescantium*, just published) were dispatched from Kirby.[31] The pruning knives cost 10s, Tradescant's book only 1s 6d, a bargain, for it would have enabled him to find out the most recent introductions from all parts of the world, and to obtain them from nurserymen such as Pierre Morin. Hatton would send the plants and trees along with descriptive lists and planting notes to London, presumably to one of the household servants. A memorandum dated 27 March 1660 notes receipt from France of a catalogue of trees, followed a week later by the trees themselves 'in two great cases', which were then sent on to Kirby. Delivery was remarkably swift, for it is further noted that a second catalogue of trees was sent off from Paris on 5 April, arriving in London on 6 April. The following day saw the arrival of a consignment of citrus trees which was dispatched up to Northamptonshire on 9 April. Details were provided by Hatton on how to plant out the orange trees, along with appropriate references to the plant catalogues of John Gerard and John Tradescant. A third consignment of fruit trees came with a list annotated to accord with a plan of planting, and detailed notes, such as 'a rare unknown plant called by Morin hydrophallia because it loves to be in a moist place and therefore it must be planted in moist ground.'[32]

Charles also acted as his brother's agent in London, making good use of his circle of horticultural friends. A list dated July 1658 is headed 'at Mr Rose's Garden', and includes 'All the sorts of best Julyflowers, many kinds of Amaranthus', purple and white oleanders, clematis, 'Merveille of peru the yellow, the white, ye striped', 'Maricock [Marigold] of Virginia', laurels, Turkey Oak, myrtle, and dwarf fig.[33] Mr Rose is thought to be John Rose, so the garden is presumably Essex House on the Strand. In the following month the Hattons were buying flowers and herbs from Mr Walker's St James's nursery. Walker followed this order up with seeds such as the 'Hiacanthe of Peru', 'Lobell's Catch-fly' and Indian canes, yellow and red, along with 'the best Indian tobacco'.[34] Plants were also acquired from the opposite side of London, from Mr Steppings in Colman's Alley and Goodman Hilliard in Brick Alley, 'against White Crosse Street' – both these nurseries were located in Finsbury Fields just to the north east of the City. From his South Lambeth nursery John Tradescant the Younger supplied trees, such as 'sweet leafed Maple & the large leafed Laurustinus', along with substantial orders for fruit trees.[35]

One of the gardens referred to in this catalogue is 'Hatton's Garden', followed by a list of fruit trees. In 1656 Christopher III Hatton returned from exile in France and set about recouping his fortunes which had been severely damaged by the Civil War. Hatton Garden in Clerkenwell, today the centre of London's diamond trade, offered an ideal opportunity for residential development, and he began to subdivide it into plots. It may be that the fruit trees noted were to be transplanted up to Northamptonshire. The most intriguing of all the lists is one dated 28 July 1658, 'at Goodwife Cantrey's Garden in Flower'. The list includes what we would describe as cottage flowers: lupins, larkspurs, scabious, sweet Williams, honeysuckle, and double camomile.[36] This sounds like a bucolic Northamptonshire garden, but the presence of London Pride in the order may make it yet another London nursery. All these trees, plants and flowers were to be used by Christopher IV Hatton for the recreation of the gardens at Kirby, which through 'benign neglect' in the following centuries have retained their original layout, and are now looked after by English Heritage.

After all the alarums and excursions of Edmund Waller's early life, he turned to creating a grand formal landscape at his Buckinghamshire estate of Hall Barn. It is not known exactly when he began to lay out the gardens, but Christopher Hussey has surmised that he set about the task soon after his return to England in January 1652, his head full of the ideas that he had seen during his five years of exile in France and Italy.[37] A visitor to Hall Barn in 1724 recorded that the gardens 'put us in mind of those at Versailles'.[38] Louis XIV began to lay out his spectacular gardens at Versailles in 1661, a decade after Waller had returned to England, but during his stay in Paris, he must have visited the great royal gardens such as St Germain and the Tuileries in Paris, and Cardinal Richelieu's projects at the Palais Royal and at Rueil near St Germain. At Hall Barn Waller established a formal canal garden surrounded by a landscape of woodland extending over 20 hectares. The walks and groves cut through this woodland may still be seen there, adorned with temples probably added in the early eighteenth century. The kind of garden he was creating is reflected in a poem that he wrote in 1661 as a panegyric to Charles II for his layout of a formal landscape in St James's Park in London:

> For future shade young trees upon the banks
> Of the new stream appear in even ranks . . .
> Near this, my Muse, what more delights her, sees
> A living gallery of aged trees;
> In such green palaces the first kings reigned,
> Slept in their shades, and angels entertained;
> With such old counsellors they did advise
> And by frequenting sacred groves grew wise.
> Free from the impediment of Light and Noise,
> Man thus retired his nobler thoughts employs.[39]

It would be fascinating to know the response of his fellow poet Andrew Marvell to Waller's ideas. As tutor in languages to Mary, daughter of General Sir Thomas Fairfax, Marvell had ample opportunity to reflect on the gardens of Nun Appleton, the home of the Fairfax family in North Yorkshire. Although he was one of Oliver Cromwell's leading generals, Fairfax had become distressed by the country's political situation and retired to Yorkshire in 1651. Marvell records in his long poem 'Upon Appleton House' how Fairfax:

> ...when retired here to Peace,
> His warlike Studies could not cease;
> But laid these Gardens out in sport
> In the just Figure of a Fort;
> And with Five Bastions it did fence,
> As aiming one for ev'ry Sense.[40]

He goes on to describe the General's flower garden:

> See how the Flow'rs as at Parade,
> Under their Colours stand displaid:
> Each Regiment in order grows,
> That of the Tulip, Pinke, and Rose.[41]

In another poem, 'Mower against Gardens', Marvell takes an interesting stance, looking from the fields and woods of the estate into a garden, with the man who scythed the meadow grass commenting on what he observes. He begins:

> Luxurious man, to bring his vice in use,
> Did after him the world seduce,
> And from the fields the flowers and plants allure,
> Where nature was most plain and pure,
> He first enclosed within the garden's square.

Marvell, or rather the mower, then talks of the way that florists intervened in the nature of plants, and the Dutch mania for the tulip:

> The pink grew then as double as his mind;
> The nutriment did change the kind.
> With strange perfumes he did the roses taint
> And flowers themselves were taught to paint.
> The tulip, white, did for complexion seek,
> And learn to interline its cheek:
> Its onion root they then so high did hold,
> That one was for a meadow sold.

The taste for exotic plants then comes under scrutiny:

> Another world was searched, through oceans new,
> To feed the marvel of Peru.

He ends by looking at the formal landscape:

> 'Tis all enforced, the fountain and the grot,
> While the sweet fields do lie forgot:
> Where willing nature does to all dispense
> A wild and fragrant innocence.[42]

Marvell, in his dislike of artifice in gardening, echoes the sentiment expressed by John Milton in *Paradise Lost*, who felt that it embodied the fallen world:

> . . . the crispèd brooks
> Ran nectar, visiting each plant, and fed
> Flow'rs worthy of Paradise which not nice art
> In beds and curious knots, but Nature boon
> Poured forth profuse on hill, and dale, and plain.[43]

These were some of the murmurs against the strict formality and artifice of the fashionable style of gardening that increased in volume over the years to follow.

Yorkshire, kinship and a love of gardening linked Lord Fairfax with another of Cromwell's generals, Major-General Sir John Lambert. Born in 1619 in Calton in the West Riding, Lambert studied at Cambridge and the London Inns of Court before rising to the fore as a dashing cavalry commander during the Civil War, and playing a major role in the politicisation of the New Model Army. After the execution of Charles I he became the most prominent upholder of the army, drawing up Britain's first written constitution that made Cromwell Lord Protector in 1653, yet stopped him becoming king four years later. His interests extended well beyond the military and politics, however, and he was a keen botanist. One of the soldiers under his command, Thomas Willisel, became plant hunter for the Royal Society in the 1660s. No doubt Willisel was encouraged in his skills and knowledge by Lambert.

In May 1652 Lambert bought Wimbledon Manor, the Italian-style villa with gardens of 'many ascending and descendings' that had been laid out at

78 Major-General Sir John Lambert as the Eight of Hearts in a pack of playing cards produced as propaganda by Royalist exiles in Holland. Famous for his love of flowers, especially tulips, he is shown as the Knight of the Golden Tulip in his garden at Wimbledon.

the end of the sixteenth century by Thomas Cecil, and recreated in magnificent style by Queen Henrietta Maria just before the outbreak of the Civil War. His particular enthusiasm was for the tulip, and when a satirical pack of playing cards was produced by the Royalists to denigrate Oliver Cromwell and his colleagues, Lambert was shown as the Eight of Hearts, the Knight of the Golden Tulip, standing in his garden holding his favourite flower. This was a very gentle satire compared to that meted out to his wife, who, as the Queen of Hearts, was shown dallying with the Lord Protector.

Lambert clearly aroused mixed feelings in the breasts of his fellow countrymen, for Sir Thomas Hanmer rose above the political affray to present him with three tulips for his garden at Wimbledon: Belle Isabelle, Belle Susanne and Agate Hanmer. As Hanmer's *Garden Book* shows, he loved the colours of these flowers, carefully distinguishing between them. Thus Isabelle was a greyish yellow and Agate Hanmer combined greyish purple, deep scarlet and pure white, described by John Rea as 'commonly well parted, striped, agated and excellently placed, abiding constant to the last, with the bottom and stamens blue'. Agate Hanmer was a particular triumph for Hanmer, who had introduced it to England, and he noted in his pocket book in June 1655 that he had sent to Lambert 'a very great mother-root'.

The death of Oliver Cromwell on 3 September 1658 pitched the country into a febrile chain of events. Lambert became a leading member of the Committee of Safety, the executive organ of government, but quarrelled with the Rump Parliament and was arrested in March 1660 and imprisoned in the Tower of London. When the return of Charles II to the throne became an increasing possibility, Lambert escaped from the Tower in the guise of chamber maid to stage a last republican stand, described by Samuel Pepys in one of the first entries in his diary: 'I hear that the Phanatiques have held up their heads high since Lambert got out of the Tower, but I hope all that will come to nothing'.[44] Indeed, it did come to nothing and, with the Restoration, Lambert was convicted of treason but spared the horrible fate of a traitor's death through the intervention of the King, who recognised his integrity. Instead Lambert was sent to Castle Cornet on Guernsey, where he came under the care of the Hatton family, a benign fate because of their shared interest in botany. Christopher III had even suggested that Lambert's daughter Mary should become the bride of either the King or his younger brother, James, Duke of York, but in a romantic twist she instead married Charles Hatton.

While on the island Lambert continued with his gardening, and is thought to have introduced the *Nerine sarniensis*, or Guernsey Lily. Originating from South Africa, this lily is said by some to have been part of a consignment en route to Holland, washed up on the shore when the ship was wrecked. However, the painter Alexander Marshall depicted the flower with a note that he had been sent it by Lambert from Wimbledon, so it would seem that *Nerine sarniensis* had been growing there from the 1650s and that he took it with him when he was sent to Guernsey.

The triumphal arrival of Charles II into his restored kingdom in May 1660 marked the end of the long winter for many, but for John Lambert there was to be no happy end. His imprisonment on Guernsey was made bearable by the Hatton family as governors of the island. However, as the years passed, he became prone to increasing fits of melancholy. The various plots that were hatched against Stuart rule once the initial euphoria of the Restoration subsided made it impossible for the King to consider Lambert's release, and in 1670 he was transferred to St Nicholas's Island off Plymouth Sound. Here he remained for another fourteen years, dying in 1684 from a chill caught when he changed out of his gardening clothes to greet some guests. Spring had arrived at last for the Knight of the Golden Tulip.

Epilogue
Springtime

I N MAY 1660 CHARLES II RETURNED TO HIS KINGDOM after nine years'
absence, and nearly a year later, on 22 April 1661, he made his way across
London from the Tower of London to Westminster, where he was to be
crowned the following day. As he passed through the City of London he
encountered a series of triumphal arches that had been designed as a display
of propaganda for the new regime. The fourth and last of these was the
Garden of Plenty in Fleet Street. An engraving made to record the event shows
pillars entwined with leaves, garlands of fruit, and flowers in vases. A statue
representing Flora gave her red and white roses, lilies and a garland of various
flowers. Above her, a garden was painted with walks, statues, fountains and
more flowers. Pomona, crowned with a garland of fruits, carried in one hand
a pruning hook, in the other the Sun, while all sorts of gardening tools lay
at her feet. As the King approached the arch, a representation of Plenty
promised:

> The glitt'ring Plenty of this Golden Age
> The Clouds blow o're, which long our joys o'recast
> And the sad Winter of your absence past
> See! the three smiling Seasons of the Year
> Agree at once to bid You Welcome here.[1]

It was not lost on observers that Charles II was the grandson of Henri IV, the
gardener king of France, and hopes were high that he, like his ancestor, would

prove a generous patron, encouraging the prosperity of the nation. These hopes were given a boost when in the following year he granted a charter of incorporation to the Royal Society. No money was forthcoming from the royal purse, but the Society was given similar status to the City companies. Although the King treated the activities of the Society with a certain amount of regal disdain, the founding members had enough curiosity and seriousness of purpose to make this immaterial. The importance of the Society was that it was the first modern scientific academy, connected neither with the universities, nor subject to the control of the nobility, though, that said, the membership was very much gentlemen rather than players. The roll call of the early members is filled with the names of important thinkers and doers of the seventeenth century, including Christopher Wren, Robert Boyle, John Evelyn, Robert Hooke and, from across the Atlantic, John Winthrop Junior.

Information was exchanged through correspondence amongst members in the tradition established by the European Republic of Letters in the sixteenth century, and in England, the networks established during the Commonwealth period by Samuel Hartlib. On the first Monday of each month, the *Philosophical Transactions* were issued, in English. No longer could Latin be regarded as the natural language for 'citizens of the world' as Francis Bacon had put it to Charles I. The Society insisted on studies in the field, embracing every branch of science. One of the areas of horticulture that particularly exercised the Society was the classification of plants, providing an opportunity for conflict that every so often seizes the scientific community. Here the main protagonists were Robert Morison and John Ray.

John Ray was born in 1627, the son of a village blacksmith in Essex. After attendance at the grammar school in Braintree he entered Trinity College, Cambridge, holding a series of college appointments in Greek, mathematics and humanities. In the 1650s Trinity suspended the requirement that its fellows should take holy orders, but this was reinstated in 1658, and Ray was ordained two years later. However, he felt unable to take the oath required by the Act of Uniformity introduced at the Restoration. Although he remained a loyal member of the Anglican Church, Ray forfeited his fellowship of Trinity, casting himself upon the good nature and generosity of friends. These proved doughty supporters, but Ray remained in a vulnerable position financially for the rest of his life.

In 1667 Ray, by now one of the country's leading botanists, was elected to the Royal Society and entered into the discussions about the classification of plants. Sixteenth-century botanists had evolved various theories, concentrating on visible features, so that Matthias L'Obel looked to leaves, Cesalpino to fruit,

Rivinus to flowers. Ray followed the instincts of Cesalpino, taking the seed to account for the whole structure, and in 1666 was persuaded by John Wilkins, the influential Warden of Wadham who was now Dean of Ripon, to produce a Table of Plants for a book that he was planning on 'the regular enumeration and defining of all the families of plants and animals'.[2] Ray was obliged to do this in a matter of three weeks, and although his arrangement was ingenious, it was made to order and artificial. As a result it roused the ire of Robert Morison, the king's physician and professor of botany, and keeper of the Royal Physic Garden in St James's Park. Morison seems to have been an intemperate and arrogant character and, although he did not name Ray, he wrote: 'I saw there only a chaotic muddle of plants: I learnt nothing: I will show you the faults and confusion some other time'. Ray, desperately hurt, poured out his feelings to a friend, describing Morison as 'sneering so fatuously at the Royal Society', although in public he maintained a dignified silence.[3]

Yet Morison would not let go, and in public lectures described Ray as one who 'studied plants more in his closet than in gardens and fields'. Here the Oxford professor of botany was landing a double low punch, for Ray was not officially connected with Cambridge, and the university itself lacked a botanical garden, acquiring one only in 1762. The presence of a botanical garden was an important step in the study of medical botany, as the physician Robert Sibbald recognised when in 1670 he founded the Royal Botanic Garden in Edinburgh. At first it was a small patch, no bigger than a tennis court, at Holyrood, but by 1683 the Intendant, James Sutherland, was able to publish a descriptive catalogue of some two thousand plants growing in the garden. Three years after the establishment of the Edinburgh garden, the London Society of Apothecaries founded a physic garden in Chelsea. The site, upriver from London, was chosen to house the society barge, but also enabled apprentices to make botanising expeditions to Battersea and Putney Heath. The gardeners at the Physic Garden liaised with their colleagues in other botanic gardens and initiated an international botanic plant exchange with Leiden which is maintained to this day.

Robert Morison as professor initiated lectures three times a week in spring and autumn in the Botanic Garden in Oxford, sitting at a table covered with specimens of plants. His great project was to produce a comprehensive herbal of 2,450 plants in a series of monographs, each dealing with a particular family based on his new principles of taxonomy. He began with umbelliferous plants in a handsome folio with metal engravings, published in Oxford in 1672, with the idea that three volumes would follow, financed by securing subscriptions of £5 from interested parties. Subscribers would receive a free set of the great

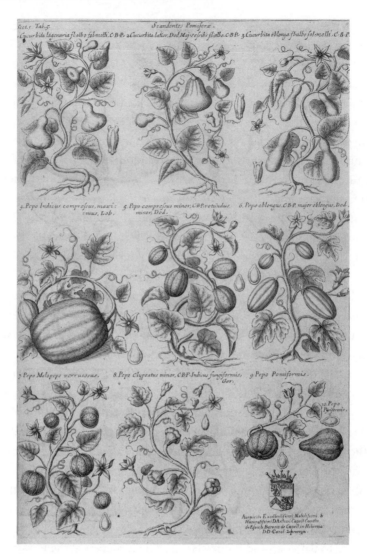

79 Cucumbers, melons and gourds from Robert Morison's *Plantarum Historia Universalis Oxoniensis*. This elaborate catalogue was the work of many years for Morison, professor of botany at Oxford. The expense of using engravings in metal by leading Dutch artists left him in huge debt, despite the fact that the university press organised a subscription scheme. Donors were acknowledged at the bottom of each page: this one is credited to Arthur Capel, Earl of Essex, whose garden at Cassiobury in Hertfordshire was one of the most celebrated of the time.

work, and have their name, and coat of arms if appropriate, engraved at the bottom of one of the pages. Although he was able to attract interest from several noblemen and many members of the Royal Society and the London College of Physicians, the ambitious scheme foundered through lack of money. The first volume never reached the presses, the second appeared in 1680, but three years later Morison was badly injured by being struck on the chest by the pole of a coach while crossing the Strand in London, and died the following day. The third volume was eventually completed in 1699 by Jacob Bobart the Younger, who somehow managed to combine the role of super-intendent of the botanic garden with giving the university's lectures on botany after the professor's untimely death.

Although John Ray was desperately keen that his own contribution to botanical literature, *Historia plantarum*, should be illustrated so that readers would understand the different parts of plants, he was in an even weaker financial position. The Royal Society tried to raise subscriptions but failed, so that the project was never the popular success Ray had hoped for. The first volume, published in 1686, was in Latin, no longer the exclusive language of scholarly discourse, and Ray found that the printers in London could not be trusted to set up accurate text. It is ironical that William Turner's herbal, published in the mid-sixteenth century, lacked popular success for precisely the opposite reason, because it was written in English and therefore did not have an international market. And, of course, neither Morison nor Ray established the system of classification that was to be univer-sally adopted: this honour went in the eighteenth century to the Swedish botanist, Carl Linnaeus.

The first book sponsored by the Royal Society was John Evelyn's great trea-tise on trees, *Sylva*, which appeared in 1664. This very influential book arose from a paper that Evelyn had read to the Society two years before, to answer questions posed by the principal officers and Commissioners of the Navy, concerned about the shortage of timber for His Majesty's ships. Although Evelyn's purpose was not primarily an aesthetic one, his timing was impec-cable as far as the fashion in gardening was concerned. This was the very time that the King was organising the planting of avenues of trees in the park of St James's Palace in London.

During their years of exile in France, the King and members of his court had been able to witness at first hand the creation of some of the most spec-tacular gardens by the master of design, André le Nôtre. Le Nôtre was born in 1613, in a house in the Tuileries gardens, where his grandfather was the gardener-in-chief of the parterres, and his father the royal master gardener. Apprenticed under his father and Claude Mollet, he not only learnt his skills as a gardener at royal gardens, but also studied the principles of architecture, painting and design. In 1657 Louis XIV appointed him one of his three Contrôleurs Générals du Bâtiments, and in that same year Le Nôtre began to create the spectacular garden at Vaux-le-Vicomte for the King's finance minister, Nicolas Fouquet. The format that Le Nôtre established at Vaux-le-Vicomte was a grand, symmetrical arrangement of parterres, pools and walks flanking a wide and sweeping central vista. This style was used to even greater effect at Versailles, where the King extended his hunting lodge into an enormous palace as his primary residence and seat of power.

When Charles II returned to England, he asked his cousin Louis whether he might have the services of Le Nôtre in laying out gardens at his various palaces. The French king duly gave him leave to come to England, but apparently he never did so. However, he drew up plans and corresponded with Charles about the park at Greenwich, and these were carried to fruition by Claude Mollet's sons André and Gabriel who had remained in England throughout the 1650s. In addition, two of Charles's gardeners, John Rose and George London, went on different occasions over to France to observe the gardens being created by Le Nôtre at Versailles. Charles II's avenues in St James's Park were not a revolutionary concept. As mentioned in Chapter 6, Sir Francis Bacon had laid out walks in the gardens at Gray's Inn in the 1590s, and a few years later, Moorfields to the north of the City of London was levelled and laid out with walks lined with trees, probably at the behest of the merchant Nicholas Leate. However, where the King led, his wealthier subjects followed, and walks and groves were planted all over the country, as can be seen in the bird's-eye views of gardens engraved by Kip and Knyff. Keith Thomas memorably describes this national planting as a mix of social assertiveness, aesthetic sense, patriotism and long-term profit, comparing it to the English aristocrat's obsession with his dogs and horses.[4] The trees that Evelyn particularly commended in *Sylva* were the walnut, 'they render most graceful avenues to our country dwellings', the lime with 'its unparalleled beauty for walks' and the cypress, which despite its vulnerability to cold winds, he assured would become 'endenizon'd among us', a prediction that proved unfounded when nearly every tree was killed during the harsh winter of 1683–84.

In later editions of *Sylva* Evelyn added an ideal plan of a garden. Following Le Nôtre's maxim, a main vista ran from the house down to a wooded area through which paths were cut, every so often breaking out into a small area of verdure.

Nearer the house in Evelyn's ideal plan were formal gardens with fountains, and areas for growing fruit and vegetables. The florist John Rea, in his *Flora, seu de Florum Cultura* published in 1665, provided plans for less grandiose gardens along with the proviso that skill was required in their creation: 'I have seen many gardens of the new model, in the hands of unskilful persons, with good walls, walks and grass plots; but the most essential adornments so deficient, that a green meadow is a more delightful object; there, nature alone, without the aid of art, spreads her verdant carpets, spontaneously embroidered with many pretty plants and pleasing flowers, far more inviting than such an immured nothing'. Rea recommends a walled rectangle divided into two gardens, one for flowers, the other for fruit, with the kitchen garden set in a more remote place. Trees such as elms or sycamores should be planted at some little distance as a wind break. The garden should not be too big: for noblemen eighty yards for fruit and thirty for flowers; for a private gentleman, forty and twenty yards.[5]

One of the best-known paintings of an English gardener, of which there are several versions, has been traditionally described as 'John Rose, the Royal Gardener', presenting to Charles II the first pineapple growing in England'. But this description is fraught with problems: the pineapple was not cultivated in England until after the death of Charles; the identification of the gardener with John Rose was made only in the eighteenth century; and the background could even be Dutch. The one fact that has not been challenged is that the figure receiving the pineapple is the King, and Evelyn recorded in his diary in 1661 that Charles ate a Queen pineapple imported from Barbados, one of Britain's expanding collection of colonies.

To the original North American colonies of New England and Virginia were added the settlements of the Carolinas, Baltimore and Maryland, and in August 1664 the Dutch city of New Amsterdam was taken by the British and renamed New York after the King's brother, James. Barbados had been acquired from the Portuguese in 1625, and Jamaica was captured from the Spanish thirty years later. From these colonies, along with the traditional trading contacts with the Mediterranean, South America and the Far East, exotics were being imported in ever increasing quantities, and developments in technology enabled gardeners to protect the delicate plants against the rigours of the British climate. In 1684 the physician and indefatigable collector Hans Sloane wrote to John Ray about the heated greenhouse erected by the gardener at the Chelsea Physic Garden. This he described as

a new contrivance, at least in this country: viz. he makes under the floor of his greenhouse a great fire plate, with grate, ash-hole, etc., and conveys the warmth through the whole house, by tunnels: so that he hopes, by the help of weather-glasses within, to bring or keep the air at what degree of warmth he pleases, letting in upon occasion the outward air by the windows. He thinks to make, by this means, an artificial spring, summer and winter.[6]

Botanical gardens were natural recipients of exotic plants, but private collections were also being made. Henry Compton, Bishop of London, built up an impressive collection at Fulham Palace. Charles Hatton wrote to his brother Christopher of how Fulham had oaks and walnuts and Jesuit's bark [quinine] from Virginia, and urged him to find out from the bishop about the construction and management of stoves. But Bishop Compton's collection was dwarfed by that of one of the great horticulturalists of the late seventeenth century, Mary, Duchess of Beaufort. She had gardening in her blood, for her father was Arthur, first Baron Capel, the creator of the notable Italianate garden at Hadham Hall in Hertfordshire, and her brother, also Arthur, had a fine garden at Cassiobury. At the time of the Restoration, Mary's second husband, Henry Somerset (created Duke of Beaufort in 1682), inherited the Badminton estate in Gloucestershire and embarked upon a major building project there. While he concentrated on the house, Mary turned her attention to the gardens, installing extensive conservatories, where she gradually amassed a huge collection of exotic plants from all over the world. These rare specimens brought the Duchess into correspondence with the foremost botanists of her time, linking her to a network of foreign suppliers and ensuring that her plants were identified and published, including two illustrated albums produced by the artists Everhard Kychique and Daniel Frankcom, which are still at Badminton.

But it was not just the aristocracy who were creating new gardens. The whole nation was hard at it, helped by the proliferation of books being published in England. Practical information was being dispensed not only by John Evelyn and John Rea, but also in titles such as Stephen Blake's *Compleat gardener's practice*, 1664, and Leonard Meager's *English Gardener*, 1670. The first Scottish gardening book, *The Scots Gard'ner*, by John Reid, gardener to Sir George Mackenzie of Rosebaugh, was published in Edinburgh in 1683. John Worlidge in his *Systema horti-culturæ: or the art of gardening*, published in 1677, declared:

Neither is there a noble or pleasant seat in England but hath its gardens for pleasure and delight; scarce an ingenious citizen that by his confinement to a shop, being denied the priviledge of having a real garden, but hath his boxes, pots, or other receptacles for flowers, plants, &c . . . there is scarce a cottage in most of the southern parts of England but hath its proportionable garden, so great a delight do most of men take in it; that they may not only please themselves with the view of the flowers, herbs and trees, as they grow, but furnish themselves and their neighbours upon extraordinary occasions, as nuptials, feasts, and funerals, with the proper produces of their gardens.[7]

Many of the hopes aroused at the Restoration were to be dashed by the profligacy of the King and his court. Despite his many children by mistresses, Charles lacked a legitimate heir, so that at his death the throne would pass to James, Duke of York. The Duke's conversion to Roman Catholicism in 1668 plunged the nation into political turmoil which was to dog the rest of Charles's reign and beyond. In matters horticultural, however, the King did not disappoint, and as Worlidge observed, the English, or rather the British, had become a nation of gardeners.

The most fashionable gardens were now French, and with the arrival in 1688 of Mary Stuart and her co-regent, William of Orange, the 'Holland way' became popular. But in July 1666, when Samuel Pepys walked up and down Whitehall with the architect Hugh May, who had spent his Civil War in exile in Holland, their thoughts turned to gardens:

among other things, discoursing of the present fashion of gardens to make them plain [the style of Le Nôtre] – that we have the best walks of gravel in the world – France having none, nor Italy; and our green of our bowling-alleys is better than any they have. So our business here being ayre, this is the best way, only with a little mixture of Statues, or pots, which may be hand-some, and so filled with another pot of such or such a flower or green, as the season of the year will bear.[8]

The stage was now set for the English garden to become the envy of the world.

Notes

Introduction – The Pattern in the Quilt

1. First published in London in 1939.
2. See Margery Corbett, 'The emblematic title-page to "Stirpium adversaria nova" by Peter Pena and Matthias l'Obel', *Archives of Natural History*, 1981, 10(1), pp. 111–17.
3. John Evelyn, *Numismata*, London, 1697, p. 322.
4. E.F. Benson, *Queen Lucia*, London, 1920, pp. 10–12.
5. 'Learning by Experience', in *Rooted in History: Studies of Garden Conservation*, London, 2001, p. 31.
6. Prudence Leith-Ross, *The John Tradescants: Gardeners to the Rose and Lily Queen*, revd edn, London, 2006; Jennifer Potter, *Strange Blooms: The Curious Lives and Adventures of the John Tradescants*, London, 2006; Philippa Gregory, *Earthly Joys*, London, 1998.

1 Fit for a Queen

1. Roger Manners in a letter to his nephew, the Earl of Rutland, 2 June 1583, HMC Rutland MSS, London, 1880, Appendix 12th report, Part IV, vol. 1, pp. 150–1.
2. An exception could be argued for the water gardens created at Bindon in the grounds of a former Cistercian Abbey in Dorset by Thomas Howard, the second son of the third Duke of Norfolk. See Timothy Mowl, *Historic Gardens of Dorset*, Stroud, 2003.
3. William Harrison, *The Description of England*, ed. Georges Edelen, London, 1994, p. 271.
4. John Cloake, *Palaces and Parks of Richmond and Kew*, I (The Palaces of Shene and Richmond), Chichester, 1995, p. 61.
5. See David Jacques, 'The Compartment System in Tudor England', *Garden History*, vol. 27, no. 1, 1999, pp. 32–53.
6. Daniel Lysons, *The Environs of London*, 4 vols, London, 1792–3, vol. 2, 1795, pp. 86–8.
7. There was a fifth sister, Margaret, who died young before she could achieve the potential of her excellent education.
8. Today's equivalents would be £210,000 and £32,560.
9. Paul Hentzner, *A Journey into England in the Year 1598*, ed. Horace Walpole, Strawberry Hill, 1757, p. 54.
10. Paula Henderson, *The Tudor House and Garden*, New Haven and London, 2005, p. 197.
11. *The Diary of Baron Waldstein: A Traveller in Elizabethan England, 1600*, trans. G.W. Gross, London, 1981, pp. 83, 87.

12. Dedication in John Gerard's *Herball*, London, 1597.
13. One version is at Hatfield House, another in the Bodleian Library.
14. Gerard, *Herball*, pp. 111, 151.
15. William Camden, *Annales, the true and royall History of Elizabeth Queene of England*, London, 1625–29, book 3, p. 288.
16. Dudley Papers at Longleat, vol. II, fol. 321.
17. There is debate about the true identity of the author of the letter, and it has been suggested that it could have been written by one of William Cecil's men. For details, see Trea Martyn, *Elizabeth in the Garden: A Story of Love, Rivalry and Spectacular Design*, London, 2008, pp. 95ff.
18. Robert Tittler, *Nicholas Bacon: The Making of a Tudor Statesman*, London, 1976, p. 215.
19. Vita Sackville-West, *Knole and the Sackvilles*, London, 1922, p. 54.
20. Camden, *Annales*, 'Tomus Alter', p. 60.
21. John Norden, *Speculi Britanniae pars altera; or A Delineation of Northamptonshire*, London, 1720, pp. 49–50.
22. E. St John Brooks, *Sir Christopher Hatton*, London, 1946, p. 216. Brooks also proposed that this Hugh Hall was the priest and gardener involved in the Somerville Plot to assassinate the Queen in 1583, as a result of which one of William Shakespeare's relations, Edward Arden, was executed. The priest-gardener was pardoned, perhaps because of his connections in high places.
23. Letter of 18 October 1561, quoted by E.C. Till in 'The Development of the Park and Gardens at Burghley', *Garden History*, vol. 19, no. 2, 1991, p. 129. I am grateful to Andrew Eburne for giving me this reference.
24. Edmund Lodge, *Illustrations of British History*, London, 1791, vol. 1, p. xvii.
25. Devonshire MSS, *Book of Maps* by William Senior, Chatsworth, 1610, fol. 54.
26. Ibid., Hardwick, 1610, fol. 18.
27. Harrison, *The Description of England*, p. 199.
28. The Cesariano edition of 1521, published in Como, and the Philander edition published in Paris in 1545.
29. Alberti, *De re aedificatoria*, book IX, part iv, translated by Joseph Rykwert, Neil Leach and Robert Tavernor as *On the Art of Building in Ten Books*, Cambridge, MA, and London, p. 300.
30. Sir Thomas Hoby, *Travels & Life*, Camden Miscellany, vol. 10, ed. E. Powell, Royal Historical Society, 1902, p. 35.
31. Quoted by Martyn, *Elizabeth in the Garden*, p. 37.
32. According to the guidebook for the Villa Lante, the frescoes may have been undertaken by Zuccaro's pupils, supervised by Raffaelino da Reggio.
33. Martyn, *Elizabeth in the Garden*.
34. G. Anstruther, *Vaux of Harrowden. A Recusant Family*, 1953, p. 112.
35. British Library, Add. MS 39831, fols 66–71.
36. Ibid.
37. British Library, Add. MS 39829, fol. 165.
38. Anthony Watson, *Magnificae et plane regiae domus quae vulgo vocatur Nonseusch descriptio*, c. 1582. Hondius's drawing was reproduced by John Speed in his map of Surrey, 1610. The Red Velvet Book is in the collection of the Earl of Scarborough.
39. Royal Institute of British Architects, SC230/I/24.
40. *Calendar of State Papers: Relating to English Affairs in the Archives of Venice*, vol. 15 (1617–19), ed. Allen B. Hinds, London, 1909, p. 271.

2 The Men on the Ground

1. John Harvey, *Early Nurserymen*, Chichester, 1974, p. 33.
2. British Library, MS Royal 18, C.III.
3. The letters referring to this were noted in the Public Record Office in the late nineteenth century, but have since been destroyed in a fire. However, the curator at the British Museum who catalogued the Royal manuscripts was scrupulous in his references so that the identification with Hugh Hall can be relied upon.

4. Letters and Papers Foreign and Domestic of the Reign of Henry VIII, cited in C. Paul Christianson, *The Riverside Gardens of Thomas More's London*, New Haven and London, 2005, pp. 110–11.
5. Drawing by Hugh Alley for *A Caveatt for the City of London*, 1598, now in the Folger Shakespeare Library.
6. William Lambarde, *A Perambulation of Kent*, reprinted London, 1826, pp. 222–3.
7. British Library, Lansdowne MS 89, fols 92v–93.
8. British Library, Add. MS 39831. For a transcript see Andrew Eburne and Katz Fetuś, eds, *Lyveden New Bield Conservation Management Plan*, The National Trust, 2008, p. 208.
9. See Richard Altick, *The English Common Reader*, Chicago and London, 1957, p. 22.
10. Statute of Artificers, 1563, 5 Elizabeth C.4, section xi.
11. Harvey, *Early Nurserymen*, p. 29.
12. Letter, 2 November 1584, Henry E. Huntington Library, Pasadena, MS HM 21714.
13. See Simon Adams, ed., *Household Accounts and Disbursement Books of Robert Dudley, Earl of Leicester, 1558–61, 1584–86*, Camden Fifth Series, vol. 6, Cambridge, 1995, p. 102 (1559) and p. 220, n. 467 (1585).
14. Ibid., pp. 196–7 (November 1584); p. 215 (January 1584/5); p. 296 (August 1585); and p. 60 (1558).
15. Calendar of State Papers Domestic, 1547–80 (1856), p. 171: order of 7 March 1561.
16. Chatsworth MS 4: August 1577, p. 25r; March 1578, p. 41r; May 1578, p. 72r; July 1578, p. 49v.
17. Bodleian Library, MS Engl. History, b.192 fol. 27.
18. Calendar of Letters and Papers of the Reign of Henry VIII, XXI.i.523.
19. Brian Dietz, *The Port and Trade of Early Elizabethan London*, London, 1972, pp. 63, 78.
20. The Johnson papers are used in Barbara Winchester, *Tudor Family Portrait*, London, 1955.
21. 'An Elizabethan Seed-list', *Garden History*, vol. 23, no. 2, 1995, notes, pp. 242–5.
22. Tusser, *Five Hundred Points of Good Husbandry*, facsimile of 1580 edition, ed. Geoffrey Grigson, Oxford, 1984, pp. 39, 121.
23. Registers of St Margaret's Westminster: Westminster Public Library, Peculiar Court of Westminster, 163 Bracy Will of John Banbury.
24. Gerard, *Herball*, p. 1269.
25. Public Record Office C.142/125/74, quoted in Harvey, *Early Nurserymen*, p. 63.
26. Listed in Harvey, *Early Nurserymen*, p. 30.
27. *The Countrie Farme*, trans. Richard Surflet, London, 1600, p. 325.
28. Thomas Hill, *The Gardeners Labyrinth*, London, 1577, pp. 81–2.
29. *L'Art et manière de semer, et faire des sauvageaux* by Davy Brossard, a Benedictine monk at the abbey near Le Mans.
30. Syon House MSS W.II, 1, printed in E.B. de Fonblanque, *Annals of the House of Percy*, London, 1887, vol. II, pp. 626–30.
31. Thomas Tusser, *Five Hundred Pointes of Good Husbandrie*, 1580 edition collated with those of 1573 and 1577, and the 1557 edition of *A Hundreth Good Pointes*, ed. W. Payne and S.J. Herrtage, London, 1878, p. 229.
32. Tusser, *Five Hundred Points of Good Husbandry*, facsimile of 1580 edition, p. 320.
33. John Strype, *The Life of the Learned Sir Thomas Smith, Knight*, London, 1698, p. 218.
34. A.B. Appleby, *Famine in Tudor and Stuart England*, Liverpool, 1978, pp. 138–9.
35. Samuel Hartlib, *His Legacy of Husbandry*, London, 1655, p. 8.
36. Ronald Webber, 'London Market Gardens', *History Today*, December 1973, vol. 23, p. 874.
37. Hartlib, *His Legacy of Husbandry*, p. 9.
38. William Harrison, *The Description of England*, ed. Georges Edelen, London, 1994, pp. 263–4.
39. John Parkinson, *Paradisi in Sole*, London, 1629, p. 509.
40. Samuel Pepys, *Diary*, ed. Robert Latham and William Matthews, London, 1972, vol. VII, p. 235.
41. Quoted in Sara Paston-Williams, *The Art of Dining*, London, 1993, pp. 29–30.
42. Guildhall Library, MS 3396, Appendix I, letters patent.
43. See Arnold F. Steele, *The Worshipful Company of Gardeners of London: A History of its Revival, 1890–1960*, London, 1964; and David Marsh, 'A Fellowship on the Fringes: The Gardener's

Company of London in the Seventeenth Century,' in Ian A. Gadd and Patrick Wallis, eds, *Guilds and Association in Europe, 900–1900*, London, 2006.

44. Cited in J.T. Cliffe, *The World of the Country House in Seventeenth-Century England*, New Haven and London, 1999, p. 56.

3 Strange Encounters

1. William Harrison, *The Description of England*, ed. Georges Edelen, London, 1994, p. 265.
2. Brian Dietz, *The Port and Trade of Early Elizabethan London*, London, 1972, pp. 6, 34, 85.
3. Harrison, *The Description of England*, p. 269.
4. *Les Observations de plusieurs singularitez et choses memorables, trouvées en Grèce, Asie, Judée, Egypte, Arabie et autres pays éstrangèrs*. A later edition was published by Christopher Plantin in Antwerp in 1555.
5. Rauwolff's memoirs, entitled *Aigentliche beschreibung der Raisz inn die Morgenländerin*, were published in Germany in 1582. Nicholas Staphorst's English translation was published in the first volume of John Ray's *Collection of Curious Travels and Voyages*, London, 1693, pp. 2, 92, 53, 113.
6. Charles Thornton Forster and F.H. Blackburne Danielle, eds, *The Life & Letters of Ogier Ghiselin de Busbecq*, London, 1881, vol. 1, pp. 107–8.
7. Translation by Otterspeer, cited in Harold J. Cook, *Matters of Exchange: Commerce, Medicine, and Science in the Dutch Golden Age*, New Haven and London, 2007, p. 105.
8. The gardens attached to the ninth-century palace of Madinat al-Zahra, just outside Cordoba in Andalusia, may be regarded as the earliest botanical gardens in Europe.
9. With the title *Aromatum et simplicium aliquot medicamentorum apud Indos nascentium historia*.
10. Costa's text was *Tratado de las drogas medicinas y plantas de las Indias Orientales*. Clusius's translation, entitled *Aromatum et medicamentorum in Orientali India nascentium liber*, was published by Plantin in Antwerp in 1582.
11. Entitled *Nova plantarum, animalium et mineralium Mexicanorum historia*.
12. The Latin translation was called *Plurimarum singularum et memorabilium rerum observationes*.
13. John Aubrey, *Aubrey's Brief Lives*, ed. Oliver Lawson Dick, London, 1949, p. 123.
14. Gerrit de Veer, *The Three Voyages of W. Barents to the Arctic Regions, 1594, 1595 and 1596*, translated by W. Phillip, London, 1876.
15. Anna Pavord, *The Naming of Names*, London, 2005, p. 258.
16. Conrad Gesner's *Horti Germaniae*. This was included in Valerius Cordus, *Annotationes in Pedacii Dioscoridis Anazarebi de materia medica libros*, published in Strasbourg in 1561.
17. *Chronyke van Vlaenderen. Derde en Leste Deel*, Bruges, 1736, p. 430. The translation comes from *Botany in the Low Countries*, ed. F. de Nave and Dirk Imhof, Antwerp, 1993, p. 30.
18. Somer's adventures, along with the *liefhebbers* of Middelburg, are recounted by Anne Goldgar in chapter 1 of *Tulipmania: Money, Honor and Knowledge in the Dutch Golden Age*, Chicago and London, 2007. The second edition of Somer's memoirs, *Beschrijivinge van een Zee ende Landt Reyse Naer de Levante*, was published by Joost Hargers in Amsterdam in 1649. The quotation about the Constantinople flower market is from 4–4v, p. 29.
19. University Library, Leiden, Vulc. 101, 8 May 1597.
20. Clusius acknowledged the receipt of the portrait of the yellow fritillary with a citation to Somer in *Rariorum plantarum historia*, II, cap xi, 153, Antwerp, 1601.
21. Deborah Harkness, 'Living on Lime Street', chapter 1 in *The Jewel House: Elizabethan London and the Scientific Revolution*, New Haven and London, 2007.
22. *Syntagma herbarum encomiasticum*, the first edition of which was published in 1606.
23. Quoted by Charles Raven, *English Naturalists from Neckam to Ray*, Cambridge, 1947, p. 136.
24. Justus Lipsius, *Two Books of Constancie*, tr. Sir John Stradling, London, 1595, vol. II, chapter 3, p. 64.
25. For the prosecution, Raven, *English Naturalists*, pp. 205–17; for the defence, Robert Jeffers, *The Friends of John Gerard*, Falls Village, CT, 1967, pp. 49, 67.

4 Spreading the Word

1. Blanche Henrey, *British Botanical and Horticultural Literature before 1800*, Oxford, 1975.
2. Theophrastus's *Historiae Plantarum* and *De Causis plantarum* were translated by Sir Arthur Hort and published as *Enquiry into Plants and minor works on odours and weather signs*, 2 vols, London, 1916.
3. Quoted in Pavord, *The Naming of Names*, p. 74.
4. Turkish Letter IV, 16 December 1562, in *The Turkish Letters of Ogier Ghiselin de Busbecq*, ed. E.S. Forster, Oxford, 1927, pp. 417–8.
5. Agnes Arber, 'From medieval herbalism to the birth of modern botany', in *Science, Medicine and History: Essays written in honour of Charles Singer*, ed. E. Ashworth Underwood, London, 1953, vol. I, p. 318.
6. Quoted in Pavord, *The Naming of Names*, p. 162.
7. Ibid., p. 17.
8. *Dienerbuch*, a record of the town, from Klaus Dobat and Karl Mägdefrau, '300 Jahre Botanik in Tübingen', *Attempto*, 55–56, Tübingen, 1975, pp. 8–27.
9. Charles Raven, *English Naturalists*, p. 196 and n. 1 quoting from Jacques Delamain's *Why Birds Sing*, English translation (by Anna and Ruth Sarason), London, 1931.
10. Raven, *English Naturalists*, p. 63, translated into modern English from William Turner's *Libellus de re Herbaria novus*, London, 1538, sig. B iii.
11. William Turner, *Newe Herball*, vol. II, Cologne, 1562, p. 77, where he points out about the opium poppy, 'If a man take too much of it, it is hurtful, for it taketh a man's memory away and killeth him'.
12. Francis Thynne's continuation of Holinshed's *Chronicles*, London, 1587, p. 1512.
13. William Turner, *The Names of Herbes*, London, 1548, sig. A iii, which I have here translated into modern English.
14. Letter of 9 October 1574, *Correspondence IV*, no. 566, pp. 158–9. Quoted and translated in Karen Lee Bowen and Dirk Imhof, *Christopher Plantin and Engraved Book Illustrations in Sixteenth-Century Europe*, Cambridge, 2008, p. 31.
15. Entitled *Rariorum aliquot stirpium per Hispanias observatorum historia*.
16. *Rariorum aliquot stirpium, per Pannoniam, Austriam & vicinas quasdam provincias observatorum historia*.
17. *Kruydtboeck*.
18. Dodoens's *Histoire des Plantes*, tr. Clusius, Antwerp, British Library, 442.h.9.
19. Gerard, *Herball*, 1557, p. 782.
20. Ibid., p. 613.
21. Ibid., pp. 1077, 1082.
22. Serlio, *Five Books of Architecture*, London, 1621; Palladio, *I Quattro Libri*, Venice, 1616; Barozzi, *Le Due Regole dela prospettiva*, Rome, 1611.
23. Devonshire MSS CHA 10 1597–1601.
24. Andrew H. Anderson, 'The Books and Interests of Henry, Lord Stafford (1501–1563)', *The Library*, fifth series, vol. XXI, no. 2 (June 1966). The catalogue and letter book are in the Bagot MSS in the William Salt Library, Stafford.
25. Sir John Fitzherbert, *Boke of Husbandry*, pp. 87–8 in the English Dialect Society edition, London, 1882.
26. *Thesaurus pauperum* by Petrus Hispanus.
27. Lord Herbert of Cherbury, *Autobiography*, ed. William H. Dircks, London, 1888, pp. 36–7.
28. David McKitterick, *The Library of Sir Thomas Knyvett of Ashwellthorpe, c. 1539–1618*, Cambridge, 1978.
29. Alberti's *Architettura*, Florence, 1550; Palladio's *I Quattro libri*, Venice, 1570; Serlio's *Architettura*, Frankfurt, 1575.
30. Andrew Maunsell, *The Catalogue of English Printed Bookes*, 2 parts, London, 1595; photographic reprint, London, Gregg Press, 1965.

31. Shute, published in folio in 1584 by Thomas Marsh; *The Great Herbal* of Peter Treveris, first published in 1529 in folio with pictures, 'since reprinted without'; Birckmann's edition of William Turner's herbal in folio, 1568; Henry Lyte's translation of the herbal of Dodoens 'for Gerard Dewe with pictures in folio, 1578 and since, in 1586, without pictures in quarto by Ninian Newton'; Thomas Hill reprinted for Henry Binneman in quarto in 1579; John Maples's *The Green Forest* printed by Henry Denham in octavo, 1567.
32. *Gardeners Labyrinth*, printed by John Woolfe in 1586; Mascall printed for John Wight in 1580; Scot, 1578, published by Henry Denham.
33. Sears Jayne, *Library Catalogues of the English Renaissance*, Godalming, 1983, Appendix I: Misc. Book Lists, 1500–1640.

5 House and Garden

1. Alberti, *Ten Books of Architecture*, ix, iv.
2. Quoted in W.B. Rye, *England as seen by foreigners in the days of Elizabeth and James the first*, London, 1865, p. 77.
3. G. Dyfnaallt Owen, ed., *Calendar of the Mss of the Most Hon. The Marquess of Bath*, vol. V: Talbot, Dudley and Devereux Papers, 1533–1659, London, 1980, p. 149.
4. See note 2 above.
5. Thomas Tusser, *Five Hundred Pointes of Good Husbandrie*, 1580 edition, p. 40.
6. The miniature is in the Victoria and Albert Museum, while a large group portrait hangs at Nostell Priory in Yorkshire.
7. Hugh Platt, *Floraes Paradise*, London, 1608, pp. 30–9.
8. The painting is now in the National Portrait Gallery in London.
9. Quoted in Rye, *England as seen by foreigners*, p. 44.
10. Barnaby Googe, *Foure Bookes of Husbandry*, a translation of Conrad Heresbach, first published in London in 1577.
11. Emily Sophia Hartshorne, *Memorials of Holdenby*, 1868, pp. 15–16, quoted in Mark Girouard, *Robert Smythson*, London, 1966, p. 33.
12. Probably from the edition published in Venice in 1568 or the Lyons edition of 1572. See John Nevinson, 'An Elizabethan Herbarium', *National Trust Year Book, 1975–76*, ed. Gervase Jackson-Stops, London, 1976, pp. 65–9.
13. See pp. 182–5 in Santina M. Levey, *The Embroideries at Hardwick Hall: A Catalogue*, National Trust, 2007.
14. Devonshire MSS, CHA, Hardwick MSS, Bess and Earls Misc. Box 2.
15. See Rachel Weigall, 'An Elizabethan Gentlewoman: The Journal of Lady Mildmay', *Quarterly Review*, ccxvi, 1911, pp. 119–38; and Linda A. Pollock, *With Faith and Physic: the Life of a Tudor Gentlewoman, Lady Grace Mildmay, 1552–1620*, London, 1993, pp. 127 and ff.
16. Joanna Moody, ed., *The Private Life of an Elizabethan Lady: The Diary of Lady Margaret Hoby, 1599–1605*, Stroud, 1998, pp. 194, 18, 211.
17. Hilary Spurling, ed., *Elinor Fettiplace's Receipt Book: Elizabethan Country House Cooking*, London, 1986, pp. 98, 163.
18. Platt, *Floraes Paradise*, pp. 28–30.
19. Philip Stubbes, *Anatomy of Abuses*, London, 1583, pp. 48–9.
20. John Cloake, *Palaces and Parks of Richmond and Kew*, vol. I, Chichester, 1995, p. 61.
21. British Library, Add. MS 17025, fols 50r and 52v.
22. Laneham's letter, p. 70, in John H. Drew, *Kenilworth: An Historical Miscellany*, Kenilworth, 1969.
23. Sir Philip Sidney, *The Countess of Pembroke's Arcadia (The New Arcadia)*, ed. Victor Skretkowicz, Oxford, 1987, p. 14.
24. Stanza 100. I have translated the names of the flowers into modern English for clarity.
25. Book II, canto xii, verse 77, ll. 1–4.
26. See Michael Leslie, 'Spenser, Sidney and the Renaissance Garden', *English Literary Renaissance*, vol. 22, no. 1 (Winter 1992), pp. 3–36.
27. Jayne Elisabeth Archer, Elizabeth Goldring and Sarah Knight eds, *The Progresses, Pageants, and Entertainments of Queen Elizabeth I*, Oxford, 2007, p. 216.

6 Court and Country

1. J.W. Neumayr, *Des Durchlauchtigen Hochgebornen Fürsten und Herrn Johann Ernsten des Jüngern zu Sachsen . . .*, Leipzig, 1620, p. 184. English translation quoted by Roy Strong in *The Renaissance Garden in England*, London, 1979, pp. 90–1.
2. Fynes Moryson, *An Itinerary*, Glasgow, 1907, vol. I, pp. 327–30.
3. Francesco de' Vieri, *Delle maravigliose opere di Pratolino & d'Amore*, Florence, 1586.
4. Published in Latin in 1501 by Lorenzo Valla, and in an illustrated edition in 1589 in Italian by Aleotti.
5. *Institution harmonique*, dedicated to Anne of Denmark and published in Frankfurt, 1615; *La Pratique et demonstration des horloges solaires*, Paris, 1624.
6. Quoted in *The King's Arcadia: Inigo Jones and the Stuart Court*, exhibition catalogue by John Harris, Stephen Orgel and Roy Strong, London, 1972, p. 43.
7. Hatfield House Bills 58/2 and 58/3.
8. Hatfield House Gen 11/25 and Bills 58/31.
9. British Library, Lansdowne MS 89, fols 92v–93.
10. Hatfield House Cecil Papers Dom/48/136, 27 October 1609.
11. Brian Vickers, ed., *Francis Bacon*, Oxford, 1996, pp. 54–5.
12. See Paula Henderson, 'Sir Francis Bacon's Essay "Of Gardens" in context', *Garden History*, vol. 36, no. 1, 2008, pp. 59–84.
13. British Library Add. MS 27278, fols 24–5.
14. James Spedding, Robert Leslie Ellis and Douglas Denon Heath, eds, *Collected Works of Francis Bacon*, Philosophical Works, vol. 11, London, 1996, pp. 76–7.
15. Aubrey, *Aubrey's Brief Lives*, ed. Dick, p. 13.
16. Francis Bacon, 'Of Gardens', in *Essays*, ed. Michael J. Hawkins, London, 1972, p. 137.
17. Quoted in Strong, *The Renaissance Garden in England*, p. 132.
18. Ibid., p. 134.
19. Royal Commission for Historical MSS, Salisbury MSS, London, 1964, vol. 19, pp. 129–30.
20. Bacon, *Essays*, p. 195.
21. Thomas Tenison, *Baconiana*, London, 1679, p. 57.
22. Aubrey, *Aubrey's Brief Lives*, p. 81.
23. John Donne, Elegy IX: 'The Autumnal'.
24. Bodleian Library, Aubrey MS 2, fols 53r, 56r, 59r.
25. Sir Henry Wotton, *The Elements of Architecture*, London, 1624, p. 109.
26. Bodleian Library, Aubrey MS 2 fol. 56v.
27. Roy Strong, *The Artist and the Garden*, New Haven and London, 2000, p. 56.
28. Edward Hyde, Earl of Clarendon, *The History of the Rebellion and Civil Wars in England . . .*, Oxford, 1717, vol. I, part i, p. 74.
29. *Portrait called Sir Francis Walsingham*, by an unknown artist, *c.* 1625, in the collection of the Marquess of Bath, Longleat House, Wiltshire. See Strong, *The Artist and the Garden*, pp. 46–7.
30. Gervase Markham, *The English Husbandman*, book II, London, 1614, p. 13.
31. Ibid., book I, London, 1613, A5.
32. Francis Bamford, ed., *A Royalist's Handbook*, London, 1936, pp. 84, 207.
33. See note 30 above.
34. Henderson, *The Tudor House and Garden*, p. 109.
35. See Malcolm Thick's introduction to William Lawson, *A Newe Orchard and Garden with The Country Housewifes Garden*, facsimile edition, first published together in 1618, Totnes, 2003.
36. The influence of the works of Gervase Markham and William Lawson is detailed in Judith Roberts, 'The Gardens of the Gentry in the Late Tudor Period', *Garden History*, vol. 27, no. 1, 1999, pp. 89–106.
37. Henry Peacham, *Minerva Britanna*, London, 1612, p. 61.

7 Curious Gardeners

1. Visit to Paris, 23 May 1651, *The Diary of John Evelyn*, 6 vols, ed. E.S. de Beer, Oxford, 2002, vol. III, p. 33.

2. Cited in the *Oxford English Dictionary* as from Isaac Walton, *Reliquiae Wottonianae*, p. 407.

3. Samuel Gilbert, *Florists Vade-Mecum*, London, 1682, p. 116.

4. Quoted by Robert Thornton in his *Temple of Flora*, London, 1799. In 'a group of carnations', fn. 2.

5. Peter Mundy, relation XXXII, 'A Passage from England over into Holland, with some Particularities of thatt Country', in *Travels in Europe, 1639–1647*, vol. IV, *The Travels of Peter Mundy in Europe and Asia, 1608–1667*, ed. Lt.-Col. Sir Richard Carnac Temple, 2nd series, no. lv, London, 1925, p. 75.

6. Gervase Markham, *English Husbandman*, book II, London, 1614, p. 35.

7. Jacob van Swanenburch's album is in the Nederlandsche Economisch-Historisch Archief, Amsterdam; Judith Leyster's illustrations are in an album in the Frans Hals Museum, Haarlem; Pieter Cos's album is in the University Library, Wageningen.

8. Ralph Knevet, *Rhodon and Iris*, Bodleian Library, Mal.174(4).

9. Bodleian Library, E.325, fol. 129.

10. Bodleian Library, Douce S7. See also Ruth Duthie, *Florists' Flowers and Societies*, Aylesbury, 1988, and 'English Florists' Societies and Feasts in the Seventeenth and the First Half of the Eighteenth Centuries', *Garden History*, vol. 10, no. 1, 1982, pp. 17–35.

11. Sir Thomas Hanmer, *The Garden Book*, introduction by Eleanour Sinclair Rohde, London, 1933.

12. Letter of 21 August 1671, quoted in the introduction to Hanmer, *The Garden Book*, p. xv.

13. See Karen Hearn, *Nathaniel Bacon: Artist, Gentleman and Gardener*, London, 2005.

14. A.C. Edwards, ed., *English History from Essex Sources, 1570–1750*, Chelmsford, 1952, p. 35.

15. John Parkinson, *Paradisi in Sole*, London, 1629, p. 6.

16. Ibid., pp. 63–4.

17. Ibid., pp. 206, 213.

18. Ibid., commendation, translation in Anna Parkinson, *Nature's Alchemist: John Parkinson, Herbalist to Charles I*, London, 2007, p. 195.

19. John Parkinson, *Paradisus*, epistle to the reader.

20. Ibid., p. 52 (Tradescant), p. 152 (Tradescant), p. 312 (Tuggie).

21. Ibid., p. 88 (Le Veau), p. 126 (Boel), p. 365 (Marvel of Peru).

22. Ibid., p. 30.

23. Ibid., p. 96 (Fludd), pp. 122–3 (Barnesley), p. 213 (Packington), p. 348 (Tunstall), p. 348 (Danvers).

24. John Parkinson, *Theatrum Botanicum*, London, 1640, epistle to the reader (Johnson), p. 1064 (Boel).

25. Richard Hakluyt, *The Principal Navigations, Voiages, and Discoveries of the English Nation*, London, 1589, p. 530.

26. James I, *Counterblaste to Tobacco*, London, 1605, pp. 1–8.

27. Gerard, *Herball*, p. 286.

28. See R.T. Gunther, *Early British Botanists and their Gardens*, Oxford, 1922, p. 34.

29. This appeared as *Instructions for the increasing of mulberie trees*, printed by Edward Allde for Eleazar Edgar, London, 1609.

30. Nicholas Geffe, trans. de Serres, *The perfect use of Silk-wormes, and their benefit*, London, 1607, p. 21.

31. Jennifer Potter, *Strange Blooms: The Curious Lives and Adventures of the John Tradescants*, London, 2006, p. 213.

32. Now in the Bodleian Library, Antiq.c.E1629.1.

33. Parkinson, *Theatrum Botanicum*, p. 1477.

34. 'Rais'd from Seeds which were brought back from *Virginia* many Years since by Mr. *John Tradescant*, in his Garden at *South Lambeth* near *Vaux-hall*'. Philip Miller, *The Gardeners Dictionary*, London, 1731, under *Acer Virginianum*.

35. Public Record Office State Papers, Domestic, Charles I, 4, 1625, pp. 155–6.

36. Peter Mundy, *Travels in England, India, China, etc.*, 1634–38, vol. III, part i, *The Travels of Peter Mundy in Europe and Asia, 1608–1667*, ed. Lt.-Col. Sir Richard Carnac Temple, 2nd series, no. xlv, London, 1919, pp. 1–3.

37. Bodleian Library, MS Ashmole 1461.

38. The book is listed in John Tradescant's *Musaeum Tradescantium*, London, 1656.

8 The Sun and the Moon

1. Marginal note in Jones's copy, now at Chatsworth, of Daniello Barbaro's *I dieci libri dell'architetura di M. Vitruvio*, Venice, 1567, p. 22, quoted in Nicholas Tyacke, ed., *Seventeenth-Century Oxford*, Oxford, 1997, pp. 169–70.
2. Anthony Wood, *The History and Antiquities of the University of Oxford*, vol. 2, part 2, Oxford, 1796, pp. 897–8.
3. Potter, *Strange Blooms*, p. 251.
4. Louise Allen and Timothy Walker, *The University of Oxford Botanic Garden*, Oxford, 1995, p. 56.
5. *Diary of John Evelyn*, vol. III, 12 July 1654, pp. 109–10.
6. John Gauden, *Eikon Basilike*, London, 1649, p. 34.
7. Tyacke, ed., *Seventeenth-Century Oxford*, p. 70.
8. *Aubrey's Brief Lives*, ed. Dick, p. 186.
9. Montagu Burrows, ed., *The Register of the Visitors of the University of Oxford, from A.D. 1647 to A.D. 1658*, Camden Society, new series, XXIX (1881), p. xc.
10. Bodleian Library, MS Ashmole 1810.
11. *Diary of John Evelyn*, vol. III, 13 July 1654, pp. 110–11.
12. From Thomas Hearne's diary, quoted by Gunther, *Early British Botanists and their Gardens*, Oxford, 1922, p. 80.
13. Stonehouse's catalogue and plan of the garden at Darsfield were acquired by John Goodyer and are now in the archives at Magdalen College, Oxford, MS 239. The notes about the garden are from R.T. Gunther's *Early British Botanists and their Gardens*, Oxford, 1922, pp. 348–51.
14. A.R. and M.B. Hall, eds, *Correspondence of Henry Oldenburg*, 13 vols, Madison, Wisconsin and London, 1965–8, vol. 1, p. 113.
15. Quoted in Trea Martyn, *Elizabeth in the Garden: A story of love, rivalry and spectacular design*, London, 2008, pp. 54–5.
16. Annals of the Comitia of Physicians, The Royal College of Physicians of London, October 1589.
17. W. Ryves, *The Life of the Admired Physician and astrologer of our times, Mr Nicholas Culpeper...*, London, 1659, sig. C3r.
18. Nicholas Culpeper, *Catastrophe Magnatum*, London, 1652, p. 20.
19. Nicholas Culpeper, *Semeiotica Uranica*, London, 1651, p. 182.
20. L. Fioravanti, *Three Exact Pieces*, London, 1652, preface.
21. *Culpeper's school of physick*, London, 1696, sig. C6r.
22. William Fulke, *Anti-prognosticon contra inutiles astrologorum praedictiones Nostradami, Hilli*, London, 1560.
23. Hugh Platt, *Floraes Paradise*, London, 1608, p. 80.
24. Sir Thomas Hanmer, *The Garden Book*, London, 1933, p. 17.
25. Quoted by Eleanour Rohde in her introduction, ibid., p. xx.
26. Parkinson, *Paradisi in Sole*, pp. 461–2.
27. Gerard, *Herball*, p. 282.
28. *Philosophical Transactions*, no. 137, January and February, 1677/8.
29. This concept was revived by Rudolf Steiner, with his theories of anthroposophy. See, for example, Hilary Wright's *Biodynamic Gardening for Health and Taste*, London, 2003.
30. Benjamin Woolley, *The Herbalist: Nicholas Culpeper and the Fight for Medical Freedom*, London, 2004, p. 176.
31. *Historia hortensium quatuor opusculis methodicus contexta; Alexicepus seu auxiliaris et medicus hortus;* and *Artificios methodus comparandorum hortensium fructuum.*
32. C.J. Fordyce and T.M. Knox, 'The Library of Jesus College, Oxford', *Oxford Bibliographical Society, Proceedings and Papers*, vol. V, part 2, 1937, pp. 53–115.
33. William H. Dircks, ed., *Autobiography*, London, 1888, p. 28.
34. *De Plantis Aegyptiis observationes et notae ad Prosperum Alpinum.*
35. Walter Charleton, *The Immortality of the Human Soul Demonstrated by the Light of Nature*, London, 1657. In this work, Charleton recorded the contemporary research being undertak-

en at the College of Physicians in London and at the university in Oxford, written in the form of dialogues between himself as Athanasius, John Evelyn as Lucretius, and Lord Dorchester as Isodicastes. See Lindsay Sharp, 'Walter Charleton's Early Life', *Annals of Science*, vol. 30, no. 3, 1973, p. 338.

36. Royal College of Physicians, 2000/81/a.
37. The controversy over this book is detailed in Harold J. Cook, *Matters of Exchange: Commerce, Medicine, and Science in the Dutch Golden Age*, New Haven and London, 2007, pp. 212 and ff.
38. *Diary of John Evelyn*, vol. II, 1 March 1644, p. 114.
39. G.W. Wheeler, ed., *Letters of Sir Thomas Bodley to his librarian, Thomas James*, Oxford, 1926, pp. 219, 221–2.

9 Secrets Revealed

1. William George Hoskins, *The Making of the English Landscape*, London, 1970, pp. 154–5.
2. John Partridge, *Treasurie of commodious conceits and hidden secrets*, London, 1633, sig. B3v.
3. Hilary Spurling, ed., *Elinor Fettiplace's Receipt Book: Elizabethan Country House Cooking*, London, 1986, p. 97. I have adapted it into modern English.
4. Ibid., p. 146.
5. William London, *A catalogue of the most vendible Books in England, 1657, 1658, 1660, originally printed in London for sale in his shop in Newcastle*, reprinted English Bibliographical Resources, London, 1965, sig. A3; sig. G3v; sig. H3v.
6. Ralph Austen, *A Treatise of Fruit-trees*, Oxford, 1665, dedicatory epistle.
7. C. Anne Wilson, ed., *A Book of Fruits & Flowers*, facsimile edition, London, 1984.
8. Shirley Sherwood, *A New Flowering: 1000 Years of Botanical Art*, Oxford, 2005, pp. 50–3.
9. R.T. Gunther, *Early British Botanists and their Gardens*, Oxford, 1922, p. 14.
10. Magdalen College Archives, Goodyer MS 11, fol. 117.
11. Prosper Alpinus, *De plantis Aegypti*, Venice, 1592, and Johan Vesling, *Paraeneses ad rem herbariam*, Padua, 1638; Juan Fragoso, *Aromatum fructuum et simplicium*, Strasbourg, 1601, and Garcia ab Orto, *Aromatum et simplicium*, Antwerp, 1574; Nicolas Monardes in the Latin edition by Clusius, *De simplicibus*, Antwerp, 1574 and in English by John Frampton, *Joyfull newes out of the newe-found worlde*, London, 1596; Joannes Lerius, *Historia navigationis in Brasiliam*, Geneva, 1586 and Willem Piso, *De Medicina Brasiliensi*, Leiden, 1648; Francisco Hernández, *Nova Plantarum*, Rome, 1651; and Jacobus Cornutus, *Canadensium plantarum*, Paris, 1635.
12. Magdalen College Archives, Goodyer MS 11, fol. 117.
13. Basil Besler, *Hortus Eystettensis*, Nuremberg, 1613; Peter Paaw, *Hortus publicus Academiae Lugduno-Batavae*, Leiden, 1601; Guy de la Brosse, *Description du jardin royal des plantes médicinales*, Paris, 1636.
14. R.T. Gunther's *Early British Botanists and their Gardens*.
15. Evelyn's papers are in the British Library: see Thedore Hofmann, et al., 'John Evelyn's Archive at the British Library', in Anthony Kenny et al., *John Evelyn in the British Library*, London, 1995; his library catalogue of 1687 was analysed by Geoffrey Keynes, *John Evelyn: A Study in Bibliophily*, Oxford, 1968; the auction documents at Christies relating to the sales of Evelyn's books, 1977–8: A–C, 22–3 June 1977; D–L, 30 November–1 December 1977; M-S 15–16 March 1978; T-Z, 12–13 July 1978. Many of his horticultural books were bought for the British Library at the Christies sale.
16. Samuel Hartlib, *Considerations tending to the happy accomplishment of England's reformation . . .*, London, 1647, pp. 46, 48.
17. Samuel Hartlib, *Samuel Hartlib His Legacy*, London, 1651, p. 9.
18. *Oxford Dictionary of National Biography* entry, Oxford, 2004, vol. 6, p. 228.
19. *Traité compendieux et abrégé des Tulippes et de leurs diverses sortes et espèces*, Paris, 1617.
20. Quoted in Anna Pavord, *The Tulip*, London, 1999, p. 93. Her translation is taken from Henry van Oosten, *The Dutch Gardener*, London, 1711.

21. *Diary of John Evelyn*, vol. III, 6 December 1658, p. 225. According to the *OED*, this is the first use in English of 'olitorie'.
22. Translated by June Taboroff in '"Wife, unto thy Garden": The First Gardening Books for Women', *Garden History*, vol. 11, no. 1, 1983, p. 4.
23. John Evelyn, *Elysium Britannicum, or The Royal Gardens*, ed. John H. Ingram, Philadelphia, 2001, p. 42.
24. See D.J. McKitterick, 'Women and their Books in Seventeenth-century England: the case of Elizabeth Puckering', *The Library*, 7th series, vol. 1, 2000, pp. 359–80.
25. British Library, MS Egerton 2983, fol. 79.
26. Philip L. Barbour, ed., *The Jamestown Voyages*, vol. 1, Cambridge, 1969, p. 139.
27. Philip L. Barbour, ed., *The Complete Works of Captain John Smith*, vol. 1, Williamsburg, 1968, pp. 151–3.
28. John Josselin, *An Account of Two Voyages to New England*, London, 1674, p. 59.
29. William Wood, *New England's Prospect*, London, 1634, p. 14.
30. Journal, 8 June 1630, *Winthrop Papers*, 2nd series, vol. II, Boston, MA, 1931, p. 259.
31. Ibid., vol. III, p. 153.
32. Letter, 29 March 1634, ibid., vol. III, p. 158.
33. *Winthrop Papers*, 4th series, vol. VI, Boston, MA, 1863, p. 474.
34. *Winthrop Papers*, 2nd series, vol. III, Boston, MA, 1943, p. 73.
35. *Winthrop Papers*, 5th series, vol. I, 1871, p. 153.
36. Stephen Switzer, *Nobleman, gentleman, and gardener's recreation*, London, 1715, pp. 44–5.

10 The Long Winter

1. John Rea, *Flora, seu de Florum Cultura*, London, 1665, p. 2.
2. *Diary of John Evelyn*, vol. II, 18 August 1641, p. 41.
3. Ibid., 1 April 1644, pp. 128–31.
4. Ibid., 4 April 1644, p. 132.
5. Ibid., 29 November 1644, p. 287.
6. Illustrated in Anthony Kenny et al., *John Evelyn in the British Library*, London, 1995, p. 29 as unnumbered manuscript.
7. Andrew Marvell, *Works*, ed. Thomas Cooke, 2 vols, London, 1726, vol. I, p. 5.
8. John Dixon Hunt, *Andrew Marvell: His Life and Writings*, London 1978, pp. 26 and ff.
9. *Diary of John Evelyn*, vol. II, 24 March 1646, p. 478.
10. Robert Crab, *Dagons Downfall, or the Great Idol digged up Root and Branch*, London, 1657, p. 20.
11. Ralph Austen, *The Spirituall use of an Orchard*, proposition 93; John Prest, *The Garden of Eden: The Botanic Garden and the Re-Creation of Paradise*, New Haven and London, 1981, p. 85.
12. Hartlib Papers, Sheffield University Library, 51/23a, 27 September 1658.
13. Quoted in Rosemary Hill, *Stonehenge*, London, 2008, p. 30.
14. British Library, Add. MS 78342.
15. Michael Leslie, 'The Spiritual Husbandry of John Beale', in *Culture and Cultivation in Early Modern England: Writing and the Land*, ed. Leslie and Timothy Raylor, Leicester, 1992, p. 163.
16. Letter, 28 January 1660, *The Works of Sir Thomas Browne*, ed. Keynes, 4 vols, 1964, vol. IV, p. 274; Sir Thomas was the author not only of the very influential *Religio Medici* but also of *The Garden of Cyrus*, published in 1658, where he also put forward ideas about horticulture, considering the occurrence of the quincunx in man-made objects, including the plantations of the ancients, and in plants and animals.
17. 3 September 1659, *Diary and Correspondence of John Evelyn*, ed. William Bray, 4 vols, London, 1859, vol. III, pp. 262–4.
18. Letter to William Prettyman, 2 December 1651, British Library, Add. MS 78298, fol. 48.
19. *The Diary of John Evelyn*, ed. de Beer, vol. III, 10 February 1652, pp. 58–9.
20. British Library, Add. MS 78221, fol. 56.
21. British Library, Add. MS 78628A. Sayes Court survived, albeit in a battered state, until 1884 when W.J. Evelyn tried to offer the house and garden to Octavia Hill and Robert Hunter. Sadly

there was no public body with the necessary statutory power to preserve it for the uses that Evelyn intended. In the ten years that it took to bring such a body, the National Trust, into existence, the chance to save Sayes Court was lost. However, many important and fine gardens have been preserved as a result. For details, see Merlin Waterson, *The National Trust: the First Hundred Years*, London, 1994.

22. *Fumifugium*, facsimile edition, Exeter, 1976, p. 14.
23. This explanation and many others are given by Maggie Campbell-Culver in her edition of *John Evelyn: Directions for the Gardiner and other Horticultural Advice*, Oxford, 2009, p. 27.
24. Ibid., pp. 41–2.
25. British Library, Add. MS 78316.
26. British Library, Add. MS 78298, in a letter dated 12 January 1659.
27. Sir Thomas Hanmer, *The Garden Book*, facsimile edition, London, 1933, pp. 18, 19.
28. Sir Henry Wotton, *Elements of Architecture*, facsimile editon, Farnborough, 1969, p. 110.
29. The Finch Hatton papers, now in the Northamptonshire Record Office.
30. Morison's remark is from *Plantarum Historia Universalis Oxoniensis*, and Evelyn's from *Acetaria*, both quoted in Miles Hadfield, *A History of British Gardening*, London, 1979, p. 136.
31. Finch Hatton 2504.
32. Finch Hatton 3440.
33. Finch Hatton 2448, 2450.
34. Finch Hatton 2454.
35. Finch Hatton 2423.
36. Finch Hatton 2455.
37. *Country Life*, 20 and 27 March 1942.
38. Letter by Lord Perceval, first Earl of Egmont, 9 August 1724, British Library, Egmont MSS.
39. G. Thorn Drury, ed., *The Poems of Edmund Waller*, London, 1905, vol. II, p. 40.
40. Stanza XXXVII, 283–8.
41. Stanza XXXIX, 309–12.
42. Frank Kermode and Keith Walker, eds, *Andrew Marvell*, Oxford, 1990, pp. 40–1.
43. John Milton, *Paradise Lost*, book IV, ll. 237 and 240–3, London, 2000, p. 80.
44. Pepys, *Diary*, ed. Latham and Matthews, vol. I, 15 April 1660, p. 109.

Epilogue – Springtime

1. John Ogilby, *The Entertainment of His Most Excellent Majestie Charles II in his passage through the City of London*, London, 1662, pp. 139 and ff.
2. William Derham, *Philosophical Letters*, London, 1716, p. 366.
3. Robert Morison, *Praeludia Botanica*, p. 476. The translation from Latin was made by Charles Raven in *John Ray*, Cambridge, 1942, p. 184. John Ray's letter is in *The Correspondence of John Ray*, ed. Edwin Lankester, London, 1848, pp. 41–2.
4. Keith Thomas, *Man and the Natural World: Changing Attitudes in England, 1500–1800*, London, 1983, p. 109.
5. John Rea, *Flora, seu de Florum Cultura*, p. 3.
6. Quoted in Sue Minter, *The Apothecaries' Garden: A History of Chelsea Physic Garden*, Stroud, 2000, p. 5.
7. Worlidge, *Systema horti-culturæ: or the art of gardening*, London, 1677, pp. 4–5.
8. Pepys, *Diary*, ed. Latham and Matthews, vol. VII, p. 213.

Select Bibliography

Primary Manuscript Sources

Cavendish Family papers at Chatsworth:
    Northaw inventory, Hardwick MSS, Bess & Earls Misc., Box 2
    Wages books, 1578–80, Chatsworth MS 4
    William Senior's *Book of Maps*, Chatsworth & Hardwick, 1610

Cecil Family papers at Hatfield:
    Bills 58/2; 58/3; 58/31
    Gen 11/25
    Dom/48/136

Lord Dorchester's catalogue of books:
    Royal College of Physicians, London, MS 2000/81/a

John Evelyn's papers at the British Library:
    Elysium Britannicum, Add. MS 78342
    Sayes Court plan, Add. MS 78628A
    Correspondence, Add. MSS 78221, 78298, 78316

Finch Hatton papers at Northamptonshire Record Office:
    FH 2423; 2448; 2450; 2454; 2455; 2504; 3440

Primary Printed Sources

Dates refer to first publication, unless subsequent editions are significant.

Austen, Ralph, *A Treatise of Fruit-trees*, Oxford, 1657.
Brunfels, Otto, *Herbarium vivae eicones*, Strasbourg, 1530–36.
Clusius, Carolus, *Rariorum plantarum historia*, Antwerp, 1601.
Culpeper, Nicholas, *The English Physitian (Culpeper's Complete Herbal)*, London, 1652.
    A Physical Directory, London, 1649.
De Passe, Crispijn, *Hortus Floridus*, Arnhem, 1614.
Evelyn, John, *The French Gardiner*, London, 1658.

Kalendarium Hortense, London, 1664 (published with *Sylva*, and then separately from 1666).
    Sylva or a Discourse of Forest-Trees, London, 1664.
Fitzherbert, Sir John, *Boke of Husbandry*, London, 1533 (transcript by English Dialect Society, London, 1882).
Frampton, John, *Joyfull newes out of the newe-founde world*, London, 1577.
Fuchs, Leonhart, *De Historia Stirpium*, Basel, 1542.
Gardiner, Richard, *Instructions for manuring, sowing and planting of kitchin gardens*, London, 1603 (facsimile, Amsterdam and New York, 1973).
Gerard, John, *Herball*, London, 1597.
Googe, Barnaby, *Heresbach's Foure Bookes of Husbandry*, London, 1577.
Hartlib, Samuel, *His Legacy of Husbandry*, London, 1651.
Hill, Thomas, *The Gardeners Labyrinth*, London, 1577.
Josselin, John, *An Account of Two Voyages to New England*, London, 1674.
Lawson, William, *A New Orchard and Garden*, London, 1618.
Le Moyne, Jacques, *La Clef des Champs*, London, 1586.
L'Obel, Matthias and Peter Pena, *Stirpium adversaria nova*, London, 1570.
Lyte, Henry, *A Niewe Herball or Historie of Plants*, London, 1578.
Markham, Gervase, *The English Husbandman*, London, 1613–14.
Mascall, Leonard, *Booke of the Art and Maner, howe to Plante and Graffe All Sortes of Trees*, London, 1569.
Parkinson, John, *Paradisi in Sole*, London, 1629.
    Theatrum Botanicum, London, 1640.
Partridge, John, *Treasurie of commodious conceits and hidden secrets*, London, 1573.
Peacham, Henry, *Minerva Britanna*, London, 1612.
Platt, Hugh, *Floraes Paradise*, London, 1608 (*Garden of Eden*, 1653).
Rea, John, *Flora, seu de Florum Cultura*, London, 1665.
Scot, Reginald, *A Perfite Platforme of a hoppe garden*, London, 1574.
Stallenge, William, *Instructions for the increasing of mulberie trees and the breeding of silk wormes for the making of silk in this kingdom*, London, 1609.
Surflet, Richard, *The Countrey Farme*, London, 1600.
Turner, William, *Herbal*, London and Cologne, 1551–68.
    Libellus de re herbaria, London, 1538.
    The Names of Herbes, London, 1548.
Tusser, Thomas, *Five Hundreth Pointes of Good Husbandrie*, London, 1573.
    A Hundreth Good Pointes of Husbandrie, London, 1557.
Wood, William, *New England's Prospect*, London, 1634.
Wotton, Sir Henry, *The Elements of Architecture*, London, 1624.

Secondary Sources

Adams, Simon, ed., *Household Accounts and Disbursement Books of Robert Dudley, Earl of Leicester, 1558–61, 1584–86*, Camden Fifth Series, vol. 6, Cambridge, 1995.
Alford, Stephen, *Burghley: William Cecil at the Court of Elizabeth I*, New Haven and London, 2008.
Anderson, Andrew H., 'Henry, Lord Stafford: his Books and Interests 1501–1563', *The Library*, 5th series, vol. 21, 1966.
Archer, Jayne Elisabeth, Elizabeth Golding, and Sarah Knight, eds, *The Progresses, Pageants, and Entertainments of Queen Elizabeth I*, Oxford and New York, 2007.
Aubrey, John, *Aubrey's Brief Lives*, ed. Oliver Lawson Dick, London, 1949.
Bacon, Francis, 'Of Gardens', in *Essays*, ed. Michael J. Hawkins, London, 1972.
Bamford, Francis, ed., *A Royalist's Handbook*, London, 1936.
Baridon, Michel, *A History of the Gardens of Versailles*, tr. Adrienne Mason, Philadelphia, 2008.
Barker, Nicolas and David Quentin, eds, *The Library of Thomas Tresham and Thomas Brudenell*, London, 2006.
Barnard, John, 'Politics, Profits and Idealism: John Norton, the Stationers' Company and Sir Thomas Bodley', *Bodleian Library Record*, vol. 17, 2002, pp. 385–408.

Batho, G.R., 'The Library of the Wizard Earl: Henry Percy, Ninth Earl of Northumberland', *Library History*, 5th series, vol. 15, 1960, pp. 246–61.

Beck, Thomasina, *Embroidered Gardens*, London, 1979.

Bending, Stephen and Andrew McRae, eds, *The Writing of Rural England, 1500–1800*, London, 2003.

Biddle, Martin, 'The Gardens of Nonsuch: Sources and Dating', *Garden History*, vol. 27, no. 1, 1999, pp. 145–83.

Bird, Sarah et al., 'A Late Sixteenth-Century Garden: Fact or Fantasy – The Portrait of Sir George Delves in the Walker Art Gallery, Liverpool', *Garden History*, vol. 24, no. 2, 1996, pp. 168–83.

Blunt, Wilfrid and William T. Stearn, *The Art of Botanical Illustration*, new edition, Woodbridge, Suffolk, 1994.

Bowen, Karen Lee and Dirk Imhof, *Christopher Plantin and Engraved Book Illustrations in Sixteenth-Century Europe*, Cambridge, 2008.

Brighton, Trevor, 'Chatsworth's Sixteenth-Century Parks and Gardens', *Garden History*, vol. 23, no. 1, 1995, pp. 3–55.

Bushnell, Rebecca, *Green Desire: Imagining Early Modern English Gardens*, Ithaca and London, 2003.

Campbell-Culver, Maggie, ed., *John Evelyn: Directions for the Gardiner and other Horticultural Advice*, Oxford, 2009.

—— *The Origin of Plants*, London, 2001.

Christianson, C. Paul, *The Riverside Gardens of Sir Thomas More's London*, New Haven and London, 2005.

Cliffe, J.T., *The World of the Country House in Seventeenth-Century England*, New Haven and London, 1999.

Cook, Harold J., *Matters of Exchange: Commerce, Medicine, and Science in the Dutch Golden Age*, New Haven and London, 2007.

Croft, Pauline, ed., *The Early Cecils: Patronage, Culture and Power*, New Haven and London, 2002.

—— *King James I*, Basingstoke, 2003.

Dannenfeldt, Karl H., *Leonhard Rauwolf*, Cambridge, Mass., 1968.

Darley, Gillian, *John Evelyn: Living for Ingenuity*, New Haven and London, 2006.

Dash, Mike, *Tulipomania*, London, 1999.

De Nave, F. and Dirk Imhof, eds, *Botany in the Low Countries (end of the 15th century–ca. 1650)*, Antwerp, 1993.

Dietz, Brian, *The Port and Trade of Early Elizabethan London*, London, 1972.

Duthie, Ruth, 'English Florists' Societies and Feasts in the Seventeenth and the First Half of the Eighteenth Centuries', *Garden History*, vol. 10, no. 1, 1982, pp. 17–35.

—— *Florists' Flowers and Societies*, Aylesbury, 1988.

Eburne, Andrew and Kate Feluś, *Lyveden New Bield Conservation Management Plan*, The National Trust, 2008.

Farr, David, *John Lambert, Parliamentary Soldier and Cromwellian Major General, 1619–84*, Woodbridge, Suffolk, 2003.

Fehrenbach, Robert, ed., *Private Libraries in Renaissance England: A Collection and Catalogue of Tudor and early Stuart Book-lists*, with E.S. Leedham-Green, Binghamton, NY, 1992.

Fettiplace, Elinor, *Elinor Fettiplace's Receipt Book: Elizabethan Country House Cooking*, ed. Hilary Spurling, London, 1986.

Findlen, Paula, *Possessing Nature: Museums, Collecting, and Scientific Culture in Early Modern Italy*, Berkeley, CA and London, 1994.

Fordyce, C.J. and T.M. Knox, 'The Library of Jesus College, Oxford', *Oxford Bibliographical Society, Proceedings and Papers*, vol. V, part 2, 1937, pp. 53–115.

Forster, Charles Thornton and Francis Henry Blackburne Daniell, trs, *The Life and Letters of Ogier Ghiselin de Busbecq*, London, 1881.

Frank, Roger G., *Harvey and the Oxford Physiologists*, Berkeley, CA and London, 1980.

Gadd, Ian A. and Patrick Wallis, eds, *Guilds and Association in Europe, 900–1900*, London, 2006.

Gent, Lucy, ed., *Albion's Classicism: The Visual Arts in Britain, 1550–1660*, New Haven and London, 1995.

—— *Picture and Poetry, 1560–1620*, Leamington Spa, 1981.

Girouard, Mark, 'Elizabethan Holdenby', *Country Life*, 25 October 1979.

Goldgar, Anne, *Tulipmania: Money, Honor, and Knowledge in the Dutch Golden Age*, Chicago and London, 2007.

Goodchild, Peter, '"No Phantastical Utopia, But a Reall Place": John Evelyn, John Beale and Backbury Hill, Herefordshire', *Garden History*, vol. 19, no. 2, 1991, pp. 105–27.

Goose, Nigel, and Lien Liu, eds, *Immigrants in Tudor and Early Stuart England*, Brighton, 2005.

Gristwood, Sarah, *Elizabeth and Leicester*, London, 2007.

Gunther, R.T., *Early British Botanists and their Gardens*, Oxford, 1922.

—— *Early Science in Oxford*, Oxford, 1926.

—— *Oxford Gardens*, Oxford, 1912.

Hadfield, Miles, *A History of British Gardening*, revised edition, London, 1979.

Hanmer, Sir Thomas, *The Garden Book*, facsimile edition, introduction by Eleanour Sinclair Rohde, London, 1933.

Harkness, Deborah, *The Jewel House: Elizabethan London and the Scientific Revolution*, New Haven and London, 2007.

Harvey, John, *Early Nurserymen*, Chichester, 1974.

Hassall, W.O., 'The Books of Sir Christopher Hatton at Holkham Library', *The Library*, 5th series, vol. 5, no. 2 (1950–51), pp. 1–13.

Henderson, Paula, 'Sir Francis Bacon's Essay "Of Gardens" in Context', *Garden History*, vol. 36, no. 1, 2008, pp. 59–84.

—— *The Tudor House and Garden: Architecture and Landscape in the Sixteenth and Early Seventeenth Centuries*, New Haven and London, 2005.

Henrey, Blanche, *British Botanical and Horticultural Literature before 1800*, Oxford, 1975.

Herbert, Edward, first Baron, *Autobiography*, ed. William H. Dircks, London, 1888.

Herring, Peter, *Godolphin: An Archaeological Historical Survey*, Cornwall, 1997.

Howarth, David, *Lord Arundel and his Circle*, New Haven and London, 1985.

Hoyles, Martin, *Bread and Roses: Gardening Books from 1560–1960*, vol. 2, London, 1995.

Gardener's Delight: Gardening Books from 1560, London, 1994.

Hunt, John Dixon, *Andrew Marvell: His Life and Writings*, London, 1978.

—— *The Genius of the Place: The English Landscape Garden, 1620–1820*, London, 1975.

Hunter, Michael, *Establishing the New Science: the Experience of the Early Royal Society*, Woodbridge, Suffolk, 1980.

Jacques, David, 'The Compartment System in Tudor England', *Garden History*, vol. 27, no. 1, 1999, pp. 32–53.

Jayne, Sears, *Library Catalogues of the English Renaissance*, Godalming, 1983.

Jeffers, Robert, *The Friends of John Gerard*, Falls Village, CT, 1967.

Knight, Leah, *Of Books and Botany in Early Modern England: Sixteenth-century Plants and Print Culture*, Farnham, Surrey, 2009.

Leighton, Ann, *Early English Gardens in New England*, London, 1970.

Leith-Ross, Prudence, 'The Garden of John Evelyn at Deptford', *Garden History*, vol. 25, no. 2, 1997, pp. 138–52.

—— *The John Tradescants: Gardeners to the Rose and Lily Queen*, revised edition, London, 2006.

—— 'A Seventeenth-century Paris Garden', *Garden History*, vol. 21, no. 2, 1993, pp. 150–7.

Leslie, Michael, 'Spenser, Sidney and the Renaissance Garden', *English Literary Renaissance*, vol. 22, no. 1, Winter 1992, pp. 3–36.

Leslie, Michael and Timothy Raylor, eds, *Culture and Cultivation in Early Modern England: Writing and the Land*, Leicester, 1992.

Levey, Santina, *An Elizabethan Inheritance: The Hardwick Hall Textiles*, London, 1998.

—— *The Embroideries at Hardwick Hall: a Catalogue*, National Trust, 2006.

Martyn, Trea, *Elizabeth in the Garden: A Story of Love, Rivalry and Spectacular Design*, London, 2008.

Mawdsley, William Norman Hargreaves, *Oxford in the Age of John Locke*, Oklahoma, 1973.

McKitterick, D.J., *The Library of Sir Thomas Knyvett of Ashwellthorpe, c. 1539–1618*, Cambridge, 1978.

—— 'Women and their Books in Seventeenth-Century England: The Case of Elizabeth Puckering', *The Library*, 7th series, vol. 1, 2000, pp. 359–80.

Minter, Sue, *The Apothecaries' Garden: A History of Chelsea Physic Garden*, Stroud, 2000.

Moody, Joanna, ed., *The Private Life of an Elizabethan Lady: The Diary of Lady Margaret Hoby 1599–1605*, Stroud, 1998.

Nevinson, John, 'An Elizabethan Herbarium', *National Trust Year Book, 1975–76*, ed. Gervase Jackson-Stops, London, 1976.

Nichols, John, *The Progresses and Public Processions of Queen Elizabeth*, London, 1823.

Nicolson, Adam, *Earls of Paradise*, London, 2008.

Parkinson, Anna, *Nature's Alchemist: John Parkinson, Herbalist to Charles I*, London, 2007.

Pavord, Anna, *The Naming of Names: The Search for Order in the World of Plants*, London, 2005.

—— *The Tulip*, London, 1999.

Pollock, Linda, *With Faith and Physic: the Life of a Tudor Gentlewoman, Lady Grace Mildmay, 1552–1620*, London, 1993.

Potter, Jennifer, *Strange Blooms: The Curious Lives and Adventures of the John Tradescants*, London, 2006.

Prest, John, *The Garden of Eden: The Botanic Garden and the Re-Creation of Paradise*, New Haven and London, 1981.

Raven, Charles, *English Naturalists from Neckam to Ray*, Cambridge, 1947.

—— *John Ray*, Cambridge, 1942.

Roberts, Judith, 'The Gardens of the Gentry in the Late Tudor Period', *Garden History*, vol. 27, no. 1, 1999, pp. 89–108.

Sherwood, Shirley, *A New Flowering: 1000 Years of Botanical Art*, Oxford, 2005.

Sidney, Philip, *The New Arcadia*, ed. Victor Skretkowicz, Oxford, 1987.

Strong, Roy, *The Artist and the Garden*, New Haven and London, 2000.

—— *The Renaissance Garden in England*, London, 1979.

—— 'The Renaissance Garden in England Reconsidered', *Garden History*, vol. 27, no. 1, 1999, pp. 2–9.

Stuart, David, *The Plants that Shaped our Gardens*, London, 2002.

Sweerts, Emanuel, *Early Floral Engravings*, ed. E.F. Bleiler, London, 1976.

Taboroff, June, ' "Wife, Unto thy Garden": the First Gardening Books for Women', *Garden History*, vol. 11, no. 1, 1983, pp. 1–5.

Thick, Malcolm, *The Neat House Gardens: Early Market Gardening around London*, Totnes, 1998.

Thomas, Keith, *Man and the Natural World: Changing Attitudes in England, 1500–1800*, London, 1983.

Till, E.C., 'The Development of the Park and Gardens at Burghley', *Garden History*, vol. 19, no. 1, 1991, pp. 128–45.

Tinniswood, Adrian, *His Invention So Fertile: A Life of Christopher Wren*, London, 2001.

Tyacke, Nicholas, ed., *Seventeenth-Century Oxford*, vol. IV of *The History of the University of Oxford*, Oxford, 1997.

Uglow, Jenny, *A Little History of British Gardening*, London, 2004.

Voet, Leon, *The Golden Compasses: The History of the House of Plantin-Moretus*, Amsterdam, 1969.

Webber, Ronald, 'London Market Gardens', *History Today*, vol. 23, 1973, pp. 871–8.

Wells-Cole, Anthony, *Art and Decoration in Elizabethan and Jacobean England*, New Haven and London, 1997.

White, Eileen, ed., *The English Cookery Book: Historical Essays*, Totnes, 2004.

Williams, Neville, *All the Queen's Men: Elizabeth I and her Courtiers*, London, 1972.

Wilson, C. Anne, *Banquetting Stuffe*, Edinburgh, 1989.

—— ed., *A Book of Fruits & Flowers, 1653*, facsimile edition, London, 1984.

Wilson, Derek A., *Sweet Robin: A Biography of Robert Dudley, Earl of Leicester, 1533–88*, London, 1981.

Wood, Anthony, *Survey of the Antiquities of the City of Oxford, composed in 1661–2*, ed. Andrew Clark, Oxford, 1889.

Woodhouse, Elizabeth, 'Kenilworth, the Earl of Leicester's Pleasure Grounds Following Robert Laneham's Letter', *Garden History*, vol. 27, no. 1, 1991, pp. 127–44.

—— 'Spirit of the Elizabethan Garden', *Garden History*, vol. 27, no. 1, 1999, pp. 10–31.

Woodhuysen, H.R., 'Leicester's Literary Patronage: a Study of the English Court, 1578–82', unpublished thesis, Oxford University, 1981.

Woolley, Benjamin, *The Herbalist: Nicholas Culpeper and the Fight for Medical Freedom*, London, 2004.

Worsley, Lucy, *Cavalier: A Tale of Chivalry, Passion and Great Houses*, London, 2007.

Index